Temporalities, Texts, Ideologies

Temporalities, Texts, Ideologies

Ancient and Early Modern Perspectives

Edited by Bobby Xinyue

BLOOMSBURY ACADEMIC

Bloomsbury Publishing Plc, 50 Bedford Square, London, WC1B 3DP, UK
Bloomsbury Publishing Inc, 1385 Broadway, New York, NY 10018, USA
Bloomsbury Publishing Ireland, 29 Earlsfort Terrace, Dublin 2, D02 AY28, Ireland

BLOOMSBURY, BLOOMSBURY ACADEMIC and the Diana logo are trademarks of
Bloomsbury Publishing Plc

First published in Great Britain 2024
This paperback edition published 2025

Copyright © Bobby Xinyue and Contributors, 2024

Bobby Xinyue and Contributors have asserted their rights under the Copyright,
Designs and Patents Act, 1988, to be identified as Authors of this work.

Cover image: Giovan Battista Beinaschi, *Allegoria del Tempo*, 1675–80

All rights reserved. No part of this publication may be: i) reproduced or transmitted in any form, electronic or mechanical, including photocopying, recording or by means of any information storage or retrieval system without prior permission in writing from the publishers; or ii) used or reproduced in any way for the training, development or operation of artificial intelligence (AI) technologies, including generative AI technologies. The rights holders expressly reserve this publication from the text and data mining exception as per Article 4(3) of the Digital Single Market Directive (EU) 2019/790.

Bloomsbury Publishing Inc does not have any control over, or responsibility for, any third-party websites referred to or in this book. All internet addresses given in this book were correct at the time of going to press. The author and publisher regret any inconvenience caused if addresses have changed or sites have ceased to exist, but can accept no responsibility for any such changes.

A catalogue record for this book is available from the British Library.

Library of Congress Cataloging-in-Publication Data
Names: Xinyue, Bobby, editor.
Title: Temporalities, texts, ideologies : ancient and early-modern perspectives / edited by Bobby Xinyue.
Description: London : Bloomsbury Academic, 2024. | Includes bibliographical references and index.
Identifiers: LCCN 2023030515 (print) | LCCN 2023030516 (ebook) | ISBN 9781350257221 (hardback) | ISBN 9781350257269 (paperback) | ISBN 9781350257238 (pdf) | ISBN 9781350257245 (ebook)
Subjects: LCSH: Classical literature–History and criticism. | Time in literature. | European literature–Classical influences. | Comparative literature–Themes, motives.
Classification: LCC PA3015.T6 T46 2024 (print) | LCC PA3015.T6 (ebook) | DDC 880.09—dc23/eng/20230727
LC record available at https://lccn.loc.gov/2023030515
LC ebook record available at https://lccn.loc.gov/2023030516

ISBN:	HB:	978-1-3502-5722-1
	PB:	978-1-3502-5726-9
	ePDF:	978-1-3502-5723-8
	eBook:	978-1-3502-5724-5

Typeset by RefineCatch Limited, Bungay, Suffolk

For product safety related questions contact productsafety@bloomsbury.com.

To find out more about our authors and books visit www.bloomsbury.com
and sign up for our newsletters.

Contents

List of Contributors	vii
Acknowledgements	x
Introduction *Bobby Xinyue*	1

Part One The Presence of Time

1. Dialectic at a Standstill: Homer, Image and the Nature of Temporality *Ahuvia Kahane* — 17
2. Historical Ontology, Texts and Interpretation: Protagorean Reflections *Duncan F. Kennedy* — 35
3. Roman Temporalities of Presence *James Ker* — 53

Part Two Time, Space and Relations in Greek Literature

4. '… how you first went over the earth': Interactions of Human and Divine Time in the *Homeric Hymn to Apollo* *Anke Walter* — 71
5. The Apotheosis of Time: Challenging Tradition and Anachronism in Pherecydes' *Heptamychos* *Susannah Ashton* — 89
6. Pindar and the Nature of Contemplation *David Fearn* — 107

Part Three Temporal Patterns and the Politics of Latin Literature

7. Rivers as the Embodiment of Disrupted Time: Ovid's *Metamorphoses*, Ecological Chronotopes and the Apocalypse *Rebecca Batty* — 127
8. More than a Lifetime: Temporal Patterns in Roman Biography – Nepos, Tacitus, Suetonius *Martin Stöckinger* — 143
9. Short Long / Long Short: Brevity, Power and Epigrammatic Temporality *Tom Geue* — 159

Part Four The End of Time

10 The Day of Reckoning: Seneca's Epistolary Time *Catharine Edwards*   177

11 Engendering the Christian Age: Ovid's *Fasti* and the Annunciation in Renaissance Poetic Calendars *Bobby Xinyue*   195

12 *Respice finem*: Fast-Forwarding to the End of Time in Lucretius, Virgil, Ovid, Milton and Early Eighteenth-Century Poems on the Last Judgement *Philip Hardie*   217

Bibliography   233
Index of Passages   259
General Index   267

Contributors

Susannah Ashton is a Senior Teaching Fellow at Royal Holloway, University of London. Her research interests focus on early Greek conceptions of time, Presocratic philosophy and anthropological approaches to Classics. Her most recent publication is 'Chance, Relativity, and Empedocles' Cycle(s) of Time' (2022).

Rebecca Batty teaches at St Mary's Catholic High School, Lancashire, UK. Her research interests focus on Latin literature, ecocriticism and depictions of the natural environment in the late Republic and early Roman Empire. She completed her doctoral thesis, titled 'Rivers and the Redefinition of Time in Ovid's Poetry' in 2021 at the University of Nottingham. Most recently, she reviewed Irby's *Water in Antiquity* (2021) in *The Classical Review* 72 (2022).

Catharine Edwards FBA is Professor of Classics and Ancient History at Birkbeck, University of London. She has written books and articles on Roman cultural history, Latin literature and the reception of Rome in the eighteenth and nineteenth centuries. Among her research interests, Seneca features particularly. Her edition of *Seneca: Selected Letters* was published in 2019.

David Fearn is Professor of Greek at the University of Warwick. He has published widely in Greek lyric poetry, including monographs on both Bacchylides and Pindar. He is particularly fascinated by the inherent vitality of ancient Greek literary texts, and in current work seeks to push the formalisms of classical poetics into dialogue with contemporary critical-theoretical approaches to literature, and the phenomenology and historicities of contemporary experience and reading practices.

Tom Geue teaches Latin at the Australian National University. His 2019 book, *Author Unknown*, proposed some new ways of working with anonymous authorship. His current project, *Major Corrections: The Materialist Philology of Sebastiano Timpanaro*, lies between intellectual history and classical scholarship. It seeks to show technical philology and militant Marxism working together towards a future of full human flourishing.

Philip Hardie is a Fellow of Trinity College, Cambridge, and Emeritus Honorary Professor of Latin Literature in the University of Cambridge. He has published widely on Latin literature and its reception. His most recent book is *Celestial Aspirations: Classical Impulses in British Poetry and Art* (2022).

Ahuvia Kahane is Regius Professor of Greek and A. G. Leventis Professor of Greek Culture at Trinity College Dublin. His research interests include temporality, complexity theory, ancient literature and the relations between antiquity and contemporary critical thought. In press work includes 'Ancient Narrative Time' (in *The Oxford Handbook of Ancient Literary Theory and Criticism*) and *A Cultural History of Time Vol. I: The Ancient World*. Recently published work on time includes 'Narratology and the Temporality of Emotions in Homer' (2022), 'Homer and Ancient Narrative Time' (2021), and 'Theses on the Geometry of the Ruin' (2020).

Duncan F. Kennedy is Emeritus Professor of Latin Literature and the Theory of Criticism at the University of Bristol. He is the author of *The Arts of Love: Five Studies in the Discourse of Roman Love Elegy* (1993), *Rethinking Reality: Lucretius and the Textualization of Nature* (2002) and *Antiquity and the Meanings of Time* (2013). He is currently writing a monograph provisionally entitled *The Emergence of Ontological Styles of Thinking in Ancient Greece*.

James Ker is Professor of Classical Studies at the University of Pennsylvania. He specializes in imperial Roman literature and culture, including Roman conceptions of time and their reception. His most recent book is *The Ordered Day: Quotidian Time and Forms of Life in Ancient Rome* (2023).

Martin Stöckinger is a lecturer ('Wissenschaftlicher Assistent') in Classics at the University of Cologne. He is a co-editor of *Horace and Seneca: Interactions, Intertexts, Interpretations* (2017) and the author of *Vergils Gaben: Materialität, Reziprozität und Poetik in den Eklogen und der Aeneis* (2016) as well as articles on Republican and early imperial Latin literature. His research interests focus on Latin literature, and especially Virgil, post-Virgilian pastoral, intertextual concepts and relations, historiography, and biography. From there derives his current project which is concerned with the depiction of writing in Roman historiography from the beginnings to the early Middle Ages.

Anke Walter is Senior Lecturer in Classics at Newcastle University. The focus of her research is ancient epic, especially Flavian epic, the construction of time in literature, ancient stories of origin and festivals in Latin literature. She has published monographs on storytelling in Flavian epic (*Erzählen und Gesang im flavischen Epos*, 2014) and *Time in Ancient Stories of Origin* (2020). She has just completed a book manuscript on *Festivals in Latin Literature – The Poetics of Celebration* and is currently working on a German translation of Statius' *Thebaid*.

Bobby Xinyue is Lecturer in Roman Culture at King's College London. His research focuses on Latin literature and Roman political thought. He has published on Virgil, Horace, Propertius and Ovid, as well as a number of early modern Latin authors such as Battista Mantovano and Julius Caesar Scaliger. His most recent book is *Politics and Divinization in Augustan Poetry* (2022). His current research is on Ovid's *Fasti* and its reception in the Renaissance.

Acknowledgements

This volume began its life as a conference held in Venice in September 2019. Some of the chapters here are based on papers presented at the conference, others are commissioned at a later stage. I would like to offer heartfelt thanks to Ovanes Arkopyan, Siobhan Chomse, Elena Dahlberg, Helen Dixon, Stephen Harrison, Andrew Laird, Tiziana Lippiello, Marco Sgarbi, and Caroline Stark for their contribution and stimulating discussion at the conference; and David Fearn and James Ker for offering excellent chapters on topics which give this volume much-needed balance and variety.

Among the many people who helped me with putting together this volume, I would like to thank firstly Ingrid De Smet. As my mentor during my British Academy Postdoctoral Fellowship, Ingrid played a critical role in the organization of the conference and kept a close eye on the intellectual quality of the volume. Without her input, this volume would not have been possible. Secondly, I would like to thank Lily Mac Mahon and Zoe Osman at Bloomsbury for supporting me every step of the way. Their enthusiasm for this volume certainly made my life much easier. Of course, I must also thank the press's readers for their constructive criticism and incisive comments, which undoubtedly improved the quality of the work presented here. Furthermore, I would like to thank Louise Chapman and Michael Hendry for compiling the indices (a horrendous task which I shall never attempt by myself again); and Sacha Scott for copyediting and proofreading. Tom Coward deserves a special mention for his outstanding hospitality in Venice.

Last but not least, I would like to thank the British Academy and Ca'Foscari University of Venice for the organization of the conference; the University of Leicester for offering me a home when things were looking a bit bleak; and King's College London for bringing this project to a satisfactory conclusion.

BX, November 2023

Introduction

Bobby Xinyue

> *nos manet Oceanus circumvagus: arva beata* (41)
> *petamus, arva divites et insulas,*
> *reddit ubi cererem tellus inarata quotannis*
> *et inputata floret usque vinea,*
> ...
> *non huc Argoo contendit remige pinus*
> *neque impudica Colchis intulit pedem;*
> *non huc Sidonii torserunt cornua nautae,*
> *laboriosa nec cohors Ulixei.* 60
> *Iuppiter illa piae secrevit litora genti,* 63
> *ut inquinavit aere tempus aureum,*
> *aere, dehinc ferro duravit saecula, quorum* 65
> *piis secunda vate me datur fuga.*

The encircling ocean awaits us. Let us seek the blessed fields, the fields and rich isles where every year the earth unploughed returns grain, and the vine unpruned continually flowers ... Not to this land did Argo's oarsman drive the pine, nor did the unchaste Colchian set her foot; not to this land did Sidonian sailors turn their yardarms, nor Ulysses' toiling crew. Jupiter set those shores apart for the righteous race when he debased the Golden Age with bronze, then hardened that age with iron, from which a blessed escape is offered to the righteous with me as their seer.

Horace, *Epodes* 16.41–66[1]

In a manner typical of literary golden ages from antiquity onwards, Horace's famous description of the Blessed Isles revisits an idealized past, suspends the present, and seeks an imagined future all at once.[2] Against the backdrop of Rome's civil war in the 30s BCE, *Epode* 16 imagines stepping out of political reality and setting sail for a blissful eternity, one that is removed from the real world yet conceived directly in opposition to it.³ Life on the Blessed Isles represents a different kind of temporality – the long march of history is interrupted by a mythic age which is both past and future – but not a total suspension of time (*quotannis*, 43). But where there is timekeeping, there is also inequality and exploitation: nature produces *for* mankind *on time*, while humans don't have to pick up a single shift (*inarata*, 43). The utopian bliss of the poet's escapist fantasy (*fuga*, 66) is a patchwork of different literary, philosophical and religious concepts of time. There are echoes of the utopian imagery in Homer, Hesiod, Pindar, Plato and near-contemporary Roman texts (such as Virgil's *Eclogue* 4), as well as traces of Eastern thought on epochal cycles and notions of redemption.⁴ Horace's vision, moreover, holds a mirror up to the poet's present. As impiety marked the end of man's Golden Age (57–8; cf. Hes. *Op*. 134–7, 236–7),⁵ so, too, has it brought a stop to Rome's Republican era; but good times await those who are pious (66). Time is moralized, polarized and even politicized. Nor is time a linear process that proceeds unidirectionally, uninterruptedly and neutrally along the past–present–future axis.

This volume shows that the exploration of time as a locus of philosophical and political thought has been an important activity in Greek and Latin literature; and this in turn served to shape the conceptualization of macro and historical time in the literary imagination of the early modern period. Approaching this topic through four distinct themes (presence, spatialized time, temporal patterns and finality), the essays in this volume highlight the ways in which time is construed as relational, contestable and politically inflected across a number of texts and intellectual cultures. As the contributors to this volume represent a wide range of research specialisms, covering a variety of authors, genres and periods, engaging with different critical theories and interpretive models, each chapter speaks to specific debates and offers fresh perspectives on the literary figuration of time in a particular subfield of ancient or early modern studies. At the same time, this book offers a reading of time in literature not as a backdrop to or component of storytelling, but as a lively site of contemplations on ontology, relationhood and ideology, enabling the reader to locate a text's philosophical and political activities in its temporal fabric.

This collective approach is underpinned by a point of conceptual common ground. The investigation carried out here seeks to understand how time and temporal relationships are imagined and negotiated in specific cultural and historical contexts. That is to say, we set out to investigate *temporality* rather than metaphysical time per se. The distinctive characteristic of temporality identified by modern scholarship – namely, its twofold concern with relationality (i.e. how different periods and aspects of time relate) and with the imaginary (i.e. the subjective perception and experience of time)[6] – offers an ideal analytical framework to elicit the concept that the positioning, shaping and delineation of time in literary discourses are no mere artistic arrangement but a process of intellectual negotiation and a potentially political one at that.

The volume's core strength and key contribution to scholarship and critical debate lies in its consistent offering of alternatives to or modifications of narratological modelling of time.[7] The contributors set out to achieve this through considered implementation of modern philosophical theories (such as phenomenology and historical ontology) and urgent dialogue with current political issues (such as the ecological crisis and labour market exploitation). By engaging directly with ongoing conversations in contemporary science, philosophy and politics, several of the volume's chapters demonstrate the relevance and ready applicability of the product of these conversations as innovative interpretive tools for literary figurations of temporality. At the same time, this volume takes forward the crucial insights of classical scholarship on topics such as aetiological discourses,[8] timekeeping in antiquity,[9] the production of temporality in Greek and Roman epic,[10] and the development and manipulation of calendars in ancient Rome,[11] and illustrates how these insights can propel fresh understandings of temporality in a broad range of literary texts and historical situations. In a number of cases, the contributors also draw on the techniques and technologies of cinema and photography to render apparent the ways in which the study of temporality thrives on interdisciplinary openness. The volume's explicit engagement with contemporary intellectual developments and political issues dovetails with its consistent exploration of the wider impact of classical scholarship on critical approaches to time in literature. It is through this combination that the volume both maps out new ways for studying temporality in ancient and early modern texts and expands the conceptual frameworks of modern critical theory.

Entering a crowded field, this volume differentiates itself from some recent contributions to the question of time in literature in a number of ways.[12] First, the majority of the texts studied here lean towards the non-narrative (or at least not straightforwardly narrative), in particular philosophical dialogues and treatises, didactic and lyric poetry, epistles, epigrams and versified calendars. While conventional narrative genres such as epic occupy the attention of a number of chapters, and foundational texts such as the *Odyssey*, *Metamorphoses* and *Paradise Lost* remain the subject of enquiry, the volume's intentional coverage of non-epic and non-historiographical texts serves to demonstrate its principal claim that time functions not merely as a mechanism in the ordering of narrative but as a critical space for texts to interrogate the order of things.[13] Indeed, as a number of subsequent chapters show, the examination of how time operates or manifests itself in literary genres that are not driven by a plot or the sequentiality of events can jolt the reader into fresh considerations of questions of temporality and relationhood, such as: does the temporal fabric of a text inform us of how time is perceived and understood? What does a text have to say about having a relationship with time and with forces and phenomena that are always already there? How does a text articulate the significance of recognizing this relationship? These and other cognate questions propel the volume's attempt to steer the discussion of literary time away from the province of narrative.

Second, this volume identifies the value of ancient and early modern texts for critical discussions on temporality in the future – both within and beyond the confines of academic research. The texts examined here have much to offer to current scholarship on the non-linearity of time, the production and experience of time and the existentially incomplete nature of texts (and their interpretations) – topics which occupy a notable space in modern philosophy. A number of essays in the volume also respond directly to recent approaches to the study of time in the humanities and social sciences, exploring how they may help to shed new light on or find new uses for ancient texts in contemporary contexts. Specifically, the contributors engage with critical trends that have productively expanded on Bakhtin's concept of the 'chronotope' and offered new ways of conceptualizing time informed by sociocultural and environmental criticism.[14] The key proposition of anthropological studies on time – namely, time is an ongoing process of 'construction' being made and remade at multiple individual, social and cultural levels – underpins the analysis of the ideology of time in this volume, enabling the interpretations of specific texts to speak to broader social and political issues in antiquity, early modernity and beyond.[15] At the same time, the emergence of a more spatialized and (in recent years) ecologically oriented conception of time, with special emphases on the historical layering of landscape and the interactions between human and natural activities over time,[16] is here taken further by several chapters. These essays in particular urge readers to consider how ancient and early modern texts have already raised – and will continue to raise – important questions about the place of mankind in the world and broader ideas of progress, inevitability and decline.

Third, the essays in this volume situate the literary figuration of temporality at the crossroads of narratology, historicism and theories of genre, treating it as a phenomenon that encapsulates – and engenders further considerations for – the interconnection of these areas of study. As the subsequent chapters show, the interrogation of how time attains presence through narration, and how time is conceptualized and negotiated by the author of a text, raises questions about the extent to which we can situate a text in (an author's consciousness of) a particular historical moment or (the 'evolution' of a specific) literary category. Specialist studies focused on each one of these aspects have enriched our understanding of the ways in which the literary presentation of time sheds light on the mode of narration,[17] the poetics of a genre,[18] and the sense of historical consciousness in Graeco-Roman antiquity.[19] However, as Allen demonstrates in *Time and Literature*, the study of time has been a site where some of the most important methodological debates of literary scholarship were conducted (e.g. formal analysis vs historicist approaches; whether literature works to collude with or disrupt structures of power).[20] By foregrounding how the study of time is situated within this nexus of key critical and theoretical concerns, the present volume offers a more dynamic understanding of temporality in the classical and early modern periods, and casts into relief the extent to which different perspectives on temporality are interrelated. It is precisely this desire to promote dialogue between different approaches, in and across literary genres from different fields, that the format of a collected volume has been chosen to disseminate the result of our research.

The four thematic parts that make up this volume exhibit in depth the critical and intellectual contexts outlined above. Part One, 'The Presence of Time', examines a number of ancient texts which contain striking insights into the nature of time which are otherwise not rediscovered until late modern science and recent ontological studies. Ahuvia Kahane's essay (Chapter 1) is an attempt to observe the invisible 'structure of time' in the diction, verbal imagery and thought of Homer's verse. Most studies of time and temporality in Homer, in ancient Greek and Latin epic, and more generally in antiquity interpret time as a linear structure. Yet, the trajectory of epic time, as Kahane points out, cannot be described in terms of linear, homogenous, 'empty' time. Through a close analysis of one specific example – the epithet-and-noun formula δολιχόσκιον ἔγχος and the image of 'long-shadowed spears' (*Iliad* 5.15 and 616) – Kahane argues that we are drawn towards 'cinematic' readings of Homer's verbal imagery and to what may be referred to as 'dialectics at a standstill'. In turn, Homer's time and the 'genealogy' of temporality in the ancient world in general can be more convincingly understood and visualized in non-linear, complex forms like those presented in topology and phenomenology.

Next, Duncan Kennedy (Chapter 2) explores how recent thinking on 'historical ontology' may change our interpretation of texts, in particular ancient philosophical texts that explore the idea of 'being'. Historical ontology, as Kennedy demonstrates, encourages us to imagine what it was like when new things – especially concepts and ideologies – were emerging into the intellectual and experiential landscape before they were taken for granted as having been simply 'there' or 'present' all along. This raises a whole range of issues about interpretation, its 'timeliness' and the shifting meaning and authority of a text. With these concerns foregrounded, Kennedy reads a series of passages on 'being' from the works of Parmenides, Plato and Protagoras; and illustrates that the ideas that are thought to be *there* in these texts become 'maximally present' or 'minimally present' as readers perpetually bring to texts their own changing assumptions about what reality is and what constitutes 'being'. Kennedy's essay thus offers not only important insights into how ideas come into being over time, but also a new understanding of *interpretation* as bringing to maximal presence fresh ontological concerns.

James Ker (Chapter 3) rounds off the discussion of Part One by focusing on the ways in which time is 'present' in Roman literature and culture. Ker construes 'present' as both the *present* time (as opposed to the past and future) and the *presence* of time (as opposed to its absence); and his essay explores both of these branches of 'present' and how they entwine. Ker argues that the exploration of the different senses of time's presence can be a useful way to grasp the wide range of Roman times and temporalities: that is, both the different parts, units, qualities and parameters in Rome's cultural inventory of time concepts, and the broader social, intellectual and political implications of Roman temporal concepts. As Ker shows, it is by tracing both branches of Roman concepts of time's presence that we begin to get a firmer idea of the mentalities and ideologies that course through Roman culture from the Republic to the principate.

Part Two, 'Time, Space and Relations in Greek Literature', explores the interactions between non-human time and human-historical time in Greek literature. The essays in this section show that the coming together of different temporal and ontological frameworks in a text affords readers with a means to understand how a text conceives of the relationship between human and divine, earth and cosmos, mankind and nature. Anke Walter (Chapter 4) presents a nuanced reading of the *Homeric Hymn to Apollo* and argues that the way human and divine time interact shifts from the first to the second half of the hymn. While both divine and human actions remain temporally unspecific in the poem's first half, a clear sense of order and sequence for both divine and human actions emerges in the second half. Indeed, when Apollo at the end of the poem mentions the 'other men' who might become the masters of the Cretans, the god appears to think in human-historical time as he acknowledges the shifting of power among men. As Walter argues, while there is something characteristically archaic about the way that the poem constructs human time as subordinate to and responding to divine time, the notable variations and interactions of different temporalities in the *Homeric Hymn to Apollo* point to the conception of distinct temporal frameworks for gods and humans, which represents an important step in the development of ancient religious and metaphysical thought.

Susannah Ashton's essay (Chapter 5) tackles an important issue in a sorely under-appreciated text: the figure of Chronos/Kronos in Pherecydes' *Heptamychos*, a sixth-century BCE cosmo-theogonical treatise that has often been read through a retrospective lens informed by later Platonic ideas about time. By considering the text's presentation of Chronos in relation to sixth-century ideas about time and eternity, Ashton sheds new light on Pherecydes' understanding of the nature of divinity and the cosmos. In particular, she suggests that Chronos' creation in five cosmic nooks, later used as sites for metempsychosis, not only reflects Pherecydes' pioneering conceptualization of Chronos' role in the temporal organization of the cosmos, but even anticipates his eventual transformation into Kronos. The significance of the *Heptamychos*, as Ashton argues, thus lies in its daring reimagining of the nature of divinity, through which Pherecydes puts forward an innovative conception of a cosmos in which time and eternity were not distinct but unified.

The question of what object-oriented ontology and ecocriticism can do for our appreciation of Greek lyric and its relevance for today is the subject of David Fearn's essay (Chapter 6). Pindar's *Olympian* 10 presents, in part at least, a meditation on temporal processes of transformation of space into place, within and beyond the parameters of human cultural cognition. By attending to Pindar's lyric language, sound and imagery with fresh ontological concerns, Fearn shows that a 'traditional' philological close reading of *Olympian* 10 – or indeed of any lyric poem – can become integral to a broader ecocritical project reassessing human-world relations in ethical as well as aesthetic terms that intersect directly with pressing issues of environmental philosophy. In posing the question of how we even understand what Olympia is as a space or place, Pindar's poem, as Fearn points out, involves the reader in a process of reconfiguring the security of their own subjectivity in relation to nature.

Part Three, 'Temporal Patterns and the Politics of Latin Literature', considers the figuring of chronological patterns and progressions in Latin literature, and enquires into the ideological thrust behind each author's handling of these temporal configurations. The overall claim of this section is that the varied textual presentation of the motion, order and quantity of time goes to the core of where a text positions itself in relation to authority, whether that is literary orthodoxy or political hegemony. Just as David Fearn's study of Pindaric landscape extends Duncan Kennedy's exploration of the uses of ontological studies for ancient texts, the ecocritical angle of Fearn's chapter finds further expression in Rebecca Batty's reading of the interaction of time and the environment in Ovid's *Metamorphoses* (Chapter 7). Combining fresh dialogues with recent ecological theories and in-depth engagement with Bakhtin's 'chronotope', Batty argues that the extreme flooding and drying behaviour of the rivers in the *Metamorphoses* can indicate moments of timelessness in the narrative, which are key to Ovid's fluid epic temporality. The focus of her essay is the spatiality of river behaviour, both in the sense of spatial excess in flooding and in the retrogressive journey of the rivers retreating from the apocalyptic heat caused by Phaethon's fall (*Met.* 1.279–347 and 2.241–59). In particular, Batty notes that the depiction of the movements of specific rivers – the Nile, Rhine and Tiber – can be seen to encapsulate not only Ovid's playful manipulation of narrative time, but also the poet's negotiation of literary tradition and political time. Batty's essay thus sheds new light on the extent to which the natural environments in the *Metamorphoses* serve as a stomping ground for the poet's critique of time and power in the Augustan period.

Questions of temporality have usually stood in the background of scholarship on Roman biography. Martin Stöckinger (Chapter 8) suggests that a re-examination of temporal patterns in the works of Suetonius, Nepos and Tacitus enables us to better appreciate Roman biography as a genre deeply concerned with human agency, political introspection and the values of history. Stöckinger elicits the 'messy' chronology and shifting focalization of Suetonius' *Life of Tiberius* (72–74) through a narratologically informed examination; but the conclusion he reaches highlights that the patterning of time in biography serves to explore the tension between contingency and determinism. Likewise, Stöckinger's reading of Nepos and of Tacitus' *Agricola* underlines the extent to which Roman biography is thoroughly preoccupied with not just the career of the written individual, but broader questions of Roman identity and Rome's political trajectory and future.

Can the length of a text be in some way connected to the transition of political power in the Roman world? Tom Geue (Chapter 9) shows us that the brevity or lengthiness of Latin literature at the turn of the Domitianic and Nervan-Trajanic periods is a reflex of social hierarchy. Branching from James Ker's work on the politics of 'time pressure' as figured in the imperial-era *clepsydra* (water-clock) and its different valences across Pliny and Martial,[21] Geue brings out further the connection between time, class and textual length. Pliny's repudiation of brevity in speech-making (*Epistles* 1.20) shows that shorts and longs in this era are heavily politicized aesthetic signals: brevity is closely tied to the insufferable subjection and self-curbing of the Domitianic blackout, whereas an explosion in length is hitched to the new dawn. Against this backdrop, Geue explores how Martial tries to ape this move from brevity to length in Book 10, but ends up shrinking under the weight of comparison with the man himself in the famous epigram dedicated to Pliny (*Ep.* 10.20). Pliny then returns the temporal squeeze on epigram when he sends Martial off with a letter on his death (*Epistles* 3.21), in which he trims this very epigram by half. At stake here, as Geue neatly illustrates, is nothing short of a power tussle over who and what political class has the right of access to time.

Moving from Graeco-Roman antiquity to the early modern period, Part Four, 'The End of Time', focuses on the different kinds of endpoints in time, and examines how literary negotiations of these endpoints are interwoven with contemplations of morality, progress and spirituality. Catharine Edwards (Chapter 10) examines the ways in which time, in Seneca's *Epistulae morales*, is conceived of as an expendable resource and is corporealized and moralized. In his opening letter, Seneca reminds the reader that *se cotidie mori* ('he dies each day', Letter 1.2), a paradoxical message which Seneca elaborates in subsequent letters in relation both to the importance of the individual day and to the perpetual presence of death. Later on, Letter 12 opens with a poignant acknowledgement of the effects of time on the individual human body. For Seneca, as Edwards shows, the single day is the unit of time on which a philosophical approach to life should focus, while epistolary writing, rooted in the individual day, offers the ideal medium through which to put this approach into practice. Edwards suggests that it is through this pointed assertion of the paramount importance of the day that the *Epistulae morales* challenge the shadow cast by imperial displeasure over their author's immediate future.

The importance of Ovid's *Fasti* and the role it played in shaping early modern poetic responses to the evolution of the calendar are the subject of Bobby Xinyue's essay (Chapter 11). Using the Feast of the Annunciation (25 March) as a case study, Xinyue shows how Italian humanist poets (Ludovico Lazzarelli, Battista Mantovano and Ambrogio 'Novidio' Fracco) explored this day's significance as the inception of Christianity, and variously presented it as the moment when Christian 'modernity' put an end to and surpassed pagan antiquity. Xinyue demonstrates that in their presentation of this episode the Renaissance calendrical poets engaged closely with Book 3 (March) of Ovid's *Fasti*, drawing parallels between the women who mothered the first Romans and Mary the Mother of Christ, and between Romulus' foundation of Rome and the beginning of Christianity with the conception of Christ. Through this dialogue, Xinyue argues, the Italian humanist poets not only underscored the superiority of Christianity and the Church's calendar, but also asserted their own intellectual and religious authority at a time when both Renaissance humanism and the Roman Church came under sustained challenge from the Reformation.

The volume's final essay by Philip Hardie (Chapter 12) explores what happens to temporality when time comes up against the end of time, in the eighteenth-century fashion for poems on the Last Judgement. These poems look back to classical models, especially Virgil, Ovid and Lucan; their authors share in a wider taste for cataclysmic upheavals of nature; their poetic imagery draws repeatedly on Milton's great epic of sacred history, *Paradise Lost*, which extends the temporal scope of Virgil's universalizing *Aeneid* by looking beyond the Virgilian 'end of history' to the Christian end of history at the Second Coming. Hardie brings out the various strategies employed by the authors of Last Judgement poems to call the reader to engage with that seemingly distant and alien moment in the future. In particular, as Hardie notes, these poems set the termination of nature and seasonal variety in counterpoise with an image of ripening fruit in order to contemplate the possibilities *after* the end of history. Both in terms of its theme and the timeliness of the topic, Hardie's essay provides a fitting conclusion to the volume.

In keeping with the spirit of the volume, the twelve studies outlined above are arranged in an order that is broadly chronological but not chronologically linear. The essays move steadily from the time of Homer to the eighteenth century; but they also jump forwards and backwards in time to establish salient connections across different periods. A sequential reading of the volume rewards the reader with a strong sense that the main contention of the volume – that is, time in literature serves as a locus of philosophical and political critique – is the result of a critical examination of the rich history of Western literary culture. Of course, the volume can also be consulted piecemeal according to each reader's individual interests or the specific demands of a given syllabus. However, by deliberately disrupting a strictly linear chronology and grouping the twelve essays into four themes, this volume works to bring ideas about time from different periods into fresh dialogue, and invites the reader to make new juxtapositions and identify further connections. For instance, one could consider the wide appeal and different applications of ecocritical approaches to time in literature by reading the contributions of Fearn, Batty and Hardie together; the politics involved in the manipulation of or innovative play with time are treated in the essays of Ashton, Stöckinger, Geue, Edwards and Xinyue; original observations on the metaphors used to conceptualize time are offered by Kahane, Ker, Fearn, Batty, Edwards and Hardie; new efforts to trace how ideas emerge over time can be found in the works of Kennedy, Walter and Ashton. These and other possible ways of reading this volume not only attest to the richness of the topic, but also serve as the starting point of identifying future directions of research.

Notes

1 Text is taken from Klingner's edition, *Q. Horati Flacci Opera* (Leipzig: Teubner, 1959). Translation is my own.
2 For an overview of the Golden Age in the Graeco-Roman tradition, see Gatz (1967).
3 Essential scholarship on *Epode* 16 include: Hierche (1974: 99–108), Kraggerud (1984: 129–68), Nisbet (1984), Fitzgerald (1988), Mankin (1995: 10–12, 244–72), Oliensis (1998: 77–98), Watson (2003: 2–3, 20–30, 479–533), Harrison (2007: 130–4) and Stocks (2016: 153–74).
4 See esp. Hom. *Od.* 4.563–8, 7.112–32, 9.116–41; Hes. *Op.* 109–26, 225–37; Pind. *Ol.* 2.61–75; Pl. *Ti.* 24e–25a; *Criti.* 114d–115c, 120e–121a; Verg. *Ecl.* 4.18–45. It is thought that some combination of Sibylline prophecies and Eastern religious traditions, which appear to have informed Virgil's fourth *Eclogue* (Nisbet 1978), may also be at work in this epode. Furthermore, the unmistakable similarity between Horace's description of the Blessed Isles and Plutarch's *Life of Sertorius* 8.2–3 points to a common source, most likely Sallust's *Historiae*. Also relevant perhaps is Diod. Sic. 5.19 and 6.1.4 (the latter records Euhemerus' account of an imaginary journey to the utopian island of Panchaea). See Watson (2003: 480–3, 512–30) with further references.
5 Note esp. the Hesiodic expression ὕβριν . . . ἀτάσθαλον ('wicked outrage', *Op.* 134), with discussion by West (1978: 185) and Clay (2003: 87–8). On the association between the invention of seafaring and impiety, see West (1978) on Hes. *Op.* 236–7; Kraggerud (1984: 152), Mankin (1995: 267–8) and Watson (2003: 525–6).
6 Ogle (2019: 314–15).
7 See esp. Genette (1980). While it would be unfair to describe Genettian narratology as mere taxonomy, its fundamental concern – and dominant influence in today's literary criticism – is the *formal* dynamics of narrative temporality. For Genette, narrative linearity gives way to diversity when there is variation in the order,

duration and frequency of narrative temporality. However, the extent to which narrative temporality doubles up as a force for ideological closure, whereby the teleological drive of narrative time mirrors ideological determinism, is not thoroughly considered in Genette's *Narrative Discourse*, but forms the basis of Miller's argument in *Narrative and Its Discontents* (1981).
8   E.g. Walter (2020).
9   E.g. Hannah (2009), Ker (2009a) and Ben-Dov and Doering (2017).
10 E.g. Greensmith (2020) and Phillips (2020).
11 E.g. scholarship on the calendar reforms of Caesar and Augustus and literary responses to them, in particular Ovid's *Fasti*; see esp. Beard (1987), Wallace-Hadrill (1987), Newlands (1995), Barchiesi (1997) and Feeney (2007).
12 See esp. Kennedy (2013), Allen (2018), Miller and Symons (2019), Rood, Atack and Phillips (2020) and its journal counterpart (*Classical Receptions Journal* vol. 12 (2020)), Goldhill (2022), Faure, Valli and Zucker (2022). In addition, the exploration of queer temporality has intensified in recent years, see e.g. Atack (2020), Herring (2020) and McInerney (2020). A key proposition of queer temporality is that queer lives do not unfold in the same way as non-queer lives: events such as coming out, transitioning and the AIDS epidemic 'warp' time and thus refract it in ways that cannot be aligned with notions of linear progress. The connection made by scholars of queer time between temporal linearity and heteroreproductivity further underscores the need to interrogate the ideology of time. See further Edelman (2004) and Halberstam (2005).
13 The near-total omission of ancient historiography in our investigation is a deliberate choice, not least because a volume of this size cannot hope to be exhaustive, but also because the very topic of time in ancient historiography demands, and has indeed received, standalone treatments: see e.g. Grethlein and Krebs (2012).
14 Bakhtin (1981). First developed in 1937–8 and amended significantly in 1975, Bakhtin's notion of the 'chronotope' draws attention to the interconnection of time and space in the literary imagination. The 'chronotope' is concerned with how time manifests itself in different literary genres, and shines a light on the nature and ideology of the literary 'space' within which narrative time unfolds (or rather, is allowed to unfold). Bakhtin's main focus is the novel, a highly narrative genre; and critics of Bakhtin often point to the overly static understanding of both time and genre in his conception of the 'chronotope'. Compelling extensions of Bakhtin's work have centred around the notion of 'foreshadowing': see Morson (1994) on 'sideshadowing' and Bernstein (1996) on 'backshadowing'. Each of these 'shadows of time' raises important questions about what literature says about causality, possibility and freedom.
15 See Bergmann (1983) on time as a social construct; Bender and Wellbery (1991) on 'chronotypes' (conceived in response to Bakhtin's 'chronotope'); Miller and Symons (2019) on the mutual interference of 'chronotope' and 'chronotype' in antiquity.

16 See Zapf (2016) on ecocriticism.
17 See esp. de Jong (1987).
18 See esp. Lowrie (1997) on Horatian lyric.
19 See Kennedy (2013) and most recently Rood, Atack and Phillips (2020), which offers a systematic study of the concept of anachronism in Graeco-Roman antiquity and Western intellectual history, and argues that the notion of anachronism played a role in the formation of the idea of antiquity itself.
20 Allen (2018).
21 Ker (2009a).

Part One

The Presence of Time

1

Dialectic at a Standstill

Homer, Image and the Nature of Temporality*

Ahuvia Kahane
Trinity College Dublin

Introduction

In this essay, I want to consider time and temporality in Homer's verse, at the notional beginning of narrative in the literary traditions of the West. *Pace* common conceptions of the linear (or largely linear, day-by-day, notwithstanding flashbacks, etc.) progression of events in Homer's verse (ἦμος δ' ἠριγένεια φάνη ῥοδοδάκτυλος Ἠώς, etc.), and drawing above all on an analysis of visual attributes, I argue that Homer's time is inherently inseparable from the complex, multitemporal structure of cognition and action and their relation to the phenomenal world.

In practical terms, I focus on just one word, δολιχόσκιος, 'long-shadowed', as it is usually translated, which in Homer is often used to describe spears. At first glance, this epithet may seem unremarkable. Indeed, it has attracted only passing critical attention in the past. But let us not forget that throughout history, shadow, and indeed light, have always been used to tell time.[1] That, as we shall see, is what δολιχόσκιος, does, in Homer and beyond.

I begin with brief preparatory general comments in Section 1, on linear chronology and on more complex forms of temporality. In Section 2, I introduce the sequence of events in *Iliad* 5.15–19, a short battle scene between Phegeus and Diomedes, which I will discuss in detail. At first glance, time seems to progress step by step in a linear manner in this scene which encapsulates Homer's narratives of victory and death. Nevertheless, considering the scene's most distinct verbal element, the common epithet–noun phrase δολιχόσκιον ἔγχος, suggests, unavoidably, I argue, a different form of temporality. I show that this expression is made up of separate visual components that can only be united if we think of the expression as epistemically transparent and as 'an image of cognition'. This is the foundation of the main part of the analysis which follows in Section 3. Emphasizing cognition and the wider formulaic use of δολιχόσκιον ἔγχος in Homer and appealing, again, to visual reasoning, I argue that this phrase distinctly invokes more than one moment in time, indeed, by its visual logic, the full temporal extension of action in Homer's world and the multiple outcomes of combat, both survival/victory and death/defeat, in which Homer's ethics reside.

The concluding part of this essay is a brief attempt to demonstrate, first (in Section 4) that our reading of δολιχόσκιον ἔγχος is of general import and can be used to characterize Homeric temporality as a whole, and (in the Conclusion) to comment on the place of Homeric temporality as a reference point for the perception of time in antiquity and its legacies.

1. Chronology and Temporality

In antiquity as, indeed, in history and life, we often think of time as an abstract, uniform continuum, plotted and quantified on a linear (Cartesian) axis: $t^1, t^2, t^3 \ldots t^n$, along which events (776 BCE – the first Olympic games; 730 – the First Messenian War; 621 – Draco; 594 – Solon; 515 – Hippias; 490 – Marathon; etc.) are set. Indeed, already Aristotle (*Physics* 219a22–6) suggests that we perceive time as change, or rather as 'movement' (κίνησις, thus expressed in direct, sensory terms[2]) with regard to the 'before' and the 'after'. He famously defines time as 'the number of change' (ἀριθμός κινήσεως, *Physics* 220a24–6), a quantified, sequential process.[3]

There are many practical uses for well-ordered, linear time.[4] It allows us to normalize and regulate literary, juridical, scholarly, ideological and political narratives of history, culture, value and the self. As Bonnie Honig, for example, suggests:[5]

> Belief in a linear time sequence is invariably attended by belief that that sequence is either regressive (a Fall narrative) or progressive ... the time sequence itself is seen to be structured by causal forces that establish meaningful, orderly connections between what comes before and what comes after (Decline or Rise), such that one thing *leads* to another.

Perhaps even more importantly, as Stephen Tanaka emphasizes: 'While such linearity might appear neutral and natural, it has usually been deployed with some value system.'[6]

Examples of naturalized linear time as the vehicle of value systems abound.[7] And, as Aristotle, in the *Nicomachean Ethics*, for example, says (1174a19–22, X.6.2):[8]

> ἐν χρόνῳ γὰρ πᾶσα κίνησις καὶ τέλους τινός, οἷον ἡ οἰκοδομική, καὶ τελεία ὅταν ποιήσῃ οὗ ἐφίεται· ἢ ἐν ἅπαντι δὴ τῷ χρόνῳ ἢ τούτῳ. ἐν δὲ τοῖς μέρεσι τοῦ χρόνου πᾶσαι ἀτελεῖς, καὶ ἕτεραι τῷ εἴδει τῆς ὅλης καὶ ἀλλήλων.

> Every motion or process of change exists in time, and is a means to an end, for instance the process of building a house; and it is perfect when it has effected its end. Hence a motion [κίνησις, i.e., the process of change] is perfect either when viewed over the whole time of its duration, or at the moment when its end has been achieved. The several motions occupying portions of the time of the whole are imperfect, and different in kind from the whole and from each other.

Literary accounts, 'imitations of action', are likewise often perceived in linear terms. In Aristotle's *Poetics* (though itself probably not read in antiquity), the notion of 'plot' (*muthos,* an 'imitation of action') as the sequence of beginning, middle and end, and the notion of causal, teleological chains of events, play a central role in linear views of literary time since the Renaissance.[9] In contemporary studies of narrative, it is not infrequently assumed that[10]

> most narrative texts display an order that is chronological. This phenomenon is hardly surprising, since the very definition of a narrative [i.e. as a sequence of events arranged along an axis of time] is to some extent built on the notion that time progresses.

And yet, students of temporality have, for a very long time, offered substantive challenges to linear conceptions of time and of time in narrative, arguing instead, in different ways, for 'plural temporalities and tempos'.[11] Forty years ago, in his widely influential *Time and Narrative*, Paul Ricoeur, for example, invoking Martin Heidegger's seminal *Being and Time*, set out a basic phenomenological perspective:[12]

> As is well known, Heidegger reserves the term temporality (*Zeitlichkeit*) for … the dialectic of coming to be, having been, and making present. In this dialectic, time is entirely desubstantialized. The words 'future', 'past', and 'present' disappear, and time itself figures as the exploded unity of the three temporal *ekstases*.

Such time is, by and large, more complex, more unruly, less easy to deploy in the name of regulatory ends, and in this sense, perhaps more ethically responsible.[13] In this essay, focussing on just one example from Homer's *Iliad*, I want to suggest that, *pace* linear readings, 'plural temporalities and tempos' are, in fact, at the very heart of Homer's language and thought. Ultimately, such plurality can help us understand the values and the ethics of Homer's world and worlds further afield.

2. 'Long-Shadowed Spears' and the Image of Cognition

Consider the following compressed scene of a battle between Phegeus and Diomedes in the *Iliad* (5.15–19):[14]

Φηγεύς ῥα πρότερος προΐει δολιχόσκιον ἔγχος
Τυδεΐδεω δ' ὑπὲρ ὦμον ἀριστερὸν ἤλυθ' ἀκωκὴ
ἔγχεος, οὐδ' ἔβαλ' αὐτόν· ὃ δ' ὕστερος ὄρνυτο χαλκῷ
Τυδεΐδης· τοῦ δ' οὐχ ἅλιον βέλος ἔκφυγε χειρός,
ἀλλ' ἔβαλε στῆθος μεταμάζιον, ὦσε δ' ἀφ' ἵππων.

Phegeus then first cast a long-shadowed spear,
and the spearhead passed over his right shoulder
but did not hit him. And he, second, attacked with the bronze,
the Son of Tydeus. And his missile did not flee his hand in vain,
But struck Phegeus his chest between the nipples, and hurled him from his chariot.

But for the fact that the narrative is made of words, this scene unfolds rather vividly, somewhat like a cinematic (indeed, *kinematic* – from *kinêsis*, thus 'of the movement of time') sequence.[15] It also seems, at first, to attest to a linear temporality in which time, parsed by grammatical clauses and by verbs marking spatial movement, can be described as the 'number of change'. In the opening clause (T^1) Phegeus 'first' (πρότερος) throws (προΐει) his 'long-shadowed spear' (δολιχόσκιον ἔγχος); in the next clause (T^2) the spearhead, (ἀκωκή | ἔγχεος) flies (ἤλυθ') past its target; the spear misses (οὐδ' ἔβαλ', T^3); Diomedes attacks (ὄρνυτο) 'second' (ὕστερος) with his 'bronze' (χαλκῷ) spear (T^4); the 'missile' (βέλος) does not fly from his hand (ἔκφυγε) in vain and hits home (T^5); it strikes (ἔβαλε) Phegeus between in the nipples (T^6); Phegeus is cast (ὦσε) to the ground (and dies, T^7).[16] It's a 'typical' battle scene.[17] The sequence seems to establish a natural, isomorphic overlap between the ordered (πρότερος ... ὕστερος ...) movement of time ($T^1 ... T^n$), numbered lines of verse (15, 16, 17, 18, 19 – only in the written text, of course[18]), and plot action that is propelled by the force of martial virtue, that leads up to the endpoint (an Aristotelian τέλος) of victory/

death, and that implicitly embodies Homeric ideology and its ethical/political values: excellence (*aretê*), fame (*kleos*) and the so-called heroic-code by which heroes live and die.[19] All this is vividly presented in flurry of verbs of movement and verbalized visual descriptions of weapons, of shadows and flashes of bronze.[20]

Nevertheless, I want to suggest, this linear reading and, fundamentally, the visual imagery that sustains it collapse under scrutiny and point, profitably, to a different perception of time. Let us focus on the epithet δολιχόσκιος, 'traditionally translated as long-shadowed' (Beck, LfgrE).[21] The epithet is notable for its distinct, highly formulaic usage.[22] In our passage in particular, the epithet stands out in the very first line of this exchange, not least in relation to other nouns, adjectives, verbs, adverbs and conjunctions in the passage, which are among the most general (semantically) and most common (in terms of frequency) in Homer and in epic. Regardless, it is understandable that the visual description of a spear should attract some of our attention. After all, the spear is an instrument of death. And death, the engine of 'pity and fear', is at the heart of battle scenes, heroic life and the *Iliad*. It is exactly what we want to see in our mind's eye.[23]

At first glance, δολιχόσκιος may nevertheless seem like something of a disappointment. The sense 'long-shadowed' is widely accepted but already the scholia (Σ D *Il.* 6.44), for example, were dissatisfied with this meaning, and have also suggested, albeit unconvincingly, 'that can be cast to a long *distance*', or 'having grown in the shade and therefore long'.[24] Rouse was more direct. He thought that 'long-shadowed' was, 'not appropriate to a spear, which suggests a "flash" rather than a "shadow."'[25] Kirk sourly dismisses the matter: 'there is no real objection to this epithet's most obvious meaning, "with long shadow," to which no reasonable alternative has been proposed'.[26]

Within Rouse's reservations and Kirk's unenthusiastic verdict, let me nevertheless suggest, lies an acute problem which has to do, not simply with style or semantics, but with the nature of vision and language, cognition, time and the world.

At the beginning of our scene in *Iliad* 5.15–19, Phegeus casts his δολιχόσκιον ἔγχος. Flying through air, the spear's 'long shadow' must be trailing on the ground. Strictly speaking, spear and shadow are in two different places (Figure 1.1).

The fact of the matter is that the physical human eye cannot literally focus on two different objects in material space at a single point in time or look at two images at once. We can only depict such complex objects in a picture, or in the

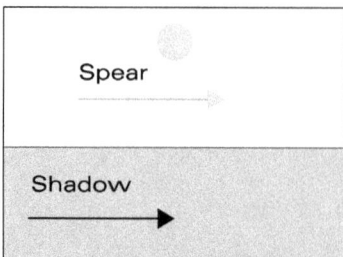

Figure 1.1 Spear and Shadow.

mind, where, needless to say, we combine multiple images as a matter of course: we, and most other animals, look at the world with two eyes.[27] Indeed, as every neuroscientist, experimental psychologist and philosopher will confirm, in this sense, it is the mind that 'sees'. Combining images in the mind is such an embedded process that we do not normally account for it as such. We tend to 'forget' the multiplicity of the world.[28]

In *Iliad* 5.15, we are certainly looking at a typical epic spear flying through the air. Yet, the verbal phrase δολιχόσκιον ἔγχος, being, as Rouse, for example, says, 'inappropriate' (we expect a flash, not a shadow), forces a separation of the images of spear and shadow. It thus reveals that, in our mind, we are combining multiple images.[29] My first point, then, is that the words δολιχόσκιον ἔγχος expose our forgetfulness of the deeper multiplicity of the world.

Let me slightly rephrase: in *Iliad* 5.15, the epithet–noun phrase δολιχόσκιον ἔγχος is *epistemically transparent*. It is a verbal expression that, in non-philosophical terms, directly forces us to confront what we might describe as the complex nature of vision, images and words and the relation between perception, knowledge and the world. Phegeus' 'long-shadowed spear' flying in mid-air is, in truth, a double image, simultaneous yet separate. It is an image in the real world, yet – precisely because of our assumptions about vision in the world and regardless of the fact that these are verbal descriptions – *not* an image we can focus on or grasp with a single glance of our eyes.[30] We can and do combine this double image into one in the mind. But, properly speaking, δολιχόσκιον ἔγχος, because of the visual nature of what it describes in words, because it reveals the practice of our mind, may be said to be a verbal image of cognition, an image that helps us to 'un-hide' or 'un-forget' the complexity of relations (whatever exactly such relations are) between the ontic and the epistemic, between ontological and epistemological questions.[31]

As we shall see in the next section, such relations between cognition and the world are inseparable from the nature of time and from the essence of Homeric temporality. Herein, I will suggest, lies the most important function of the epithet.

3. Cognition and Time

'Long-shadowed spears' may be images of cognition, but they are not simply invisible thoughts or transcendental objects in our minds. The moment of flight separates the image of a spear and the image of its long shadow trailing on the ground, but there are many other moments in the trajectory of a spear that are part of 'what it is to be a spear'. Such moments occur, for example, in the past of a spear's flight, before it is cast, when it may be stuck upright, deep in the ground, with its shiny point in the air (*Od.* 10.151–4), leaning against a wall outside of the house (*Od.* 17.29), indoors in a spear-stand (*Od.* 1.127–8), or on the ground – with or without a visible shadow which may or may not be accounted for.[32] There are also moments in the future of a spear's flight, when it reaches the end of its trajectory, either missing its mark (as in *Od.* 5.15–17), or, most notably, when it has hit its designated target. At such moments, in the real world, spear and shadow unite at a single point in space and can be observed as a single visual object (Figure 1.2).

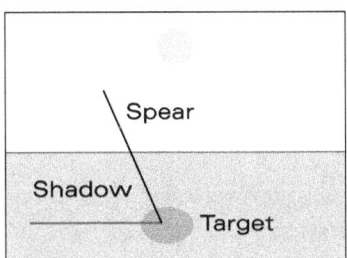

Figure 1.2 Spear and Shadow.

Now, descriptions of spears at rest and of spears that miss their mark can be interesting. Nevertheless, as we have already noted, one of the focal points of combat scenes and of heroic life in general is death. Spears that hit home are, in this sense, exactly what we want to see: that point in space and that moment in time when one epic hero meets his fate and another gains immortal fame.

In Book 5 of the *Iliad*, for example, Ajax' 'long-shadowed spear' strikes Amphios in the belly and kills him (616–18):

νειαίρῃ δ' ἐν γαστρὶ πάγη δολιχόσκιον ἔγχος,
δούπησεν δὲ πεσών· ὃ δ' ἐπέδραμε φαίδιμος Αἴας
τεύχεα συλήσων·

The long-shadowing spear stuck in his lower belly,
and he fell with a crash. And illustrious Ajax ran forward
to strip him of his armour.

Similarly, in *Iliad* 13, Idomeneus kills Oinomaus. Idomeneus then tries to remove the spear from his victim's body (*Il.* 13.509–11):

Ἰδομενεὺς δ' ἄρα Οἰνόμαον βάλε γαστέρα μέσσην,
ῥῆξε δὲ θώρηκος γύαλον, διὰ δ' ἔντερα χαλκὸς ἤφυσ'·
ὃ δ' ἐν κονίῃσι πεσὼν ἕλε γαῖαν ἀγοστῷ.
Ἰδομενεὺς δ' ἐκ μὲν νέκυος δολιχόσκιον ἔγχος
ἐσπάσατ', οὐδ' ἄρ' ἔτ' ἄλλα δυνήσατο τεύχεα καλὰ
ὤμοιιν ἀφελέσθαι· ἐπείγετο γὰρ βελέεσσιν.

Now, Idomeneus struck Oinomaus in the middle of his belly,
and broke through the hollow of his breastplate
and his entrails burst through the bronze.
He fell to the dust clutching the earth with his hand.
Idomeneus wrenched the long-shadowing spear
from the corpse, but could not remove the splendid armour
from its shoulders, held back by enemy missiles.

Likewise, in the *Odyssey*, we find a description of the killing of Amphinomus (22.92–6):

Τηλέμαχος κατόπισθε βαλὼν χαλκήρεϊ δουρὶ
ὤμων μεσσηγύς, διὰ δὲ στήθεσφιν ἔλασσε·
δούπησεν δὲ πεσών, χθόνα δ' ἤλασε παντὶ μετώπῳ.
Τηλέμαχος δ' ἀπόρουσε, λιπὼν δολιχόσκιον ἔγχος
αὐτοῦ ἐν Ἀμφινόμῳ·

Telemachus struck him [Amphinomus] from behind with a spear
between the shoulders, driving it through his chest,
and he fell with a crash and kicked up dust with all of his forehead.
Telemachus sprang away, leaving his long-shadowed spear
in the body of Amphinomus.

These are seminal moments that capture the essential condition and values of violent conflict and heroic life. Crucially for us, these are also moments when the all-important function of the spear as an instrument of death and the visual image of the spear and its shadow unite, with absolute prominence in our mind.

Already in the previous section we have established that the expression δολιχόσκιον ἔγχος exists, not as a simple reflection of visual reality or of what we see with our sensory eye, but as a multiplex image of cognition.

Now, in cognition, just as a multiplicity of images can coalesce, so instants in time multiply and coalesce, simply because without recollection and anticipation, without memory of the past, without knowledge of the present and without thinking, in fear or in hope, about what might happen in the future, without the unity of all these temporal *ekstases* (as Heidegger would call them), no action would have any meaning (we'd be living in a never-ending state of oblivion in the present). This applies to the big ideas just as it applies to minute details of the narrative.

In the scene from *Iliad* 13 (above), for example, there is no actual description of that point in time when Ajax cast his spear, nor of the spear flying through the air. We are, in lines 506–8, given a point-by-point description of the wounding and death of Oinomaus, though, again, Ajax' spear is not itself mentioned at this crucial moment. It is, of course, neither possible nor necessary to give an account of all details. Every text contains 'gaps'.[33] We know that Ajax cast the spear, that it flew through the air, that it was the spear that burst through Oinomaus' breastplate. We surely see all this in our mind's eye. These verses, like other visual descriptions in Homer and many other descriptions and images, would have no meaning at all if we were not capable of viewing the whole sequence somehow, if images and events in time, past, present and future, were not fluid and entangled attributes of our memory, knowledge, reason, imagination and cognition.

My second point, then, is that when we read words such as Φηγεύς ῥα πρότερος προΐει δολιχόσκιον ἔγχος in *Iliad* 5.15 and other verses that contain this epithet–noun formula, we are, in truth, reading a visual description that expresses, not a static point in linear time, not an instant, but the image of a compound, dynamic temporal event (Figure 1.3).[34]

We should note, of course, that Muybridge's image is, in fact, a fragmented 'hiding' of reality, a heuristic which artificially unpacks the entangled plurality which δολιχόσκιον ἔγχος keeps correctly whole.[35]

Because the words 'long-shadowed spear' are an image of cognition, because they describe entangled moments, and because the words themselves are formulaic and thus highly memorable and distinct,[36] our reading of δολιχόσκιον ἔγχος is inherently multitemporal.

Figure 1.3 Eadweard Muybridge: 'Horse Gallop.'

Within the instant of this formula a whole *duration* (*durée*)[37] exists, moments before the battle, real but sometimes unaccounted-for in the literal text, when the spear might have been lying on the ground or leaning against the side of a hero's hut; the formula incorporates those entangled multi-image, multiple moments of the spear being cast, moments of the spear in flight (a trajectory, not single points in space), moments when a spear misses its target, as in *Odyssey* 5.15–17, those moments, sometimes told (e.g. *Il.* 11.572, etc.) but at other times untold when, as 'spent munitions', the spear lies unnoticed in some corner of the battlefield, moments when its shiny point lodges itself deep in the body of a hero, when shaft and shadow are united as a single, terrible visible image, and, as we have seen, moments when the spear is wrenched out of the hero's corpse.[38]

The time of all these moments, let me suggest, cannot be defined as 'the number of change'. It cannot be measured with a stopwatch.[39] We could, of course, say that so-and-so cast the spear at 10:45:00 AM; that the spear was at point X in the air at exactly 10:44:59; that it struck Y in the belly at exactly 10:45:03; that Y died at 10:55:21; that the spear was pulled out at 10:59:17; and so on. But such numbered representations of Homeric time do not exist in Homer's world. They are un-Homeric and patently meaningless.[40] They destroy, not the *illusion* of Homeric narrative representation, but the *reality* of Homer's narrative and Homer's time.

Phegeus' death, like, *mutatis mutandis,* those of Achilles and many other heroes, is a moment that unites a hero's past, present and future, it is a heroic *life*, indeed, a whole narrative *bios*, a 'biography'. A deflected flying spear is always a narrative that binds the past and the future of song. Time in such narratives does not progress step by step or in straight lines or strictly by causes that precede effects, nor does such time constitute a single *muthos*. 'Long-shadowed spears' sometimes find their target, but at other times they miss their mark. The outcome of many battle scenes is typical, and is in one sense 'known'. But such knowledge is a function of our cognition, and, by the complex and multiple nature of cognition (as well as the complex nature of oral *mouvance*[41]), it is never fully aligned with language 'in itself' or with any formulaic expression, no matter how rigidly patterned in formal terms. Yet, precisely this misalignment allows language, indeed Homer's formulaic language, to reflect and expose the fluid nature of cognition and its relation to the world and to the precarity of events, both in general and in many detailed variations. Thus, for example, expression δολιχόσκιον ἔγχος sometimes *marks a successful hit* and the death of the spear's intended victim. In 5.15–19, however, the exact same expression ironically marks a diametric opposite outcome: the spear has *missed its mark* and failed to kill Diomedes. A moment later, the one who has cast the spear, Phegeus himself, meets his death. My point, then, is that the formula, δολιχόσκιον ἔγχος, can, and must be read phenomenologically, as a verbal image of cognition and of the 'plurality of temporalities and tempos' in the world.

Or rather, let us rephrase this conclusion in the words of one of the influential critics of both temporality and of the image of late modernity, Walter Benjamin, and his famous definition of the image. As he says:[42]

> It is not that what is past casts its light on what is present, or what is present its light on what is past; rather, *image is that wherein what has been comes together in a flash with the now to form a constellation*. In other words: *image is dialectics at a standstill*. [My emphasis.]

That bright 'flash' and 'shadow' of the bronze spearhead of Homer's 'long-shadowed spear' and the futures and the pasts which it reveals to us are, I suggest precisely, 'dialectics at a standstill', a true image that casts its light on Homer's temporality and, in this sense, since it is an image of life and death, of a trajectory of being, also on the precarity of life in the Homeric world.

4. Homer and the Ethics of Temporality

Two penultimate points must be made, if only in brief. To do them justice one would have to write a very long book.

First, let me stress that the phenomenology of time I have tried to describe, though inescapably attested in the formula δολιχόσκιον ἔγχος (and thus a distinct example), is in no way unique. Once we know what to look for, we will find it prominently attested everywhere in Homer's diction and thought.

Consider, for instance, the formula πόδας ὠκὺς Ἀχιλλεύς, which denotes, of course, Achilles' future victory (significantly, with divine assistance and thus, even here, not a static attribute) over Hector in the mortal footrace in *Iliad* Book 22. Yet this epithet is frequently used in Book 1 of the poem (48, 84, 148, etc.), in Book 9, where Achilles is stationary and sulking in his hut (197, 307, 606, etc.), and it marks important moments in Achilles' meeting with Priam in Book 24 (559, 649, 751), clearly pointing, as a matter of basic poetic sensibility, not merely to the hero's bodily swiftness, but to the tragedy of his killing of Hector, to his quick, destructive and self-destructive anger, his restless temper, his fated swift death in a future beyond the end of the *Iliad* and so on.[43] Similarly, the formula πολύμητις Ὀδυσσεύς, (*Il.* 1.311, 23.755; *Od.* 2.173, 24.406) signals, not only the many devices of Odysseus, both his resourceful and his vicious politics in the *Iliad*, not only his past suffering, his clever if selfish survival, his inability to save his men, his release from suffering in the *Odyssey*, his future triumph over the suitors in *Odyssey* Book 22, the manner in which, after that triumph, he is outwitted by Penelope in Book 23, his cruel excess in the encounter with his father in Book 24 of the poem and ultimately, his fated death, *ex halos* (11.143), in the future of the *Odyssey*, in the *Telegony* (and in Sophocles' lost *Odysseus Akanthoplex*), which all his 'many devices' could not avert and so on. Apollo, by the same token, is 'far-shooting' whether he holds the bow in his hand or not. Penelope's suitors are 'noble' whether they misbehave in Odysseus' palace or not. Ships are 'swift' even when they are beached.[44] They are 'hollow' both before and after they have disgorged their deadly human cargo on the shores of Troy, when they are filled and emptied and filled again with spoils and so on. Such filling and emptying are precisely a dialectic at a standstill, a single, verbal image of time. In one way or another, every word in Homer's verse resonates with multiple temporalities of this type. Cognition and language are exponents of reality, and reality is multiple (at least as we, following many pivotal contemporary philosophical and scientific accounts see it). Cognition and language are not simply a matter of psychology or perception but, much more fundamentally, a matter of truth and existence and of a relation of the *ontic* and the *epistemic*.

Paolo Vivante and many other students of Homer have long argued that epithets signal the whole identity of a hero.[45] What I am suggesting is that formulaic diction, by its very nature, expresses far more than that. Homer's diction is not a matter of poetics or of style, but is, fundamentally, a verbal embodiment of the phenomenology of Homer's existential time.

Time, we should nevertheless stress, as, indeed, Bonnie Honig, Stephen Tanaka and many other critics point out, is not simply a matter of ontics or epistemics or of ontology and epistemology, but is (as one would expect, if time is an attribute of existence and knowledge) in Homer, as elsewhere, inherently ethical and political. Clearly, for instance, questions of Fate, of one's allotted portion in mortal life, of the outcome of abductions and expeditions, of quarrels and military campaigns, are the very substance of the *Iliad* and *Odyssey*. It is likewise clear that in Homer, Fate and the Fates exist, and are represented and perceived, not as single, numbered moments *in time*, but *over time*, as 'time itself'. Achilles is a dead-man-walking long before his death, which lies unseen yet in full view, well beyond the end of the *Iliad*. The full trajectory of his existence, of his refusal, of his death, is a statement about *ethics*. Likewise, Odysseus' death (*Od.* 11.134–5) is foretold well before he reaches Ithaca and well before he dies. The entanglements of Odysseus' past(s), present(s) and future(s) take on deep *ethical* meaning with regard, for example, to identity and freedom of will, authority and truth. Are Achilles, Odysseus and other epic characters free to choose their fate? Achilles' actions on the island of Skyros, his discussions with his mother Thetis in the *Iliad*, Odysseus' violent response to Thersites, his attempts to woo Achilles back in Book 9 of the *Iliad*, his destructive curiosity, his journeys past the end of the *Odyssey* suggest that free will is not a meaningless term in Homer's world even if we know how Homer's plots develop and end.

But are Homer's epics, epic tradition and, indeed, epic rigid formulaic language itself free to choose its own fate?[46] I have elsewhere argued in considerable detail that, indeed, epic formulaic language is, in the most rigorous and technical sense and consequently politically and ethically free.[47] Viewed from the methodological perspective of contemporary science, usage-based linguistics, cognitive-functional grammar, the study of complex dynamic systems, and, indeed, the history of Homeric scholarship in the last hundred years or so, even the most formally patterned epic language can be shown to be as free to express individual will, and thus individual ethics and politics as any other form of discursive expression.[48]

More specifically, in this essay itself we have seen that the very phrase δολιχόσκιον ἔγχος is not bound by what John Foley once termed as 'traditional referentiality'.[49] This highly repetitive formula marks both a spear that hits home and a spear that misses its mark and thus the precarity of heroic life, the tragedy of death and the triumph of survival and victory. Homeric diction *is* bound by patterns of formal repetition. But such patterns are *not* bound by universal determinative rules. Tradition, we might say, is inherently epiphenomenal. It is stochastic, non-deterministic and (paradoxically, perhaps) unbound.

5. Conclusion

My concluding comment is the briefest of all, but is of widest import and directly responds to the historical scope of this book. I want to suggest that tracing Homer's multiple temporality provides us with a point of reference by which to explore a much wider swathe of literary works in antiquity, in traditions of the West and beyond.

Such traditions, we have to stress, like time itself, are categorically 'not one object, idea, moment or trajectory', but rather, genealogies of temporality – multiple, non-linear, non-deterministic and historical. They, too, are inherently epiphenomenal, stochastic and non-deterministic.

There is never one Homer and always more than one Homer.[50] Yet, Homer – this hardly needs saying – was a pillar of ancient literature, thought and pedagogy. It is safe to say that many ancient writers, politicians, historians and critics, including Aristotle, will have been schooled in Homer's verse and thus – since nothing exists out of time – schooled in a tradition (a *stochastic* tradition, let us stress) of the temporality of epic.

Indeed, we might stress, not only those voices within the tradition, but also those that have been silenced by the inheritors of antiquity and their exclusive practice, by later eras in the history of an education in the classics and the 'great tradition', can be usefully measured not in relation to Homer as a trope of time but in their *non-relation* to Homeric tradition and its temporality.[51] In such cases, let us stress, Homer, ceases to be a privileged originary trope which he should never have been and perhaps never was. Instead, Homer and his temporality recede, quietly and comfortably, truthfully, into the open traditions of diffracted, democratic spaces and of our many different ways of telling time.

Notes

* I am grateful to Matthew Ward for helpful suggestions. Any faults with the argument nevertheless remain my own.

1 The bibliographies on vision and visual aspects and, separately, on time in Homer, are large and often comment on the relation between daylight, night-time, darkness and the passage of time. See Kahane (2022b), Zanker (2019), Beck (2017), Garcia (2013), Purves (2010a, 2010b), Grethlein (2014), Grethlein and Krebs (2012), Foxhall, Gehrke and Luraghi (2010), Lucci (2011), Christopoulos, Krantzakis and Levaniouk (2010), Calame (2009), Bergren (2008, esp. chs 2–4), Kim (2008), de Jong and Nünlist (2007), Dunn (2007), Bassi (2005), Holford-Strevens (2005), Bakker

(2002a), Theunissen (2002), and Csapo and Miller (1998). Earlier work, see Degani (1961) and Fränkel (1931). More generally, Holford-Strevens (2005), Wilcox (1987) and Meister and Schernus (2011). Existing work, however, rarely attempts to explore the fundamental links between vision and the ontology (and phenomenology) of time, which is the focus of this essay.

2   Time is otherwise 'the element of invisibility itself' (Derrida 1992: 6).
3   See recent discussions, e.g. in Sentesy (2018) and Stein (2015). More generally, for Aristotle on time, see Roark (2011), Bowin (2009) and Coope (2005).
4   Fundamental arguments within the philosophy of science in Galison (2003).
5   Honig (2009: 15).
6   Tanaka (2016: 161), usefully cited in Holmes (2020: 63).
7   In Aristotle, there are many examples of naturalized, linear, teleological time within the hierarchy of domestic, economic and political orders. E.g. in the *Politics*, with regard to the regulation (ἐπιμέλεια) of procreation and its social and political consequences. Measures must be taken, Aristotle says (1335a6–7, trans. H. Rackham.) 'to ensure that the children produced may have bodily frames *suited to the wish of the lawgiver*' (my emphasis) (. . .ὅπως τὰ σώματα τῶν γεννωμένων ὑπάρχῃ πρὸς τὴν τοῦ νομοθέτου βούλησιν). Remarking on the appropriate ages of male and female maturity by the standard of 'all animal species', Aristotle advises (1335a28–37) that it is 'fitting (ἁρμόττει) for the women to be married at about the age of eighteen and the men at thirty seven . . . Moreover *the succession of the children to the estates* (ἡ διαδοχὴ τῶν τέκνων), if their birth duly occurs soon after the parents marry, will take place when they are beginning their prime, and when the parents' period of vigour has now come to a close, towards the age of seventy' (my emphasis).
8   Trans. H. Rackham.
9   Esp. Ludovico Castelvetro (1505–71). The *Poetics* itself (in contrast, for example, to *On Poets*) was almost certainly not read in antiquity. See Tarán and Gutas (2012: 3–76); cf. Zucker (2016: 362 n. 19) on Themistius and the *Poetics*; Falcon (2016); also Janko (2011). The question of whether linear conceptions of time did, or did not otherwise characterize antiquity requires separate, extended consideration.
10 Distinctly in narratological studies, of course: de Jong and Nünlist (2007: 505).
11 The phrase is borrowed from Honig (2009: 15), who links such plurality to politics.
12 Ricoeur (1984–8: 61). NB, immediately following:

> This dialectic is the temporal constitution of Care [*Sorge,* a key term in Heidegger's phenomenology]. As is also well known, *being-towards-death* imposes, counter to Augustine, the primacy of the future over the present and the closure of this future by a limit internal to all anticipation and every project.

'Death' figures prominently in the discussion below and Heidegger and Ricoeur are a basic point of departure for the conception of time that underpins the present essay. I invoke Ricoeur and Heidegger who mark a better-acknowledged point of reference. The critical perspectives that guide my discussion differ on several points of ontology and method but to set them out in detail would have required extended, separate discussion. See (*mutatis mutandis*) phenomenological perspectives in Husserl, Bergson, Benjamin, Derrida, Deleuze (also in relation to cinema), Merleau-Ponty and Nancy, Rancière, Badiou, Meillasoux and others, for example, with regard to notions of *becoming* and the *event*. Discussions of time in the sciences fundamentally underpin the intuitions of this essay but would have required an extended, and rather technical separate presentation. Suffice it to note that Newtonian calculations still work in many 'ordinary life' contexts, but since the twentieth century, especially in the study of astrophysics, gravity, quantum mechanics, etc., time ceases to be a linear constant and becomes a variable dimension. Work by Barad (2007), Latour (1999), De Landa (2000), Daston (2000), Bachelard (1984) and others is particularly helpful in linking contemporary science to historical and critical thought.

13 See e.g. Derrida (2005) and his notion of *à-venire* (the 'future-to-come'), 'democracy-to-come', etc.; also Protevi (1996). Cf. Kahane (2022a), Kahane (2022b) and Kahane (forthcoming).
14 Translations of the Greek, unless otherwise stated, are my own.
15 For the idea of 'frame-by-frame' movement in Homer, see e.g. Purves (2010a: 35) who, nevertheless, eschews the fundamental philosophical complexities of cinematic temporality, for which see, e.g., Deleuze (1989).
16 In full:

T^1 (clause 1): Phegeus throws his spear *'first'* – Φηγεύς ῥα πρότερος προΐει δολιχόσκιον ἔγχος

T^2 (clause 2): The spearhead flies past Diomedes – Τυδεΐδεω δ' ὑπὲρ ὦμον ἀριστερὸν ἤλυθ' ἀκωκὴ // ἔγχεος.

T^3 (clause 3): The spear *misses* – οὐδ' ἔβαλ' αὐτόν.

T^4 (clause 4): Diomedes attacks *'second'* with the bronze (='spearhead') ὃ δ' ὕστερος ὄρνυτο χαλκῷ.

T^5 (clause 5): Diomedes' missile *does not miss* – τοῦ δ' οὐχ ἅλιον βέλος ἔκφυγε χειρός,

T^6 (clause 6): Phegeus is struck in his chest between the nipples – ἀλλ' ἔβαλε στῆθος μεταμάζιον,

T^7 (clause 7): Phegeus tumbles from the chariot to the dust – ὦσε δ' ἀφ' ἵππων.

17 Fenik (1968) and Arend (1933) on 'typical/type scenes'; more recently Grethlein (2007) and Louden (2002); but discussions of formal type scenes incorporate Parryan notions of oral style. Like the idea of formulaic composition (see Kahane 2018b), the patterning of scene elements require fundamental methodological refiguration, which I will present in future work.

18 Linear temporality is not unrelated to the emergence of alphabetic writing and linear scripts.
19 That 'code' has long been challenged – perhaps to be taken also as a hint that we should likewise question the idea of linear temporal movement in Homer.
20 See e.g. Grethlein and Huitink (2017) and a large bibliography on *enargeia*.
21 *Sub voc.* 328.
22 Beck, LfgrE, M (*Metrik*), 26x neut. acc. sing only, 25x δολιχόσκιον ἔγχος, 24x verse terminal, u u – u u | – x //. Otherwise, (c) – u u | – x //, χάλκεον/μείλινον ἔγχος; (v) – u u | – x //, ὄβριμον ἔγχος.
23 See e.g. Griffin (1980) on the pathos of death, especially of heroes who appear only briefly.
24 See also Beck LfgrE, *sub voc.*
25 Rouse (1890: 183).
26 Kirk (1985: 316) on 3.346–7. Cf. more recently, Bowie (2019: 346): 'Why the shadow should be highlighted is not clear: the epithet may simply be a poetic way of saying "long".'
27 We see in parallax. Likewise, as the world moves, we see many images, from many different angles; etc. I make no assumptions here beyond the basic facts. See e.g. *The Oxford Handbook of Philosophy of Perception* (Hilbert 1984).
28 See below, n. 31.
29 Cf. Purves (2010a: 34–5) who, discussing *eusynoptic* views of the poem as a whole, notes that: 'Homeric scholarship has also emphasised, however, that the *Iliad* is difficult to visualise as a single, coherent entity. Not only do we run into problems connected with sequence and simultaneity when attempting to "see" the plot as if it were a picture, but we are also given very few examples of clear-sighted human vision within the poem.'
30 A *demonstratio ante oculos* in the tick-tock world of linear time visible to our eyes.
31 The terms are Heideggerian, of course, and refer to the ontology of his phenomenology and his use of the term *aletheia*; see Heidegger (1962: 133, 220); Dahlstrom (2013: 11–13) for overview and references.
32 *Od.* 10.151–4 is particularly interesting for its visual description though Book 10, a nighttime adventure, contains no instances of the epithet 'long-shadowed':

> ἀμφὶ δ' ἑταῖροι
> εὗδον, ὑπὸ κρασὶν δ' ἔχον ἀσπίδας· ἔγχεα δέ σφιν
> ὄρθ' ἐπὶ σαυρωτῆρος ἐλήλατο, τῆλε δὲ χαλκὸς
> λάμφ' ὥς τε στεροπὴ πατρὸς Διός·

> And around him (i.e., Diomedes), his companions
> slept, with their shields beneath their heads. Their spears
> upright on their end-spikes, *and the bronze tips*
> *shone like the lightning of father Zeus.*

Cf. also e.g. the image of 'Achilles and Ajax Playing a Board Game' with their spears at rest (Exekias, amphora, 540–530 BCE, Musei Vaticani, Rome). Aristotle says (*Poet.* 1461a3): 'this was then their custom, as it still is among Illyrians'; thus, a 'real-world' depiction.

33 Cf. Ingarden (1973).
34 Eadweard Muybridge, public domain, via Wikimedia Commons: https://commons.wikimedia.org/wiki/File:Muybridge_horse_gallop.jpg (accessed 13 June 2023).
35 The reference, again, is to Heidegger's phenomenology. See n. 31, above.
36 As words, as signifiers, *not* as signifieds or meanings.
37 For *duration* as I use it in this essay, see, e.g., Bergson (1913).
38 See Bielfeldt (2014: 33 n. 31).
39 See e.g. F. G. Lorca's famous, 'Lament for Ignacio Saches Mejias' (1935). The poem narrates a long, dramatic sequence of events in the *corrida* and the death of the matador, opening with and repeating the refrain 'At five in the afternoon. // It was exactly five in the afternoon'.
40 See Kahane (2022b).
41 For *mouvance*, see Zumthor (1990).
42 Benjamin (1999: 463, N3, 1). Benjamin does not speak of Homer in this passage.
43 See esp. Lynn-George (1988: 170–1) on *Il.* 18.94–100 on Achilles' demand *autika* for his death: 'The intensity of the wish would abolish the intervals of time's sequence – even the short succession which will culminate in Achilles' own swift and early death after Hektor – in a death which would be present instantly' and on 'the timing of death, that which always comes either too early or too late, even – as in the case of the hero Achilles – both too early *and* too late.'
44 For 'hollow' ships, see Ward (2019).
45 On the epithet, see core bibliography in Reece (2010: 259).
46 *Pace*, e.g. views by Hegel, Lukács, Auerbach, Bakhtin, etc., regarding the authority and fixity of epic.
47 See Kahane (2021).
48 See Kahane (2018b), Kahane (2019) and Kahane (2018a).
49 See Foley (1991).
50 See e.g. Most (2005), Porter (2004), Porter (2021).
51 For the arguments, see e.g. The Postclassicisms Collective (2020) and esp. section on 'Untimeliness'.

2

Historical Ontology, Texts and Interpretation

Protagorean Reflections

Duncan F. Kennedy
University of Bristol

Ontology studies the question of being, of what exists, of what is or is not ('really') *there*. Interest in the verb *to be* arose in the fifth century BCE and the question of *being* became central for the discourse set in motion in the fourth by Plato to which he gave the name 'philosophy', and was taken up by Aristotle in the series of texts that were later gathered together under the title *Metaphysics*. Recently, a number of prominent thinkers in different disciplines have turned afresh to ontology. Their studies take perspectives that are often explicitly at odds with the styles of metaphysical thinking associated with Plato and Aristotle and render visible just how shot through with unexamined 'Platonic' and 'Aristotelian' ontological assumptions 'modern' thinking remains. Their approaches offer different emphases and operate under different labels: speculative realism (Tristan Garcia); object-oriented ontology (Graham Harman); modes of existence (Bruno Latour); new realism or neo-existentialism (Markus Gabriel); and new materialism (Thomas Nail).[1] Drill down and significant differences (even antagonisms) become apparent; still, many overlapping concerns emerge. Most relevantly here, in contrast with ontological approaches that (looking back to Parmenides of Elea) seek out the transcendental and timeless, things in themselves, being as against becoming, these ontological approaches see entities – scientific (Latour [2000]; Daston [2000]), conceptual (Koselleck [2002]), indeed ontological styles of thinking themselves (Kennedy [2020]) – as *coming into being* and sometimes fading away, and this is the focus of their concern. New things – artefacts, technologies, concepts, ideologies – are coming into being constantly, and these affect what it is to be a human being. Historical ontology encourages us to imagine what it was like when such things were emerging into the intellectual and experiential landscape before they were taken for granted as having been simply 'there' all along.

This chapter has two purposes. Section 1 fleshes out the styles of thinking sketched here; then Section 2 explores the implications of this ontological turn for texts and their interpretation in reconsidering the famous dictum of Protagoras, 'Man is the measure …'

1. Discourses of Coming-to-Be

The world is full of a bewildering variety of 'things' that – in various ways and to a greater or lesser extent – have being, are *there*, for us. Markus Gabriel offers the following provocative list (2015b: 1): 'There are planets, my dreams, evolution, the toilet flush, hair loss, hopes, elementary particles and even unicorns on the far side of the moon, to mention only a few examples.' His list includes physical objects, concepts, events, objects of the imagination. Crucially for Gabriel, these things do not exist *in themselves* or *in the same way*. Something 'exists' – etymologically it 'stands out' – within what Gabriel (2015b) calls a 'field of sense' populated by other things. His most obviously playful example, unicorns on the far side of the moon, exists in the field of sense constituted not simply by the list in which it appears, but more broadly by the argument he puts forward in his book: unicorns on the far side of the moon do not exist *in the same sense* as elementary particles, but both exist in some (field of) sense. The toilet flush exists in a field of sense that is not simply, as philosophers might put it, mereological, the parts (handles, levers, ballcocks, valves, stoppers) that make it what it is and do what it does. This would be physically reductive, and the ontologists we are concerned with are very resistant to any forms of reductionism. The field of sense in which a toilet flush exists can be one that also contains supply chains, piped water, public health legislation, germ theory, sewerage systems, fatbergs, plumbers, the Herculean labours of Thomas Crapper, amongst much else.[2] Nothing exists in splendid isolation, per se, but any thing you care to name acquires its distinctive properties, what makes it what it is (a 'new' or 'better' flush), *in relation to* whatever else populates the field of sense within which it 'stands out'. Elementary particles exist in a different field of sense from the toilet flush, one populated by things like the Large Hadron Collider, institutions like CERN, research scientists, readouts of data, grants, academic papers and peer review and so on, in accordance with which something like the Higgs boson is instituted as an entity that is *there* – and wouldn't be *there* for us without them.

The question of being, then, is not what exists (for things without number exist, and new things are continually coming into being that were not there before), but *how* what exists exists, what Latour calls their 'modes of existence'.[3] Along the lines of Gabriel's fields of sense are two of Latour's intersecting modes of existence, which he terms Network and Attachment. Human beings are a case in point. 'We are what we are attached to' is a recurrent mantra of Latour's. The networks of attachments that make us who we are, individually and collectively, change over time and in relation to events in which we are involved and the things we encounter. Gabriel puts it thus (2018: 39):

> Some of the things human agents do can be accounted for only with adequate reference to the fact that they do them in the light of an historically variable conception of what it is for them to be human. Humans live their lives in the light of a conception of what the human being is. This conception does not pick out a natural kind.

Human beings develop fresh conceptual schemata, often as hypothetical ideas, but as ontological investment in them becomes more intense (the sense that, yes, they are *there*), these ideas become embedded in human belief and practice. Hacking (1994) calls this 'the looping effects of human kinds'.[4]

Many of the things to which we are attached escape our attention, perhaps because we have not (yet) observed them or are unaware of their effect on us (such as microbes before Pasteur demonstrated their agency). They exist, but are not *present* for us; they 'are' not 'in front' of us. We exist in the midst of so many things that make us what we are and that we *make to be,* in some (field of) sense or other (like the toilet flush or unicorns on the far side of the moon), but while fields of sense may overlap (CERN surely has toilets that flush), there is no single field of sense that encompasses everything, and that we could observe, as it were, from the outside – a God's-eye view. This is, as the title of Gabriel (2015b) asserts, *Why the World Does Not Exist*, where 'the world' is imagined as a field of sense that would embrace every thing that has ever existed or will ever exist.[5] As we exist within fields of sense, we observe them only from the inside.

Fields of sense are irreducibly plural and change over time and circumstance as they are populated by new things. It is the task of ontologists who explore the question of being in this manner not to prejudge what may or may not be included (recall Gabriel's list). Methodologically, this is sometimes referred to as 'flat ontology' (Harman 2018: 54–8), which considers things in no pre-ordained hierarchy. Tristan Garcia emphasizes that, formally, ontological study should seek to embrace anything whatsoever to which being is or has been attributed, no matter what – 'n'importe quoi' (2014: 19–30). This does not leave us with fields of sense that are littered indiscriminately with stray things. Another of Latour's modes of existence is Organization: when arranged within fields of sense things acquire properties and values in respect of whatever relationships they have with other things that occupy any particular field, their networks of *attachments*. Garcia theorizes thus as he asks (2014: 105; original emphasis): 'Can one be without being *something*? Being this or being that is belonging to this or that, being *in* this or that. We say that this or that "comprehends" that which is this or that … Being is *being comprehended*.' For human beings, comprehension can be epistemic, but for Garcia it embraces many different sorts of relations, for example 'spatial containment, mereological constitution, and being an instance of' (2018: xvi). The key term here is *relations*, which can, but need not, involve human observation. Comprehension epistemologically (as in human comprehension) is but an instance of comprehension ontologically. Ontologically, a thing exists *in some relation or other to* something else: it is not enough for something to *be*, it must be *there* for something else. On its own, being, or comprehension, Garcia suggests (2014: 168–9; original emphasis), 'is not enough to account for the fact that things are *there* … More precisely, the connection between a thing's two senses, being and comprehension, constitutes its presence.' Likewise absence is relational: absence is the absence of something *for* something else.

This way of thinking about being leads Garcia to question prevalent ways of thinking about time, in particular how we think of the terms *past*, *present* and *future*. The past has, in some sense, gone away; it is absent. Present (what 'is in front') and future (what 'is about-to-be'), as their etymology suggests, are ontologically inflected – indeed, are the product of particular ontological styles of thinking that are open to rethinking. He says (2014: 177):

> The problem of defining time concerns the status attributed to the present. Since at least Saint Augustine [*Confessions* 11.20], understanding time only from the present only leads to confusion. The past is not, since it is no longer present; the future is not, since it is not yet present; and the present is only insofar as it slips by and is already no more, since its being is to become.

Received approaches to understanding time, which assume a binary distinction between is/is not, 'all divide time into temporal extension, considering past, present, and future as temporal parts of a whole – some real, others illusory. Since these philosophies of time lead to impasses, we ought to consider past, present, and future not as extensive parts, but perhaps as *intensive* variations' [of presence, in Garcia's sense]. Thus, what is called the present is for Garcia (2014: 182; original emphasis) 'always the *maximum of presence*', but never an *absolute* presence. What gets called the past is not an absolute non-presence, but a *relative* non-presence. And what gets called the future is not a non-existence, but an absence that could not be greater, a maximum of absence.

Garcia's notion of *intensity* refreshes for us comprehension of what time is as a process. 'Insofar as it is a process, the past is all that weakens in presence'; [we can] 'understand the presence of the past as an *intensive variation* of presence'. Thus he suggests: 'The continuous intensive variation of presence is what we call time' (2014: 183). Latour has a similar take. What gets called the present is not a point 'in' time, the marker of a chronological measure (e.g. 2013), in which time is thought of in quasi-spatial terms as an extension, a 'fourth dimension' (1993: 74): 'Time is not a general framework but a provisional result of the connection between entities.' It is the systematic organization of entities, some of which may be 'very old', some 'very recent', that constitutes *a* 'present', and it is the replacement of some entities by others that gives the sensation of time having passed.

For Garcia, things come into being, but never entirely pass away, though the intensity of their presence may have become so weak for us as to escape our awareness of them. A corollary of this is that the universe is getting fuller of things. More things exist in 2023 than did in 1900 or 400 BCE, and it is through variations in intensity, relative presence or absence (for 'us' and for 'others', say 'Greek thinkers in 400 BCE'), that we 'comprehend' them and accommodate them to different fields of sense (e.g. 'the history of Greek thought'). Many things that have come into being are not 'there' for us, which is not to say that they do not affect us, as, for example, anthropogenic climate change was not 'there' for many a generation ago. And, once we start to have an intense ontological investment in some thing, the belief that, yes, it is really there, as with anthropogenic climate change, we look for hitherto undetected traces of its presence in the 'past'. Meanwhile, we coexist with things whose agency will only be *there* for those who come after us, and they may experience their relative intensity in pointing out their relative absence for us, just as we experience the relative intensity of certain things by pointing out their relative absence for those who have 'passed away' (e.g. 'Greek thinkers of 400 BCE').

Degrees of intensity of presence or absence make ontological enquiry into a historical study no less than a philosophical one. This has been an active and salient aspect of scholarship for some years now. In a collection of essays from 2000, *Biographies of Scientific Objects*, its editor Lorraine Daston assembled a range of studies across the natural and social sciences under the rubric of 'applied metaphysics', how 'whole domains of phenomena – dreams, atoms, monsters, culture, mortality, centers of gravity, value, cytoplasmic particles, the self, tuberculosis – come into being and pass away as objects of scientific inquiry' (2000: 1). Such comings-into-being are historical, and in surveying associated fields of study and their philosophical affinities Hacking suggests (2002: 4–5) that 'the catchphrase "historical ontology" helps us to think of these diverse enquiries as forming part of a family'.[6] Likewise, modes of thinking or, as Hacking has it, 'styles of reasoning' are regarded as phenomena that have come into being at certain times and certain places; new fields of sense are brought into being (1996: 72):'Each style of reasoning brings into being new standards for objectivity, and indeed new objects.' In the cases of 'philosophy', 'metaphysics', 'the question of being' or 'history', this was Greece over the course of the fifth and fourth centuries BCE. But, as ontological investment in such styles of reasoning deepens, they are often projected back into periods when they did not yet exist in the (fields of) sense that would subsequently come into being, as we shall explore in Section 2.

Although it is possible to draw distinctions between these styles of reasoning – the 'historical' from the 'philosophical', say – such distinctions from this perspective are articulated in the service of some argument or other, some field of sense, and are not final; 'history' or 'philosophy' are not regarded as existing *per se* but in relation to each other, and neither has dominion over the other. Within the perspective Daston adopts, history and philosophy, ontology and epistemology remain linked: the 'domains of phenomena' that 'come into being and pass away *as objects of scientific inquiry*' actively engage attention as they *become* present to us. Daston (2000: 1) cites not Aristotle's writings on being, the *Metaphysics*, but his treatise on becoming, *On Generation and Corruption* (1.3, 317b34) in describing 'applied metaphysics' as 'a sublunary metaphysics of change, of the "perpetuity of coming-to-be"'. Daston invokes a separation of worlds characteristic of metaphysical thinking: superlunary, 'up there', is the domain of static, changeless Parmenidean being (e.g. the Forms in Plato's writings, *ousia* in Aristotle's); sublunary, 'down here', is the domain of dynamic change, of appearance and disappearance. In applied metaphysics, our perspective is from down here, the domain of perpetual coming-to-be of which we are a part, where no sets of relations, no distinctions are ever final, as new things emerge and become present to us that change the fields of sense we experience.

How does the interpretation of texts look from the perspectives put forward in historical ontology? A text does not exist 'in itself', its meaning encoded once-and-for-all at some moment deemed its 'creation', a term that attributes God-like qualities to its author who can view it in its entirety and is the ultimate arbiter of its sense.[7] Rather think of a text as perpetually coming into being within an extensive and changing field of sense that contains its author, perhaps its characters and setting, as maximally present within an immense network of attachments that includes other texts, crucially those that come *after* the moment of inscription (though maximally absent at that moment, they become present later), no less than those that came before. The reception of the text, unforeseen and largely unforeseeable, works to determine what the text is thought to be about, what is thought to be *there* in it. This field of sense exists in time, a perpetuity of coming to be without finality. What was maximally, but not absolutely, present fades as other things maximally absent enter the field of sense: new texts, future readers not-yet-being, who will come to the text with their (unkn)own attachments. Garcia's take on time as intensive rather than extensive makes him cautious about conventional ways of ordering past, present and future as successive extensions of a whole. What he says about determination in relation to his own life is suggestive for how the meaning of texts becomes determined (2014: 184):

> The future is indeed the greatest possible absence of determination. It is what the present can dissolve. On our view, counter-intuitively, my future was closer to me at my birth, at the moment when, even defined by my familial history and my social situation, I could become all or nothing: dying young, being famous, anonymous, good or evil. This future will in reality be further from me at the moment of my death; I will die, determined and completed by a past.[8] The past, to the extent that it extends, therefore separates the future from the present, which is increasingly loaded with determinations – whereas the future remains the maximal indetermination.

In this way, the present moves away from (what was) the future, dissolving it as it goes, effacing futures that could have happened. Such 'futures past' (to use the phrase that gives Koselleck [2004] its title) are, emphatically, not non-existent. Even if their presence may not have been keenly felt for long periods, that presence can be freshly brought to our attention in newly organized fields of sense.

Derrida had a nice play on ontology as relative presence and absence: hauntology. Peter Salmon succinctly comments on this 'near homonym of ontology', 'the not non-existent' (2020: 171):

> All words carry with them that which they are not; this was, after all, Saussure's original insight. So it is that life carries with it things that are *not*: the ghosts of

the dead, of possible futures not realized, pasts that could have been. Every decision is a renunciation, and the path renounced still in some sense exists, commenting on the choice taken.

Derrida calls the discourse that engages with relative being/non-being *spectrality*.[9] Reading and interpretation are performative processes that *resuscitate* and restore different degrees, *shades* even, of presence and absence, to aspects of the text (authors, words, ideas, arguments, settings, personalities, roads not taken) in relation to those attachments maximally present for a reader – Garcia's *intensity*. Writing of historical ontology Thomas Nail seeks to characterize how this happens (2019: 14):

> The past is not an objective set of fixed events. Depending on the conditions of the present, different aspects or dimensions of the past will appear or disappear. New lines of development between the past and the present can be put forward on the basis of new social, scientific, and aesthetic discoveries or events that emerge in the present ... As the present changes, however, so do the lines of the past that lead to it. This does not mean that history is illusory and false but rather that it is composed of multiple real and divergent historical series. There is no other starting point outside of the present from which to begin.

As Garcia has suggested, the present – *this* particular field of sense that constitutes a 'present' – is always a maximum of presence, never an absolute presence. Let us explore this in terms of the concerns of this present essay, the emergence of ontological styles of thinking across a range of texts from the fifth and fourth centuries BCE. From a starting point of the field of sense called 'historical ontology', one must not take for granted, or regard as inevitable, developments which were not *there* for the authors of these texts. Meaning is not yet determined as a text comes into being but – recall what Garcia said about his own life – becomes 'increasingly loaded with determinations', none of which definitively establish that meaning once-and-for-all. New lines of development, to use Nail's phrase, can be put forward in respect of which different aspects and dimensions of the past can appear.

2. Resuscitating Protagoras

In the course of the fifth century BCE, the verb *to be* is not only used in statements and assertions, it becomes an object of enquiry. Prominent was the poem of Parmenides of Elea, *On Nature*. Fragment 8.6–11 reads:

μοῦνος δ᾽ ἔτι μῦθος ὁδοῖο
λείπεται ὡς ἔστιν· ταύτῃ δ᾽ ἐπὶ σήματ᾽ ἔασι
πολλὰ μάλ᾽, ὡς ἀγένητον ἐὸν καὶ ἀνώλεθρόν ἐστιν
οὖλον μουνογενές τε καὶ ἀτρεμὲς ἠδ᾽ ἀτέλεστον·
οὐδέ ποτ᾽ ἦν οὐδ᾽ ἔσται, ἐπεὶ νῦν ἔστιν ὁμοῦ πᾶν,
ἕν, συνεχές·

There only remains the word of the path [scil. that says] 'Is'. On this one there are signs, very many of them: that being, it [or: that which is] is ungenerated, indestructible, complete, single-born, untrembling and unending [scil. probably: in time]. And was not, nor will it be at some time, since it is now, together, whole, one, continuous.

Trans. Laks and Most

The verb *to be* is made to flex its muscles here – some of them, at least. Charles H. Kahn remarks (2009: 204): 'In these verses a modern commentator may classify the first occurrence as existential or veridical (*hōs esti*), the second as locative-existential (*tautēi d'epi sēmat'easi*), the third and fourth as copulative (*agenēton eon kai anōlethron estin*). But an ancient reader would probably recognize only more or less emphatic uses of a single verb with a single (unanalyzed) meaning.' The kind of grammatical analysis 'a modern commentator' might be familiar with is maximally absent, and would only gradually emerge in antiquity over subsequent centuries (cf. Ildefonse [1997]); the field of sense of the verb over time will become populated by fresh distinctions and categories to which it will be variously related. Nonetheless, with the repeated use of the form *esti* Parmenides establishes the characteristics of what we can call 'is'-being: not subject to creation or destruction, time, change or movement.

This treatment of 'is'-being by Parmenides would become the central concern for the emergent discourse Plato in the fourth century was to call 'philosophy',[10] and drove the discussion of some of its most famous concepts (the Forms in Plato's own works, and *ousia* in Aristotle's), which trace the line of development, in Nail's sense, from their presents back to Parmenides. But the significance of that reception should not lead us to overlook the intense interest in the verb *to be* and a lively debate on its uses, before there was a 'thing', an organizing discourse and style of thinking, called 'philosophy' – or indeed 'history' – as they have become familiar to us. The emergence of the style of thinking associated with the verb is characterized by robust, indeed polemical, disputation, and so it has continued through Plato to 'the present'. Melissus of Elea (and thus a compatriot of Parmenides) wrote a work entitled *On Nature, or on What there Is* (Περὶ φύσεως ἢ περὶ τοῦ ὄντος). The title of Empedocles' major work, according to the entry on him in *Suda*, was not simply *On Nature* but *On the Nature of Things that Are* (Περὶ φύσεως τῶν ὄντων). David Sedley (1998: 22) has drawn attention to the contrast between the singular Melissus uses ('proclaiming his Eleatic monism') and the plural in Empedocles ('for what was above all else a pluralist manifesto'). In turn, Gorgias, a follower of Empedocles, plays slyly on Melissus' title, and the lofty Parmenidean dismissal of non-being, in his *On What there is Not, or on Nature*. Sadly, these treatises are largely – though not wholly – absent for us. However, the fragments we have do not exist 'in themselves' but are the product of selection and discussion in relation to styles of thinking that, sometimes friendly, sometimes hostile, draw attention to these extracts in contexts their authors cannot have anticipated.[11]

Parmenides works to decouple 'is'-being from what we might call 'am'-being or 'we'-being, the human experience, individual *and* collective, of coming into being, of time, change and movement. From the perspective of historical ontology, such a distinction is not final or absolute, but rather seeks to enquire how first- and third-person being might be related. At this point, let us present another text from the mid-fifth century BCE, Protagoras' dictum 'Of all things the measure is man, of the things that are, that they are, of those that are not, that they are not' (πάντων χρημάτων μέτρον ἐστὶν ἄνθρωπος, τῶν μὲν ὄντων ὡς ἔστιν, τῶν δὲ οὐκ ὄντων ὡς οὐκ ἔστιν, DK 80 B1), in which the experience of 'man' is included, not excluded, from the question of the being of 'the things that are'. Parmenides' poem may be a shadowy presence here. This well-known saying has been subjected to intense exegesis ever since,[12] notably in Plato's *Theaetetus*, where Socrates quotes a version of it (152a–b) and asks Theaetetus if he knows it. Theaetetus responds that he has come across it often, and they then engage in a lengthy discussion of what the saying might mean, to which we will return. But first, a third text.

The fifth century offers multiple examples of *to (e)on* to express what the writer or speaker thinks to be the case (cf. Kahn 2009: 22). Thus in Herodotus 1.30, when Croesus asks Solon, as one who has travelled far and wide seeking wisdom (φιλοσοφέων)[13] if he has ever seen the most prosperous of all men (thinking the answer must be himself), Solon would not flatter him but said 'Tellos the Athenian'. Herodotus uses a striking phrase – difficult to translate – to characterize Solon's reply: τῷ ἐόντι χρησάμενος. Solon tells it as it is? Solon makes use of the *to eon* argument? Croesus invites Solon to use his unmatched personal experience of the world to answer the question he poses. Thrown by his reply, Croesus retorts: κοίῃ δὴ κρίνεις Τέλλον εἶναι ὀλβιώτατον; ('How *do you judge* Tellos *to be* the most prosperous?'). 'Is'-being is to be determined by the informed judgement of an 'am'-being, Solon. Astonished though Croesus is by Solon's reply, it is not capricious, and draws on Solon's unparalleled wealth of observation. The Parmenidean isolation of 'is'-being is relatively absent, and Solon is obliged to give his reasons that this is the case, as he goes on to do. Croesus' question puts him on the spot, and Solon 'has recourse to *to eon*', perhaps anachronistically for someone who lived a century and more before Herodotus was writing.

Might one posit some relation between Herodotus' χρησάμενος and Protagoras' χρημάτων? Mauro Bonazzi (2020, §2.1) comments:

> *Chrema* (sic) derives from the verb *chraomai*, meaning 'to treat', 'to use', 'to entertain a relation with': according to its original meaning, the term describes not so much 'things' in themselves (in this case Protagoras could have used *onta* or *pragmata*), as in relation to us; the emphasis is on the way in which we relate to things, use them, judge them, and so on.

The observation he makes about the relational contexts in which the word is used is interesting, but one could take issue here with the notion of 'original meaning', the sense that *khrēmata* (let's insist on the plural) can be isolated as having a meaning in itself, if only we could pin it down once and for all (time), or with the notion that Protagoras would have been (anachronistically, like Solon in Herodotus?) concerned with 'things in themselves'. Protagoras was interested in techniques of public argumentation (a title *Kataballontes logoi*, 'Knockdown Arguments', an image associated with wrestling, was attributed to him); *epideixis*, the public display of argumentative skill, was his preferred mode of performance, and is a possible context for an opening dictum (Bonazzi 2020, §1.2 and §2) well calculated to grab his audience's attention and get them arguing. If so, Protagoras' dictum has certainly succeeded in provoking discussion, in ways he may not have foreseen, and with a lack of finality that continues to prove a source of exasperation for some.

Now a fourth text, in which pinning down stable meaning over time has become a matter of intense concern, Thucydides' account of the Peloponnesian War. Thucydides expresses the hope (1.22.4) that his words will be *judged* useful (ὠφέλιμα **κρίνειν**) by those who want to see clearly 'the things which came to be, and are going to be' (τῶν τε γενομένων . . . καὶ τῶν μελλόντων ποτὲ . . . ἔσεσθαι) again at some time or other in the same, or nearly the same, way, 'in accordance with the human' (κατὰ τὸ ἀνθρώπινον). 'Man' is very much in the frame in the discourse of Thucydides, not only in the issue of those men (plural) judging his words 'useful' ('whoever they are [ὅσοι] who will want [βουλήσονται] to contemplate the clear thing [τὸ σαφὲς σκοπεῖν]' – they will be the measure of whether it is useful or not), but the reason for doing so. He posits something – 'the human thing' – regarded as (more or less) transcending time and circumstance, one not subject to change, investing it with the associations of Parmenidean *esti*. In an emphatic combination of the neuter definite article and an adjective (the formation that would do so much work in Plato's writings in pointing to some 'thing' such as 'the good' or 'the beautiful'), he reduces the plurality of human beings to *one* thing, which expresses the grounds on which his words may become not a 'competition piece for immediate hearing' (ἀγώνισμα ἐς τὸ παραχρῆμα ἀκούειν) but 'a possession for always' (κτῆμά τε ἐς αἰεί). τὸ παρα**χρῆμα**, which has a temporal aspect of immediacy, has resonances of παρὰ τὸ χρῆμα, something to which recourse is made as the need arises in, say, an epideictic argument.

This mode of ontologizing 'the human', reducing plural humans to one thing and removing it from time and change, works to bring into being an explanatory concept that claims to transcend the here and now. It seems to offer the prospect of reaching back into the events which came to be and forward into those that are going to be, and seeks to wrest some stability of interpretation from perpetual coming-to-be. Could such a sense of explanatory reach across space and time also underlie Protagoras' assertion that *man* (singular) is the measure of all things? Socrates in *Theaetetus* will contentiously try to resolve Protagorean judgement into a matter of each individual's perception (152a), what I think and what you think to be the case, 'and you and I are, each of us, a man?' More on this in a moment. But it could be argued that *man* expresses the outcome of the process of *collective* judgement: first-person being as 'we'-being, the considered judgement of those who assemble around a particular question or inquiry, those who, like Thucydides' prospective readers, will want (βουλήσονται – does one just hear an echo of the *boulē*, the Athenian assembly in this word?) to contemplate/examine (σκοπεῖν) 'the clear thing' (τὸ σαφὲς) and come to a judgement. Protagoras is thought to have had a great interest in democracy. In particular, as Bonazzi §5.4 (referencing Farrar [1988]) says, 'the parallel between the vindication of opinions implied by [the dictum that 'man is the measure . . .'] and another key motive of Athenian democracy, *isegoria* (everyone's right to express their idea in the assembly), need[s] to be taken into account: the right for everyone to express their ideas seems to rely on the assumption that all opinions are legitimate'. All opinions are legitimate, but some may be 'better', 'more useful' or 'more to the point' than others, and it is the role of public debate to come to a judgement on which these may be.

A remarkable thing about some texts of the late-fifth century is the way in which figures long dead are made vividly *present*: Croesus and Solon are *there* for the readers of Herodotus' enquiries (whenever they happen to read the text), walking and (especially) talking, being put on the spot, arguing their case; as Derrida would put it, they *haunt* the readers of these texts. Such will become a major feature of the discourse that morphs from Herodotean ἱστορίαι, 'enquiries', into a single thing, a style of thinking Aristotle calls ἱστορία, 'history', in *Poetics* 1451b6. But we see the same techniques put to work in the texts in which the processual search for wisdom, φιλοσοφέων (recall Solon in Herodotus 1.30), becomes a particular style of thinking, a 'thing', φιλοσοφία, in the field of sense of the dialogues of Plato.[14] Not only Socrates, recently dead, is *there*, but other figures are conjured 'back into life' in the dialogues that bear their name, such as Parmenides in the *Parmenides* and Protagoras himself in the *Protagoras*. But Protagoras is a conspicuous absence in the *Theaetetus*, the dialogue in which his dictum is discussed at such great length (152a–171d). Protagoras could not participate because, at the dramatic date of this dialogue shortly before the death of Socrates in 399 BCE (cf. *Tht.* 142c), he had been dead for about twenty years. Socrates, Theaetetus and Theodorus seek to pin down the meaning of Protagoras' saying, but succeed more in revealing the challenges that poses through the dialogue's dynamic staging of this exercise in performative reading and interpretation.

In *Theaetetus* 152a–b, Socrates quotes the saying and asks Theaetetus if he knows it. Theaetetus responds that he has come across it often. Socrates suggests an interpretation. 'And so, he says something along these lines' (οὐκοῦν οὕτω πως λέγει): 'as individual things seem to me, such are they to me (οἷα μὲν ἕκαστα ἐμοὶ φαίνεται τοιαῦτα μὲν ἔστιν ἐμοί), and for you in turn such as they appear to you (οἷα δὲ σοί, τοιαῦτα δὲ αὖ σοί); you and I being "man" (ἄνθρωπος δὲ σύ τε κἀγώ)?' Socrates drops in the example of a wind that feels cold to one person and not to another, and suggests that this equates perception of that which is (αἴσθησις ... τοῦ ὄντος) and knowledge (ἐπιστήμη). Before going further, Socrates suggests that the saying is deliberately designed to bamboozle the likes of them. He remarks (152c) that perhaps the πάσσοφός Protagoras 'uttered this riddle (τοῦτο ... ἠνίξατο) to us the multitudinous mob (πολλῷ συρφετῷ), while he told the truth (τὴν ἀλήθειαν) to his pupils on condition that it was not to be spoken of (ἐν ἀπορρήτῳ)'. Aha, the real meaning known only to true initiates! Socrates' own statement here is hard enough to pin down. Is he joking? Is πάσσοφός 'all-wise' or 'know-it-all'? Is the reference to 'truth' playing on the title attributed to Protagoras, *Alētheia*? Is the reference to 'telling the truth to his pupils' a teasing dig at one of his interlocutors, Theodorus, one of Protagoras' followers (i.e. 'if anybody knows, you should')?[15] This banter (if such it is) is doing quite a lot of work, before Socrates offers his take and admits that it is 'no bad argument' (οὐ φαῦλον λόγον) (152d, trans. McDowell):

> It's to the effect that nothing is one thing just by itself, and that you can't correctly speak of anything either as some thing (ἓν μὲν αὐτὸ καθ' αὑτὸ οὐδέν ἐστιν) or as qualified in some way. If you speak of something as big, it will also appear small; if you speak of it as heavy, it will also appear light; and similarly with everything, since nothing is one – either one thing or qualified in one way. The fact is that, as a result of movement, change and mixture with one another, all the things we say are (εἶναι) – which is not the right way to speak of them – are coming to be (γίγνεται); because nothing ever is, but things are always coming to be (ἔστι μὲν γὰρ οὐδέποτ' οὐδέν, ἀεὶ δὲ γίγνεται).

Socrates goes on to remark that all the wise men (οἱ σοφοὶ; he names Protagoras, Heraclitus and Empedocles and the poets) agree on this, with the exception of Parmenides, who was striving to speak of one thing in itself (ἓν ... αὐτὸ καθ' αὑτὸ, as Socrates puts it), and to strip out movement and change. This offers a very neat genealogy of the distinction between the one and the many, between being and becoming, with Parmenides, the proponent of unchanging 'is'-being, appropriately in splendid isolation over against the many, the multitudinous mob (including 'you' and 'me' and 'us') and their reluctance to bracket off 'am-/we'-being in their search for *Alētheia*, to bracket off 'perception of what is' from 'knowledge'. To translate this title as (singular) 'Truth' – as most modern scholars do – is perhaps to load the argument in favour of Parmenides, and marshal against Protagoras something as monolithic, as univocal, as the term *truth* has *become* in philosophical discourse 'after' Plato. Might we rather hear some of the historical resonances of the word, not letting things escape our attention (*a-lētheia*), and translate it 'Awareness' or 'Not Overlooking'? The human search for knowledge, individual and collective, arguably involves noticing not only things that are emphatically there for us, but things whose presence is unnoticed or has faded, yet affect us.

Surely the *truth* is out there *somewhere* ... or is it? Socrates, Theaetetus and Theodorus discuss the meaning of the dictum at length. Socrates even puts what he thinks Protagoras must have meant into Protagoras' mouth in an extended *prosopopoeia* (*Tht*.166a–168c). Socrates ends up by arguing that it is self-refuting (*Tht*. 171c): 'So then, since it is disputed by everyone, Protagoras' *Truth* wouldn't be true for anybody – not for anyone else nor for the man himself.' Theodorus objects that 'we are running *down* (**καταθέομεν**) my friend too hard'.[16] Socrates responds by picking up on the verb Theodorus has used, but changing the prepositional prefix to say that it isn't clear that we are running *past* (**παραθέομεν**) what is correct (τὸ ὀρθόν, 'the correct thing'), thus countering an accusation of personal disparagement with an appeal to the (albeit elusive) 'correct' meaning. But is there a 'correct' meaning? Protagoras is not there to defend himself, Socrates takes Theodorus to be saying. But would even his physical presence to put his side of the argument be a sufficient guarantee of the 'correct' meaning of his statement, outside of the contexts in which it is discussed (as in *Theaetetus*)? Socrates responds with a rather grotesque flight of fancy (*Tht.* 171d): 'it's likely that he, being older than us, is wiser than us; and if he suddenly popped up (ἀνακύψειε) out of the ground, from the neck up, he'd condemn me for talking a lot of nonsense, in all likelihood, and you for agreeing with me, and then he'd duck down and get away at a run'. Socrates presents his pop-up Protagoras as a slippery customer, quick to deny and pour scorn – perhaps as a ploy to avoid 'saying what he really means'? But even if he wanted to, could Protagoras settle the issue for once and for all? Does historical ontology have a lesson here for interpreters of Plato's dialogues? Notably Plato never appears (nor even sticks his head up out of the ground!) in his writings (for Diskin Clay [2000], he is 'the silent philosopher'), and those who seek to establish univocal meaning, of 'the truth' or of the meaning of Plato's texts, are forever working against the grain of these multivocal, dialogic, performative texts in which, however well the speakers grapple with 'the truth', there is no 'knockdown' argument.

Protagoras: 'I'm Still Standing'

The search for the 'original meaning' looks like the ('philosophically' inflected) quest in this sublunary world for the crock of gold at the end of the rainbow, as Socrates in the *Theaetetus* seems to imply. Furthermore, as van Berkel remarks (2020: 104): 'Plato's engagement with the statement in *Theaetetus* 151e9–160d2 seems to have sealed its fate as an epistemological thesis in its philosophical *Nachleben*.'[17] The phrase 'sealed its fate' recalls our discussion in Section 1 of Garcia's description of the way 'the future' is at its most undetermined at the moment of birth, and 'its philosophical *Nachleben*' suggests how the passage of time and circumstance lay down determinations on meaning, but do not, finally, determine it once-and-for-all. 'Philosophy' is but one line of development, as Nail would put it. The meaning of texts (Protagoras' dictum, the dialogues of Plato) cannot be fully circumscribed in any field of sense and remain open to new considerations. The sense of what is, or is not, 'really' there in such texts changes over time and circumstance. The approach put forward by the historical ontologists we looked at in Section 1 can plot a line to Protagoras' statement as one early instantiation of a set of concerns in this present *now*, in which ontology is not viewed as exclusively the preserve of its 'philosophical' reception, and Protagoras not treated as a punchbag, his provocative dictum drained of its capacity to challenge. The Parmenidean/Platonic pursuit of an 'is'-being separate from human experience is but one response to 'the human thing'; but an insistence on it may lead us to overlook much of what makes us human, a condition characterized by an overlooking, an unawareness or a forgetting of so many of the myriad things that affect us and make us the 'am/we'-beings that we happen to be, but open to new *realizations* of what that might be (there). Historical ontology offers a field of sense that treats *a-lētheia* not as a 'thing', to be translated as 'the truth', but as an ongoing and urgent quest for awareness of those things that have escaped our notice but could inform our (always imperfect, always incomplete, always shifting) sense of what is, or is not, the case.[18]

Notes

1 I have explored the work of Latour in Kennedy (2020).
2 This list is unashamedly inspired by Latour's account (1988) of the complex processes by which microbes were *instituted as entities*, rendered *there* and 'real' (for us), by Pasteur and others; see Kennedy (2020: 44–6).
3 Latour (2013: 488–9) summarizes the fifteen such modes he suggests.
4 Hacking explores such 'looping effects' in relation to recently emergent, and, in Latour's sense, instituted, entities as 'recovered memory syndrome', 'trauma' and 'child development': Hacking (1995) and Hacking (2002: 1–26). Ontological investment can be particularly strong when something is regarded not as a 'human' kind, but what Gabriel called a 'natural' kind.
5 'The world' exists only *within* the field of sense we have come to call 'metaphysics'.
6 The most prominent figure in the field of sense Hacking constructs is Foucault, particularly *The Archaeology of Knowledge* (Foucault 1972). One important figure he does not mention is Koselleck (2002), who explores 'the history of concepts' (*Begriffsgeschichte*).
7 For the theological entailments of much current philological practice, cf. the essays in Conybeare and Goldhill (2020).
8 Here I disagree: what Garcia's life or reputation will mean will not be *completely* determined at the moment of his death.

9   Most notably in *Spectres of Marx* (Derrida 1994).
10 Cf. Nightingale (1995), Nightingale (2004) and Moore (2020).
11 As explored in Cassin (2014: 297–316).
12 The material from antiquity is collected in Laks and Most (2016: VIII.80–113). For a list of the sources in which the dictum (with some variations) is cited cf. van Berkel (2020: 78 n. 18). A number of titles of Protagoras' works are transmitted, but, as van Berkel remarks (2020: 78): 'We do not know what our source authors are "quoting" from. We do not know if they consulted Protagoras' writings in the original, nor, for that matter, if such originals were available at all – even in the early stages of Protagoras' reception. This has exasperating consequences for the likelihood of reconstructing the original philosophical meaning [of the dictum].' Nowhere is the quest for 'the original philosophical meaning' more relentlessly pursued than in Plato's *Theaetetus*, to which we shall return below.
13 On this use here cf. Moore (2020: 128–32). For further analysis of this episode, cf. Kennedy (2020: 63–5).
14 Cf. Nightingale (1995), Nightingale (2004) and Moore (2020).
15 Blondell (2002: 255) says that Socrates 'is only mildly ironic towards the recalcitrant Theodorus' only to remark in footnote 18 (my emphasis): 'In fact it is questionable how ironic any of these passages *really* is.' Is irony *there* or not? 'Really' stands as a marker of ontological presence or absence *for* someone.
16 For the loyalty of Theodorus to his old teacher here, cf. Blondell (2002: 282, 286–7).
17 Cf. van Berkel (2020: 81 n. 32): 'The classical analysis of the differences between the Protagoreanism in Plato (relativism) and that in Aristotle (subjectivism) is set out in two articles by Myles Burnyeat [Burnyeat 1976a and 1976b].' van Berkel's own field of sense for reading the fragment is organized around ethics.
18 I am currently exploring the issues raised here in a book – a larger field of sense – provisionally entitled *The Emergence of Ontological Styles of Thinking in Ancient Greece*.

3

Roman Temporalities of Presence

James Ker
University of Pennsylvania

Introduction

Time may be 'present' in two primary ways. Present time is of course distinguished from the past and future, but time itself may be said to be present (salient, marked, recognized, etc.) in a given context, rather than absent. The first of these senses, the present, invites questions about time-differentiation: what distinguishes the time being experienced now? how does this relate to times not being experienced now? The second sense, that time itself is present, invites questions about time's definition: what is time? what produces time? how are we made aware that time is there? In this essay I propose to trace some instances in Roman literature and culture in which time is marked as present in one or both of these senses, and this presence is marked as significant.

Consider, for example, Lucretius' *On the Nature of Things*, where the Epicurean poet explains that time does not exist independently but is a secondary attribute – an 'accident' (*eventum, DRN* 1.470) – of the material objects that are constituted exclusively by atoms and void. Some verses in that passage define the qualified sense in which time itself exists: 'Time, likewise, does not exist in its own right, but from things themselves ensues sensation' (*tempus item per se non est sed rebus ab ipsis | consequitur sensus*, 1.459–60). But he is also concerned with explaining how the past events of the Trojan War do not exist: we should not allow ourselves to be forced to say 'that these things *are* in their own right' (*haec per se . . . esse*, 1.466). The poet, then, toggles between the question of whether (or in what sense) time exists and the question of what conditions are required for past events to be present, all the while applying the same Epicurean analysis which withholds *per se* existence from both.

Below we will look more closely at this Lucretius passage alongside passages in Plautus and Seneca. My purpose in these case studies will be to examine the ways in which time's presence – especially in the two senses distinguished above – is configured, as well as how these two senses relate to one another. I will take each passage on its own terms, but there are some recurring tendencies in all three cases that can help us to get a better sense of Roman thinking about the presence of time overall, and especially the symbiotic relationship between time and the present.

These articulations of time's definition and internal differentiation are what I term 'temporalities of presence'. I use 'temporality' as a term that can highlight time's relational and subjective or imaginary dimensions.[1] This can be supplemented by proximate concepts that also go beyond mere time. Bakhtin's notion of 'chronotope' – in which 'time, as it were, thickens, takes on flesh, becomes artistically visible' – allows us to focus on the genre-specific and site-specific presence of time fused with space.[2] The more recent critical term 'timescape' is equally concerned with spatialized time, but points toward a more subtle and complex assessment of environmental context.[3] 'Chronotype', as distinct from chronotope, invites an appreciation of tendencies as well as variations of time-behaviours among a population,[4] while 'time-orientation' focuses more on the profile (or profiling) of the persons involved.[5] Such concepts capture how sociocultural realities are shaped by time-dynamics and how time, in turn, is given existence, shape and meaning by society.

Below we will encounter various 'temporalities of presence' in which one or more aspects of time's presence are encoded in the literary contexts of our three case studies. Here I can only gesture toward the broad realm of Roman time-phenomena that serve as backdrop, and perhaps corrective, to the relatively limited patterns I will identify. Time's presence, for example, is established through a vast range of timekeeping devices, spatial arrangements, cultural notions, historical developments and literary representations that have been thoroughly explored elsewhere and which include consideration of how the history of Roman times has been narrated within the context of modern times.[6]

Less systematic attention has been given to Roman *present* time, and so I will sketch the terrain in more detail. First, there are the methods by which present time is thrown into relief against a backdrop of times that are not present – methods as simple as the use of a deictic such as *nunc* ('now') or idioms such as *cum maxime* ('at this [that] very moment', *OLD* s.v. *cum* 13b) or *in re praesenti* ('at the scene of action', *OLD* s.v. *praesens* 11). The scale and quality of the present time being delimited depends very much upon concepts relevant to a given context, extending from the instantaneous *in vestigio* ('[still] in [one's own] footprint', i.e. immediately; cf. *OLD* s.v. 2c) to the expansive notion of overlapping lifetimes or a shared era signified by *saeculum* (*OLD* s.v. 3: 'the present time, the contemporary generation').

Certain modern theorizations of present time are worth keeping in mind here. The specious present, for example, involves the extension of present time to include the recent past,[7] and is relevant to the usage of Latin *modo* ('just now') to treat as virtually present something that is actually past. And in postmodern studies of the late-twentieth century, the substitution of an open-ended present time for any genuine future is echoed in Shaw's claim that to some extent the ancient Romans did not possess a complex sense of the future relevant to various specific social and economic projects.[8]

These different scopes of present time in turn entail different calibrations of the past–present–future axis. In some instances the relationships present-to-past and present-to-future are roughly symmetrical. For example, the term *olim* is notoriously open as to whether its 'at some time' belongs in the indefinite past or indefinite future (cf. *OLD* 1, 3), while *repraesentare* can refer to acts of presencing that bring past *or* future entities to the fore.[9] Most often, however, these two relationships are asymmetrical, due to time's unidirectional arrow. Bettini has traced Roman conceptions of time that include the notion of 'the future at our back', in which the subject faces the past, and of a spatial arrangement of *antiqui* and *posteri* that is comparable to a funeral procession in which the oldest ancestors walk at the front.[10]

So far, we have been discussing the separation between present and non-present time, but often the presencing of non-present times is at issue. In Roman exemplarity, present actions emulate (or avoid) past models,[11] and within linguistic usage we see the historic present, in which selected past events are described as if occurring in the present, and the epistolary past tense,[12] in which the letter-writer refers to the time of writing from the time-perspective of the recipient for whom that time is already in the past.

There are also instances in which time-discourse is concerned with the coordination or synchronization of multiple times in a shared present. One example is the double-indication of one and the same time, in two different modes, such as when the autumn date of the emperor Claudius' death is told both in poetic circumlocution (*iam Phoebus breviore via contraxerat arcum*, 'Already the sun had contracted its arc in shorter path') and in bathetic quotidian prose (*mensis erat October*, 'It was the month of October', Sen. *Apocol.* 2).[13]

Another is what Luckmann called the 'interpenetration' of 'non-identical diachronies', such as one's inner time, the time of the body, the time of others in social interaction, etc.[14] We see this type of superimposition at work in Ovid's *Fasti*, where the poet draws attention to the coincidence of several distinct time schemes such as the discourse-time of the poem and the time of the civic calendar being described: *cum carmine crescit et annus* ('the year grows together with the poem', *Fast.* 2.1).[15]

Lastly, what are we to make of modern scholarly practices that invite us, for the sake of analysis, to conceptualize ancient events within a scholarly 'now', or to make ourselves at home in an ancient now? O'Donnell draws attention to the tendency to excessive temporal familiarity in classical scholarship and teaching, and suggests instead: 'Let us try as well to stop forgetting the lapse of time'.[16] This critique asserts the value of historicizing our relationship with the deep past rather than syncing with it.

One thing to reiterate before we proceed is the symbiotic relationship between time's presence and the present time. For whenever we begin exploring how time stands out in the Roman universe in one way or another, becoming present in the foreground of cultural life in close connection to other features of the Roman imaginary, we soon brush up against time's inherently extensional dimension – that is, time as a quality of reality that is concerned with, and defined by, change and contrast, both in the temporariness of the present (as time moves on) and in the absence of past and future (as parts of time that were previously present or will be present later). Whenever we survey time-phenomena involving the contrast of present time and non-present time, we are certainly shifting focus from time's existence overall to the experiencing of time in some 'now', and how its relationship to other times is experienced. Yet, the presence of time itself is primarily experienced through the interface of present time, and the absence of time altogether is to some extent analogous either to the remoteness (from now) of the past and the future or to the impact of an enduring present. Present time is sometimes just a metonym or synecdoche for time itself, while references to 'time' are sometimes most concerned with temporal dynamics that are characteristic of present time.

As already noted, a vast range of cultural areas would need to be explored in order to give a thorough account of Roman temporalities of presence. Yet, each of the three case studies considered below provides signal opportunities to glimpse how the workings of presence, in all its senses, are central to Roman time-discourse – and even more so when we consider them together.

1. A Culture-History of Time's Presence (Plautus)

Our first case study concerns an oft-quoted fragment from Plautus that includes an early reference to the Romans' adoption of hours and sundials, featuring a lengthy complaint by a hungry parasite who is not happy that he must now wait until the scheduled time for dinner (Gell. *NA* 3.3.5).[17] Here we will be concerned with time made present in the novel form of horological timekeeping and the perceived impact of this innovation as it defines present times in contrast with past and future.

The fragment begins with a curse against the putative first-inventor of both a new time-unit and the device for measuring it: 'May the gods destroy the one who first discovered hours and who also first set up a sundial here!' (*ut illum di perdant, primus qui horas repperit,* | *quique adeo primus statuit hic solarium!*, lines 1–2). As indicated by *hic* ('here'), it is not simply the invention that is being lamented, but the resulting presence of a sundial in the parasite's local environment. He specifies the impact this has had on him personally: 'He has reduced my day to pieces' (*qui mihi comminuit misero articulatim diem*, line 3). This statement alludes to a prior time in which the parasite's day was pristine and whole. He then goes on to describe what this time before sundials was like: 'For when I was a boy my belly was my sundial, by far the best and more truthful than all those ones. You would eat when it told you, except when there was nothing' (*nam <unum> me puero venter erat solarium* | *multo omnium istorum optumum et verissumum:* | *ubi is te monebat, esses, nisi quom nil erat*, lines 4–6). Although these lines describe the belly metaphorically as an archaic sundial, the belly's time-telling function is anchored not in time-units and scheduling but in the authority of the body's sensation of hunger and in its power to command eating at any moment. Finally, in the last verses of the fragment, the parasite returns to evoke the present suffering in which he shares: 'Now even what there is, is not eaten, except with solar approval. And so the town is now so stuffed with sundials, most of the people are on their knees, parched with hunger' (*nunc etiam quom est, non estur, nisi soli lubet.* | *itaque adeo iam oppletum oppidumst solariis,* | *maior pars populi <iam> aridi reptant fame*, lines 7–9). The image of a city 'replete' with sundials but overcome by starvation encapsulates the unique degradation of the present time.

The fragment, then, is first of all concerned with a historical event in which time – the clock-time marked by sundial and hours – has become present. This historical event may be understood in a few ways. To begin with, there is the discovery of hours by the primordial first inventor in a *Kulturgeschichte* in which timekeeping has arrived in a world where hitherto this form of timekeeping, and in some sense time itself, had been absent. Then there is the importation of sundials into the city of the play – whether this is to be understood as a fictional version of Rome, where sundials were indeed fairly novel in the time of Plautus, or as Athens (or Boeotia) in an earlier Greek play that Plautus may have been adapting, perhaps from the time of Menander, when sundials were, correspondingly, still novel in the Greek world.[18] There may also be more specific moments in the lost play to which the parasite is alluding – if, for example, his host had recently set up the sundial at or near his house in recent times. And then there is the literary-historical evolution of dramatic time-conventions in Middle Comedy, which may add a metatheatrical dimension to the parasite's complaint.[19] In any case, the fragment is very much concerned with this immediate, tangible and consequential presence of horological time within the dramatic scenario.

Inseparable from this, however, is the parasite's account of how the clock's presence defines his own experience of the *nunc* (now) of present time. This degraded present is portrayed along two distinct axes. First, in a more concrete realization of the Kulturgeschichte timeline, there is the periodizing contrast between the present time and the good old days within the parasite's own lifetime, when he was a boy (cf. *me puero*). As noted above, in the good old days the body held free sway over determining the time of eating. This past is cut off from the present time by the fact that the day is now articulated (a culinary image that also, however, suggests the network of hour-lines on the sundial), and it is now the sun that has sole say on whether eating can take place. In Plautus' pun *nunc etiam quom est, non estur* ('Now even what there is, is not' – eaten, that is), beyond the wordplay between *esse* (to be) and *ēsse* (to eat) there are suggestions of a present time that is inauthentic and insubstantial in contrast to the past, all because of the presence of clocks.

In this critique of the present there is also a second contrast. This is the contrast between the present moment, which is experienced with such misery by the parasite, and the future moment when hunger can be satisfied. The deferral of this desperately awaited future is thematized more prominently in a much later text from the second century CE or later, Alciphron's satirical letter in which a parasite named 'Noonchaser' (Ἐκτοδιώκτης) observes that 'the gnomon is not yet (οὔπω) casting its shadow on the sixth [hour]' and suggests bending the gnomon so that 'it will be able to indicate the hours [viz. for eating] more quickly (τάχιον)' (3.1.1–2).[20] And so the parasite's perspective on the presence of horological timekeeping is inextricably bound up with an experience of present time that stands in contrast with his past experience and equally suffers the agony of separation from a future mealtime.

We may say, then, that time makes its presence felt, in the parasite's comedic world, through the specific degraded experience of present time in relation to both past and future, and this problematic experience in turn bolsters the condemnation of time's presence – or at least of the presence of clock-time. One further perspective worth keeping in mind here concerns the impact of this fragment within the literary work where it is preserved, the *Attic Nights* of Aulus Gellius written in the second century CE. The parasite's primordial encounter with timekeeping technology adds detail to an antiquarian past which, through the eyes of Gellius' contemporary readers, may seem like a rudimentary contrast for the technological sophistication of their present-day imperial elite world but may also seem to anticipate an old-fashioned Roman's resistance to the imposing social schedules of that same imperial world.

2. An Ontology and Epistemology of Time's Presence (Lucretius)

Our second case study is the Lucretius passage briefly cited above, from early in the opening book of *On the Nature of Things* where the poet has been arguing that there is no 'third nature' (*tertia ... natura*, DRN 1.432) that exists beyond atoms and void, and that things such as weight, servitude and war are all to be understood in each case as an *eventum* – his term for Epicurus' notion of σύμπτωμα (accidental attribute, 'accident') – of things that are compounded exclusively from atoms and void.[21] A prominent item on this list is time, and he explains its ontological status at greater length (*DRN* 1.459–63).[22] The passage gives us an opportunity to consider the qualified presence of time as a secondary attribute of the material world yet still a significant reality, and how non-present times relate to the present.

Lucretius begins by emphasizing that time exists only secondarily: 'Time, likewise, does not exist in its own right, but from things themselves ensues sensation of what was completed in the past, then what thing is immediate, further what will follow next' (*tempus item per se non est, sed rebus ab ipsis | consequitur sensus, transactum quid sit in aevo, | tum quae res instet, quid porro deinde sequatur*, 1.459–61). In case this was not clear enough, he reiterates the point in slightly different terms: 'Nor must it be said that anyone senses time in its own right, separate from the motion of things and from calm rest' (*nec per se quemquam tempus sentire fatendumst* | *semotum ab rerum motu placidaque quiete*, 462–3). If, though, this grants time only a qualified presence, as something that is never present *per se*, the poet also signals here time's connection both to the alternation of atoms' motion and rest (cf. *motu ... quiete*) and to our experience of *sensus* (sensation). The latter is a dynamic experience in which *res* themselves that are present to our perception (atoms and things compounded from them) can show us all of time's three parts: 'what has been done in the past, then what thing is immediate, further what follows next' (*transactum quid sit in aevo,* | *tum quae res instet, quid porro deinde sequatur*, 460–1).

While in some sense the Epicurean analysis demotes time to an epiphenomenal status, Lucretius does not at all undermine the significance of time as a unique and complex component of our experience of the world. Admittedly, as Zinn observes in a lucid discussion of the time-sense to which Lucretius here refers, the ways in which we can know times beyond the present are limited.[23] With reference to times prior to the invention of writing and to the history (*res gestae*) commemorated by poets, the poet observes: 'our age cannot look back upon what was done before unless our reason somehow reveals traces' (*quid sit prius actum respicere aetas* | *nostra nequit, nisi qua ratio vestigia monstrat*, 5.1446–7). And of the future, 'one can only predict' by using prior experience as a guide.[24] Yet, despite all such limitations, Zinn notes: 'past, present, and future time are all real', unaffected by our knowledge thereof.[25]

The second major point Lucretius makes about time uses the example of the past: he is concerned to point out that past events do not exist *per se* in present time. His progression to this point suggests that to some extent he is inviting us to think of the past's non-existence in the present on analogy with the previous point – that is, *time's* lack of independent existence in the world – such that both time and the past are categorized in parallel terms as not existing '*per se*' (1.459, 466; cf. 1.479). Yet, Lucretius has already asserted above that time has a real (if secondary) existence, as an object of time-oriented *sensus* that can perceive past, present and future happenings. And so, to this extent, past events can be present – to the senses.

This stands in contrast, however, with the somewhat bolder claim of *per se* existence that certain others – Lucretius uses an anonymous 'they' – assert for past events (cf. *dicunt*, 1.465). The poet refutes that notion using an example: 'In short, when they say that having-been-abducted-daughter-of-Tyndareus is and that the-nations-of-Troy-defeated-in-war are, we must ensure that they do not happen to force us to say that these things *are* in their own right' (*denique*

Tyndaridem raptam belloque subactas | *Troiiugenas gentis cum dicunt esse, videndumst* | *ne forte haec per se cogant nos esse fateri*, 1.464–6). Here the delayed position of *esse* is highly emphatic: taking advantage of the periphrastic form of Latin's perfect passive, Lucretius parcels out the idea 'that Helen was abducted' to say 'that having-been-abducted-Helen . . . *is*', and ditto for the entire Trojan war, and then argues against the idea that the past event has its own present existence. He then attacks the reasoning that 'they' might use when arguing for the present independent existence of such past events, namely, 'because (they argue) an age now past, which cannot be called back, has taken away the generations of human beings whose happenings these were' (*quando ea saecla hominum, quorum haec eventa fuerunt,* | *inrevocabilis abstulerit iam praeterita aetas*, 1.467–8). The idea seems to be that the only way 'they' can see for past events to persist beyond the deaths of the protagonists involved is if the events somehow persist on their own. As for the identity of 'they', some scholars have seen here a possible reference to Stoics, given their analysis of time as something incorporeal but 'a thing conceived of in its own right' (καθ' αὑτό τι νοούμενον πρᾶγμα, Sext. *Adv. M.* 10.218) and given Stoics' willingness to treat past events as in fact corporeal (cf. Sen. *Ep.* 117.7), while others have not been so sure.[26] Doxography aside, it seems plausible that epic poets also are implicated in 'they', given that Lucretius is in part countering the capacity of epic narrative to establish facts about the historical past, as Nethercut has argued.[27]

Lucretius' rebuttal rests upon the idea that the persistence of the past is neither interrupted by the mortality of the protagonists nor does it necessitate an independent existence for the past. Rather, events will always be able to have a secondary existence perceptible to the senses so long as there is some material basis in a space or place: 'for it will be possible to say, whatever has been done, that it came about in one case in the world, in another case in the spaces themselves' (*namque aliud terris, aliud regionibus ipsis* | *eventum dici poterit quod cumque erit actum*, 1.469–70) – where *terris* perhaps stands in for body/atoms while *regionibus* stands in for space/void.[28]

The rest of Lucretius' discussion elaborates time's subtle status between two extremes. On the one hand, he reasserts the status of time, and of the past, as a secondary quality of the material world: *res gestae* (things done, accomplishments, 'history') do not exist *per se* in the way that atoms and void do (1.478–80), and he adds here a 'figura etymologica' for *res gestae* by describing void/place as *res in quo quaeque gerantur* ('that in which each thing is done', 482). On the other hand, he revels in the capacity of the material world to generate real events (*DRN* 1. 471–7):

> denique materies si rerum nulla fuisset
> nec locus ac spatium, res in quo quaeque geruntur,
> numquam Tyndaridis forma conflatus amore
> ignis Alexandri Phrygio sub pectore gliscens
> clara accendisset saevi certamina belli   475
> nec clam durateus Troiianis Pergama partu
> inflammasset equos nocturno Graiiugenarum.

> In short, if there had been no matter consisting of things and no place or space (in which each thing is done), never would the fire fanned in love by the beauty of Tyndareus' daughter have swollen beneath the Phrygian breast of Alexander and kindled the bright contests of fierce war, nor would the wooden horse, in secret from the Trojans, have secretly given birth to Greeks by night and set fire to Pergamum [= Troy].

From start to finish, then, the entire Trojan War sequence can be retold as a tale of elemental and biological processes.

In this passage, Lucretius provides a philosophical account in which he defines time's qualified presence and he also qualifies the sense in which past events may be considered present. Neither exists *per se*. But both time and the past *are* present as an *eventum* of atoms and void and can be accessed through *sensus*. And Lucretius so celebrates the movement and rest of atoms and void, and their capacity to generate temporally dynamic narrative sequences with their beginnings, middles and ends, that his passage makes time and its parts vividly present even as he denies their independent existence.

In a fuller account of Lucretius' interest in time's presence we would need to contextualize this passage within his broader narrativization of the poem's present time, beginning with the invocation of Venus in the poem's first words as *Aeneadum genetrix* ('Mother of the descendants of Aeneas', *DRN* 1.1) and his allusion to 'this unjust time in our country' (*hoc patriai tempore iniquo*, 1.41). We would also need to attend to the Epicurean appreciation of the present time that is best known from Horace's *carpe diem* but is also, as Hadot points out, expressed by Lucretius as the finitude of experiences available to us in nature: 'The same things always remain (*eadem . . . omnia restant*), even if you surpass all the ages in your living' (*DRN* 3.947–8).

3. An Ethics of Time's Presence (Seneca)

Hadot's 1995 essay 'Only the Present is our Happiness' savours the 'extraordinary structural analogy' between the privileging of present time in both Epicurean and Stoic doctrine, while also emphasizing their different motives. For the Epicureans, the present is a source of pleasure and freedom from pain, while for the Stoics it is, in general, a focus of duty and 'vigilance' so as 'not to miss anything that is contrary to reason'.[29] But in our third and final case study, a sequence in Seneca's *On the Brevity of Life*,[30] we find the Stoic philosopher giving an especially detailed account of temporal presence and its ethical possibilities that is perhaps not reducible to such a simple contrast.

The main contention of Seneca's work is that 'we do not receive life brief but make it so' (*non accipimus brevem vitam sed fecimus*, 1.3) and 'life is long if you know how to use it' (*vita, si uti scias, longa est*, 2.1). The key is to know the difference between merely existing and *living*, to avoid being one of whom it might be said: 'he did not live long, he existed long' (*non ille diu vixit, sed diu fuit*, 7.10). Time in the normative sense of life well lived is key to Seneca's contrasting portraits of a life in which time is absent or in short supply – which lends qualified truth to his opponents' complaint that life is brief – and a life in which time is present in abundance. This text gives us an opportunity to consider the normative definition of time in terms of time well spent and the unique ethical opportunities provided by present time.

Seneca's antagonists in the dialogue are the various time-wasters he refers to *en masse* as *occupati*, and he diagnoses their problem primarily as a failure to perceive time's presence and unique value (8.1):

> I am always amazed when I see some people requesting time and those asked being fully compliant (*facillimos*). Both parties have in view the thing for which the time was requested, and neither has in view time itself (*spectat . . . ipsum . . . neuter*). It is as though nothing is being requested and nothing given (*quasi nihil petitur, quasi nihil datur*). They are playing around with the most precious of all things (*re omnium pretiosissima luditur*), but it escapes their detection because it is an incorporeal thing, because it does not come before our eyes and therefore is judged to be of very little value – in fact, its price is set at virtually nothing (*fallit autem illos, quia res incorporalis est, quia sub oculos non venit ideoque vilissima aestimatur, immo paene nullum eius pretium est*).

Seneca here concedes time's incorporeality in Stoic doctrine: for the Stoics, time, like void, is one of the things that have only a qualified existence (*quasi sunt*, cf. Sen. *Ep.* 58.22). But this is merely a foil for his effort to have us see, value and hold on to time.[31] The uniquely superlative valuation he gives to time here elaborates his assertion a few chapters earlier that time is 'the one thing about which it is right to be miserly' (*cuius unius honesta avaritia est, Brev.* 3.1) and will be echoed also in *Moral Epistles* 1, where he asserts: 'Everything [else], Lucilius, belongs to others. Time alone is ours' (*omnia, Lucili, aliena sunt, tempus tantum nostrum est, Ep.* 1.3).[32] That exceptionalist language, as I have noted elsewhere,[33] parallels Seneca's exceptionalist account of virtue as the sole possession of the wise person that is inalienable (cf. *Const.* 5.5). And so, at least in this protreptic context, Seneca is keen to play up the presence of time as an ethical resource.

Not much later in the work, Seneca goes on to support his assertion about the quantity of (ethically normative) time that is present in a person's life by focusing on the question of how a person uses present time specifically. Urging his readers to avoid the mistakes of the *occupati,* he provides advice on meaningful use of time through a technical analysis of the different qualities of time's three parts (*Brev.* 10.2):

> Life is divided into three times: what was, what is, and what will be. Of these, that which we are doing is brief (*quod agimus breve est*), what we are going to do is doubtful (*dubium*), what we have done is certain (*certum*) – for this is what Fortune has lost jurisdiction over, what cannot be brought under anyone's authority.

In this analysis, the certainty of the past makes it substantial and significant.

The fundamental error of the *occupati,* however, is that they fail to take advantage of the present, which is brief but unique as an opportunity for action (*Brev.* 10.4–6):

> Single days only are present, and these through moments.... The present time is extremely brief (*praesens tempus brevissimum est*), so much so that to some[34] it seems to be nothing. For it is always on the move, it flows and it hurtles. It stops before it arrives, and it is no more tolerant of a pause than are the universe and the stars; their movement, always restless, never remains in the same spot. And so only the present time belongs to the *occupati.* Yet, present time is so brief that it cannot be seized (*tam breve est ut arripi non possit*), and even this is pilfered from them as they are distracted by many things.

Here the *occupati*'s failure to seize hold of the fleeting present gives a more precise point to Seneca's earlier observation that they fail to perceive and value time in general (cf. 8.1). There the relevant Stoic doctrine to be addressed, and in many ways counteracted, was the incorporeality of time (see on *Brev.* 8.1

above).³⁵ More relevant here, in turn, is a Stoic doctrine ascribed to Chrysippus, that 'only the present "belongs"' (μόνον ὑπάρχειν τὸν ἐνεστῶτα), making the present available and relevant in a way that the other parts of time are not – the latter merely 'subsist' (ὑφεστάναι; Long and Sedley 1987: 51B4). That distinction seems conceived in part with reference to the way in which predicates 'belong' to their subjects in linguistic propositions.³⁶ But also relevant are Stoic ideas about the brevity of the present, distinguishing between a 'broad' (κατὰ πλάτος) distinction of the present and the idea that 'no time is wholly present' (οὐδεὶς ὅλως ἐνίσταται χρόνος; Long and Sedley 1987, 51B3); in one formulation ascribed to Posidonius, the present is 'the briefest perceptible time' (τὸν ἐλάχιστον πρὸς αἴσθησιν χρόνον, Long and Sedley: 51E5).³⁷

In chapter 10, however, Seneca's analysis of time's three parts allows him not simply to spotlight the *occupati*'s failure as regards the present, but to problematize their relationships to future and past respectively. For it is their distraction by the future (cf. *districtis in multa*, 10.6) that is responsible for their neglect of the present. And their neglect of the present results, in turn, in a past time empty of accomplishments: 'Unwillingly, then, they recall their minds to times poorly spent (*ad tempora male exacta*) and do not dare to re-explore those things whose vices upon reflection are plain to see – even the ones that crept up through some seduction of present pleasure (*aliquo praesentis voluptatis lenocinio*)' (10.3). Seneca's emphasis on the security of the past is a distinctive theme of this dialogue – it is absent when he discusses time in the later work *Epistulae morales*.³⁸ Indeed his satirization of the *occupati* losing past time to oblivion and death is a tactic he elsewhere uses to characterize the experience of *all* people.³⁹ Here, though, he claims that the philosopher's effective use of present time has a quantitative benefit, which Williams convincingly associates with the Epicurean practice of *revocatio*, the recollection of past pleasures in the present.⁴⁰ Seneca's Stoic philosopher assembles a storehouse of significant past accomplishments that can be commanded to appear before him (*Brev.* 10.3–5):

> No one willingly turns himself back toward the past unless all his actions were performed under his own 'censorship', which is never deceived.... Single days only are present, and these through moments. But all the days of past time will be present when you command; they will let themselves be inspected and detained before your authority (*praeteriti temporis omnes, cum iusseris, aderunt, ad arbitrium tuum inspici se ac detineri patiantur*) – something the *occupati* do not have the time to do. A secure and peaceful mind can run out into all the parts of one's life (*in omnes vitae suae partes discurrere*). The minds of the *occupati*, cannot turn and look back at themselves.

Another counter to *brevitas vitae* comes later in the work, where Seneca presents a more systematic inversion of the *occupati*'s problematic relationship to past, present and future. For he claims that the philosopher's effective use of present time can transcend the limits of mortality altogether (15.5):

> The wise person's life is broad and capacious: he is not confined by the same limit as others. Only the wise person is released from the laws of the human race; all the ages serve him as they would a god (*omnia illi saecula ut deo serviunt*). Some time has passed: he grasps this in his memory. Some time is present: he uses this. Some time is to come: he anticipates this. His life is made long by a gathering of all times into one (*omnium temporum in unum conlatio*).

Again Seneca contradicts the claim that life is brief. The answer lies in a dynamic use of present time that allows for a presencing of all time's parts.

In Seneca, then, we see an alternating focus on time's presence and relevance as an ethical focus, especially the normative notion of time lived well, and on the unique value of present time as an opportunity for ethical actions – this being both a remedy against future-oriented distraction and a pathway to accumulating a memorable past.[41] These two areas of focus are mutually entailing. As in our other two case studies, the project of defining time is inseparable from the project of differentiating time's parts, and time's presence is felt above all through the dynamic relationship of present time to past and future.

Conclusion

It will likely have come as no surprise to the reader that Roman authors most often define time in close conjunction with exploring the differences and divides between present time, on the one hand, and the non-present times of future and past. If time is recognized as a present dynamic of Roman social and personal experience, then of course it makes sense that the form it takes should be one in which different parts of time are differentiated. The presence of time is, ultimately, predicated on the absence of times. But this simple and potentially simplistic observation has also allowed us to describe a recurring pattern in three otherwise quite disparate passages whose contributions to Roman time discourse are all important but otherwise somewhat distinct. The Plautine parasite provides a window into technology-history in an archaic comedic scenario, while Lucretius' poetic philosophical analysis primarily concerns the physics and epistemology of time and its parts, while Seneca's moralizing dialogue seeks to reorient the reader to a normative ethics of time-use. As we have seen, however, each of them reads a special significance into the presence of time that in each case is most fully articulated through demonstrating what happens when the present is separated from past and future; and each of them focuses on this separation to demonstrate what it means for time to be present in a person's experience.

Notes

1. For these aspects of temporality see Ogle (2019: 314–15).
2. Bakhtin (1981: 84). For an interesting application of chronotope to the Roman spaces of '*forum, urbs*, and *villa*', see Wolkenhauer (2019: 217).
3. For timescape, see Adam (1998: 11).
4. For chronotype, see Bender and Wellbery (1991: 4), and on chronotope *and* chronotype in the context of ancient time culture, see Miller and Symons (2019: 5–6).
5. On time-orientation, see Bergmann (1983: 465–73).
6. See Wolkenhauer (2019), Kondoleon (1999), Hannah (2009), Feeney (2010) and Ker (2023).
7. On William James' adaptation of this notion from E. R. Clay, see the section entitled, 'The Sensible Present Has Duration,' in *The Principles of Psychology*, vol. 1 = James (1981: 573–4).
8. See Nowotny (1994) and Shaw (2019).
9. On *repraesentare*, see Ker (2007).
10. Bettini (1991: ch. 13) and Short (2016).
11. See Roller (2004).
12. On these special tense-uses, see the linguistic analysis by Pinkster (2015: 413, 401–9).
13. See Weinreich (1937).
14. Luckmann (1991: 151).
15. See Volk (1997).
16. O'Donnell (2019: 236).
17. On this passage (Plautus, *Boeotia* fr. 1), see esp. Gratwick (1979), Wolkenhauer (2011: 124–37) and Ker (2023: 25–53).
18. See Gratwick (1979: 312).
19. An important suggestion made by the late Robert Germany (see Germany (2014)).
20. See Gratwick (1979: 309).
21. On Lucretius' presentation of accidents, see Bailey (1947: 2.670–2).
22. On this passage, the Epicurean analysis of time, and the sequel passage dealing with events (*DRN* 1.464–82) also discussed below, see Bailey (1947: 2.675–80), Long and Sedley (1987: 7A), Zinn (2016), Warren (2006) and Fratantuono (2015: 35–8).

23 Zinn (2016: 130–1). See also Warren (2006) for detailed exploration of how Lucretius understands the ontological basis of past events in relation to the present (arguing against the past-present reading of Lucretius and Epicureanism): Lucretius evidently refuses 'to be drawn into the game of offering some present bearer for these [past] events' (p. 374).
24 Zinn (2016: 130).
25 Ibid. (131).
26 See Bailey (1947: 2.676) and Warren (2006: 370–1 n. 19).
27 On this passage as a whole, see Nethercut (2021: 79–83); Lucretius contends 'that the past no longer exists in a way that makes it relevant to us' (86). Nethercut himself takes *dicunt* as a possible 'Alexandrian footnote' by which Lucretius signals his engagement with prior poetic passages.
28 This is how the terms are understood by Bailey (1947: 2.677), although this reading is not universally agreed upon; see the discussion by Fratantuono (2015: 36–7); Long and Sedley (1987: 2.26).
29 Hadot (1995: 226).
30 See the commentary of Williams (2003) and discussion by Gagliardi (1998: 31–50). On time in *On the Brevity of Life* and generally in Seneca, see the overview in Edwards (2014: esp. 324–30).
31 On Seneca's 'appropriation' of time, see Armisen-Marchetti (1995).
32 See also Edwards in this volume.
33 Ker (2009c: 159–60).
34 Referring to 'unspecified Stoics' (Williams (2003: 183)).
35 On Stoic time doctrines, characterized by 'flexibility', see Long and Sedley (1987: 1.306–8, quotation from p. 308).
36 See Long and Sedley (1987: 1.308); also, on the Stoic conception of a 'retrenchable present', Schofield (1988: 357–8).
37 The influence of Posidonius in *Brev.* 10 is highlighted by Williams (2003: 182–3).
38 On Seneca's portrayal of past and present here by contrast with *Epistulae morales*, see Gagliardi (1998: 36).
39 Cf. Williams (2003: 181).
40 Ibid.
41 See also Edwards in this volume.

Part Two

Time, Space and Relations in Greek Literature

4

'... how you first went over the earth'

Interactions of Human and Divine Time in the *Homeric Hymn to Apollo*

Anke Walter
University of Newcastle

The construction of time in literature is not a monolithic phenomenon.[1] Even within one and the same text – or what has come to be transmitted as one and the same text – ideas of time, and of the interaction of human and divine time in particular, can differ quite strongly. This is in particular the case in the *Homeric Hymn to Apollo*. As I am going to show, we can see here how, between the first and the second half of just one text, the notion of 'sacred time', the locating of the present moment and the relationship between human and divine time can appear in rather different shapes.

The question of the two parts of this text, the 'Delian' and the 'Pythian,' and the place and time of their composition, as well as that of the fusion of both into one text, is old and much-debated,[2] and I am not going to enter into this debate here.[3] What I am going to show, however, is that both parts of the hymn construct the interaction of human and divine time in markedly different ways.[4] In the first part, which centres on the god's birth on Delos, there is relatively little concrete interaction between the time frame of Apollo and the humans on earth. The festival on Delos takes place in a temporal sphere somewhere between human and divine time, and the song of the Delian Maidens, in its dialogue with the song sung among the gods on Olympus, enacts the power of Apolline poetry to take humans beyond the limits of mortal time.

The realm of human time, characterized by a linear experience of time, is much more prominent in the second part of the hymn. It not only forms the backdrop of the events surrounding the foundation of Apollo's oracle in Delphi, but the god's own actions become intertwined with it. The aetiological focus of the 'Delphic' narrative is much more pronounced than that of the Delian part, where explicit *aetia* are absent.[5] In establishing his oracular cult in Delphi, even Apollo himself uses aetiological formulae to make sure that the sequence of his foundational acts will forever be commemorated. At the end of the hymn, Apollo acknowledges the characteristic human inclination towards hubris and its consequence: the possibility of changing constellations of power. By the time Apollo's oracle is established, his own deeds are already entangled with the time of men on earth. The second part of the hymn is still markedly different from, but paves the way for Callimachus' Hellenistic *Hymn to Delos*, where Apollo even before his birth lends his voice to specific historical events. Whether or not the *Homeric Hymn to Apollo* originally consisted of two parts, one belonging to an earlier period than the other, what we can conclude with certainty is that, in the archaic age, the way humans situate themselves with regard to the 'timeless' sphere of the gods, is not fixed, but remains open to very different representations.

1. The Delian Festival

I should note from the start that I take the first part of the hymn not to end with lines 177–8, as some scholars do,[6] but with line 206.[7] In the first part of the hymn, then, Apollo is born and goes up to Olympus, the second part begins with a proem (207–15) that has many parallels with the very first proem of the hymn (19–29; cf. e.g. 19=207) and with Apollo coming down from Olympus (216). The parallels between the two Olympian scenes, at the beginning and the end of the first part,[8] as well as between the scene on Delos and the second scene on Olympus (cf. below), underline this. I believe that the hymn forms a coherent whole, honouring the god in his entirety,[9] even if different strata or layers might have been involved in the composition of the hymn as we have it today.

While the beginning of the first part (with the first scene on Olympus, Leto's wanderings and Apollo's birth) is firmly located in the divine sphere, the festival on Delos and the question of its timing are central for understanding the interaction of human and divine time in this part of the hymn. This festival must have come into existence at some point after the god's birth and his setting forth on the journey to his favourite places. What is described as the 'beauty' (χάρις) of the scene of the festival, which would 'delight' the spectator (τέρψαιτο δὲ θυμόν, 153), mirrors the reaction of Delos to Apollo's birth, when the island 'was laden with golden growth' and was full of joy (γηθοσύνηι, 137).¹⁰ This suggests, together with the fact, highlighted by Richardson, that the Ionians come together 'mindful' of the god (μνησάμενοι, 150), that their gathering is a festival in commemoration of the god¹¹ and his birth. Very much in contrast to what we will see in the second part of the hymn, no *aetion* is given, and the festival is not bound to a specific moment of origin. Its coming into existence remains miraculous and looks like an extension or continuation of Delos' own supernatural reaction to the god's birth.¹² This is underlined by the characterization of the humans celebrating this festival: 'a man might think they were the unageing immortals if he came along then when the Ionians are all together' (151–2).

Note that the connection established between the festival celebrated on Delos and the visit of the god is not temporal, but spatial, as the description of the festival in the text is tied to Apollo's arrival on Delos (cf. ἔνθα 147).¹³ Apollo's wanderings themselves have their own temporality. He 'sometimes' went to Cynthus, and 'sometimes roamed the islands of the world and of men' (ἄλλοτε μέν, [...] ἄλλοτε δ' αὖ, 141–2).¹⁴ The time frame of his wanderings is not strictly circular (he does not appear to come back to the same places in the same order at about the same time), nor is it measured in terms of the linear passage of time. Instead, Apollo's visits to the world of men are part of a rather unspecific but recurring frame of time ('sometimes ..., sometimes'),¹⁵ entirely dictated by the inscrutable mind of the god.

The text, then, does not tell us at what time or in which intervals the festival takes place, but closely aligns it with Apollo's seemingly erratic wanderings. The connection between the festival and the gods is underlined by the parallels between the celebrations on Delos and those on Olympus. Apollo, the poet says after describing the scene on Delos, goes to Pytho, and from there to Olympus, 'swift as thought, to the house of Zeus, to join the congregation of the other gods' (186–8; cf. also θεῶν [...] ὁμήγυριν ἄλλων, 187, with Ἰάονες ἠγερέθονται, 147). Like the Delians, the gods, upon Apollo's arrival, 'devote themselves to lyre music and song' (188). What follows is a scene of singing and dancing (189–206) that closely resembles not only the very first scene on Olympus, with which the hymn begins (1–13), but also the festival celebrated on Delos.¹⁶ Just as Apollo's arrival on Olympus initiates the singing and dancing among the gods, so his arrival on Delos activates the description of the Delian festival.¹⁷ Both in terms of its timing and in terms of these parallels, then, the festival on Delos stands in close contact with the sphere of the gods.

2. Delian and Olympian Song

The festival on Delos forms the backdrop for the song of the Delian Maidens.[18] They are introduced as a 'great wonder' (μέγα θαῦμα, 156), which further aligns the festival with Delos' own miraculous reaction to the god's birth, its becoming all golden, and the goddesses' wonder at Apollo's birth (θάμβεον, 135). The Delian Maidens, who 'know how to mimic all people's voices and their babble' (162), transgressing the boundaries of language (cf. φωνάς καὶ βαμβαλιαστύν, 162),[19] sing of 'the men and women of old' (μνησάμεναι ἀνδρῶν τε παλαιῶν ἠδὲ γυναικῶν, 160). Although none of these people of the past are mentioned by name in the short résumé of the song given by the poet, the poet includes himself in the immortal κλέος conveyed by the song. Having praised the Maidens as a 'great wonder, the fame of which will never perish' (156), he asks them to think of him in the future and tell visiting strangers that the poet they enjoy most 'is a blind man, and he lives in rocky Chios; all of his songs remain supreme afterwards (μετόπισθεν)' (173–4).[20]

By asking the Maidens to remember him (μνήσασθ', 167), the poet establishes a connection between himself and 'the men and women of old', whom the Delian Maidens 'remember' in their song (μνησάμεναι, 160). The poet, it is suggested, will one day also belong to the people 'of old', whose fame is preserved in song and who become immortal.[21] As the emphasis on the time 'thereafter' suggests (μετόπισθεν, 166; 173), the present hymn, in which the encounter of the blind singer and the Delian Maidens is narrated, also functions as an *aetion* for the fame and afterlife of the poet. The poet and the Maidens, then, mutually guarantee each other's undying fame and memory. This happens while both the Maidens of Delos and the poet sing a hymn to Apollo (cf. 158; 177–8), whose memory forms the raison d'être of the entire festival on Delos (cf. μνησάμενοι, 150) and stands as the first word in the first line of the poem (μνήσομαι).[22] The poetic fame of both the Maidens and the poet, then, is inextricably intertwined with the power of the god of poetry, which is proven time and time again when the hymn is recited and the commemorative and laudatory power of this poetry is enacted.[23]

The song of the Delian Maidens pleases the audience and fills them with delight (they 'sing a song that charms the peoples', 161). The hymnic text, by indirectly transmitting their words, conveys some of that pleasure to its own audience. This joy is mirrored a little later in the scene on Olympus, when, hearing the song of the Muses to the sound of Apollo's lyre, and watching the dance of the gods, Leto and Zeus are 'delighted in their great hearts' (204).[24] For a split second, the charm and beauty of the song brings the audience – both the

Delians mentioned in the text and each new present audience of the hymn – in touch with the sphere of the gods.[25]

Yet, the same joy that unites gods and men also fundamentally divides them. Whereas the Delian Maidens sing of the fame of 'men and women of old' (160), what delights the immortals is the inability of men to find a defence against old age (γήραος ἄλκαρ, 193).[26] The song that delights the gods, then, is a reminder of the power of linear time over the life of men, who inexorably move from birth to old age to death.[27] Also, while song for the mortals is the only way to overcome the limits of their lives and gain poetic immortality, song has a merely entertaining and ornamental function among the eternal gods. The two songs mirror each other, shining a light on the human condition from two opposing points of view: the human and the divine. The common bond between the two songs sung on Delos and on Olympus is Apollo.

The same god who gives the gift of immortalizing poetry to men, once arrived back on Olympus, accompanies a song about human mortality, stressing the limits set to mortal existence. To a certain extent, however, the song sung among the gods underlines the power of poetry even more: first, because it gives the human audience of the hymn access to the content of the song sung among the gods, and second, because, given the limitations of mortal existence, poetry's power to preserve the 'famous men and women of old' is all the more astonishing – and the very hymn, as it is read or heard, proves that power by preserving the fame of the 'blind man from Chios' and the Delian Maidens. The first part of the hymn, then, both reminds the audience of, but ultimately lifts it beyond the linear passage of time on earth, by describing a festival that is located between mortal and immortal time, and by enacting the power of poetry to convey immortal κλέος.

3. Pythian Apollo

The second part of the hymn is dedicated to the narrative of how Apollo, having established himself on Olympus, goes on to found his oracle, in order to prophesy 'Zeus' unerring will to humankind' (132).[28] This deed is crucial for the relationship of gods and men: it gives humans access to the divine sphere – not unlike poetry, as we just saw – thus taking them beyond the limits of their knowledge and establishing a means of communication between gods and men.[29] But even in the narrative of how the oracle is first founded, the time frame inhabited by Apollo comes to be much more closely tied to the linear time of men on earth than anything that happens in the first part of the hymn. This creates a special kind of sacred time: the distinction between divine foundation and human commemoration is obliterated, the god's and the poet's gaze converge in one meaningful moment, and the god himself ultimately has to acknowledge the power of change in human affairs.

Apollo begins 'to walk on the broad-wayed earth' (133) after his birth and his very first prophecy (131–2).[30] Yet, as we saw, in the first part, Apollo's wanderings remain fairly unspecific, with the god wandering 'sometimes on rugged Cynthus, sometimes on the islands and the world of men' (ἄλλοτε μέν ... ἄλλοτε δ' αὖ', 141–2). This changes in the second part when the poet again sets out to narrate how Apollo 'first went over the earth, in search of a place for his oracle for humankind' (214–5). In this case, Apollo's itinerary is described in much more detail and with particular emphasis on the sequence of the god's wanderings.[31] Apollo 'first came down to Pieria from Olympus' (πρῶτον, 215), 'soon' (τάχα, 218) he reached Iolcus, 'from there' (ἔνθεν, 222) he crossed the Euripus, 'from there he quickly reached Mycalessus and grassy Teumessus' (τάχα δ' ἷξες ἀπ' αὐτοῦ, 223) and reached Thebes,[32] 'from there' he went on (ἔνθεν, 229) and so forth.[33] Compared with the voyages described in the first part of the hymn, this one is more firmly tied to the actual conditions on earth and the locations of the individual places. The god's wanderings are thus more accessible to the human mind than the unspecific 'sometimes ... sometimes'. Yet, there is still something notably divine about this itinerary, and that is the speed with which Apollo crosses the distance between these places (cf. τάχα, 218; 223; καρπαλίμως, 281; αἶψα, 377) – a speed and ease that no mortal can hope to attain.[34]

Once Apollo has arrived at Delphi, the text keeps its linear structure, being organized by the sequence of Apollo's thoughts and actions. Apollo decides to build his temple and kills the Python,[35] 'then' (καὶ τότ', 375) he realizes that Telphousa has tricked him, and, after founding his own cult there, 'then' (καὶ τότε δή) Apollo 'started to consider what men he should bring in as his ministers' (388–90). As the repeated καὶ τότε shows, the mind of the god here works in a sequential way, with one thought following the other. The poet – just like, for instance, Homer or Hesiod or the poets of the other *Homeric Hymns* – has privileged access to that divine mind. The structure of his text follows the sequence of divine thought, which thus becomes accessible to the mind of men.

The linear framework of the god's travels, thoughts and actions is then closely intertwined with commemorative actions, which leave their traces in human time well into the poet's present.[36] After Apollo has reached Crisa,[37] he declares that there he wants to 'make his beautiful temple as an oracle for humankind' (287–93). 'So saying, Phoibos Apollo laid out his foundations (διέθηκε θεμείλια) in broad and very long, unbroken lines' (294–5).[38] Two humans, Trophonius and Agamedes, mimic the god's action and lay a stone threshold (λάινον οὐδὸν ἔθηκε Τροφώνιος ἠδ' Ἀγαμήδης).[39] As the echo of the same verb suggests (διέθηκε; ἔθηκε), divine and human action are here closely intertwined. With the mention of two named mortals, including the name of their father, Erginus (297), this part of the hymn goes much further than the first one towards connecting the actions of the god with a particular moment in the time of men.[40] Around these foundations, the people build the god's temple, 'to be a theme of song for ever' (298–9).[41] The present hymn too prolongs this axis of foundational activities, by 'laying out' in words the foundations of the temple, and by making sure that the temple remains 'the theme of song for ever' that it was supposed to be. As in the first part of the hymn, the commemorative function of poetry can be seen in action. But rather than meditating on human mortality or immortality in more general terms, it is here bound up with – and takes an active part in commemorating – a specific divine foundation, which is closely connected with human activity.

After Apollo has killed the Python,[42] he tells the corpse to 'rot away', and prophesies that it 'will be rotted away here by the dark earth and the blazing sun' (363; 368–9). The poet then establishes as close a connection as possible between the rotting away of the corpse and the place name Pytho, saying that the sun's divine force rotted her down (κατέπυς, 371); hence the place is now named Pytho (ἐξ οὗ νῦν Πυθὼ κικλήσκεται, 372), and the people call the god Pythios (Πύθιον αὖ καλέουσιν ἐπώνυμον, 373), 'because it was here that the keen sun's force rotted the monster away' (πῦσε, 374). This way of phrasing the *aetion* closely aligns the speech acts of the god and the humans. The words of the humans, who 'call' the god and the place by this name (cf. κικλήσκεται; καλέουσιν) echo those of the god, who insists on the rotting away of the snake's corpse. The name of the place, as well as the god's name Pythios, are still in use 'now, from that moment on' (ἐξ οὗ νῦν), but they do more than commemorate a divine deed of the past. Instead, whenever these names are used, they echo and re-enact the words spoken by the god himself, such as πύθε' and πύσει. On the one hand, then, Apollo's words form the beginning of a linear 'arrow of time', extending from the beginning into the poet's present (cf. ἐξ οὗ νῦν). On the other hand, whenever the words in question are used, they reactivate the very words spoken in the past. Time on earth does move forward in a linear fashion, but the words of the god keep on resonating throughout. What is thus created is a particular kind of 'sacred' time – in which time does move forward, but in which the voice of the god keeps being heard.

The close correspondence between the god's deeds and their commemoration is again confirmed by the establishment of the Delphian altar and of Apollo's cult name Delphinios. After Apollo has led the Cretan sailors towards Delphi (more on which below), having jumped onto their ship in the form of a dolphin (400–1), he later tells the Cretans to build an altar on the seashore (490–6).[43] The altar, then, acts as a central intersection between the divine and mortal spheres: it is a monument to the divine epiphany on earth, but it also allows the mortals to cook their food[44] – one of the acts that most clearly separates them from the gods, who have no need for it. Although it is left to the humans to actually build the altar of which Apollo speaks (which they do piously, in a description which closely echoes the god's command, 508–10[45]), it is here the god himself who performs a role that would normally be that of humans: he commemorates his own past deed. Again, as with the references to Pytho and Apollo Pythios, the god's speech ('even as I originally leapt onto your ship in the misty sea in the form of a dolphin, so you are to pray to me as "the Dolphin god," and the altar itself will be "Delphian," and a permanent landmark', 495–6), implies that whenever his worshippers use the cult titles Delphinios and Delpheios, they will not only commemorate the god's deed, but echo his own words.[46]

The final step in the sequence of the foundation of Apollo's cult in Delphi is that Apollo starts to watch out for ministers who could serve in his new cult (388–90). He notices a ship on the sea, 'and in it were many fine men, Cretans from Cnossos the city of Minos, the ones who perform sacrifices for the god, and who announce the rulings of Apollo [...], whatever he says when he gives his oracles from the bay tree down in the glens of Parnassus' (391–6). The present tense in 'they perform' and 'they announce' (ῥέζουσι καὶ ἀγγέλλουσι, 394), at first sight, seems peculiar. A few lines earlier, Apollo had considered who his ministers should be, who *would* serve him in Pytho (οἳ θεραπεύσονται, 390). The future tense correctly characterizes the temporal relationship between Apollo's seeing the Cretans and the actions they are later to perform. Some of the manuscripts in line 394 transmit the future tense: ῥέξουσι καὶ ἀγγελέουσι. However, the present tense is kept by many editors,[47] and, as we will see, it is the more interesting reading, since it gives an additional nuance to the hymn's construction of divine time.

With the present ῥέζουσι καὶ ἀγγέλλουσι, the voice focalizing these lines is first and foremost the poet himself: it is his present, presumably, in which the Cretans 'perform sacrifices for the god and announce his rulings'. The observations of Apollo (cf. ἐνόησ', 391),[48] then, are blended with those of the poet: Apollo is the one who 'noticed a swift ship on the wine-faced sea, and in it were many fine men', which then leads to the remark about the present occupation of the Cretans (or rather, their descendants).⁴⁹ At the same moment when the poet refers to the present function performed by the Cretans, the god must be anticipating what for him is their future function (as suggested by θεραπεύσονται earlier). He must already have made or be making his plans for the future role of the Cretans, whom he then immediately starts to divert from their course towards Pylos. The poet and the god, then, must be seeing almost exactly the same thing: the Cretans as serving in Delphi. Located at opposite spectrums in time – the god at the foundational moment of the past, the poet looking back on it from the point of view of his present – and at opposite ends of the divide between gods and mortals, the poet and Apollo still see the same. Linear time collapses as the god's and the poet's gaze converge, and as the present and the future are seen together in the same moment.

Yet, time soon returns to its usual passage, as it becomes clear that, for the Cretan priesthood to be fully established, a number of events have to unfold through time. This time frame too turns out to be manipulated by the gods. The Cretan ship's voyage to Crisa under the guidance of Apollo is described in another catalogue,⁵⁰ which closely resembles Apollo's own journey from Olympus to Delphi in its clear sequential order (cf. πρῶτον, 409; ἔνθα, 412; βῆ δὲ παρὰ [...] καὶ παρὰ [...], 425). Just like the poet insisted that 'far-shooting' Apollo travelled from one place to the next with super-human speed, so the ship of the Cretan sailors is blown forward miraculously, both 'effortlessly' by Apollo himself, and by a wind coming from Zeus.⁵¹ While the sequence of places passed by the Cretan ship belongs to the world of human experience, their speed does not. Again, then, the encounters between the god and humans, as well as their impact for 'all time' are firmly embedded in the notion of a linear passage of time, even while the distinctions between human and divine speed, between original deed and commemoration, as well as between the gaze of the god and the gaze of the poet, are blurred in various ways.

4. Human ὕβρις

There is one final twist to this interaction of divine and human time. After Apollo has revealed himself to the Cretans, he declares that they are to occupy his rich temple and to know the gods' intentions. 'By their will you shall be held in honour for all time' (βουλάς τ' ἀθανάτων εἰδήσετε· τῶν ἰότητι / αἰεὶ τιμήσεσθε διαμπερὲς ἤματα πάντα, 484–5). This promise stresses the close contact between the

Cretans and the sphere of the gods, who are equally honoured among men 'for all time'. Later, however, once the Cretans have exactly obeyed the gods' orders for the building of his altar and once they have started worrying about how to sustain themselves on the infertile soil of Delphi (526–39), it becomes clear that the Cretans' condition could well be modified in the future. If they do not respect Apollo's orders and commit any insolence, the god tells them, the Cretans will be under the yoke of other masters 'for all time' (ἤματα πάντα, 540–3).[52] Apollo now has to reckon much more with human temporality than in his earlier prophecy. He has to acknowledge that it is 'the manner of mortal folk' to commit acts of ὕβρις (541).[53] The words ἤματα πάντα in the god's final speech, then, modify the same expression he had used earlier.[54] The phrase 'for all time', in the mouth of the god, has become tinged with mortal time, as these words now acknowledge the (seemingly inevitable) tendency to hubris and the resultant change in the distribution of power among men.[55]

The last lines of the hymn thus open up the god's words for the mutability of human affairs, in which human hubris and 'the manner of mortal folk' are prone to bring about change, which the gods in turn are not used to. By the somewhat paradoxical logic of this hymn, Apollo's own honours are finally fully established when he tells the Cretans to remember these orders (544) – which, the god himself had suggested, they might not do. Even while he acknowledges the role of change and instability in human affairs, his own status as the Olympian god who 'prophesies Zeus' unerring will to humankind' (cf. 132) – a status that will truly be his 'for all time' – is fully established.

If Apollo in his last speech of the hymn acknowledges a characteristic feature of human time, this hymn could be seen as paving the way for later, Hellenistic representations of the god. In Callimachus' *Hymn to Delos*, Apollo, after first prophesying the establishment of his oracle in Delphi and the fate of Thebes (88–98), then prophesies historical events – the birth of Ptolemy II on Cos and his victory over Magas of Cyrene (162–95) – closely aligning his own story with that of the Ptolemaic monarch.[56] It could well be that Callimachus himself did indeed take the end of the *Homeric Hymn to Apollo* as an allusion to the First Sacred War and to historical events around Delphi, which he then developed into a much larger prophecy of historical events to come. In contrast to the *Homeric Hymns*, however, he makes it clear what he is referring to by 'sealing' his prophecy by naming the historical protagonist he has in mind (ἐσσόμενε Πτολεμαῖε, 188).

The extended references to historical events give this Callimachean hymn a direction that strongly distinguishes it from the *Homeric Hymn to Apollo*. Apollo's prophecy establishes a direct connection between the foundation of his own oracle and Ptolemy's victory, which is underscored by Apollo's announcement that Ptolemy will 'greatly praise in all the days to be him that prophesied while yet in his mother's womb' (189–90). The foundation of Apollo's oracle does not so much look back to and complete the establishment of the Olympian order, but it looks forward to human history and the oracle's involvement with it. By the Hellenistic period in general, the gods seem to be much more compatible with human time and more prone to closely interact with it.[57] The specific kind of sacred time created in the second part of the *Homeric Hymn to Apollo* is still far removed from this, but, especially at its end, it starts paving the way for this development.

Conclusion

As the different constructions of time in the two parts of the hymn show, there is no such thing as '*the* time of the gods' and '*the* time of men.' Instead, what matters is how in every individual case these two spheres and their interaction are described. As we saw, the scene on Delos, for instance, implicitly does have an aetiological meaning, but the festival is placed in a peculiar time frame somewhere between the mortal and the immortal sphere. Within this framework, every moment when this hymn is performed or read enacts and gives proof of the power of Apolline poetry to raise certain mortals, including the poet himself and the Delian Maidens, beyond the limits of death and old age.

The second part of the hymn, by contrast, is based on a different notion of 'now': the present moment of the hymn's performance is here figured as a present that is full of the traces of the god's foundational activities. These are all anchored in a time frame that comes close to the linear experience of human time: the god's itineraries, thoughts and actions are all organized in a sequence, in which his individual foundational deeds find their place. A specific kind of 'sacred time' is created through the interaction of Apollo's acts and words with the time of men: two named mortals mimic the god's own foundational action and lay the foundation of his temple, which is then built by men, while Apollo first speaks the words which will resonate throughout all later time – as Pytho and Pythios – and he himself verbally remembers his appearance on the Cretan ship in the form of a dolphin. Apollo's τιμή as the god who 'prophesies Zeus' unerring will to humankind' can only become fully realized through a clearly marked sequence of divine actions on earth, which are tied to human actions, and which blur the distinction between divine action and human commemoration. Even the god's and the poet's gaze converge for a moment. Ultimately, the god himself has to acknowledge the impact of change in human affairs. This construction of time paves the way for the Hellenistic hymns of Callimachus, where, in the *Hymn to Delos*, Apollo fully engages with specific events on earth, events of the poet's present.

The fundamental questions underlying all of this are ones that we cannot fully answer. Is there indeed a development, and is it as tidy as it could seem from my argument: a development in which poets, in their presentation of the gods, become aware of and engage more and more with a more human, linear sense of time, ending in a vision of 'historical time' placed in the mouth of a god? Do we indeed have two different halves of the *Homeric Hymn to Apollo*, one earlier, one later, which would explain these differences between the two parts? Or are they due to other factors – differences between the Delian and the Delphic cult of the god, or, more fundamentally, between his functions as god of poetry and god of prophecy? Is poetry less 'earth-bound,' whereas an oracular cult inherently requires a temple, an altar and human priests who can fall prey to ὕβρις? For now, I hope to have shown at least that 'archaic time' is not a uniform phenomenon. What distinguishes it from other periods is that the time of men does not yet fully emerge as an independent category, but remains entangled with the time frame of the Olympian gods.[58] But within this framework, the notion of 'sacred time', the locating of the present moment and the relationship between human and divine time can take on a wide variety of different shapes.

Notes

1 I would like to thank Bobby Xinyue and the anonymous referees for their help in improving this paper. I am also very grateful to the participants of the conference *Time and Eternity: The Conception of Time in Archaic Greek Literature*, University of Virginia, 22–24 September 2017, for their very helpful comments.
2 Miller (1979: 173–5) has a useful overview over the central positions in this debate; see also Drerup (1937: 81–99) and Unte (1968: 10–18). Among those who defend Ruhnken's thesis of the partition of the hymn into a Delian and a Pythian half are Janko (1982: 99–132) and more recently Chappell (2011). Stehle (1996: 177–96) sees the existence of two originally separate parts underscored by the fact that '[t]he performer . . . establishes a different relationship with the audience in each poem' (p. 178). For a defence of the unity of the hymn, see Allen, Halliday and Sikes (1963: 186–93), Miller (1979), Baltes (1981), Sowa (1984: 172–84), Thalmann (1984: 64–73), Clay (1989: 17–94) and Clay (1994). The list of correspondences between the two

halves of the hymn drawn up by Heiden (2013) is too narrowly focused on the structural properties of the 'topics' he identifies to support his argument for unity. West (1975) thinks that the Pythian part of the hymn was the original text and that the Delian part was composed later. Burkert (1979) suggests that a combined Delian and Pythian festival, held by Polycrates in 523/2 BCE, was the setting of the combined hymn.

3   I am here going to refer to the two 'parts' of the hymn (with the second part beginning with line 207; see below), leaving open the question of the order in which they were composed; see the conclusion below.
4   The split between the two parts of the hymn, and the difference between their constructions of sacred time, coincides with what has been described as a split between the 'lyric' and 'epic' or 'hymnic' and 'descriptive' parts of the hymn. See, however, for the way these aspects complement each other if the hymn is perceived as a unity, Miller (1986: 175 n. 6).
5   As noted, e.g. by Kirk (1981: 175, 180–1).
6   See esp. Kakridis (1937).
7   As argued e.g. by Drerup (1937: esp. 117–20) and Miller (1986); cf. Forderer (1971: 151–2).
8   See Forderer (1971: 137–9) and Bakker (2002b: 80–1).
9   See esp. Clay (1989: 17–94) and Clay (1994).
10 Translations are by West (2003). On terror and joy as a characteristic reaction to Apollo's power, see Clay (1989: esp. 33–46).
11 Richardson (2010: on 150).
12 This is not to say though that there was not also a political meaning to this festival and to the hymn as a whole; Burkert (1979), for instance, argues that the hymn was composed for a unique combined Delian-Pythian festival, and it has also been proposed that this gathering of the Ionians was the reflection of a regular Delian festival, probably celebrated in the Delian month Hieros (February to March); see Bruneau (1970: 89), Forderer (1971: 127) and Richardson (2010: on 135–6).
13 In the version of the text quoted by Thucydides, the connection is temporal: ἀλλ' ὅτε (instead of ἄλλοτε) [...] ἔνθα (Thuc. 3.104.4). Yet, the text as transmitted by the manuscripts (ἀλλὰ σύ [...] ἔνθα) is clearly preferable, and here ἔνθα functions as a relative and has spatial meaning, 'where'; see Allen, Halliday and Sikes (1963: ad loc.). On the Thucydidean and other receptions of this scene, see Nagy (2011). The same scheme is repeated later, when Apollo reaches Poseidon's grove at Onchestus, 'where' (ἔνθα) Poseidon is honoured (229–38).
14 See Miller (1986: 57) for parallels to this in Hymn 19 to Pan; see Janko (1981: 18), Thalmann (1984: 206 n. 91) for the tenses used in 140–5.
15 See Forderer (1971: 95), Förstel (1979: 113–14) and Miller (1986: 51, 56–7); also Heubeck (1972: 136–7) and Thalmann (1984: 206 n. 91).

16 For the second scene on Olympus as a general 'timeless' event, see Heubeck (1972: 141), Förstel (1979: 104–9, 223) and Miller (1986: 66 n. 170) with further literature. For the discussion whether the first scene on Olympus is to be imagined as a habitual action or the god's first appearance on Olympus after his birth, see the bibliography in Miller (1986: 12 n. 26).
17 The fact that Apollo goes from Pytho to Olympus 'swift as thought' (ὥς τε νόημα, 186) further underlines the divine dimension of this journey.
18 For the Delian Maidens and how they bridge the gap between the mythic past and the present, see Kowalzig (2007: 56–80) and Passmore (2019: 138–45).
19 On the various interpretations suggested for these lines, see Clay (1989: 50 n. 102); Peponi (2009: esp. 60–8), with further literature; Papadopoulou and Papadopoulou-Belmehdi (2002: 172–5).
20 On the relationship between the poet, the Delian Maidens and the gods, see Forderer (1971: 104–5, 108–9), Miller (1986: 61–5), Clay (1989: 46–56), Stehle (1996: 184–5), Capponi (2003) and Calame (2011: 350–2); see Passmore (2019) for past, present and future with respect to the performance and reperformances of the hymn; on the identity of the speaker as Homer and on how the hymn anticipates its own reception abroad, see the excellent observations by Spelman (2018a).
21 Like the Delian Maidens, the poet too, early on in his hymn, salutes 'blessed Leto, for you bore splendid children, the lord Apollo and Artemis profuse of arrows' (14–15, cf. 158–9, cf. also 199), and he, too, is 'hymning Apollo', just like the Maidens do at the beginning of their song (158). These two songs are interwoven even more closely when the hymnic poet addresses Apollo, Artemis and the maidens themselves (165–6). Cf. Heubeck (1972: 137–8, 142 n. 18).
22 See Forderer (1971: 98, 102, 142).
23 See also Miller (1986: 59) on the way the scene on Delos underlines Apollo's power.
24 See Forderer (1971: 123, 133) on this parallel.
25 See Petrovic (2013) for how hymns, and the *Homeric Hymn to Apollo* in particular, mimic the essence of the gods through the device of false closure that imitates the endlessness of the gods' existence.
26 Kakridis (1937: 105) rightly draws attention to the way the phrase ἀθανάτους καὶ ἀγήρως (151), referring to the way the humans might seem, is echoed by ἀμφραδέες καὶ ἀμήχανοι (192) in the song of the Muses; see Forderer (1971: 119, 129) and Thalmann (1984: 80). This reflects the fundamental gap between mortals and immortals, which had been temporarily obfuscated by the seeming semblance between the two.
27 On the parallels between the two scenes, see Kakridis (1937), Unte (1968: 52–6), Forderer (1971: 17–34), Heubeck (1972: 142–4), Förstel (1979: 223–34), Niles (1979: 39), Thalmann (1984: 66, 79–82), Miller (1986: 68–9, 119), Richardson (2010: on 186–206) and Spelman (2020).

28 See Miller (1986: 54, 81) on the way these words look forward to and are fulfilled in the Pythian narrative; Förstel (1979: 223–34) on how the festivals on Delos and Olympus anticipate the foundation of the Delphic oracle; see also Thalmann (1984: 69) on correspondences between the cult foundations on Delos and in Delphi.
29 See Clay (1989: 44, 55–6, 75, 91, 94); Clay (2011: 242–3). See, however, Clay (1983) on the characteristics of the – often conditional and ambiguous – knowledge conveyed by prophecies coming from the gods.
30 On the correspondences between these two geographical catalogues as well as the later one in 409–39 (see below), see Drerup (1937: 124), Thalmann (1984: 68–9) and Clay (1989: 57–8, 81–2).
31 On the catalogue of Apollo's wanderings, see Kolk (1963: 14–23), Förstel (1979: 211, for the parallels with the *Odyssey*; 239–40), Baltes (1981: 31–4), Sowa (1984: 219–21) and Miller (1986: 72–5); on the difficulty of the geography involved, see Altheim (1924: 443–5) and Allen, Halliday and Sikes (1963: on 240).
32 On the meaning of this reference to Thebes, see Förstel (1979: 243–5) and Clay (1989: 58–9).
33 See also Miller (1986: 72), Förstel (1979: 239) and Sowa (1984: 187, 228–9).
34 For the references to speed in the catalogue, see Baltes (1981: 33).
35 The text here most conspicuously deviates from a linear order, including a flashback to the story of the Pytho and Typhaon (300–54). Yet my main point is that Apollo's own actions clearly remain sequential.
36 See Thalmann (1984: 72): 'in each [of the three sections], Apollo or his place of worship receives an epithet to commemorate the occasion: Pytho (ll. 371–4), Telphousios (ll. 385–7) and Delpheios ([...], ll. 495–6)'.
37 On the identity of Crisa, see Förstel (1979: 202–9) and Richardson (2010: on 269).
38 Clay (1989: 62–3, 82) draws attention to Apollo's own active involvement in his cult foundations; see also Förstel (1979: 218) and Sowa (1984: 245).
39 For the different interpretations of λάϊνον οὐδὸν, see Kolk (1963: 24 n. 5).
40 See also Kolk (1963: 24: 'wieder fließen Mythos und Historie ineinander'). For the mythological traditions surrounding Erginus, see Förstel (1979: 252–3). On some of the references to humans in the second part of the hymn – and the anachronisms connected with that – see Kolk (1963: 39 n. 15) and Förstel (1979: 237).
41 The temple thus resembles Apollo himself, who is introduced in lines 19 and 207 as 'fit subject for song in every respect' (πάντως εὔυμνον ἐόντα). On the textual problems of lines 294–9, see Kolk (1963: 24 n. 6). See Miller (1986: 81) for the way 'the range of participation expands from the god alone [...], to heroes and specialists [...], to the generality of men [...]' and to 'future generations, among whom are the present singer and his audience'; see also Clay (1989: 62–3).
42 On this scene and the Python's close connection with the establishment of the Jovian order of the world, see Förstel (1979: 260–3), Thalmann (1984: 72), Miller (1986:

84–91), Clay (1989: 63–74; also 36–9) and Felson (2011: esp. 271–9). Stehle (1996: 192–3) examines the interplay of the god's and the poet's voice in terms of gendered aspects of performance.
43 Kolk (1963: 33 n. 18) draws attention to the meaning of ἐπόψιος (496), which commemorates the fact that Apollo had become visible to the Cretans first in the shape of a dolphin, then in his own.
44 On these two functions of the altar, see Kolk (1963: 33–4).
45 See ibid. (332) on this correspondence.
46 There is a likely connection here of this cult title with the name Delphi; see ibid. (29) and Förstel (1979: 254). This fits in with other implicit *aetia* in the second part of the hymn: for instance, the Cretans' and Apollo's march from the shore to the temple and the singing of paeans (514–19) has been understood as the origin of the Pythian festival; see Kolk (1963: 34–5), Förstel (1979: 225), Thalmann (1984: 69–70) and Richardson (2010: *ad loc.*). For other implied *aetia* in the second part of the hymn, see Förstel (1979: 253–6).
47 By Richardson (2010: *ad loc.*) on the grounds that these future tenses 'would not follow so naturally after the simple statement of 392 as the future tense in 390 does after 388–9'. Cf. the text as printed by Allen, Halliday and Sikes (1963), with their commentary *ad loc.*, Càssola (2010) and Miller (1986: 91 n. 238) on other solutions that have been proposed.
48 On the god's perspective, in contrast with that of the humans, see Clay (1989: 79–80).
49 See also Miller (1986: 91), who draws attention to 'the generalizing τε (393)', and who reads the relative clause referring to the Cretans as 'parenthetical flash-forward to "present general" time'. On the role of the Cretans, and especially the question why the Pythia is absent from this hymn, see Clay (1989: 75–8), Clay (2009) and Chappell (2006: 337–48).
50 On which, see Förstel (1979: 265–6) and Baltes (1981: 35–9).
51 Cf. esp. 420–1, 427, 433–4, 437; on the meaning of Zeus' intervention, see Miller (1986: 93) and Clay (1989: 82).
52 Apollo's reference to the potential new masters of the Cretans as σημάντορες is not devoid of irony. The one who gives σήματα in a place like Delphi is actually the god, the source of oracular 'signs' for men – again, then, the divine and human spheres are blurred. For the connection between the voice of Apollo and the voice of the hymnic speaker here, see Capponi (2003: 19–21). This is not to say though that there is not also a potential political background to these lines, based on an allusion to the First Sacred War, as the result of which new masters were established in Delphi (though scholars like West (1975: 165 n. 2), Clay (1989: 87–9) and Chappell (2006: 331–4) are sceptical).
53 See also Miller (1986: 94–108) on the 'contrastive juxtaposition' of the divine and human conditions in the final part of the hymn.

54 See ibid. (102). For the use of this phrase to describe the gods' 'immortal and ageless' existence, see Clay (1981: esp. 112) and Clay (1983: 141–8, esp. 141).
55 On the contrast between mortals and the god Apollo, 'in whom respect for natural limit and hostility toward *hubris* are innate' (Miller 1986: 49, cf. p. 39), see ibid. (104–8) and Càssola (2010: on 541).
56 See Stephens (2015: 18, 162).
57 As I argue in Walter (2020: 90–136).
58 Cf. the discussion by Purves (2006).

5

The Apotheosis of Time

Challenging Tradition and Anachronism in Pherecydes' *Heptamychos*

Susannah Ashton
Royal Holloway, University of London

In the sixth century BCE, Pherecydes of Syros composed a theogony which commences with a remarkable statement: 'Zas and Chronos always were and Chthoniē …' (Ζὰς μὲν καὶ Χρόνος ἦσαν ἀεὶ καὶ Χθονίη . . .).[1] This work, variously designated the *Heptamychos*, *Theokrasia* or *Theogony* in the *Suda*, is extremely poorly preserved.[2] Alongside this opening line of the text, only two columns of papyrus remain as secure records of Pherecydes' own words. Despite this dearth of evidence, it is clear that Pherecydes was a polemic respondent to traditional theogonies, illustrated here through a revolutionary portrait of time.[3] Not only does Pherecydes claim for the first time in surviving Greek literature that some gods eternally exist, but one of those gods, Chronos, signifies the divine embodiment of the concept of 'time'.[4] Despite indicating a significant ideological shift in early Greek comprehensions of divine temporality, as well as an unprecedented interest in the agentive properties of χρόνος, Pherecydes' depiction of time is predominantly understood by portraying Pherecydes as a proto-Platonist.[5] This anachronistic treatment of Pherecydean thought is not only incompatible with the surviving evidence, it also tells us little about how Pherecydes utilized the concept of time to mount a serious challenge to established theological ideas.

In this chapter, I address the challenges which ensue from anachronistically situating Pherecydes' *Heptamychos* within a Platonic framework, which I argue obscures Pherecydes' no less innovative response to traditional theogonies. For reference, I broadly follow the order of events suggested by Schibli:[6]

1. The eternal existence of Zas, Chronos and Chthoniē.
2. Chronos produces fire, *pneuma* and water from his seed.

3. The three elements, in various mixtures, are distributed in five nooks.
4. A second generation of gods, associated with five cosmic regions, arise from these nooks.
5. Zas weds Chthoniē, whose name becomes Gē when Zas gives her a robe embroidered with Gē and Ogenos.
6. A battle takes place between Kronos and Ophioneus, Kronos succeeds.
7. The division of portions among the gods.

Through a close reading of the opening line, in which I interrogate the conceptual significance of 'time' and 'eternity' for a sixth-century thinker, I argue that the cosmological roles of Chronos, Zas and Chthoniē are unnecessarily obscured by prematurely assuming the dichotomy of χρόνος and αἰών. Following this, I attempt to shed more light upon how Chronos, as the deification of 'time', is an innovation upon traditional depictions of the gods. In particular, I propose that Chronos' creation in five cosmic nooks, later used as sites for metempsychosis, gestures towards his role in temporally structuring the cosmos and anticipates his eventual transformation into Kronos. By delving into these fragmentary clues, I hope to demonstrate that Pherecydes is no mere intermediary between more established modes of thought, but a thinker of notable philosophical and theological merit.

1. Platonic Eternity

In the *Timaeus*, Plato instigated a conceptual paradigm which has had a pervasive legacy in Western thought, with his proclamation that time (χρόνος) was established as an 'image' (εἰκόνα) or 'imitation' (μιμουμένου) of eternity (αἰών).[7] Although there remains controversy over Plato's distinction between χρόνος and αἰών, the popular interpretation – and the one which is discernible in Pherecydean scholarship – is that eternity (αἰών) is atemporal. Existing outside the tensed framework of past, present and future, strong readings of the *Timaeus* state that there is no duration within αἰών.[8] This is set in contrast with χρόνος, a facet of the changing and sensible world, by virtue of the created measurements derived from heavenly motions.[9] Time and eternity are thus drawn into the metaphysical commitments of the *Timaeus*, subject to the ontological rift which separates 'being' and 'becoming' between the intelligible and sensible worlds.

Although Parmenides' distinction between being and becoming indicates the cultivation of these ideas in the early fifth century BCE, Plato was the first to explicitly embrace χρόνος and αἰών within this dichotomy. This treatment of time and eternity, although enfolded within the complexes of Plato's distinct metaphysical commitments, has had a profound impact which lingers in the Western consciousness to this day, due in part to its enduring popularity in Christian theological thought.[10] This can be clearly discerned from the scholarly reception of Pherecydes' opening line.

With the ostensible exception of Schibli, whom I will address shortly, Pherecydes is regularly swept up within the strong tide of Platonic thought. Diels observed a clear distinction in Pherecydean thought between an eternal realm of Αἰών, in which Zas and Chthoniē exist, and a temporal sphere of Χρόνος (Chronos).[11] Recently, Breglia has pushed this assumption even further into a Platonic embrace, discerning not merely a distinction between time and eternity, but also a sensible and intelligible world.[12] As Chase remarks, 'variations on this theme were proposed by most subsequent scholars, most of whom subscribed to Diels' fundamental distinction between an eternal and a temporal realm of gods/elements'.[13] However, there are significant difficulties with committing Pherecydes to this schema.

For one, as Schibli has stressed, this entails binding Pherecydes to ideas which were not expressly formulated for another two hundred years.[14] It is certainly feasible that Plato was familiar with Pherecydes' work.[15] Yet, it is one thing to assert that Pherecydes anticipated aspects of Platonic thought and quite another to commit Pherecydes to the metaphysics of the *Timaeus*. This becomes particularly clear with Diels' understanding of Chronos who, when perceived through a Platonic lens, is something of a paradox. As opposed to a contrast between time and eternity, Pherecydes commences his work by introducing the eternally extant Chronos. In order to retain the Platonic dichotomy, Diels ignores the eternal being of Chronos, stating that only 'two of these [Zas and Chthoniē] are treated as eternal powers (ἦσαν ἀεί)', insinuating a distinction between Chronos and his fellow gods.[16] Yet, as Schibli has emphasized, in the opening line, 'Chronos, no less than Zas and Chthoniē, is said to have existed forever.'[17]

Although it has been noted that a dichotomy of 'time' and 'eternity' has inappropriately been applied to the *Heptamychos*, Platonic notions nonetheless remain implicit in scholarly readings. Indeed, Schibli himself goes on to say that Pherecydes' 'cosmogony here reveals two aspects of time: the eternal and the temporal. Chronos . . . steps out of eternity, so to speak, to create'.[18] Platonic ideas are also discernible in Schibli's attempt to resolve the perceived paradox of Chronos' eternal being: Chronos initially existed as a 'time-principle' and it is only after 'the creation of the cosmic nooks, involving a notion of sequential ordering, [that Chronos] becomes actual measured time'.[19] A similar idea has been advanced by Breglia, who argues that Chronos develops from 'pre-time' into 'full time' with this act of creation.[20]

The suggestion that Pherecydes envisioned time as an abstract principle which becomes an actualized entity is philosophically intriguing, yet it is based upon shaky textual support. Schibli maintains this argument through comparison with fragments 14 and 68, whereby Zas weaves and gifts Chthoniē with a robe embroidered with the earth and ocean, after which she becomes known as Gē. It follows that a change of name in the *Heptamychos* hints towards a development in the identity of the god in question.[21] Thus, according to Schibli, Chthoniē – the 'earth-principle' – becomes 'actual' earth (Gē) with the investiture of the robe.[22] While this idea has been subject to criticism, this proposed transformation is at least consistent with Chthoniē's change of name.[23] Yet, is the same logic applicable to the names attributed to Chronos? Breglia attempts to establish this parallel with Chthoniē/Gē by proposing that Chronos, upon becoming 'full time', transforms into Kronos.[24] Accordingly, Pherecydes' oft-discussed interest in divine etymology is explained as an attempt to distinguish these gods on an intelligible/eternal and sensible/temporal level. Yet, if Chronos' creative act entails him transforming into 'full time', one would surely expect this transformation to be the other way around. Namely, one would expect Kronos to *become* Chronos. It should be noted that the textual support regarding Chronos' name change is notoriously problematic.[25] Yet, if we admit the one generally undisputed occurrence of Kronos in fr. 78, this indicates that Chronos' name change to Kronos actually transpired far later in the text, after leading an army in the theomachy and assuming his mythical role as divine *basileus*.[26]

In addition to terminological issues, these postulations of 'proto-time' are conceptually ambiguous.[27] Indeed, what exactly is this prototypic 'time' that exists before it becomes 'full time'? And how can this contention be justified against the fact that Chronos ('time') always existed? Part of the problem here is clearly the broad application of the English word 'time', as well as uninterrogated assumptions regarding the nature of eternity. Accordingly, any examination of 'time' and 'eternity' in the *Heptamychos* must commence with an interrogation of what these concepts entailed for the sixth-century thinker, and whether it is even necessary to engage in the philosophical gymnastics which ensue from taking the time/eternity dichotomy for granted.

2. The Time God

Thus far, I have been cautious to avoid, or at best qualify with quotation marks, the claim that 'time' is deified in Pherecydes' *Heptamychos*. After all, Pherecydes does not promote 'time' into his cosmological schema, but rather χρόνος. The necessity of this distinction has been demonstrated by numerous linguistic studies, which establish that our concept of 'time' was not expressed by any single word in early Greek thought.[28] Although it is generally claimed that χρόνος was the closest approximation to our concept of 'time', it did not carry all of the same connotations, particularly in the Archaic period.[29] Sattler has neatly summarized this: 'In the very beginning of Greek thinking, *chronos* indicates solely a particular time span ... *chronos* originally does not indicate a time that is measured with the help of any units; rather we are just experiencing something as lasting for some duration or as (too) long.'[30] As for what Schibli refers to as 'actual measured time', this was portrayed with ἡμέρα, ἐνιαυτός, ὥρα etc., words which were not explicitly connected with χρόνος until around the fifth century BCE.[31] As opposed to the measurements provided by celestial bodies, Pherecydes' understanding of χρόνος was informed by the intrinsic experience of 'duration'. Accordingly, when Pherecydes announces that Chronos always existed, it is not necessary to conceive of a 'time-principle', or 'pre-time' which is yet to become 'full time'; Pherecydes' meaning is comprehensible in and of itself. Duration (χρόνος), or temporal experience, always existed.

Indeed, the fact that these three gods existed in a durational or 'temporal' framework is expressed in the very same line which articulates their eternal existence. Compounded by the presence of Chronos, Pherecydes situates these gods in an undeniably temporal framework by shifting through three verb tenses. The full line runs as follows:[32]

> Ζὰς μὲν καὶ Χρόνος ἦσαν ἀεὶ καὶ Χθονίη· Χθονίη δὲ ὄνομα ἐγένετο Γῆ ἐπειδὴ αὐτῇ Ζὰς γῆν γέρας διδοῖ.

> Zas and Chronos always were and Chthoniē; but the name of Chthoniē became Gē when Zas gives her the earth as a gift of honour.

Pherecydes begins in the imperfect (ἦσαν ἀεὶ), shifts into the aorist (ἐγένετο), and then finally moves into the present (διδοῖ). Judging by the Grenfell Papyrus, which preserves line 600 of the *Heptamychos*, Pherecydes appears to have remained in the historical or narrative present for the remainder of the text.[33]

While there are certainly narratological techniques at play here, these can only take us so far towards understanding what Pherecydes is trying to communicate. Indeed, considering that the *Heptamychos* was likely composed in response to epic, Pherecydes' gods who 'always were' (ἦσαν ἀεὶ) suggest a marked rebuke to the gods of epic who 'always are' (αἰὲν ἐόντες).[34] Three points therefore need to be made here, regarding eternal being, succession narratives and existential change.

3. Eternal Being

In contrast with the claims of Diels and even Schibli, it is important to note that Pherecydes does not actually postulate the existence of 'eternity' (αἰών) – which incidentally denoted a 'lifetime' in the sixth century BCE – but rather eternal being.[35] These gods 'always were' (ἦσαν ἀεὶ). By eternally conditioning the existence of these gods, Pherecydes is not insinuating that an intelligible world underlies his cosmology; there is no realm of Αἰών which exists in synchronic contrast with a realm of Χρόνος. Instead, as has been observed, Pherecydes was likely responding to the *ex nihilo* theogony depicted by Hesiod.[36] Although this implies a distinction between generated and ungenerated gods (a point to which I will return), a Platonic dichotomy is not required to understand this. In fact, as opposed to the *Timaeus*, a more appropriate reference point can arguably be found in Aristophanes' *Birds*.

The cosmology presented in the *Birds* features a bricolage of early theogonies, yet particularly significant with respect to the *Heptamychos* are the echoes of Orphic and Hesiodic ideas.[37] Pherecydes is not only regarded as a respondent to Hesiod, but he is also frequently associated with Orphic beliefs due to his introduction of a doctrine of metempsychosis and the divinization of Chronos.[38] Considering that Pherecydes' work seems to have been in circulation in Athens by the fourth century BCE at the latest, it would not be especially surprising to find that Aristophanes was familiar with the *Heptamychos*. This is reinforced by suggestive similarities with Pherecydes' work:[39]

Χάος ἦν καὶ Νὺξ Ἔρεβός τε μέλαν πρῶτον καὶ Τάρταρος εὐρύς·
Γῆ δ' οὐδ' Ἀὴρ οὐδ' Οὐρανὸς ἦν· Ἐρέβους δ' ἐν ἀπείροσι κόλποις
τίκτει πρώτιστον ὑπηνέμιον Νὺξ ἡ μελανόπτερος ᾠόν,
ἐξ οὗ περιτελλομέναις ὥραις ἔβλαστεν Ἔρως ὁ ποθεινός,
στίλβων νῶτον πτερύγοιν χρυσαῖν, εἰκὼς ἀνεμώκεσι δίναις.
οὗτος δὲ Χάει πτερόεντι μιγεὶς νύχιος κατὰ Τάρταρον εὐρὺν

ἐνεόττευσεν γένος ἡμέτερον, καὶ πρῶτον ἀνήγαγεν εἰς φῶς.
πρότερον δ' οὐκ ἦν γένος ἀθανάτων, πρὶν Ἔρως ξυνέμειξεν ἅπαντα·
ξυμμειγνυμένων δ' ἑτέρων ἑτέροις γένετ' Οὐρανὸς Ὠκεανός τε
καὶ Γῆ πάντων τε θεῶν μακάρων γένος ἄφθιτον.

In the beginning were Chaos and Night and black Erebus and broad Tartarus,
and no Earth, Air, or Sky. And in the boundless bosom of Erebus
did black-winged Night first of all bring forth a wind egg,
from which as the seasons revolved came forth Eros the seductive,
like to swift whirlwinds, his back aglitter with wings of gold.
And mating by night with winged Chaos in broad Tartarus,
he hatched our own race and first brought it up to daylight.
There was no race of immortal gods before Eros commingled everything;
then as this commingled with that, Sky came to be, and Ocean
and Earth, and the whole imperishable race of blessed gods.

Aristophanes' initial cosmos, inspired as it is by Orphic beliefs, begins with the infernal Chaos, Night, Erebus and Tartarus, as opposed to Pherecydes' trio of Zas, Chronos and Chthoniē. Yet, Aristophanes' carefully crafted language implies a sharp rebuke to Hesiod's *Theogony* in a manner akin to Pherecydes. As Stamatopoulou has suggested, Aristophanes uses the word ἦν 'to describe the initial state of the cosmos … in sharp contrast with the Hesiodic γένετ' that describes the dynamic emergence of the four primordial beings'.[40] In this way, Aristophanes is arguably responding to a dynamic first attested in the *Heptamychos*. There was an initial state of the cosmos which was (ἦν), wherein the earth, ocean and sky did not yet exist. This changes when Eros 'commingles' (συμμίγνυμι) everything, an act which is notably reminiscent of Chronos' 'mixing of the gods' (θεοκρασία). From this mixture, a new generation of gods came into existence (γενετ').

Despite these significant parallels, I note that Aristophanes does not claim that Chaos, Night, Erebus and Tartarus *always* were (ἦσαν ἀεὶ), and one may therefore counter that he did not outline an explicitly 'eternal' cosmological framework. Yet, it is worth pausing for a moment to consider what impact the absent ἀεὶ actually has upon the dynamics of Aristophanes' account. While Chaos, Night, Erebus and Tartarus are not explicitly positioned as 'eternal' gods, Aristophanes is equally careful not to portray them as having come-to-be via genesis. Indeed, if they did not come-to-be, and simply 'were', this must always have been the case.[41] Accordingly, even if Aristophanes is not making explicit reference here to Pherecydes' work, the linguistic structure he employs to depict his theogony is arguably indebted to the *Heptamychos*.

Despite these broad similarities between Aristophanes' and Pherecydes' initial cosmological dynamics, one would be pressed to find a scholar claiming that Aristophanes is depicting a Platonic dichotomy, with Chaos, Night, Erebus and Tartarus existing in an eternal intelligible realm. Indeed, such a notion would be especially difficult to justify considering the fact that Aristophanes explicitly (though likely parodically) positions Erebus and Night against the temporal setting of the turning seasons (περιτελλομέναις ὥραις). In the same way, although Pherecydes' original gods did not come into existence via genesis, Platonic models invoking the twofold structure of χρόνος and αἰών are not required to explain this. The familiar cosmos was increasingly embellished and ordered by virtue of the actions of these eternally extant primordial beings.

4. Succession Narratives

As suggested above, it appears that Pherecydes did formulate a distinction between his eternally extant and generated gods. However, this arguably has less to do with their experience of time than Pherecydes' contestation of the temporal frameworks which underlie traditional theogonies. This can be discerned from Aristotle's commendation of Pherecydes as a 'mixed' thinker who does not describe everything in 'mythological language' (ἐπεὶ οἵ γε μεμιγμένοι αὐτῶν [καὶ] τῷ μὴ μυθικῶς πάντα λέγειν).[42] Aristotle's praise does not simply gesture towards Pherecydes' philosophical tendencies; he specifically spotlights Pherecydes for rejecting earlier divine succession models, in which the youngest son is fated to overthrow his father. Instead, Pherecydes makes 'the first generator the best' (τὸ γεννῆσαν πρῶτον ἄριστον τιθέασι).[43] By associating power with temporal priority, Pherecydes was not drawing out a distinction between χρόνος and αἰών. Instead, he legitimized a power dynamic in which ungenerated beings remain superior to generated ones. Indeed, the one generated upstart who seeks to challenge these primordial beings, Ophioneus, is quickly dispatched by Chronos/Kronos, who casts him into the Ocean.[44] This shift in ideas concerning hegemonic priority is also discernible in the *Birds*, with the birds' right to power signified by the fact that they were 'born a long time before Cronus, and the Titans, / and even Earth' (ἀρχαιότεροι πρότεροί τε Κρόνου καὶ Τιτάνων ἐγένεσθε / καὶ Γῆς).[45] In Pherecydes, it is no accident that the three ungenerated gods each represent a prominent member from the traditional warring familial tiers:

primordial Gaia, Titan Kronos, Olympian Zeus. This point is underemphasized by scholars who instead attempt to identify these gods as mere 'principles'.[46] By presenting these particular gods as ungenerated, thus distancing them from their famed inter-generational wars, Pherecydes instantly underscores his cosmology with an inherent stability which is absent from the generational violence and disruption of the *Theogony*.

5. Existential Change

Returning to Pherecydes' opening line, the imperfect tense that introduces the gods who 'always were' does not exist as an isolated epithet like αἰὲν ἐόντες. As emphasized by the μὲν ... δὲ construction, it sets up the second half of the opening line. Scholars have yet to convincingly explain the syntactic structure of this line, particularly Chthoniē's implied distinction from Zas and Chronos (Ζὰς μὲν καὶ Χρόνος ἦσαν ἀεὶ καὶ Χθονίη). Granger, for example, has questionably assumed that this signals Chthoniē's 'inferior status in the cosmogony, in which her role is merely one of female passivity'.[47] This distinction is even more pronounced in Casaubon's 1692 edition of Diogenes Laertius, in which this fragment is preserved.[48] In Casaubon's edition, which has been edited by Laks and Most to remove a spurious εἰς, Pherecydes tells us that Ζὰς μὲν καὶ Χρόνος ἦσαν ἀεὶ καὶ Χθονίη ἦν.[49] It is understandable that scholars generally ignore this final ἦν. In addition to ἦσαν (which unproblematically applies to Zas, Chronos *and* Chthoniē), it could be regarded as redundant. Furthermore, since ἦν is not conditioned by ἀεὶ, Casaubon's edition ostensibly disrupts the Platonic picture of Chthoniē as an eternal, intelligible being.

Whether or not we choose to accept it, this final ἦν emphasizes the proper function of this line, which does not merely express the eternal existence of these gods, but anticipates the changes which they undergo. Pherecydes sets the tone of his work through Chthoniē by mapping her diachronic transformation: she always *was*, but due to this event which will take place, this is who she is *now*. These gods are not remote demiurges, or changeless and timeless beings who belong in Diels' distinct realm of Αἰών. Rather, the opening line establishes the temporality of these three eternal beings and their intimate involvement with the changing cosmos. With the gods of epic who 'always are' (αἰὲν ἐόντες) thrust into an imperfect past, Pherecydes stakes out his own territory. With this in mind, it is necessary to return to Chronos.

6. The Ordinance of Chronos

Thus far, I have argued that the eternal existence of Chronos does not necessitate any paradoxes. According to early Greek conceptions, it merely entails that duration, or temporal experience, always existed. Yet, there is another aspect of χρόνος to consider. As a divinity, it is not enough to take account of the 'passive' sense of duration which informs Chronos' identity, but also to consider the active uses of the term in the sixth century BCE. To do so, it is necessary to follow suit with a number of Pherecydean scholars and take our cue from Anaximander.[50]

Despite the arbitrary distinctions that have historically typified one as a philosopher and the other a theologian, Anaximander and Pherecydes were clearly in one another's intellectual orbit.[51] As well as being contemporaries and competitors for the distinction of being the first Greek prose writer, their existence in a shared intellectual climate has often been emphasized with regards to the only surviving fragment of Anaximander's prose:[52]

> ἐξ ὧν δὲ ἡ γένεσίς ἐστι τοῖς οὖσι, καὶ τὴν φθορὰν εἰς ταῦτα γίνεσθαι κατὰ τὸ χρεών. διδόναι γὰρ αὐτὰ δίκην καὶ τίσιν ἀλλήλοις τῆς ἀδικίας κατὰ τὴν τοῦ χρόνου τάξιν.

> And the things out of which birth comes about for beings, into these too their destruction happens, according to obligation: for they pay atonement and recompense to each other for their injustice according to the ordinance of time.

B1 frames the 'ordinance of time' (τὴν τοῦ χρόνου τάξιν) as being responsible for overseeing the generation and destruction of beings (οὐσία).[53] Note that this responsibility is not attributed to χρόνος itself, but the *ordinance* of χρόνος.[54] Scholars have debated whether or not τὴν τοῦ χρόνου τάξιν are Anaximander's own words.[55] However, they are generally accepted and moreover complement a prominent correlation between χρόνος and δίκη in the sixth-century works of Solon.[56] Even accounting for what Simplicius refers to as Anaximander's 'poetical language' (ποιητικωτέροις . . . ὀνόμασιν), B1 provides a useful template for evaluating Pherecydes' χρόνος away from Platonic assumptions.[57] If τάξις is taken, as it usually is, in the active sense of 'ordinance' or 'decree', χρόνος alone does not signify these periodical changes, as in Plato.[58] Rather, duration (χρόνος) *organizes* the temporal intervals which are instantiated by generation and destruction. This distinction is small but important. If we apply this template to the *Heptamychos*, Chronos (duration/temporal experience) always existed, but when Chronos performed his creative act, he actively organized that duration into the periodical changes which characterize the cosmos. This does not exempt the eternal gods from experiencing 'time' (χρόνος) or require us to resort to a conceptually vague 'time principle'. Chronos – as the embodiment of duration and temporal passage – retains the same essential significance among ungenerated and generated beings. However, under Chronos' ordinance as a cosmogonic creator, duration is mapped into regular periods of change, experienced by some beings as mortality.

It is with this point that I turn to Chronos' namesake, Kronos. Although the scarcity of fragmentary evidence means that my suggestions in this final section are inevitably grounded in some degree of conjecture, I will propose that Pherecydes' use of 'time' to challenge traditional accounts of the gods extends to Chronos' eventual transformation into Kronos. As mentioned above, it is generally accepted that Chronos' name does change to Kronos, echoing Chthoniē's transformation into Gē, as well as Zas' various names including Dis, Zen and Den.[59] The evidence indicates that this name change occurred when Chronos/Kronos took part in the theomachy, thus signifying a development in his identity when he assumed this martial role. Yet, Schibli has insisted that 'an abiding connection with Time is not easily discerned' in Chronos' transformation to Kronos.[60] In response, I would contend that an abiding connection can indeed be found with the portrait of Chronos drawn thus far, by taking account of another prominent (though less traditional) characterization of Kronos in mythic and ritual traditions: his role as a judge over the dead.

7. Kronos and the Cosmic Nooks

The scarcity of evidence leaves us with a great many questions concerning Chronos' role in the text. We know little about his creation of the 'five-nook' (πεντέμυχος) gods and their relation to the iteration of five cosmic regions (πεντέκοσμος), or indeed of Chronos' abiding influence over the temporal structure of the cosmos.[61] Yet, there survives a significant, and underdiscussed, feature of Chronos' mixture of the gods (θεοκρασία), which hints at the temporal imprint which he leaves upon the cosmos: namely, the spaces in which Chronos creates these mixtures – the cosmic nooks (μυχοί).

The nooks (μυχοί), which are likely located in the body of Chthoniē, feature in two fragments which demonstrate Pherecydes' use of 'time' to challenge established theological thought. The first is Chronos' asexual method of creating the πεντέμυχος / πεντέκοσμος generation:[62]

τὸν δὲ Χρόνον ποιῆσαι ἐκ τοῦ γόνου ἑαυτοῦ πῦρ καὶ πνεῦμα καὶ ὕδωρ, τὴν τριπλῆν, οἶμαι, φύσιν τοῦ νοητοῦ, ἐξ ὧν ἐν πέντε μυχοῖς διῃρημένων πολλὴν ἄλλην γενεὰν συστῆναι θεῶν τὴν πεντέμυχον καλουμένην, ταὐτὸν δὲ ἴσως εἰπεῖν, πεντέκοσμον.

Chronos made from his own seed fire, *pneuma*, and water, the threefold nature, I suppose, of the intelligible, out of which, having been distributed in five nooks, another numerous generation of gods came into existence, called 'the five-nook' one, which is perhaps to say the 'the five-cosmos' one.

The second is the nooks' function as transitional spaces for immortal souls on their journeys of metempsychosis:[63]

καὶ τοῦ Συρίου Φερεκύδου μυχοὺς καὶ βόθρους καὶ ἄντρα καὶ θύρας καὶ πύλας λέγοντος καὶ διὰ τούτων αἰνιττομένου[64] τὰς τῶν ψυχῶν γενέσεις καὶ ἀπογενέσεις.

Pherecydes of Syros is speaking of nooks, hollows, caves, doors and gates, and he riddles that the births and departures of souls are through these.

According to Cicero, Pherecydes was 'the first to say that the souls of humans are eternal' (*sed quod litteris exstet, Pherecydes Syrius primus dixit animos esse hominum sempiternos*), thus issuing a significant challenge to the sharp dichotomy frequently imposed upon the temporal fabric of Pherecydes' cosmos.[65]

Early Greek doctrines of metempsychosis are diverse and obscure, and the particularities of Pherecydes' own concept are unfortunately lost.[66] However, as Purves has noted, Pherecydes' 'description of the soul's journey between lives is markedly topographical', thus echoing what we know of Orphic and Pythagorean eschatology, and possibly anticipating the journeys of souls described in Plato's *Phaedo*.[67] This process of metempsychosis involved transitioning through μυχοί. Notably, these are likely the very same spaces in which Chronos mixes the five-nook generation of gods into existence.

Described by Schibli as 'dark, womb-like hollows', the μυχοί in which Chronos deposits his seed are intuitive locations for generation and birth, certifying Chronos as the 'ultimate procreative power', akin to Pindar's fifth-century characterization of χρόνος as 'father of all' (Χρόνος ὁ πάντων πατὴρ).[68] Yet, if we return to Anaximander's B1, the 'ordinance of time' does not only govern generation, but also destruction. Mansfeld has even argued that the proper emphasis of Anaximander's fragment is upon the destructive capacity of χρόνος.[69] Equally, the μυχοί do not only serve as intuitive locations for coming-to-be, but also passing away. Etymologically linked with μυέω, which connotes concealment and initiation into mystery cults, μυχοί occur frequently in early Greek texts to depict the earth's infernal recesses.[70] Hesiod's Tartarus is described as being located in the deepest nook of the earth (Τάρταρά τ' ἠερόεντα μυχῷ χθονὸς εὐρυοδείης), which is echoed in the fifth-century works of Euripides, wherein μυχοί frequently denote the underworld.[71]

Although the scarcity of evidence prevents us from claiming with absolute certainty that the πεντέμυχος nooks are those which souls later travel through, the possibility of their equivalence would certainly be consistent with evidence of initiation rituals associated with metempsychosis. Mount Ida is perhaps the most famous example. From as early as the Geometric period, the cave in which Zeus was reared was used for katabasis rituals, a journey which Pherecydes' reputed student (and fellow believer in metempsychosis) Pythagoras allegedly undertook.[72] If this proposed correlation is correct, Chronos not only created divine beings and cosmic regions within these nooks, but he also conditioned them to function as transitional spaces through which souls could later pass to and from the underworld.[73] This responsibility would undoubtedly be appropriate for a god who symbolizes the eternal nature of temporal experience. Although the mortal experience of time is ostensibly finite compared with that experienced by the gods, Pherecydes' novel proposition that their souls are immortal complements the eternal existence of Χρόνος. As opposed to a one-way ticket from life to death, the mortal experience of 'time' is instead organized into recurrent rhythms of generation and destruction. This would not only exemplify how Chronos enacts his 'ordinance of time', but it would also signify an underacknowledged continuity in Chronos' identity when he eventually transforms into Kronos.

Chronos' namesake, Kronos, was not only an ill-fated divine king. In mythologies which depict his release from Tartarus, Kronos enjoyed a far more peaceful retirement as a judge over the dead.[74] According to Pindar, he welcomes souls who have undergone metempsychosis three times in Earth and Hades to 'the tower of Kronos, where ocean breezes blow round the Isle of the Blessed' (ὅσοι δ' ἐτόλμασαν ἐστρίς | ἑκατέρωθι μείναντες ἀπὸ πάμπαν ἀδίκων ἔχειν | ψυχάν, ἔτειλαν Διὸς ὁδὸν παρὰ Κρόνου τύρσιν· ἔνθα μακάρων | νᾶσον ὠκεανίδες | αὖραι περιπνέοισιν).[75] Kronos' influence in the chthonic realm is indicated by various contemporary and later sources, including his apparent worship at the cave of Trophonius, which was used in katabasis rituals from at least the fifth century BCE.[76] Also noteworthy is a tradition recorded by Euphorion in the third century BCE in which Kronos (notably after the defeat of Ophion) is given dominion over the Giants in Erebus.[77] Indeed, scholars such as

Meuli have even suggested that the Athenian festival of the *Cronia* was a ritual celebration of life and death, signified by the god's figurative unchaining.[78] That Pherecydes may have adopted this characterization of Kronos has been suggested by Schibli to justify his proposal that Kronos peacefully transferred power to Zeus.[79] Oddly, however, the continuity that this implies with Chronos and his association with the nooks has not yet been noted.

If Pherecydes sought to emphasize this aspect of Kronos' persona, which would additionally complement Pherecydes' introduction of metempsychosis, this cosmic role as adjudicator of the dead would undeniably be reinforced by initially characterizing this god as Chronos. According to this proposal, having conditioned the nooks in which temporal order is created and maintained, Chronos transformed into Kronos to defeat Ophion, after which he retained his responsibility for the 'ordinance of time' by acting as a judge who ensures that – to borrow Anaximander's words – souls 'pay the atonement and recompense' of their mortal existence. By presenting the cosmic nooks as sites of creation and destruction, which engender the metempsychosis of souls and thus the 'ordinance of time' governed by Chronos/Kronos, Pherecydes arguably put forward a cohesive philosophical vision, structured around an innovative treatment of the concept of χρόνος.

Conclusion

By exploring the conceptual affordances of Pherecydes' depiction of χρόνος, and resisting the temptation to anachronistically revert to a Platonic template, it is possible to unravel the perceived paradoxes of this fragmentary account of cosmogony. Although the surviving evidence of the *Heptamychos* necessitates a lateral view towards external evidence, it is vital to maintain a discerning eye upon what remains of Pherecydes' prose, particularly when it comes to his treatment of 'time'. As I have proposed, the eternal existence of these gods does not presuppose a metaphysical dichotomy of 'time' and 'eternity', nor a 'sensible' and an 'intelligible' world. Instead, Chronos' eternal existence enables him to condition the diverse modes of genesis explored in the *Heptamychos*, including the creation of the next generation of gods and the metempsychosis of mortal souls within the cosmic nooks (μυχοί). Within this unique cosmological vision, Pherecydes not only asserted a distinctive challenge to the extant theological tradition, but he also drew influential attention to the temporal structure of the cosmos. By virtue of Pherecydes' divine iteration of χρόνος, cosmology, topography, theogony and eschatology are entwined into a compelling and cohesive vision. As a result, and despite its fragmentation, Pherecydes' *Heptamychos* remains a significant coordinate in the landscape of early Greek thought.

Notes

1 Fr. 14.1. Numeration of Pherecydes' fragments follow Schibli (1990). Translations are my own unless indicated.
2 Fr. 2. Henceforth the *Heptamychos*. The text is sometimes referred to as the *Pentamychos*, see Preller (1846: 378) and West (1971: 13). Schibli (1990: 46–9) plausibly defends the accuracy of *Heptamychos*, cf. Conrad (1856: 35). West (1971: 8–9) proposes an adjectival reading i.e. 'seven-nook mixing of the gods' or 'seven-nook genesis of the gods'.
3 Schibli (1990: 132–4) helpfully summarizes key divergences from tradition.
4 *Contra* Brisson (1997: 159–61). On archaic uses of χρόνος as an agentive force cf. Edmonds (2018: 93). The variance of *chi* and *kappa* spellings is perfectly in line with Pherecydes' well-attested etymological play (frr. 14, 61, 62). Cf. West (1963), West (1971) and Lopez-Ruiz (2010: 130–70) on comparable (though not parallel) occurrences of time-gods in Near-Eastern, Egyptian, Phoenician and Orphic traditions.
5 Chase (2013: 33–5).
6 Schibli (1990).
7 *Ti.* 37–8.
8 A selection of arguments for and against this view can be found in Callahan (1948: 18), Cherniss (1962: 212), von Leyden (1964: 36), Guthrie (1965: 28, 34 n. 1), Vlastos (1965a), Vlastos (1965b), Owen (1966), Whittaker (1968: 133ff), Tarán (1979: 47ff.), Sorabji (1983: 108–12), Cornford (1997: 98, 102), Palmer (2009: 140–1), Ilievski (2015: 10 ff.) and Wilberding (2016: 18–22).
9 *Ti.* 38b7, 41e.
10 See Clack and Clack (2008: 57–66) and Hannam (2009).
11 Diels (1969: 31–2).
12 Breglia (2000: 180–2).
13 Chase (2013: 34). Cf. Stamatellos (2012: 123).
14 Schibli (1990: 28 n. 38, 29).
15 See esp. *Phaedo* 107d–114c. Schibli (1990: 115–25).
16 Diels (1969: 31–2); see also Jaeger (1947: 68–70).
17 Schibli (1990: 28 n. 38).
18 Ibid. (29). Cf. Šćepanović (2012: 98).

19 Schibli (1990: 29). Criticized by Chase (2013: 34 n. 88).
20 Breglia (2000: 180–2).
21 See Schibli (1990: 135–9).
22 Ibid. (1990: 29).
23 Chase (2013) summarizes these criticisms.
24 Breglia (2000: 182).
25 See esp. Brisson (1997: 159–61) and West (1971: 20ff.).
26 Kirk, Raven and Schofield (1983: 57, 67) and Schibli (1990: 135–9).
27 Chase (2013: 34).
28 See esp. Fränkel (1955), Šćepanović (2012) and Sattler (2017).
29 Fränkel (1955) and Šćepanović (2012: 297 ff).
30 Sattler (2017: 20). See also Šćepanović (2012: 68 ff., 298–302).
31 E.g. Bacchylides fr. 7.1, Soph. *OC.* 607–15.
32 Fr. 14.
33 See West (1971: 6). Contrast the depiction of tense in Pl. *Tim.* 37e3–38a3 and Parmenides B8.5. Cf. Smyth (1920: 422) and Rijksbaron (2011) on the historical present.
34 E.g. Hom *Il.* 1.290, 1.494; *Od.* 8.306, 12.371; Hes. *Theog.* 34.
35 Šćepanović (2012) and Keizer (2010).
36 Cf. Jaeger (1947: 67–8), Kirk, Raven and Schofield (1983: 56), Schibli (1990: 15), Palmer (2009: 226), Šćepanović (2012: 93) and Santamaría (2021: 129). On Pherecydes' alignment with Milesian philosophy (esp. Xenophanes B14), see Vlastos (1952: 113 n. 77), Barnes (1982: 66), Palmer (2016: 33–4) and Macé (2017: 212–13).
37 Kirk, Raven and Schofield (1983: 26–9), West (1983: 111–12), Bernabé (1995: 195–211) and Meisner (2018: 88–94).
38 Frr. 2, 7, 88. Schibli (1990: *passim*), Breglia (2000), Lopez-Ruiz (2010: 154–6) and Meisner (2018: 144–5).
39 Ar. *Av.* 693–702. Trans. J. Henderson (Loeb), slightly amended.
40 Stamatopoulou (2017: 205 n. 87).
41 Compare Parmenides B8 and Euripides fr. 484.2–6.
42 *Metaph.* 1091b10–11.
43 *Metaph.* 1091b4–14. Jaeger (1947: 69), Diels (1969: 29–30) and Kirk, Raven and Schofield (1983: 58 n. 1) suggest the ἄριστον τιθέασι is Zeus; West (1971: 12–13, 23) and Schibli (1990: 18 n. 11) suggest Chronos. See West (1971: 12 n. 3) on Diels' emendation of ἑαυτοῦ to αὐτοῦ in fr. 60. Cf. Zeller (1932: 188 n. 1) and Vlastos (1952: 109).
44 Fr. 78.
45 *Av.* 468–9.
46 See for example Breglia (2000: 180).
47 Granger (2007: 141).

48 Casaubon, Aldobrandini and Casaubon (1692: 76).
49 Laks and Most (2016: 172 n. 2).
50 Esp. Schibli (1990: 29–38) and Riverso (1979: 7ff).
51 Santamaría (2019: 99–100) and Vlastos (1952). Rather than Pherecydes borrowing ideas from Anaximander (per Jaeger (1947: 67–8)), Schibli's common 'climate of opinion' (1990: 37) is more tenable. Cf. Hahn (2012: 50–1).
52 B1 DK. Trans. G. W. Most and A. Laks (Loeb), slightly amended.
53 On denotation of οὐσία see Mansfeld (2018: 153–60).
54 *Contra* Jaeger (1947: 35), I do not take Anaximander's χρόνος to be divine. See Vlastos (1952: 108 n. 51), Granger (2007: 145) and Mansfeld (2018: 149).
55 Deichgräber (1940: 16–17), Kahn (1994: 35, 166–70), Kirk, Raven and Schofield (1983: 118) and Mansfeld (2018: 143–4) on the beginning and end of Anaximander's words.
56 Frr. 4.15–16, 36.3–6 Gerber.
57 Simpl. *In Phys.* 24.25.
58 Jaeger (1947: 35 n. 59). Cf. Vlastos (1952: 108 n. 51).
59 Fr. 61.
60 Schibli (1990: 138).
61 See esp. Schibli (1990: 38–49) and Meisner (2018: 144–5) on the μυχοί. Their development into cosmic regions echoes the Hesiodic chasm from which the roots of earth and sea grow (*Theog.* 728, 807–10).
62 Fr. 60. Trans. Schibli, slightly amended. West (1971: 12–13, 23), Kirk, Raven and Schofield (1983: 69–71) and Schibli (1990: 28–9).
63 Fr. 88.
64 West (1971: 25 n. 3) on Porphyry's use of αἰνίσσομαι.
65 Fr. 7, cf. fr. 2.
66 On diverse ideas of metempsychosis see esp. Burkert (1972: 134–5).
67 Purves (2010a: 107). A specific echo of the μυχοί may be found in the (now lost) Orphic *Krater*. See West (1983: 10) and Kingsley (1995: 133–48).
68 *Ol.* 2.17. Schibli (1990: 22). Cf. Kirk, Raven and Schofield (1983: 70) on a possible parallel in Homeric scholia (*in* Homeri *Il.* II, 783).
69 Mansfeld (2018: 148–9).
70 See μυέω in Hdt. 2.51, 8.65.
71 Hes. *Theog.* 119; Eur. *Heracl.* 37; *Supp.* 545, 926; *Tro.* 952. In Homer, μυχοί typically denote the innermost recesses within homes and landscapes (*Od.* 5.226, 13.363), yet also feature at 24.6 in a metaphor about the descent of souls.
72 Porph. *Vita Pyth.* 17; Diog. Laert. 8. 32. See Burkert (1972: 151–5), Ustinova (2009: 218–55) and Connors and Clendenon (2016).
73 On Pherecydean topography see West (1971: 24–6, 49–50), Schibli (1990: 22 n. 18), Purves (2010a: 107) and Hahn (2012: 51).

74 Note χρόνος' judicial character in Solon (frr. 4.15–16, 36.3–6 Gerber). See Jaeger (1947: 35) and Granger (2007: 145).
75 *Ol.* 2.68–72. Trans. W. H. Race (Loeb). Hes. *Op.* 173a–e is generally regarded as an interpolation, see West (1978: 194), Solmsen (1982: 14–18) and Johnson (1999). See Graf and Johnston (2007: 100–1) and Chrysanthou (2020) on Orphic connotations.
76 Paus. 39.4. See Bonnecherre (2003) and Bonnecherre (2013).
77 P. Oxy. 3830 fr. 3 col. ii; Σ AD Il. 8.479.
78 Meuli (1975: 1034). Cf. Auffarth (1991: 19) and Versnel (1993: 113–14).
79 Schibli (1990: 96–102).

6

Pindar and the Nature of Contemplation[*]

David Fearn
University of Warwick

Ontologies of temporality and relationhood are, especially in comparativist approaches, understood to be central to the self-enactment of lyric poetry. While, with Greek lyric, questions of social contextualization remain important, it is also necessary to liberate 'context'. Reflection upon the temporal ontology of lyric form as it affects audiences and readers as the very substance of its self-instantiation may be a way of achieving this.

This chapter builds on current discussions of lyric temporality,[1] to assess how Pindar intensifies phenomenological issues arising from nature imagery.[2] Close reading of the imagistic processes of figuration is integrated into a broader ecocritical outlook. Lyric assessment of human-world relations thus also intersects with concerns in the philosophy of poetry understood as processual and relational,[3] and grants philology a basic role within contemporary theoretical Classics.[4] Specific benefits may include advancement of the theorization of exemplarity within reception studies, extending recent work.[5] And philological practice may itself be re-examined: not so much a will to mastery (an intellectual reverie opened up but also critiqued in Pindar, as well as in Pindaric reception[6]) as a willingness to reflect creatively, for the future, on the possibilities afforded by literary antiquity.[7]

The focus is Pindar's *Olympian* 10. It commemorates the Olympic victory of Hagesidamos of Western Lokroi in the boys' boxing, 476 BCE. It makes a series of moves. It starts with a focus on the mental processes of poetic remembering and forgetting in the first strophe (lines 1–3), before shifting to the contemplation of a pebble rolling in the waves (lines 9–12). It then shifts again to the positioning of celebration of Hagesidamos' victory within a vividly presented mythological showcase of the foundation of the Olympic sanctuary at the first Olympiad, involving Chronos, Time, himself (lines 24–85). It closes with further musings on fame via reflection on the youthful beauty of Hagesidamos at the specific time – κεῖνον κατὰ χρόνον – of his victory (lines 95–105, specifically 103). My aim is to reveal how, in both framing and mythological sections, the poem zooms in on the contemplation of nature within lyric temporality, and how this contributes to an unfolding of lyric as a creative cultural resource.[8]

The poem's handling of the relation between lyric temporality and the contemplation of both space and place, through details of figuration, seems fundamental for reflection on such attentiveness.[9] My approach, true to the ways in which such poems were engaged with originally,[10] offers wider reflection on the strengths of the commitments that should matter to us as humans in the world, from a contemporary perspective in which human agency is under ever-increasing scrutiny. If phenomenology is to do with 'the relation between the things of the world and the words of language', then we had better get closely to grips with the terms in question.[11]

Allow me to turn first, though, to Mikhail Bakhtin, for reasons which will become clear shortly. Before continuing into his extensive discussion of features of novelistic discourse with little point of contact with our lyric concerns, Bakhtin begins his essay 'Forms of Time and of the Chronotope in the Novel: Notes towards a Historical Poetics' with a couple of pages of wider reflection on the nature of the relation between literary form, space and time. Bakhtin is surely right, in opening his essay, to say that 'the process of assimilating real historical time and space in literature has a complicated and erratic history...'.[12] The challenges of this process of assimilation, and the unfolding of them in ongoing encounters with Greek lyric, provide an underlying structure to my focus on nature.

While Bakhtin's work is generally understood to be Marxist-formalist, what also matters for Bakhtin is the relationality of language and world, and the dynamics of the modalities of experience afforded by literature: so Bakhtin is also phenomenological. He bases his view of literary form in literary space-time, or the 'chronotope', as he calls it: 'the intrinsic connectedness of temporal and spatial relationships that are artistically expressed in literature'.[13] While Bakhtin does not outline in this essay the chronotopic situatedness of readers and audiences, he recognizes that this is an important consideration. As he says, 'In the present work we will not consider the complex problem of the listener-reader, his chronotopic situation and his role in *renewing* the work of art (his role in the process of the work's life); we will point out merely that every literary work *faces outward away from itself*, toward the listener-reader, and to a certain extent thus anticipates possible reactions to itself'.[14] Bakhtin's wording feels close to the perspective of Heidegger in his essay 'The Origin of the Work of Art' based on lectures from the mid-thirties.[15]

I was drawn back to Bakhtin not from within Classics, but from the world of art: specifically, contemporary landscape photography. *Afghanistan: Chronotopia* is a monograph by photographer Simon Norfolk.[16] It is dedicated to the depiction of Afghanistan in and ulterior to the immediate context of the so-called War on Terror. Norfolk's work is both lyrically and classically inflected – prefaced by a quotation from W. B. Yeats' 'In the Firelight', and with the strata of destruction reminding Norfolk of Schliemann's Troy; it is also methodologically driven by Bakhtin's chronotopic outlook.[17] Norfolk draws on Bakhtin as an entry-point for art-historical and photographic contemplation. He invites assessment of the relation between, on the one hand, Afghanistan as a landscape constantly reshaped with layers of scars caused by destruction across its entire history, and, on the other, the aestheticization of civilizational and archaeological decay in the history of landscape painting since the Renaissance. Norfolk's photographic explorations seem to reveal the human tragedies and the aesthetic hypocrisies exposed by the bombing of Afghanistan 'back to the stone age'.[18]

Focusing on Pindar allows us to see how his handling of victory systematically exposes and explores the nature of the relation between a specific mode of historical and cultural consciousness – 'victory' – and the broader parameters across which this might be conceptualized and ramified, within and by means of the opportunities that the victory ode as lyric form provides. In Heideggerian terms, reconfigured, victory odes are forms that 'open up' the very question of the relation between a specific historical moment and the contemplative opportunities it may afford, as part of what contemplation of the world might involve and entail through the power of art.[19] That understanding and interpretation of this necessarily involves reflection upon the shifting temporal consciousness of interpretative situatedness should neither surprise nor alarm, so long as we take full responsibility for the reading practices we bring to bear.[20]

So here we start with a phenomenological Bakhtin, inflected by Heidegger and appropriated by contemporary art. This Bakhtin provides a useful starting point for this essay about lyric contemplation of nature and landscape, for two complementary reasons. First, lyric space-time receives a particularly heightened thematization in *Olympian* 10. Second, the entry into Bakhtin, made not via classicist theorization but through the perspective of contemporary artistic-historical reflection, instantiates the useful expansiveness of a comparativist breadth of conception. Pindar's landscapes are far from being antiquarian or fragmented according to the familiar modes of modernity, let alone representing 'un musée archéologique de la guerre', as Norfolk's Afghanistan.[21] Nevertheless, both sets of encounters may jolt us to reflect upon the stakes of the conceptualization of landscape as a layering of space-time. Norfolk's discussion of Afghanistan's stratification of destruction also of course resonates in relation to Shane Butler's conceptualization of 'Deep Classics', with metaphors of geology and archaeological stratigraphy utilized for a renewal of classical reception.[22] *Olympian* 10 presents, at least in part, a meditation on nature and on temporal processes of transformation of space into place, within and beyond the parameters of human cultural cognition.[23] It does this via peculiarly lyric strategies of exposition, in its manipulations of subjective imagination and consciousness. These are strategies that may thus have contributions to make to the relation between classical philology and contemporary reception studies.

The focus of this chapter involves no aesthetic or metapoetic navel-gazing, or worse, deliberate avoidance of, for instance, the political. The affordances of both poetry and photography – and the sense that it is through individual self-reflection that we come to consider communities of value – provide a possible way forward, from the right starting point: aesthetic form.[24] Exploration of aesthetic experience through anachronic critical response to both antiquity and modernity is perhaps as good a response as any to heightened awareness of the fragmented, wounded, transitory and ephemeral. This may be especially true if reflection upon such awareness is set against more massive, temporally intractable, more automated, automatic, out of hand, structures of power and forces of disorder and destruction in the contemporary.[25] And lyric's paradoxically deep insistence on its own glitteringly persistent ephemerality is also an answer to the automatization of ephemerality in the everyday, including photography as at least widely conceived and consumed. Norfolk's photographic encounters with Afghanistan as landscape are in many ways shocking and heart-wrenching, and thus very different from Pindar's Olympic lyrics. But Pindar and Norfolk share their successes, in their ability to engage us about the potential held within human places as temporally layered environments. Such environments become ideas: affording moments not simply of contemplation but of thinking with the potential of contemplation.

The substance of my discussion involves a focus on three moments of contemplation in *Olympian* 10: a pebble, lines 9–12; moonlight, lines 72–5; snow, lines 49–51.

1. Pebble

Pindar gives us a pebble, in the immediate context of the opening lines:

Pindar and the Nature of Contemplation

Τὸν Ὀλυμπιονίκαν ἀνάγνωτέ μοι
Ἀρχεστράτου παῖδα, πόθι φρενός
ἐμᾶς γέγραπται· γλυκὺ γὰρ αὐτῷ μέλος ὀφείλων
  ἐπιλέλαθ'· ὦ Μοῖσ', ἀλλὰ σὺ καὶ θυγάτηρ
Ἀλάθεια Διός, ὀρθᾷ χερί
ἐρύκετον ψευδέων   5
ἐνιπὰν ἀλιτόξενον.

ἔκαθεν γὰρ ἐπελθὼν ὁ μέλλων χρόνος
ἐμὸν κατσίσχυνε βαθὺ χρέος.
ὅμως δὲ λῦσαι δυνατὸς ὀξεῖαν ἐπιμομφὰν
  τόκος θνατῶν· νῦν ψᾶφον ἑλισσομέναν
ὀπᾷ κῦμα κατακλύσσει ῥέον,   10
ὀπᾷ τε κοινὸν λόγον
φίλαν τείσομεν ἐς χάριν.[26]

> The Olympic victor . . . read me out his name –
>   the son of Archestratos – from my mind,
>   where it is written. For I owe him a sweet song,
>   and I have forgotten. Muse, yes, and you daughter
>   of Zeus, Truth, with a straight hand
>   keep me away from the charge of falsehoods,
>   of wronging a friend.
>
>   For from afar future time arrived and
>   shamed my deep indebtedness.
> But it is possible for mortals to undo bitter discredit through
>   payback with interest. Now like a rolling pebble
>   which a wave washes over in the tide,
>   so let us settle up our joint account
>   with the grace of friendship.

It is important to recognize that this image of a rolling pebble is itself a simile – a poetic analogy, an invitation to scrutinize the nature of any relation. It also forms part of a rhetorical scheme governed by an anachronic temporality, both a momentary event in the past (aorists ἐπελθὼν and κατσίσχυνε) and one coming uncannily from the distant future (ἔκαθεν; ὁ μέλλων χρόνος). The present temporality of 'now', νῦν, intervenes in this deep sense of temporal consciousness. The impression, at least, of present immediacy in this temporal intervention colours the sense of a contractual relationship, and transforms it into something of a wider shared temporal consciousness and coming together. κοινὸν λόγον moves from being contractual – 'joint account' in financial terms – to become something like 'shared language', thanks to the catalytic action of pebble and waves. Nature in imagery enacts interpretative transformation in and because of time.

In functional rhetorical terms, it seems that the wave washing over the rolling pebble and effacing it from our consciousness marks the wiping-clean of the financial slate in the completion of an encomiastic transaction, within a biographically interpretable historical process of poetic composition and patronage, or within a symbolic poetic economics of exchange.[27] But as a reading of Pindar's language, this is insufficient. It represents a failure to recognize how aesthetic and potentially ethical bonds are forged through formal complexity. For what Pindar's image also signifies is the aesthetic power of lyric's imagistic contemplation: it is the poetic power, instantiated in the arresting image, that mediates and enables shared experience.[28] This image continues the imaginative potential conferred by the poem's opening verb ἀνάγνωτε. There, the second-person plural imperative invites unnamed people, including us, to read out, or imagine the process of reading out, the content of the poet's mind, in seemingly beginning the poem on his behalf given how bizarrely neglectful we appear to find him. Such shared experience both anticipates and enacts the poem's formal unfolding across time for all readers and audiences.[29] And such sharing is not simply aesthetically exorbitant but also potentially ethically and even politically so, because of what such shared consciousness through time might entail. Again, formal appeals to a plurality of 'you's provide the basis of individual engagements through time in response.[30]

The poem pays us back immediately with an exorbitance of attention through the image of the seashore. It does so in a way that again reveals the rich depth of temporal layering and consciousness. This is a depth identified as such with βαθύ, 'deep', in relation to the debt that is imagined as accruing through time. But the exorbitance of the image, in the 'now' of the waves and pebble, supervenes upon that debt, as we imagine a wave breaking once again over the pebble as it rolls along the shoreline.

This 'now', in its processual context, jolts our temporal consciousness in at least two ways. First, the temporal structure of syntax is reminiscent of the way in which Greek lyric had, since Alcman, manifested its own temporal, experiential complexity through the use of the adverb δηὖτε ('now ... then', or 'now again').[31] The pebble's rolling as the wave inundates it, on Anne Carson's terms, 'intercepts "now" and binds it into a history of "*thens*"'.[32] Second, the fact that that 'now' prompts a simile jolts our temporal consciousness in the recognition that that 'now' is itself imagistic: the now of aesthetic imagination, not of straightforward environmental availability to our senses according to structures of causation that we tend to think of as ours. Compare Stephen Burt's reading of the opening of Shakespeare's Sonnet 60:

> Like as the waves make towards the pebbl'd shore,
> So do our minutes hasten to their end,
> Each changing place with that which goes before,
> In sequent toil all forwards do contend.
>
> Metaphor and simile and all the tools that say 'this is like that' work against time, and against causality; they show a resemblance at the present moment, and therefore let us hold on to a 'now.' But the 'like' in simile reminds us that we cannot hold on after all; each wave moves, in sequent toil, and all do contend.[33]

Pindar's sea-like rhythms and repetitions and onomatopoeia – the tumbling sound of ψᾶφον ἑλισσομέναν; the vivid but controlled noise of the sea in κῦμα κατακλύσσει; the repetition of ὀπᾷ ... ὀπᾷ enacting the sonic effect of temporal process as wave washes over – may seem initially perhaps to taunt us in a referentiality to a 'now' access to which seems uncertain at best. But then these rhythms also remind us that attempting to access any such ulterior space is perhaps beside the point, partly because we have, ourselves ... now ... become part of this imagistic process. Deeper, richer possibilities are opened by more careful attunement. Lyric attentiveness rescues aesthetic beauty from evanescence, while resisting and perhaps even disavowing a questing for origins and causes.[34] And reflection upon the temporal complexity of lyric's being in the world includes and indeed exposes the contemplation of nature as one of lyric's fundamental concerns. This is so even when, or perhaps rather especially when, it is set against transformations of space into place that form part of human social and cultural consciousness, as with the origins of Olympia offered by this poem.

Lyric, and photography for that matter, affords an animating and paradoxically empowering experience of transience and fragility in terms that generate a sense of empathy and connection, and desire for replication.[35] Compare here the desire felt by the angel Damiel in Wim Wenders' *Wings of Desire*, where yearning for mortal experience feels lyrical and photographically inflected, within the contemplation afforded by extraordinary cinema:

> It's great to live by the spirit, to testify for eternity only what is spiritual in people's minds. But sometimes I'm fed up with my spiritual existence, of forever hovering

above. I'd like to feel a weight in me, to end the infinity, and to tie me to earth. I'd like at each step, each gust of wind, to be able to say: 'now ..., now ..., and now ...'. No longer: 'Forever' and 'For eternity'.[36]

Lyric also strives to fix and locate in time series of remote, otherworldly things and experiences – and then gains distinctiveness through the paradox of the attempt. Part of what the lyric manifestations of natural and temporal processes and transformations in *Olympian* 10 fundamentally expose is our own working through of them as constituted by the form of the text in our experience of it. Pindaric poems enact the processual nature of human experience and agency not simply as vehicles for the articulation of wider social concerns. Moreover, the deeper, richer attunements of a poem such as *Olympian* 10 enact the kind of 'feeling of weight' for which Wim Wenders' angel yearns: the thinking sense of texture of a human bodily experience offered by the effect, for instance, of lyric sound, rhythm and onomatopoeia that we have felt – however briefly – with the poem's sonorously excessive lyrical pebble, on its terms.[37] In *Olympian* 10, the power of victory as a 'decisive moment' in time, κεῖνον κατὰ χρόνον (line 103, again, with apologies to Henri Cartier-Bresson), might have been a starting point, if we hadn't already known that the uncertainty of the poet's commitment to that in the poem's opening already served as an enormous creative impulse.

2. Moonlight

Olympian 10 provides opportunities to attend to a whole host of other momentary transitions and processes that contextualize and expand upon the temporality of victory. Evanescent shards are granted a lyric agency that allows them to become as important for the defining nature of lyric experience as the success being commemorated or the mythical narrative being set alongside it. With such shards as these, Pindar is the clear heir of Sappho, with her lingering attentiveness to potentially insignificant, fragmentary and evanescent, moments otherwise overlooked.[38] Sapphic affinity feels prominent in the attention to the alluring (indeed erotically tinged: ἐρατόν, 'lovely') quality of moonlight at the end of the events of Herakles' first Olympiad, lines 72–5:

> μᾶκος δὲ Νικεὺς ἔδικε πέτρῳ χέρα κυκλώσαις
>   ὑπὲρ ἁπάντων, καὶ συμμαχία θόρυβον
> παραίθυξε μέγαν· ἐν δ' ἕσπερον

ἔφλεξεν εὐώπιδος
σελάνας ἐρατὸν φάος.   75

Nikeus whirled the stone in his circling hand beyond all others;
and the assembled force shot out a great cheer; and on evening
        there shone the fair face
          of the moon, a beautiful light.

The discus sent spinning across the sky from the hand of Nikeus – 'Victor', the eponymously uncanny prototype for all subsequent victors – moves our attention on to linger on the moon.

Sapphic moonlight – from fragment 96 where spreading φάος (light) figures the spreading κλέος (fame) of the Sapphic poetics of loss[39] – is turned back upon itself; the κλέος of Pindaric victory not only spreads into the future but provides an opportunity here to look backwards. In the original imagistic world of Sappho, attentiveness to the details of nature provides a consolatory frisson. Lyrical beauty-cum-ephemerality of moonlit flowers stands in for aspects of our lived experience that we have irredeemably lost.[40] An ethical distantiation is built in. In Pindar now, the Sapphic trace focuses attention on the originally natural, non-human, vehicle of imagery as something which we are distanced from, but which we need, to begin to understand our selves as beings whose acculturation involves transformations of and impositions on a space-time that was not ours. These transformations of course include Pindaric lyric's own coming-into-being as aestheticization and culture, not despite but indeed because of this poem's opening of access to the primordial.

Instead of using moonlight as an opportunity to produce a simile that decoratively articulates human interrelations in the moment of success (which is what Bacchylides does elsewhere),[41] Pindar strips down the essence of traditional lyric imagery to its constituent parts. This image focuses on the natural components, appropriated for the vehicles of similes, as essences ulterior to human consciousness and not at least automatically to be appropriated for human consumption. And Nikeus' victory provides a mythologically exemplary recognition of the ulteriority of nature in our contemplation of it: not an add-on to Olympic success, but fundamental to it.

Even in traditional cases of Homeric simile, it has been argued that the relation between human tenor and natural vehicle has the effect of, as it were, 'petromorphizing' the human, as much as humanizing the natural. According to Mark Payne, 'Such similes are not merely a glimpse into kinds of human life that the martial content of the primary narrative excludes. They reveal, as a deep psychic stratum, the fundamental work of objectification that makes a human narrative possible; in Snell's words: "Man must listen to an echo of himself before he may hear or know of himself".[42] And the natural world provided in Homeric imagery is 'an alternative to – rather than a carrier of – human meanings'.[43] Complementarily, according to Wai Chi Dimock, the worlds of Homeric simile present a poetic underside, the dramatization of 'a kind of unheroic counterrhythm' to the grand narratives of the mythological actors.[44]

Pindaric imagery is heir to both the Sapphic tenderness and Homeric terror of the everyday, and admits of an imagistic range that extends beyond both Homeric and Sapphic conceptualizations. In the current example, this range serves to emphasize the inalienable-but-alien presencing of nature within foundational cultural achievement.

This observation is not simply to illustrate or list in more detail the extent of Pindar's literary traditionality as a literary-historical or antiquarian end in itself. Rather, it provides the resource for further contemplation in its own right, fitting alongside the significance of Pindaric *gnomai*.[45] In *Olympian* 10 imagery of nature seems bound, given the poem's obsession with the affordances of Olympic lyrical chronometry, to draw us in to consider the processes through which the natural becomes acculturated through human imposition. We are afforded moments to reflect upon what this means for understanding the relation between humanity and the environment, and space and place. And this happens precisely as we bring to life, in our enactment of it, the poem's own figuration of human subjective reflection upon nature.

3. Snow

On these terms, one of the most extraordinary moments in the whole poem is the encounter we have with the not-quite-primordial space of Olympia in lines 49–51, before its full athletic and religious acculturation as place: πρόσθε γὰρ | νώνυμνος, ἇς Οἰνόμαος ἆρχε, βρέχετο πολλᾷ | νιφάδι, 'for before, nameless, where Oinomaos ruled, it was drenched deep in snow'. The ruling presence of Oinomaos is important since, while Pindar allows us at least to attempt to contemplate the beauty of the snowfall, it seems pointed that this event in space is marked as something precisely not noticed or felt let alone understood by Oinomaos, whose only function here is power, not contemplation.

This is Oinomaos' only mention in the poem. Yet, what his non-attentiveness figures is the uncanny, untimely, nature of the Pindaric snowfall, as non-beholden to human experience. By the same token, Oinomaos does also present an unsettling exemplarity for our own ability to comprehend Pindar's act of figuration. Pindaric attentiveness provides a sense of the revelation of what untimely song and divine transformation can do to a literally anonymous space. But the processual snowfall whose beauty prefigures encomiastic celebration[46] thus also carries with it, alongside natural evanescence, a strong element of cognitive incomprehensibility in its seemingly wilful – at least poetic – survival. This is the visually flat, featureless, deadening quiet of a snowscape that would tend to monochrome. And yet, here it is, provided for us, a sonorous poetic excess that appears to persist.

An ecocritical reading is available, which comparative art history may help to elucidate. Pindar shares something in common with the land artists of modern conceptual art (for instance Richard Long, Hamish Fulton, James Turrell, Philip Hughes) in providing the resources for mapping the parameters of human desire for order and imposition: 'a wish to mark and differentiate from nature'.[47] Going beyond, for instance, Homer, Sappho, or contemporary poets such as Bacchylides, Pindar links us to, and opens up the question of the sense of, the very distant, elemental, mythologized past as a space, before any attempt to represent space as landscape in which for cultured human bodies to perform. This is a poetic mode that raises the question of the stakes of a human-centred aesthetic framing.[48] An Olympian ode raises both the question and the significance of what the space of Olympia has become and is, in both human and non-human terms, through the language of imagery.

On the terms of phenomenologist Edward S. Casey, a Pindaric geography of Olympia presents a layered sensual enrichment. *Olympian* 10 does not straightforwardly provide an origin story to answer descriptively the question of what this place simply 'is'; 'landscape is the presented layout of a set of places, not their mere accumulation but their sensuous self-presentation as a whole'.[49] If Pindar digs down into the origin of Olympia, what he unearths is not an objective aetiology of place, but a resonant space that both is and is not already part of us. This lyric resonance reveals itself as 'work' in a way that delves deeper than a celebration of an Olympic historical or even mythological chronology, because it draws attention to the fundamental basis of celebration, in and through its attentiveness to moments in nature that seem momentarily stilled and presented to us as objects of contemplation.

On the terms of environmental philosopher Tim Morton, Olympia's originary snow would also become a kind of lyric hyperobject (non-local in the sense that the snow is present before the idea of locality is even given a name), attunement to which helps to enact the realization of the contemplative strangeness of our own temporal consciousness as human subjects.[50] Part of what makes the product of Pindar's encomiastic ambition ultimately so strange is its continuing presence as and in the poetic encounter. Coming to terms with this is a function of our current situatedness, according to which classical philology and environmental philosophy may coincide. Again, according to Morton: 'my situatedness and the rhetoric of situatedness ... is not a place of defensive self-certainty but precisely its opposite. That is, situatedness is now a very uncanny place to be, like being the protagonist of a Wordsworth poem or a character in Blade Runner'... or, indeed, a Pindaric lyric subject.[51] What comes into question is the security of our own positionality.[52] To appropriate such a recognition has, of course, substantial political and ethical consequences, with which classical philology may feel uncomfortable. Yet, it is from the philological perspective, but in processual, landscape-oriented, temporal terms, that we are drawn to reflect upon Pindar's lyric layering: lyric snow, lyric light, lyric rhythm and sound, lyric time, lyric tides.

Conclusion

With this emphasis on layering, let me conclude by circling back to the juxtaposition I made at the outset between lyric and landscape photography. Rather than being read as subservient or shackled to referents in the world ulterior to them – athletics and celebration, politics and religion; the lacerated terrain of Afghanistan – both Pindar's *Olympian* 10 and Simon Norfolk's photographs gain their power by having their entire coming-into-being as exemplary artworks enacted in our encounters with them.

In the latter case, the frisson is provided by the relation between object in the world as perceived by the photographer and aesthetic object as produced for the photographs' consumers – for instance, the beautifully lit but damaged Taq-e Zafar archway in Kabul that looks like nothing so much as a painting by Poussin. These are artworks that reflect back on their consumers within the act of aesthetic contemplation, in ways that may destabilize the security of the ethical or aesthetic relation of consumers to what they think they are perceiving, and to attune them to their strange temporalities.

With Pindar the environmental *Bildungsroman* afforded by complex figuration is no easily detachable add-on to, or opt-out from, sport, politics, or religion qua historical sociology.[53] Both aesthetics and sociology are nonnegotiable. The challenge of lyric expression, to take up rather than ignore, concerns the stakes of our comprehension of all these terms of reference. And the challenge of *Olympian* 10 might, in object-oriented ecocritical terms, concern the security of our own subjectivity – what *is* the standpoint from which we are reading, listening, or viewing that enables us to understand what we are being presented with? *Olympian* 10 makes an exemplary gesture, not solely as an opportunity for classicists to contribute further pieces to the ongoing scholarship of intellectual historiography,[54] but as something inductively more experimental. The dive into the abyss of the mythological exemplarity of Olympia's origins produces yet more resources for subjective reflection.[55] *Olympian* 10's asking of the question of how we even understand what Olympia is as a space or place can thus involve a reconfiguration of the security of our own subjectivity in relation to nature: and thinking in contemporary environmental terms can help us to interpret Pindar.

Notes

* Many thanks to Tom Phillips and Victoria Rimell for discussion of a number of ideas in this piece.
1. Culler (2015), Michael (2017), Fearn (2017: ch. 3) and Fearn (2020: 13).
2. E.g. Payne (2014) after Snell (1953); Gurd (2016), Payne (2018a) and Matlock (2020); cf. Phillips (2020: 7–8, 95–8, 320–2) on relevant lyrical effects in Apollonius.
3. Lamarque (2009), Mitchell (2011) and Leighton (2018).
4. Bianchi, Brill and Holmes (2019), esp. Porter (2019) with Morton (2013).
5. Goldhill (2017) and Güthenke (2020).
6. Pind. *Nem.* 8.5, ἐπικρατεῖν δύνασθαι, with Fearn (2017: 101–5); Goethe's Pindar: Hamilton (2003: 237–48), cf. The Postclassicisms Collective (2020: 164).
7. See esp. Güthenke and Holmes (2018: 70). I do not consider their call for valorization of critical uncertainty to be new, integral as it is to the provisionality of a deconstructive classical outlook: see esp. Fowler (2000). But it is important to renew its force.
8. My discussion thus ramifies Spelman's (2018b: 67) observation of processual movement in *Ol.* 10 from poet's mind, to composition, to choral performance, through to implied literary artifactuality; cf. Spelman (2018b: 75, 196–203) for a brief description of the mapping of the relation of past and present in the poem. While a range of critics continue to locate meaning in reconstructions of origin (historical and literary-historical) and social interrelations – e.g. Maslov (2015), Morgan (2015), Spelman (2018b) and Agócs (2020) – there are now also consistent

signs that different approaches are making headway: e.g. Gurd (2016: 13–16) on Sappho fr. 2, Phillips (2016), Fearn (2017), LeVen (2018), papers in Budelmann and Phillips (2018) esp. Payne (2018b), and Matlock (2020).

9   Space as differentiated from place: see e.g. Casey (2001: 683): 'Both geography and phenomenology have come to focus on place as experienced by human beings, in contrast to space, whose abstractness discourages experiential explorations.'

10 A point which should be obvious given the lyric reception of Pindar from the fifth century BCE onwards, but emphasized by e.g. Payne (2006: 165), Phillips (2016), Fearn (2017: e.g. 21–2).

11 On Heidegger and the poetics of relationality, see Mitchell (2011: quotation comes from p. 217).

12 Bakhtin (1981: 84).

13 Ibid. (84). For useful discussion of Bakhtin's chronotope, see e.g. Lawson (2011) and Renfrew (2014).

14 Bakhtin (1981: 257); original emphasis.

15 Heidegger (2002 [1935–6]).

16 Norfolk (2002).

17 Norfolk (2002: 'chronotopia' preface).

18 Photographic framing enables imagined temporal juxtapositions to be highlighted. 'Ici se trouve un salon de thé modern en béton qui resemble à Stonehenge; là, un pylône de radio FM tel un mât de cocagne; les pyramides de Gizeh; l'observatoire astronomique de Jaïpur; la trésoire de Petra; même les peintures rupestres votives dans les cavernes de Lascaux': Norfolk (2002: 'chronotopia' preface).

19 Cf. Heidegger (2002 [1935–6]: 23).

20 Cf. The Postclassicisms Collective (2020: 157) for the 'contingent dynamics of relationality' involved in reading Pindar with and against Wilamowitz (1922). Responsibility: Fearn (2017: 103) with Barthes (1974); cf. Fowler (2000: esp. 7) for a discussion of classicists' obsessions with foundationalism, of specific interest given my focus on *Ol.* 10 and what can be gained from rethinking the affordances of the poem's reflections within a foundational discourse. Responsibility also includes recognition of the challenges of using Heidegger for the ecocritical project given the grim situatedness of Heidegger's own environmental outlook, as for instance outlined in Garrard (2012: 120–2).

21 Norfolk (2002: 'chronotopia' preface).

22 Butler (2016: e.g. 4–5), with Schliemann's Troy again.

23 From an object-oriented ontological perspective, literature involves a socio-politically urgent decentering of human subjectivity. For a classicist outlook, see Porter (2019: esp. 207 with n. 61).

24 See further O'Meara (2013: 188–9, 196–7) discussing the formalist aesthetics of late Barthes, and the affinities between his celebrated musing on photography (Barthes,

1982) and the work of Adorno, and the pain inscribed into Barthes' theorization of the particularities of photographic *punctum* (the attracting, but wounding, detail in a photograph).

25 For further reflection on the relation between modern conceptual art and the Heideggerian critique of technological modernity, see esp. de Beistegui (2005: 125–54).

26 Reading θνατῶν and following the text and metrical analysis of Gentili et al. (2013).

27 Cf. e.g. Norwood (1945: 111–14) for the pebble as grounding principle for the whole poem via biographical historicism and financial symbolism.

28 The diverse interpretability of κοινὸν λόγον is suggested by the scholia, who reveal ancient discussion about the extent of the bond of commonality here: ΣΣ *Ol.* 10.15ab Dr. Shared experience as ethical within the lyric event: Payne (2018a).

29 Cf. Phillips (2016: 7–9).

30 Cf. n. 24 with O'Meara (2013) politicizing aesthetics in late Barthes, via the recognition of social and political consciousness as inscribed within individual aesthetic experience.

31 Carson (1986: 117–22) and LeVen (2018: 225–32).

32 Carson (1986: 119), original emphasis.

33 Burt (2014: 19).

34 Ecocriticism itself might indeed find disavowal to be in tune with the opening up of broader non-human timescales and dangers: see e.g. Morton (2013: 5); from the perspective of a phenomenological poetics of care, see Payne (2018b: 51–4).

35 Cf. lyric epideixis via Culler (2015), Fearn (2017) and Payne (2018a). 'Animating': Barthes (1982: 20) on photographs.

36 *Wings of Desire* (1987) 0:12.35–0:13.06: both ironic meta-photographic gesture and ultimately Romantic vision of temporality inherent in modernity. And, for the broader thematic context of recuperative quasi-archaeological ruination in *Wings of Desire*, see Bordo (2008: esp. 89–90).

37 For further discussion of issues in the conceptualization of the embodied ontological relationhood of the voice, beyond a reduction to semantic phonocentrism, see Cavarero (2005: esp. §3.4, 'The Reciprocal Communication of Voices' and appendix): embodied song-like resonant vocalities as not necessitating (patriarchal) domination or predetermination, but offering up the potential for a new constitution of social being. For poetry as mediating auditory experience, however figured and imagined, see Leighton (2018), for whom lyric is (or at least 'might be') '[an] acoustic texture ... which distracts the ear with all its hums, melodies, and songs ...' (47). See also Molde (2020: 587) on the relation between lyric metrics, enchantment and risk.

38 Purves (2021).

39 Sappho fr. 96.6–10; Macleod (1974).

40 Payne (2018a: 263).

41 Bacch. 9.27–32, with Fearn (2003: 362–3).
42 Payne (2014) with Snell (1953: 201), after Schiller (1993 [1800]).
43 Payne (2014).
44 Dimock (2008: 75).
45 Cf. Payne (2006: 165): Pindaric *gnomai* as a 'repository of thought'.
46 The usage prefigures this poem's own ultimate hyperbolic gesture of encomiastic self-figuration and conferment at lines 98–9: μέλιτι εὐάνορα πόλιν καταβρέχων ('drenching with honey their city of brave men'). Cf. e.g. *Ol.* 7.33; *Ol.* 6.55.
47 Syrad (2019: 13) on Richard Long. Also Boetzkes (2010: esp. 105).
48 One might profitably compare here, as relevant to the overall effect of *Olympian* 10, the thoughts of Nersessian (2020: 133–4) on lyric's 'distributed consciousness' ('whose knowledge of the world is not centred in any one person's perspective') and modelling of commitment: the sense that poetry is committed to the world, modelling 'a certain way of being in the world and with others' in spite of the fact that poetry enacts the very sense that the world is indifferent to it. For lyric this is obviously the challenge and allure of apostrophe as a figurative mode, for which see also Culler (2015: 211–43).
49 Casey (2001: 683).
50 Pindar's snow feels like the ancient equivalent of Morton's twentieth-century TV snow, the static noise that signifies no connection but also highlights its origin. Thus, Morton (2013: 174): 'One can see the Cosmic Microwave Background from the "beginning" of the universe in TV snow.' Attunement to the depth of relations such as these is what poetry is, and is what the Pindaric encounter provides here.
51 Morton (2013: 5).
52 Cf. Merleau-Ponty (2012: 433) for the relation between the analysis of temporality and necessary revisions to human subjectivity.
53 Cf. Heidegger (2002 [1935–6]: 18): 'But the work is not a piece of equipment that is fitted out in addition with aesthetic worth adhering to it.'
54 In a sense, then, this is where I might take issue with Güthenke (2020: 52–3) on exemplarity, especially according to the comparativist poetic terms upon which Güthenke establishes the argument. While I would certainly agree that exemplarity 'is both situational and emphatically *interrupting* both context and a stable temporal relationship' (original italics), I do think that the example of Pindar I have discussed suggests something more than exemplarity as 'a mode of knowing and of organizing knowledge of the past', precisely because poetic figuration in lyric, including simile, disrupts that process of organization, of intellectual historiography, by making things unexpectedly and uncannily present to us in ways that seem to deconstruct a strict backward-looking historical temporality. Partly it depends, I think, what we suppose poetry's 'knowing' consists in: for a nuanced perspective on this issue, see again Leighton (2018: ch. 11, esp. 269).

55 The exemplarity of Pindar's myth, in its environmental reflectiveness, is therefore much less to do with any mirroring of myth and frame, than with the opening up of the very question of the relation between worlds or modes of reference and of the language used to do so: thus a particularization of Goldhill (2017) on exemplarity.

Part Three

Temporal Patterns and the Politics of Latin Literature

7

Rivers as the Embodiment of Disrupted Time

Ovid's *Metamorphoses*, Ecological Chronotopes and the Apocalypse

Rebecca Batty
St. Mary's Catholic High School

In 'Forms of Time and of the Chronotope of the Novel', Bakhtin characterizes Ovid's narrative time in the *Metamorphoses* as time which 'breaks down into isolated, self-sufficient temporal segments that mechanically arrange themselves into no more than single sequences'.[1] This view is perhaps most intriguing when dealing with the mirrored apocalyptic episodes in Books 1 and 2 of Ovid's *Metamorphoses*, where the repeated destruction of the earth would seem to undermine the view of isolated segments. As Wheeler ably demonstrates, this act of repetition forms a larger role within the narrative structure of the poem.[2] Yet, even Wheeler's argument fails to take into account the connecting element between the sections, that of the natural environment, and world-ending river behaviour in particular. With this in mind, this paper will use an ecological reworking of Bakhtin's chronotope to show the importance of repetition, particularly connected to natural cycles and rivers as chronotopes in the temporality of Ovid's *Metamorphoses*.

First, I will outline some of the key ideas for Bakhtin's concept of the chronotope, alongside a brief sketch of its ecological reworking by Müller, and a short example of the river as a 'liquid chronotope' in cultural geography practice. I will then suggest how rivers can be viewed as chronotopes more broadly in Ovid's work, before turning to the focal point of this paper, the *Metamorphoses*. Finally, I apply the ecological framework of the river chronotope to the apocalyptic episodes in Ovid's *Metamorphoses* 1.279–92, and 2.241–59, specifically looking at how the extreme flooding and drying behaviour of the rivers can indicate moments of timelessness in the narrative, which are key to Ovid's fluid epic temporality.

Through this ecological approach to the chronotope, the importance of the natural environment in Ovid's fluid temporality is made clear, alongside ideas of literary chronology, the epic genre and renewal in the *Metamorphoses*.

Bakhtin defines the literary chronotope as 'space time', referring to the inseparability of time and space in the literary imagination. He argues that the chronotope is intrinsically linked to genre, as it is the narrative needs of the genre which create the chronotope.[3] For this, Bakhtin gives the example of 'adventure time', in the ancient Greek romance novel, where the entire novel lies outside of biographical time – events happening in the novel have no interaction with everyday time, and instead events happen only to guarantee the continuation of the romance novel in its expected form.[4] As other examples he presents the parlour of a nineteenth-century bourgeois novel, allowing specific encounters in entrances and exits, or the road, as a space allowing for chance encounters and delays. The chronotope here is about a space which allows the narrative time of the particular literary genre to unfold. The chronotope as a motif of genre is significant, as it assumes a static conception of genre; in comparison, Ovid's boundary-pushing manipulation of generic tropes leads to a more fluid idea of genre, which is reflected in the chronotopes of his works.

Advocating an approach which recognizes the fundamental presence of the natural environment in the conceptualization of time, Müller suggests Bakhtin's chronotopes focus too much on 'time', the result of which is a lack of focus on space. He argues that the underestimating of spatiality privileges an anthropocentric worldview, as space itself 'does not require a refined (human) consciousness to manifest itself, nor does it need to be made visible to become perceptible'.[5] Bakhtin's chronotopes prefer historically created spaces which indicate moments of linear time, in contrast to the cyclic time he describes as 'natural'. Bakhtin separates progressive linear time, or 'historical time', associated with human achievements and unidirectional growth, from the continuity of 'natural time', linked with cyclicity and repetition through the seasons.[6] Müller suggests that this emphasis on anthropocentric episodes of time inadvertently undermines 'natural' time, and its cyclicality, in favour of an anthropocentric linear sense of time.[7] Therefore, focusing more on spatial environments allows for the presence of the natural environment in conceptualizing literary time, as natural environment actors such as rivers, plant life and animals interact within a space.

Finally, Müller argues that Bakhtin's suggestion of the chronotope does not take into account how the literary texts themselves 'preserve and revise chronotopes of the past', and how other cultural factors might contribute to the creation of a chronotope.⁸ Revision of past chronotopes is an important aspect of Ovid's poetry, where Wheeler has convincingly argued for repetition as a defining trait of the *Metamorphoses*. I would suggest further that this focus on repetition and revision also highlights a strong connection with natural time in Ovid's chronotopes, where repetition and renewal are a key component of the natural environment. With these criticisms in mind, Müller advocates an ecocritical approach to Bakhtin's chronotope, one which emphasizes space, nature and cyclicality.⁹ In this way, Müller's ecological reworking of the chronotope can shed new light on the temporal structuring of Ovid's *Metamorphoses*, and the role of natural actors within it.

I became particularly interested in the role of rivers as chronotopes through reading Peterle and Visentin's 'geographical performance', in which they describe the river Po as a 'liquid chronotope' in Gianni Celati's travel diaries.¹⁰ The term 'liquid chronotope' is used to describe the way in which the river Po influences landscape configuration and narrative voice. While this methodology is based on the specific style of Gianni Celati's travel diaries, I propose that in conjunction with the broader ecological approach to chronotopes advocated by Müller, it can be a useful framework for thinking about how the natural environment interacts with the conceptualization of time in Ovid's *Metamorphoses*, and ancient literature more broadly. Rivers are also particularly apt for thinking with ecological chronotopes as they follow an expected unidirectional path, in a similar chronotopic function to the road; yet, they also enact the process of renewal in the landscape through flooding and the wider cyclicality of the water cycle. Through this double movement, rivers create a space for consideration of conflicting or blended temporalities, where river behaviour influences spatial configuration, and so influences narrative temporality.

Rivers already have a strong connection to time in the ancient world, and Jones has shown how rivers can also reflect aspects of narrative construction.¹¹ In the *Metamorphoses*, river interactions are often key points of transition and narrative disruption: such as Peneus' council of rivers (1.568–87), Achelous blocking Theseus' journey in Books 8 and 9, and the long list of violent acts by river gods, or near rivers.¹² These interactions show rivers as key spaces for reflections on narrative time and space, particularly at moments of river disruption. This reflection on narrative time and space is clearly apparent in both of the apocalyptic episodes, where it is through the rivers' excessive flow and flooding that the earth is overcome, and similarly in the account of Phaethon's fall, the extensive catalogue of rivers highlights their necessity in the continuation of the earth. As such, I will now focus on closer analysis of the rivers in these episodes as 'liquid chronotopes', and how they can offer a space of timelessness key to Ovid's own version of the epic genre, in which repetition and renewal are distinctive markers.

Following the ecological chronotope's emphasis on spatiality, the excessive and disruptive behaviour of rivers is shown in *Metamorphoses* 1.285–92, where the river waters flow beyond their usual bounds:[13]

> exspatiata ruunt per apertos flumina campos   285
> cumque satis arbusta simul pecudesque virosque
> tectaque cumque suis rapiunt penetralia sacris.
> si qua domus mansit potuitque resistere tanto
> indeiecta malo, culmen tamen altior huius
> unda tegit, pressaeque latent sub gurgite turres.   290
> iamque mare et tellus nullum discrimen habebant:
> omnia pontus erat, deerant quoque litora ponto.

> The rivers overleap all bounds and flood the open plains. And not alone orchards, crops and herds, men and dwellings, but shrines as well and their sacred contents do they sweep away. If any house has stood firm, and has been able to resist that huge misfortune undestroyed, still do the overtopping waves cover its roof, and its towers lie hid beneath the flood. And now the sea and land have no distinction. All is sea, and a sea without a shore.

Here, the rivers have been let loose by Neptune, and rush from their fountains to the sea – an expected linear progression down and across the landscape, but with more force than normal. They spill out and fill areas of cultivated land outside their regular courses, sweeping away orchards, herds and people (285–7). The flooding river is a common simile in epic poetry, where the force of the river is often used to describe military power and destruction; here, that destructive power is purely about the force of the rivers through the cultivated areas.[14] The expanding waters tear through (*rapiunt*, 287) orchards, while buildings able to remain standing are still covered by the waves of the overflowing rivers (288–9). The destruction of orchards, livestock, people and temples specifically highlights anthropocentric markers within the landscape, where cultivated vineyards and livestock particularly reflect ordered and meticulously controlled spaces.[15] The destruction of cultivated space is important when considering the river as a liquid chronotope: as the river effectively wipes away the landscape of the present and the markers of human cultivation upon it, it simultaneously wipes away any historical temporal markers such as crops and buildings, untethering this section from any particular 'historical' moment.

As the rivers continue to flow and rise to cover buildings and towers, this absence of spatial and temporal markers is made clear by the blurring of sea and land boundaries, where 'the sea and earth have no difference; everything was sea, sea without shore' (291–2). Lateiner highlights the infinite and disorientating aspects of the spatiality of the sea in Homeric epic;[16] I would argue that this is echoed here in the *Metamorphoses*, where the endless sea caused by the flood leads to spatial and temporal disorientation. The encompassing of the earth by water flattens out the space; here there is nothing distinctive about the environment, and nothing able to identify it as set in a specific location or historical moment. In this flat, undefined space, this narrative moment now lies outside of any sense of linear time, in what Bakhtin might call an 'extra temporal hiatus', or a moment of timelessness.[17] Here the natural environment and the markers of the human cultivated environment have both been overtaken by the excess of water, creating a sense of static temporality.

The irregularity of the endless sea is played for comedic effect in the image of a man catching fish at the top of the tree, yet this comedic inversion also highlights another loss of time in this moment – the progression of time marked by the 'regular' continuation of the agricultural cycle, a collaborative process between humanity and the natural environment. The man rows the fields he used to plough, and sails over fields of grain (1.293–6):

occupat hic collem, cumba sedet alter adunca
et ducit remos illic, ubi nuper arabat:
ille supra segetes aut mersae culmina villae   295
navigat, hic summa piscem deprendit in ulmo.

Here one man seeks a hill-top in his flight; another sits in his curved skiff, plying the oars where lately he has plowed; one sails over his fields of grain or the roof of his buried farmhouse, and one takes fish caught in the elm-tree's top.

The excess of the water specifically causes this inversion and disruption of agricultural cycles, and creates a space of disrupted momentum. Drawing oars and ploughing might involve comically similar movements, but both highlight the loss of progression: the man has nowhere to row to, and the fields remain unploughed, underwater and disconnected from the next stage of the agricultural cycle. This disconnect is caused by the spatiality of the waters, where the rivers can be seen as a chronotope – the space creates the temporal conditions for this moment, and allows reflection on key aspects of the poetic temporality of the *Metamorphoses*.

The disorientated natural space here as a reflection on key aspects of the *Metamorphoses* is further emphasized through the irregularity of the endless sea, and its connection with the beginning of the poem. The specific movement of the flood waters also denies a sense of continuation, as 'new' waves are described as beating the mountain tops (310). This phrase echoes the creation of the world in the opening scenes of the *Metamorphoses*, where rivers are created to enter the earth or the sea, and 'beat' upon the shores (1.34–42). This echo initially appears to reset the timeline of the *Metamorphoses* back to the creation of the world, yet that first creation is clearly organized temporally, through stages of nature created (e.g. *principio*, 34; *tum*, 36). The imitation of the original waves beating the shores is described as *novi* (310), which, with its double connotations of newness and unnaturalness, highlights the unusual inverted spatiality of the waters which normally hit the shores, now hitting the mountain peaks.[18] This once again inverts the expected natural cycle of high to low, mountain to sea, foregrounding a lack of order. The directionless repetition of the waves denies a sense of the expected cyclic progression of flooding and returning as here the waters have nowhere to return to, but rather are stuck hitting the mountain tops they would normally flow from. The disturbed spatial patterns create a sense of discomfort, where it is clear that the earth cannot remain in this unsettled state – marking this as a moment ready for recalibration.

Repetition of an event separate from natural cycles creates an absence of the passage of time, which Bakhtin describes as lacking a 'moment in time'; 'if taken outside its relationship to past and future, the present loses its integrity, breaks down into isolated phenomena and objects making them a mere abstract conglomeration'.[19] This stagnancy is important for the temporality of this section of the *Metamorphoses*. Here both the continuation of natural time through natural cycles, and the continuation of the historical through the continued exploits of humanity are delayed by this excess of water. As such, and given this moment is the only form of movement within the narrative, the audience is forced to wait; and this delay in turn disrupts the expected flow of the narrative, leaving the audience dependent on the poet's 'recalibration' of the poem's narrative temporality. The abnormal spatiality of the waters highlights this as a moment apart from the expected progression of time, briefly denying a sense of order and direction, emphasizing the chaotic temporality of the narrative of the *Metamorphoses*.

The flood only ends at Jupiter's order, which leads to Neptune recalling the flooding rivers (324–47). It is specifically when Jupiter notices the stagnant earth (*Iuppiter ut liquidis stagnare paludibus orbem*, 324) that this renewal of natural order is put into place. Jupiter negates the timeless space of the chronotope, and resets with receding waters a return to natural cycles.[20] With the receding waters and a return to natural cycles, the space of the river chronotope also highlights continuity through renewal as a key aspect of the *Metamorphoses*' generic space and temporality. The contrast between the abnormal timeless state and the renewing natural cycles, in other words, serves to highlight the role of renewal within the *Metamorphoses*' narrative continuity. If we recall that the space of the chronotope is particularly linked to genre, then this passage can be seen to encapsulate the importance of repetition and renewal in Ovid's particular brand of epic.

This return and renewal is also marked by the remnants of the old humanity in the creation of the new, through the survival of Deucalion and Pyrrha. Feldherr suggests that Ovid uses these connections between generations of humanity to contemplate the human form in the present of the *Metamorphoses*' audience, where the new race of humanity shares the same shape as the old, and thus almost become a memorial to the old race.[21] In this way, the rebirth of humanity is driven by the remnants of the old, thus undermining the idea of a complete 'perfect' renewal motivated by total destruction. With the return of the natural cycle and the continuation of humanity, there is a sense that although the clear linear narrative of 'historical' time may be disrupted and restarted, through its connection with eternal natural cycles the past is always incorporated into the present narrative time.

The imperfect incorporation of the past into future renewal is especially observable through the natural environment, as the rivers are shown to return to their channels, and where the waters had covered and disrupted natural cycles, they now dissipate and reveal the past markers on the earth, as well as leaving their own mark – the slime on the trees (*ostendunt limumque tenent in fronde relictum*, 347). The renewal of the natural environment echoes the renewal of humanity, where elements of the past are always incorporated in any sense of resumption or restoration. In this way, the river chronotopes of the *Metamorphoses*, as both timeless space and actors of renewal, exemplify the aspect of 'revision' in Müller's ecological reworking of Bakhtinian chronotopes, and reify centrality of repetition and renewal in the narrative time of Ovid's epic.

The role of repetition and renewal is further made clear in the description of Phaethon's fall in Book 2, where the destruction of the earth is repeated, but inverted. Where the excess of water in Book 1 threatened destruction, in Book 2 it is an excess of heat which threatens the continuation of rivers and the earth. Campbell suggests that the unseasonal drying up of rivers are intrinsically linked to the end of days as they are the reversal of a river's vitality and continuity.[22] While this is not necessarily reflective of Italian rivers in reality (which often have intermittent flow), the threat to continuity through extreme loss of flow presents this moment in Ovid's poem as a potential apocalyptic event. Indeed, the image of the earth itself asking for help underscores the idea that the threat to river flow is beyond natural seasonal interruption (*Met.* 2.272–300). The river's connection with time and continuity is also important in connection with continued linear flow, where river reversal is often held as the standard for something continuing until the end of time, as an *adynaton* ('impossibility').[23] In this way, river drought and river reversal threaten future continuity, and the river behaviour in this episode, functioning as a chronotope for the *Metamorphoses*, implicates not only the characterization of the future within the poem, but also more generally the ideas of rejuvenation and continuation that underpin the *Metamorphoses*' self-positioning within the wider literary chronology.

Just as the flooding in Book 1, where a moment of timelessness is created through the disruption of expected patterns of the cultivated landscape, a similar moment of temporal stasis can be detected in the beginning of Book 2. In the previous section, I showed how the combination of a river's continuous movement from source to sea and images of ploughing link the disruption of natural time to the disruption of historical time, thereby creating a 'non-moment' of timelessness. This occurs once again through the disruption of natural patterns by the muddled behaviour of the rivers (2.241–59):

>nec sortita loco distantes flumina ripas
>tuta manent: mediis Tanais fumavit in undis
>Peneosque senex Teuthranteusque Caicus
>et celer Ismenos cum Phegiaco Erymantho
>arsurusque iterum Xanthos flavusque Lycormas,   245
>quique recurvatis ludit Maeandros in undis,
>Mygdoniusque Melas et Taenarius Eurotas.
>arsit et Euphrates Babylonius, arsit Orontes
>Thermodonque citus Gangesque et Phasis et Hister;
>aestuat Alpheos, ripae Spercheides ardent,   250
>quodque suo Tagus amne vehit, fluit ignibus aurum,
>et, quae Maeonias celebrabant carmine ripas
>flumineae volucres, medio caluere Caystro;
>Nilus in extremum fugit perterritus orbem
>occuluitque caput, quod adhuc latet: ostia septem   255
>pulverulenta vacant, septem sine flumine valles.

fors eadem Ismarios Hebrum cum Strymone siccat
Hesperiosque amnes, Rhenum Rhodanumque Padumque
cuique fuit rerum promissa potentia, Thybrin.

Nor do rivers, whose lot had given them more spacious channels, remain unscathed. The Don's waters steam; old Peneus, too, Mysian Caïcus, and swift Ismenus; and Arcadian Erymanthus, Xanthus, destined once again to burn; tawny Lycormas, and Maeander, playing along upon its winding way; Thracian Melas and Laconian Eurotas. Babylonian Euphrates burns; Orontes burns, and swift Thermodon; the Ganges, Phasis, Danube; Alpheus boils; Spercheos' banks are aflame. The golden sands of Tagus melt in the intense heat, and the swans, which had been wont to throng the Maeonian streams in tuneful company, are scorched in mid Caÿster. The Nile fled in terror to the ends of the earth, and hid its head, and it is hidden yet. The seven mouths lie empty, filled with dust; seven broad channels, all without a stream. The same mischance dries up the Thracian rivers, Hebrus and Strymon; also the rivers of the west, the Rhine, Rhone, Po, and the Tiber, to whom had been promised the mastery of the world.

The rivers are defined by their opposites, smoking (*fumavit* 241), burning (*arsit* 247), and dry (*siccat* 257). More broadly, this episode is an inversion of the flooding in Book 1, as indicated by the inverted description in lines 263–71. Where the flooding in Book 1 starts with Neptune commanding the rivers to flow uncontrollably (1.283), the present scene starts with rivers drying up, and ends with Neptune unable to lift himself out of the sea (2.220–1). The sea without shore in Book 1 becomes plain sand in Book 2, and dolphins who thrived in the flood of Book 1 suffer in the extreme heat. Where the waters rose in Book 1, the waters recede in Book 2. In this way, the two accounts mirror each other, both in terms of extreme inversion of natural patterns, but also more literally in the spatial patterning of the river behaviour. Where we might expect the rivers to flow continuously, source to sea, here they are smoking, giving the impression of evaporation and water moving upwards, disrupting expected landscape patterns.

This reversed directionality is even more extreme in the case of the Nile, which turns back to hide its source (254–6).[24] Famously in Herodotus, the Nile evokes a strong sense of ordered temporality, where the consistent, reliable flooding of the river marks the changing of the seasons, and the passing of time more broadly;[25] here, that consistency is disrupted by its reversal. Zissos and Gildenhard suggest that the outcome of Phaethon's fall, where the earth is burnt and nature in chaos, indicates chronological regression and a reversal of time to the primordial chaos of Lucretius;[26] and moreover, the idea of a return or rewind back to chaos also mimics the original creation myth in Book 1 of the

Metamorphoses, as previously discussed in relation to the formless waves beating the mountain tops. The sense of primordial chaos, and the direct inversion of the apocalypse in Book 1 once again places this in a Bakhtinian 'non-moment' of timelessness. Here, the space of the dried-up rivers, disrupting expected patterns in the landscape and causing a lack of continuity in the environment recreates the disrupted chronotope from Book 1, underlining a sense of timelessness which allows questions of genre and poetic identity to rise to the surface.

The rivers in this section differ slightly in that they are presented by name in an extended catalogue, in contrast to the abstract and ambiguous rivers of the earth in the previous episode (1.285–7). At first, this catalogue of twenty seven rivers appears to present the rivers in no clear geographical order – Jones argues that this merely reflects the 'geographical exhaustiveness' and disordered path of Phaethon's fall.[27] Yet, the expanded descriptions of some of the rivers, referring to both the literary past and future suggest a temporal connection.[28] Spencer discusses the process of 'moving through' a landscape, where 'individual landscape elements change depending on how they are connected up'.[29] Alongside the disordered path, which could reflect the chaotic narrative of the *Metamorphoses*, there is also, I would suggest, an element of temporal progression in the geographical range of rivers.

The river catalogue can be divided into three sections: mythical/literary rivers such as the Peneus, Eurotas and Xanthus; rivers with a military connotation for Romans, such as the Nile, Rhine and Rhone; and finally, the Tiber. Of course, these are not strict divisions, nor mutually exclusive categories; however I would argue that they broadly show a 'movement' from the literary-mythical past, to the rivers associated with recent military and literary endeavours of Ovid's present, before ending with the Tiber, and its future. The Peneus has already appeared near the start of the *Metamorphoses*, in Book 1, while Boyd has convincingly demonstrated how the Eurotas can be associated with Helen, and the Xanthus is naturally associated with the Trojan war.[30] The Nile and Rhine have military connotations through Ovid and his contemporaries' poetry;[31] while the Tiber is promised the world (259). Here we have three references to previous epic works, and Ovid's own, drawing together ideas of the past and future of the epic genre, and more broadly literary chronology. Through the 'movement' through the landscape in this way, and the separation of this event from 'historical' time, the chronotope of the dried up river offers an 'out of time' space where Ovid's poetic presence is retroactively inscribed into the past and future of epic chronology, through incorporating his own mythic retellings back into the literary canon. Moreover, the metaliterary journey through the river catalogue serves to highlight again that repetition and renewal, especially of previous epic motifs, are central to Ovid's own epic temporality.

To demonstrate this temporal ordering further, I will now briefly discuss three rivers in particular: the Caÿster, Xanthus and Tiber. The river Caÿster (252–3) has multiple metaliterary temporal layers: here the burning of the geese links to the simile which occurs in both the *Iliad*, the *Aeneid*, and then later in Book 5 of the *Metamorphoses*.[32] This recurrent image underscores Müller's idea that literary texts can revise and renew chronotopes of the past, where Ovid can build on the recognizable space of the river Caÿster in previous works to renew elements of the literary tradition in his own work. This is also helped by the intense metapoetic connotations of rivers in ancient literature already, which is then intensified by this specific allusion to the simile from the *Iliad*.[33] This layered allusion to the motif of the Caÿster swans recognizes the presence of past literary works in contemporary literature, much as the remnants left behind of the flood go on to form the new race of humanity. With regard to the chronotope being specific to each genre, here we can see elements of Ovid's own consideration of the epic genre reflected in this space – where one aspect is recognition and renewal of previous influences, looking to the future of the genre – all reflected in the space of the 'liquid chronotope' of the rivers.

Looking to the future from the literary past is made more apparent in the comparison of the Xanthus and Tiber. The Xanthus, is 'destined to burn again' (*arsurusque iterum Xanthos*, 245), while the Tiber is promised power over the world (*cuique fuit rerum promissa potentia, Thybrin*, 259). This refers to when the river Xanthus fights Achilles and is in turn set alight by Hephaestus in the *Iliad* (11.200–377). This repeated image of burning cements the events of the *Metamorphoses* into the literary tradition, where the retellings of previous epic stories are physicalized through the permanent presence of rivers within the landscape. As the narrative looks towards the future of the Xanthus, it also looks towards the future of the Tiber, drawing a connection between the two rivers. This is perhaps an allusion to the frequent pairing of the Xanthus and the Tiber in the *Aeneid*, where the Tiber is substituted for the Xanthus as Rome becomes the new home of the Trojans (*Aeneid* 6.88, 10.60). Both rivers have strong connections to previous epics while also looking towards the future even as they burn. This temporal connection thus conjures up both the *Iliad* and the *Aeneid* but with particular reference to Ovid's contemporary Rome, and as such it builds up to a sense of culmination with the *Metamorphoses*.

While the previous rivers in the catalogue brought out a subtle progression from the mythical literary past to the more recent military victories of Rome, the inclusion of the Tiber and its promised power firmly pins down the temporal moment in the present of the *Metamorphoses*' composition and looks towards its future (259). Anderson describes this as an 'ostentatious anachronism', where it is consciously chronologically out of place:[34] the narrative of Roman mastery is very much situated in Ovid's present. This sense of conscious temporal manipulation is expanded upon by Wheeler, who argues that anachronisms in the *Metamorphoses* 'deauthorize any single versions of mythological history by opening up alternative possibilities and force the audience to revaluate its understanding of the poem's narrative'.[35] Through this destabilization of any single mythological narrative, Ovid opens up space for his own mythological retellings in the future literary tradition; and this instance of anachronism in particular helps to bring the temporal structure of the poem to the surface. Although the Tiber has dried up at this point in the narrative, this promise of a brighter destiny looks ahead to a future towards and beyond the *Metamorphoses*. The anticipated power of the river implies a resumption of flow for the Tiber, which is flowing in the present of the poem's audience.[36]

This idea of using the past to move forward evokes the cultural turn during Augustus' rise to power. Through the chronotope of the dried up river, which considers both source and continuation, the *Metamorphoses* aligns itself with the literary tradition, laying a claim to both the past of the epic genre and its continuation. Ovid disturbs the normal flow of time and literary history, making his present part of the literary past, and Rome's landscape part of the mythic landscape – and in doing so the poet mirrors Augustus' own repositioning of himself into mythic history and time.[37]

Mirroring poetic and imperial power continues in the repetition of Jupiter's restoration of world order, recalling the end of the flood in Book 1. Schiesaro argues that Jupiter here 'is the guarantor of a poetic order, or a hierarchy of genres, which still holds in the face of Ovid's protests'.[38] Schiesaro's idea of Jupiter as 'guarantor' is especially relevant when considering the trope of river *adynata*. Here, Jupiter has restored order by allowing the rivers to flow again, and reinstates their position as a guarantee of future behaviour, seemingly leaving no room for Ovid's generic innovations. However, as I discussed, the narrative of the *Metamorphoses* has been woven into the geological time of the landscape through the mythical allusions in the river catalogue. The timeless space of the disrupted river chronotope, combined with recognizable geographical spaces represented by river names, allows the ideals of Ovid's present to be cemented into the past, creating an almost guaranteed future for both Rome and Ovid's poetry. This then links back to the *adynata* trope, where the continuity of the river is used to signal a guarantee of certainty amidst fears for the future; and here Ovid has guaranteed the survival of his own work and the perpetuation of the literary tradition, which will continue after the apocalypse has been resolved. The future-threatening flooding and drought behaviours of the rivers in these examples from the *Metamorphoses* create a space for Ovid to highlight ideas of poetic continuity through dialogues with literary predecessors. Through this self-assured engagement with the temporality of the natural environment, Ovid positions his poetry as eternal – even as natural cycles are disrupted.

Let us now return to Bakhtin's initial assessment of Ovid's *Metamorphoses* as isolated, self-sufficient temporal segments. Although it would seem reasonable to assume that the fluid temporality of the *Metamorphoses* would deprive the poem of chronotopes, I have demonstrated how rivers, particularly when disrupted, can become chronotopes, which in turn provide a timeless space integral to Ovid's particular form of epic narrative time. This aligns with Feeney's suggestion that Ovid subverts previous methods of literary chronology in favour of creating his own sense of time:[39] for in these apocalyptic episodes, we can indeed see how ideas of literary chronology, genre hierarchy and political pressures are navigated in Ovid's own form of epic. In this way, Bakhtin's chronotope, in conjunction with Müller's reworking, is useful for considering issues of genre in the *Metamorphoses*, though the space in which these chronotopes appear may be unconventional compared to Bakhtin's own examples. In the two episodes I have analyzed, the disruption of both 'natural' and 'historical' time offers a timeless space in which to consider Ovid's own fluid epic temporality, which incorporates repetition and renewal as a guarantor of future continuity. River chronotopes, as 'landscape chronotopes', can be places where the 'knots of narrative are tied and untied'.[40] Here the chronotope of disrupted river behaviour signals this process of untying the narrative strands of the *Metamorphoses*, and creating a timeless space unique to Ovid's particular form of epic, before retying them and renewing the narrative.[41]

Notes

1 Bakhtin (1981: 114).
2 Wheeler (2000) specifically argues for self-repetition within the first two books, as a characteristic of epic continuing itself. I shall argue below that it is not just self-repetition which characterizes the *Metamorphoses*' temporality, but also the repetition of other literary works, shown through landscape features.

3 Bakhtin (1981: 85).
4 Ibid. (91).
5 Müller (2016: 601).
6 See also the philosophical concept of geological time, developed by James Hutton in 1788, who argued that 'the course of nature cannot be limited by time, which must process in continual succession' (125).
7 Müller (2016: 598).
8 Ibid. (594).
9 Ibid. (599).
10 Peterle and Visentin (2017: 474).
11 Jones (2005). Drawing from Heraclitus, in M. Aur. *Med.* 4.43, time is described as a rushing torrent. Cf. Hor. *Epist.*1.2.41–3.
12 Violence around rivers in the *Metamorphoses*: Daphne and Apollo near the river Peneus (1.545); Liriope and Cephisus (3.342–3); Alpheus and Arethusa (5.572–614); Marsyas turned into a river (6.396); Orpheus' death at the Hebrus (11.50); Caicus runs red with blood (12.111); Canens' transformation at bank of the Tiber (14.462); Numicus facilitating Aeneas' apotheosis (14.598–604).
13 I cite the text and translation of Frank Justus Miller (Loeb 1916, revised by Goold 1977).
14 Epic river similes in military context: Hom. *Il.* 5.596–600, 16.384–93, 17.26–37; Verg. *Aen.* 2.304–8, 2.494–9, 10.601–4; Hor. *Carm* .4.14.25–6. See also Ov. *Am.* 1.7.43 for association with violent behaviour.
15 One only has to think of the wealth of handbooks on farming practice in Latin, see Cato, *Agr.*, Columella, *Rust.* and Varro, *Rust.*, among others.
16 Lateiner (2014: 72).
17 Bakhtin (1981: 90).
18 *OLD* s.v. *novus* 2.
19 Bakhtin (1981: 146).
20 The political implications of Jupiter restoring order are discussed further below.
21 Feldherr (2010: 127).
22 Campbell (2012: 121).
23 Examples of river *adynata* in Ovid: *Her.* 5.27–34; *Tr.* 1.8.1–14, *Pont.* 1.5.21–4, 4.5.41–4, 4.6.45–50.
24 Pl. *Ti.* 22 also details the twin events of flooding and fire, with particular reference to the Nile.
25 Hdt. 2.19.
26 Zissos and Gildenhard (1999: 35).
27 Jones (2005: 89).
28 Literary past and future in Xanthus and Tiber, amongst others, discussed below.
29 Spencer (2010: 48).

30 Boyd (1987).
31 The Nile and the Rhine represent highly militarized areas of Roman territory, with the Nile associated with Augustan victory (Hor. *Carm.* 4.14) and the Rhine representing northern Germanic territories. Campbell (2012: 26) notes the Rhine and Rhone specifically as symbolic of conquest and the acquisition of the natural environment, marking a particularly Roman aspect of river tradition – conquest.
32 Hom. *Il.* 2.461–7; Verg. *Aen.* 7.698–702; Ov. *Met.*5.386–7; see Papaioannou (2004) for swans in the *Metamorphoses*.
33 Ov. *Am.* 3.6 literalizes the river and genre connection, with comparisons between an unnamed seasonal torrent and mythical rivers.
34 Anderson (1997: 256).
35 Wheeler (1999: 128).
36 See Gildenhard and Zissos (2004) for discussion of Rome as the narrative telos of the *Metamorphoses*, and how references to Roman civilization in the first two books situate contemporary Rome as the telos of the poem. As Ovid and his poetry are situated within that contemporary Rome, I would argue that this narrative *telos* also helps to secure the future of the *Metamorphoses*, and Ovid's place in the future literary tradition.
37 Feeney (2007: 180–5) thoroughly discusses Augustus' insertion into the *Fasti*, and cyclic time, but does not connect this with natural time.
38 Schiesaro (2014: 101).
39 Feeney (1999: 18).
40 Sorall (1990: 256, 263).
41 Also worthy of consideration as a timeless space indicated by river behaviour is the Achelous episode in Books 8 and 9, where the river flood leads to a series of internal narrations.

8

More than a Lifetime

Temporal Patterns in Roman Biography – Suetonius, Nepos, Tacitus

Martin Stöckinger
University of Cologne

It comes as no surprise that the poetics of time in ancient biography has not really sparked the interest of scholarship thus far. In the wake of Friedrich Leo it has long been pointed out that Greek and Roman biographies have their roots in Hellenistic philosophy (and especially in ethical debates about the character of men) or in rhetoric (*encomion, laudatio funebris*).[1] In consequence, as Mikhail Bakhtin remarks, the arrangement of time is not at the core of an ancient biographer's interest: 'what governs from the outset is the *whole* of the character [sc. of the portrayed person]; and from such a point of view time is of no importance at all, nor is the order in which various parts of this whole make their appearance'.[2] It is always unfair to generalize, but at least, to a certain degree, this neglect of temporal issues is mirrored in studies of the last decades on ancient biography.[3]

Nevertheless, it seems worthwhile to re-examine patterns of time inherent in Roman biographies. Generally speaking, a biographer has to translate the lifetime of a person into an account which unfolds spatially over the pages of a book (or a papyrus scroll) and which, when read, also unfolds temporally.[4] Moreover, he has to bridge the temporal distance between the time the portrayed person inhabited and the time in which he himself and his intended reader live. These are but two principal problems related to temporality every biographer is faced with, and so are the three best-preserved Latin biographers from the late Republic and the early principate which I am going to examine in the following three case studies. I will not treat them in their chronological sequence but start with Suetonius. Bakhtin's quote above is particularly aimed at him, since in a sense he is the prototype of a biographer who presents a life in categories rather than in a temporally structured narrative. In the next section, I will pursue Suetonius' handling of chronology in the *Life of Tiberius* both in a passage that is organized as a rubric and in a more narrative passage. For my second case study, I will turn to Cornelius Nepos and his treatment of careers, both Roman and non-Roman. The careers of men could easily lend their biographies a temporal structure, yet strikingly Nepos seems more interested in other aspects of them such as cross-cultural differences. The final section will be devoted to Tacitus' *Agricola* and the patterns of time presented in this work. Here my argument will be that the specific temporal layering can be found not only in the Roman context of the hero, the emperors and the narrator and his audience, but also in the way how the history of the non-Romans is structured.

1. Messing with Chronology in Suetonius' *Life of Tiberius*

In most ancient biographies the respective life is not related in a strictly chronological manner. This has in most cases been explained by the authors' interest in the character of the portrayed persons, and the will to categorize the events in their lives, their actions and behaviours according to their underlying personality. This is most palpable in the case of Suetonius. People have rightly emphasized Suetonius' profession as a *grammaticus* which stands in the background of his technique of making up rubrics in order to structure both his biographical collections and the texts within them. Hans Martinet has described this way of presenting the lives of Caesars as 'slip box principle' ('Zettelkastenprinzip').[5] More recently, Dennis Pausch has complemented and revised this view by showing us that there are many passages, and indeed entire lives, that are treated in chronologically arranged narratives.[6] The *Life of Otho*, for instance, is in its entirety composed as a chronological narrative.[7] Of course, this is an exception; but as Pausch convincingly demonstrates, the rule is not a presentation strictly according to rubrics, as one might suspect, but a mixture or alternation of rubric and narrative.[8] In what follows, I will build on Pausch's insights, examining two passages from Suetonius' *Life of Tiberius*, the first of which is organized more as a rubric, while the second comes as a narrative. Specifically, I will try to show that the absence and presence of chronology does not distribute itself neatly in the two types of Suetonius' presentation, as one might expect based on Pausch's argument; rather, we find both the absence and presence of chronology in rubrics as well as in narrative sections.

In most of Suetonius' *Lives*, there are long sections about the virtues (*virtutes*) and vices (*vitia*) of the portrayed person. In the *Life of Tiberius*, we find such a catalogue of Tiberius' vices in chapters 42–67. The section is preceded by a passage about his time on Capri in the years 26 CE until his death in 37 CE. The catalogue of vices itself starts with a section on his *libidines* (*Tib.* 42–5), with remarks about his overindulgence in eating and drinking. Here the narrator tells an anecdote about Tiberius' time during his military service (*Tib.* 42.1):[9]

> in castris tiro etiam tum propter nimiam vini aviditatem pro Tiberio 'Biberius', pro Claudio 'Caldius', pro Nerone 'Mero' vocabatur.

> Even when he was a new recruit in the army camp, they used to call him 'Biberius' ['drinker'] instead of Tiberius, Caldius ['lover of mulled wine'] for Claudius, and 'Mero' for Nero ['someone who drinks wine unmixed with water', which was regarded as a sign of barbarism] because of his excessive liking for wine.

It is hard to pinpoint this anecdote about Tiberius' nicknames temporally. The word *tiro* means 'recently enrolled soldier' (*OLD* s.v. 1), but does not signify an official military rank which was bound to a specific age. It may either refer to Tiberius' time as a military tribune in Cantabria, which in chapter 9 the narrator has presented explicitly as his 'first campaign' (*stipendia prima*, *Tib.* 9.1) and which dates to the years 26–24 BCE (i.e. roughly half a century before his time on Capri), or to some sort of military training which he must have received even before his tribunate. Whatever the exact date of this anecdote is, it is clear that it refers way back to a time early in Tiberius' life, which was already narrated in the first nine chapters.

Furthermore, the narrator has introduced the entire section about Tiberius' vices with the phrase *Tib.* 42.1: *de quibus* [i.e. *vitiis*] *singillatim ab exordio referam* 'I shall give a detailed account of each [i.e. of the vices] from its inception.' The use of *exordium* has caught the attention of Wolfgang Vogt, the most recent commentator of the *Life of Tiberius*: Vogt notes that here *exordium* is used for the first time in the extant Latin literature in a modal sense.[10] His commentary stops somewhat abruptly with this observation and leaves us with the question *why* Suetonius uses this very word in such a peculiar and hitherto uncommon way. I would suggest that it is not by coincidence that Suetonius choses *exordium* here, since as a technical term it can also denote 'the introductory part of a speech or a book' (*OLD* s.v. 4, referring to *Rhet. Her.* 1.4, Cic. *Inv. rhet.* 1.20 and Quint. *Inst.* 4.1.1).[11] Read in this way, chapter 42 indeed marks an alternative starting point of Suetonius' *Life of Tiberius*.

But within this catalogue of vices, chronology is not absent. The rubric on Tiberius' *libidines* starts, as we have seen, with an episode dating back at the beginning of his adulthood (*Tib.* 42.1). Then, five examples from his time as emperor in Rome (*Tib.* 42.1–2) follow, before the narrator turns to Tiberius' sexual excesses in Capri (*Tib.* 43–5). What we can observe here is that chronology exists as a formative element within the various rubrics of the narrative, as an 'internal micro-chronology' so to speak, but not as the guiding principle for the entire *Life of Tiberius*.

While in the case of *Tib.* 42 we can attribute the narrator's departure from a chronological scheme to his overarching interest in the character of Tiberius, which is better presented in rubrics, there are other passages which need a closer and, as I will suggest, more narratological examination. By way of example, let us consider the story of Tiberius' sickness and death in *Tib.* 72–4. This section is clearly a narrative in a more conventional scheme as it is known from historiographical accounts. It begins with a more or less innocent remark about Tiberius' attempts to come to Rome during his absence from the city in the years 26–37 CE (*Tib.* 72.1–2):

> iterum Appia usque ad septimum lapidem – sed prospectis modo nec aditis urbis moenibus rediit, primo incertum qua de causa, postea ostento territus. [2] erat ei in oblectamentis serpens draco, quem ex consuetudine manu sua cibaturus cum consumptum a formicis invenisset, monitus est ut vim multitudinis caveret.

> The second time he travelled on the Appian Way, as far as the seventh mile-stone from Rome. However, he turned back, having seen the walls of the city but come no closer. With regard to the first occasion, his reasons are unclear. On the second, he was alarmed by a portent. [2] He kept a snake as a pet and when went to feed it from his own hand, as he usually did and he discovered that it had been consumed by ants, he took this as a warning to beware of the power of the many.

After this episode the narrator relates the emperor's fatal illness and death itself (*Tib.* 72.3–73),[12] before analeptically reporting three more omens which, too, must have happened before the death (*Tib.* 74):

> Supremo natali suo Apollinem Temenitem et amplitudinis et artis eximiae advectum Syracusis ut in bibliotheca templi novi poneretur viderat per quietem affirmantem sibi non posse se ab ipso dedicari. et ante paucos quam obiret dies turris Phari terrae motu Capreis concidit ac Miseni cinis e favilla et carbonibus ad calficiendum triclinium inlatis, extinctus iam et diu frigidus, exarsit repente prima vespera atque in multam noctem pertinaciter luxit.

On his final birthday, he dreamt that the Apollo Temenites, a statue of great size and wonderful workmanship which he had brought to Syracuse to place in the library of the new temple, made a sign to him that it could not be dedicated by him. And, a few days before he died, the lighthouse at Capri collapsed as the result of an earthquake. At Misenum, when the hot ashes and embers, which had been brought in to warm his dining-room had subsided and long been cold, they suddenly blazed up again in the early evening and continued to give light until late into the night.

Relating portents which concern the emperor, especially at the end of his life, is a typical task of a biographer, which he shares with historians.[13] The question I would like to pursue here is what relation the portent recounted in *Tib.* 72.2 bears to the three omens in *Tib.* 74. In terms of chronology, it is certainly possible, perhaps even probable, that they happened in a neat order: the snake portent might have happened some time before the dream of Apollo (which is dated to Tiberius' last birthday – that is 16 November 36 CE); the collapse of the lighthouse is dated not very precisely 'a few days before he died', but there is enough time left that the coal portent could have happened in between the collapse of the building and the death of the emperor. But why are the signs split up in two groups with the emperor's death presented between the snake portent and the remaining three portents, which are recounted only afterwards as a flashback?[14]

One explanation might be that the snake portent does not prefigure the death that Tiberius actually died, but rather another possible way of dying: Tiberius, who was notorious for his superstition,[15] has decoded the snake being devoured by the ants as an image for himself being assassinated by the people of Rome. Hence the episode of the snake portent is not a prodigy for Tiberius' actual death, but yet another story that helps to reinforce the image of Tiberius as a timid and superstitious character.

Nevertheless, the story of the snake portent sets the tone for the events to come. It triggers both Tiberius' depression (cf. *in languorem incidit*, *Tib.* 72.2) and the reader's expectation that the emperor's condition will deteriorate and that he will ultimately die. I would therefore argue that the splitting up of the signs into two groups and their distribution in the narrative can be explained by the way they are focalized. The snake portent in *Tib.* 72 is focalized through Tiberius himself and taken as a warning. The verb *invenisset* recreates the emperor's gaze; and the narrator's voice unites with Tiberius' thoughts when he says 'he was warned that . . .' (*monitus est ut . . .*), as if the fact that ants devoured the snake were an unquestionable portent or warning. This is different from the portents presented in *Tib.* 74. In the first of them, the statue of Apollo, we do have

Tiberius as an internal focalizer (*viderat*), but we are not told that Tiberius had decoded the dream as a warning or prophecy. As for the collapse of the lighthouse and the coal portent, we do not know whether Tiberius eye-witnessed them; but since at that point he must have already been suffering from his disease, it is not very likely that he did. Rather, we are dealing with a 'zero-focalization' here. It is the narrator who seems to present his superior knowledge as retrospective explanation for the death of Tiberius.

To sum up my point, we find in Suetonius' *Lives* passages which are more organized as rubrics and others which are presented as more conventional historical narratives. It is a somewhat natural presumption that in those cases where rubrication is at work, we find less chronology, whereas within the narrative units we find chronology as a principle of presentation. This view, however, is a bit simplifying, as we have seen in the two examples examined above. In the rubric on Tiberius' *libidines* we find at least some traces of chronology, while in the story of Tiberius' death the narrator departs from a purely chronological narrative in order to classify the different omens according to Tiberius' personal involvement.[16] It is worth bearing in mind that, in ancient biography, the question of whether a life is presented in rubrics or in a more traditional narrative does not have a direct impact on the temporal order: there can be chronological sequences in rubrics as well, and vice versa, narrative sections are often arranged in a non-chronological manner.

2. Lives, *Lives* and Careers in Nepos' *De uiris illustribus*

In the Latin, the word *vita* has (just like the Greek *bíos*) an interesting double meaning, signifying on the one hand 'the life of a person' (*OLD* 2078, s.v. *vita* 1b and 6a), but on the other also 'a written or spoken account of a person's life' (6b).[17] In the section above, I have pursued the question how 'the life of a person' with its events (1b and 6a) is transformed into a narrative text, i.e. 'a written account of this life' (6b). This way of looking at the genre of ancient biography is informed by the study of historiography, where people – not just since the seminal studies of Hayden White – likewise ask how historical events are transformed into narratives. While such an approach is justified, we must concede that in the case of biographies the relationship between these two realms is a more reciprocal one: not only are lives transformed into texts, but accounts of lives of notable persons, i.e. texts, do also have an impact on the real lives of those who come after them. People of all times have used oral or written biographies as points of orientation for their own lives, be it that they try to imitate or that they refuse (parts of) them. As the American psychologist Jerome Bruner once put it, '[n]arrative imitates life, life imitates narrative' (1987: 13). The ancient exempla tradition forms but one prominent context for this way of using biographies.[18]

However in the Roman world, there is yet another, more institutionalized, power that forms the lives of nobles, namely the *cursus honorum*.[19] With all its rules and regulations the *cursus honorum* works as an invisible script for the lives of male young-adult Romans. It determines a temporal structure, a clear sequence of the offices to achieve as well as minimum ages for election into each office. In other words, the lifetime is not open to the future nor can it be filled according to one's individual wishes and desires, but shows itself to be heavily prestructured: when a young Roman decides to follow the footsteps of a famous political leader within or without his family and to imitate his career, he – just like his model before – has to enter this *cursus honorum* and obey its inherent rules.

One could now expect that the *cursus honorum* provides a scaffold for Roman literary biographies, and to a certain degree this is the case, especially when a person of the Roman Republic is portrayed. In Suetonius' *Life of Julius Caesar*, chapters 2–23 are devoted to the military (*Iul.* 2–5) and political (*Iul.* 6–23) career from its beginnings in the late 80s down to Caesar's consulship in 59 BCE; this section is chronologically arranged and covers about a quarter of the entire biography. In Cornelius Nepos' *Vita Catonis*, a miniature – possibly an abridged version – of a longer but not transmitted biography of Cato the Elder (cf. Nep. *Cato* 3.5), the narrator likewise ticks off Cato's offices as military tribune, quaestor, aedile, praetor, consul and finally censor (*Cato* 1.2–2.3), thus covering roughly a third of the text. Nepos' *Life of Atticus* forms an exception, since Atticus famously was a man of private means who did not pursue a political career; here the narrator laconically remarks: *honores non petiit, cum ei paterent propter vel gratiam vel dignitatem*, 'He aimed at no offices (though they were open to him as well through his influence as through his high standing)' (Nep. *Att.* 6.2).[20] In biographies of persons who lived in the empire we can observe a shift of focus away from the *cursus honorum*, but this institutionalized career ladder is still mentioned as an integral part of the early lives of the portrayed persons (e.g. Tac. *Agr.* 5–6; Suet. *Tib.* 9.1–11.1, *Galb.* 6.1, *Vesp.* 2.3, *Tit.* 4).

When we look at Nepos' *Lives of Foreign Generals*, things become on the one hand increasingly more complex; yet, on the other hand, I would argue that it is precisely here that the true function of temporally prestructured career pathways for the genre of biography reveals itself. First and foremost, it is obvious that

Nepos' generals from Greece and other non-Roman parts of the ancient world follow different career pathways than the Roman readers of these texts. That means that the account of their lifetime cannot be structured as conveniently as the respective sections in Suetonius' *Life of Julius Caesar* or in Nepos' *Vita Catonis*. Sometimes Nepos' narrator refers to these cultural differences explicitly. In the *Life of Eumenes*, he reports that under the Macedonian kings Alexander and Philip, Eumenes began his career serving as a secretary (*scriba*) for twenty years in total; and here the narrator adds the important remark (Nep. *Eumenes* 1.5):

> quod [i.e. scribae locum] multo apud Graios honorificentius est quam apud Romanos. namque apud nos, re vera sicut sunt, mercennarii scribae existimantur; at apud illos <e> contrario nemo ad id officium admittitur nisi honesto loco, et fide et industria cognita, quod necesse est omnium consiliorum eum esse participem.

> It [i.e. the office of secretary] is much more honourable among the Greeks than among the Romans; for with us, secretaries are regarded as hirelings, as in reality they are; but with them, on the contrary, no one is admitted to that office who is not of good family and of known integrity and ability, because he must of necessity be the confidant of all their political measures.

Cultural differences of this kind have already been highlighted in Nepos' *Praefatio* and are part and parcel of his biographical project.[21] Whereas in the present passage from the *Life of Eumenes* the cultural difference between Greece and Rome is explained at length,[22] there are other cases where it is obscured and where the reader is faced with a Latin translation of the foreign office. In its method, this technique resembles the *interpretatio Romana* as is known from the study of Roman religion: for instance, Mithrobarzanes, the father-in-law of Datames, is reported to have served as *praefectus equitum* (Nep. *Datames* 6.3), and Hannibal's brother Hasdrubal the office of *imperator suffectus* (Nep. *Hannibal* 3.1). Both these terms have particularly Roman connotations. *Praefectus equitum* is an official rank in the Roman army, as we learn from Nepos' contemporary Julius Caesar, who uses this wording several times in his works.[23] By contrast, the phrase *imperator suffectus* is to my knowledge only attested here. Nevertheless, this formulation has a strong Roman touch, since the attribute *suffectus* is usually used of Roman magistrates who were '[a]ppointed in place of one who has died, fallen ill, or sim.' Indeed, we should note that in the relevant entries in the *OLD* the passage from Nepos' *Hannibal* is the only one to treat a non-Roman context/subject.[24]

Such remarks on the career ranks of the foreign generals, however, are few and scattered over Nepos' entire corpus of biographies. Overall they do not have the same quality in terms of structuring a life temporally and providing a scaffold for the account of this life as we have seen in the biographies of Romans. The reason for this scarcity is a relatively simple one. It derives from Nepos' concept of the genre of biography. The beginning of the *Life of Phocion* perfectly illustrates this view (*Phocion* 1.1):

> Phocion Atheniensis etsi saepe exercitibus praefuit summosque magistratus cepit, tamen multo eius notior est integritas vitae quam rei militaris labor. itaque huius memoria est nulla, illius autem magna fama, ex quo cognomine Bonus est appellatus.

> Though Phocion the Athenian was often at the head of armies, and held the most important commands, yet the blamelessness of his life is much better known than his exertions in war. Of the one, accordingly, there is no recollection, but of the other the fame is great; and hence he was surnamed The Good.

In the concessive clause the narrator hints at Phocion's impressive career, using code-words in a sequence one could also read in the biography of a notable Roman: first the military achievements (*saepe exercitibus praefuit*), then the impressive political offices (*summosque magistratus cepit*). But all this is abandoned in favour of the blamelessness of Phocion's life (*integritas vitae*). In other words, Nepos is not interested in the *res gestae* and their temporal sequence (as a historian might be), but rather focuses on the ethical qualities of his protagonists.[25] Therefore, the careers of the portrayed persons stand in the background of Nepos' biographies, and indeed sometimes shine through, yet they do not have a particularly strong formative power in terms of temporality. With his *Lives* (in the sense of *OLD* s.v. *vita* 6b) Nepos wants to influence the lives (in the sense of *OLD* s.v. *vita* 1 and 6a) of his readers, but not in the sense that they simply follow these men by setting out on the same career paths as they did. That would not have been possible, since they lived in different times and different parts of the world. But it should not be desirable either, since it is the character of the portrayed person that is to be imitated, not the deeds, however magnificent they might have been.

3. Then and Now in Tacitus' *Agricola*

In the section above I have already touched upon the productive tension between the narrated past and the present of the writer inherent in many biographies. In Nepos' *Lives of Foreign Generals*, this temporal distance is combined with a local one. But we can also find traces of this tension in his *Vita Catonis*. Chapter 2.2 reads:

> ibi [sc. in Hispania citeriore] cum diutius moraretur [sc. Cato], P. Scipio Africanus consul iterum, cuius in priori consulatu quaestor fuerat, voluit eum de provincia depellere et ipse ei succedere, neque hoc per senatum efficere potuit, cum quidem Scipio principatum in civitate obtineret, <u>quod tum non potentia, sed iure res publica administrabatur</u>.

> As he [sc. Cato] stayed there [sc. in Hither Spain] a long time, Publius Scipio Africanus, when consul for the second time, wanted to remove him from his province, and to succeed him himself, but was unable, through the senate, to effect that object, even though he then possessed the greatest authority in the state; <u>for the government was then conducted, not with regard for personal influence, but according to justice</u>.

Here the narrator contrasts Cato's lifetime (*tum*), in which the state was governed by justice, with other times in which personal influence has been more important to sort out political quarrels of the kind described here. It is quite possible that Nepos had in mind his own lifetime, when men like Caesar and Pompeius began a civil war about exactly the same issue – when to return from a province and give back one's competences.[26]

In Tacitus' *Agricola*, the interferences of different layers of time are even more pronounced and complex. Already in its first sentence (*Agr.* 1.1) there is a reference to an undefined past (*antiquitus*) and to the writer's present (*nostris temporibus*).[27] It is along these lines that in the following paragraphs, Tacitus confronts the different historical and social circumstances in which texts about the past are written (*Agr.* 1.1–4): in the old days, it was usual and easy to write on the good deeds of men since there were many good deeds by exemplary individuals to write about and since the writers were not corrupted by personal bonds or ambition; in the present, however, the genre of (auto-)biography became more and more suspect.[28] Via this comparison, Tacitus lays out the conditions of his own biographical project about his father-in-law and, as Dylan Sailor argues, of his future career as a historian.[29] The awareness of his own involvement in this temporal dynamics is reflected in the way how carefully Tacitus arranges the temporal layers in the proem: After the comparison of an undefined past and his own present in the first sentence, he contrasts the time before Domitian's death (*Agr.* 1.2–2.3) with what Tony Woodman calls 'the new dawn' (*Agr.* 3.1–2), with both portions being chiastically split up into remarks about the past (*Agr.* 1.2–3 and 3.2) and Tacitus' own day (*Agr.* 1.4–2.3 and *Agr.* 3.1).[30]

When we shift away from the proem and focus on the narrative itself, we see that here too different layers of time are intertwined: (a) Agricola's deeds, which are guided by venerable Republican values, are related against (b) the backdrop of the more recent past under Domitian. Christina Shuttleworth Kraus has recently analyzed these temporal patterns vis-à-vis their geographical situation (Kraus 2014: 228–39). Her analyses also include (c) Tacitus' 'time of writing, with its insistence on [(d)?] looking forward' (Kraus 2014: 237). The time to which Tacitus 'looks forward' can be best seen in the epilogue where the narrator uses the future tense twice (*Agr.* 46.4):

> quidquid ex Agricola amavimus, quidquid mirati sumus, manet <u>mansurumque est</u> in animis hominum in aeternitae temporum, fama rerum; ... Agricola posteritati narratus et traditus <u>superstes erit</u>.
>
> Whatever we have loved in Agricola, whatever we have admired, abides <u>and will abide</u>, in the hearts of men, in the procession of the ages, by the records of history. ... Agricola, whose story here is told, <u>will outlive death</u>, to be our children's inheritage.

In other words, we are dealing with three if not four distinct layers of time in the *Agricola*. As Kraus rightly points out, we see in the *Agricola* a 'complex interaction among time periods' at work which is 'embedded in the genre of biography itself'.[31]

The point I would like to add to Sailor's, Woodman's and Kraus' arguments is that these very temporal patterns can also be found in the *Agricola*'s history of the non-Romans. In his famous ethnographical digression, Tacitus mentions that the Gauls and some of the Britons were once brave and fierce in war, before peace has made them decadent and they have lost their courage (*Agr.* 11.4).[32] A somewhat different temporal scheme is implicit in the speech by the chieftain Calgacus to his men before the decisive battle at Mons Graupius (*Agr.* 30–2). He opens by stressing the importance of the present and looking ahead to the future (*Agr.* 30.1):

> Quotiens causas belli et necessitatem nostram intueor, magnus mihi animus est <u>hodiernum diem</u> consensumque vestrum <u>initium libertatis toti Britanniae fore</u>: ...
>
> Whenever I consider the origin of this war and the necessities of our position, I have a sure confidence that <u>this day</u>, and this union of yours, <u>will be the beginning of freedom to the whole of Britain</u>. ...

Libertas ('freedom, liberty') is a Tacitean catchword which occurs no fewer than ten times in the *Agricola*, often in decisive or programmatic passages. It is perhaps no overstatement to read the entire *Agricola* as a story of the gain and loss of *libertas*. With regard to the temporal changes of the presence and absence of *libertas*, the beginning of Calgacus' speech can best be compared to the proem of the work: in the remote past for both the narrator and Calgacus, there was freedom (perhaps even too much freedom for the narrator) – *vetus aetas vidit quid ultimum in libertate esset*, 'a former age witnessed the extreme of liberty' (*Agr.* 2.3). This changes in the more recent past under the influence of restrictive powers – for Calgacus these were the Roman occupiers, for the narrator the emperor Domitian, who took action against the freedom of speech (cf. *Agr.* 2.1–2, and here esp. *Agr.* 2.2, *vocem populi Romani et libertatem senatus ... aboleri*, 'perish ... the voice of the Roman people, the freedom of the Senate'). But in both cases the present marks a turning point, and there is the prospect or at least the hope that freedom can return (cf. *Agr.* 3.1). Throughout Calgacus' speech – just like in the proem – the opposition between *servitus* (slavery) and *libertas* plays an important role. The chieftain reminds his men of their inherited freedom and closes with a sentence which unfolds this temporal pattern in a threefold generational scheme: *proinde ituri in aciem et maiores vestros et posteros cogitate* ('Think, therefore, as you advance to battle, at once of your ancestors and of your posterity', *Agr.* 32.4). Calgacus makes reference to the present (*cogitate*), the near future (*ituri*), the past (*maiores vestros*) and the remote future (*posteros*). In their exemplarity, the ancestors seem to play a similar role for the Caledonians as Agricola for Tacitus and his intended audience. These men – non-Roman men – did not relent when faced with forces that threatened their freedom.

Conclusion

I hope it has become clear by now that Roman biographies feature complex patterns of time. The fact that writers usually approach the question of chronology quite freely while stressing the character of the portrayed persons does not mean that temporal issues are of no importance for their works. It is perhaps not all too fruitful to concentrate on the way in which the events of a life are translated into a narrative. But even if we do that, we will soon realize that things are more complicated and less clear-cut than we expect them to be (I have tried to show that in the section on Suetonius). But above all, I would like to make a plea for a widening of our perspective by turning away from the narrative presentation itself and focusing instead on the relationship of these texts and their intended audience. In doing so, we begin to see a bipolar temporal scheme emerging, which can, as in the case of Nepos' *Foreign Generals*, be further complicated by cultural tensions. These temporal and cultural gaps are also vital for Tacitus' *Agricola*. The central point here is that they take shape in a veritable tripartite temporal pattern of distant past, more recent past and a present which looks into the future. This can be expected in a writer flirting with the genre of historiography, which has an even greater affinity to issues of time; but we should be alert to find at least traces of it in other ancient biographies as well. Arnaldo Momigliano once defined biography as an 'account of the life of a man from birth to death' ([1971] 1993: 11). This can easily be – and has been – criticized from various angles as too simplistic, and I do not aim to add my voice to this choir. For the issue of temporality, it would already promote our understanding of ancient biography significantly if we acknowledge that in most cases a biography relates – or at least touches upon – more than a lifetime.

Notes

1 Leo (1901: 315–23); on these origins of ancient biography cf. e.g. also Bakhtin (1981: 130–46), Dihle (1987: 7–22), Stadter (2007: 529–31), Pelling (2012a: 232, section 3) and Pelling (2012b: 233, section 1).
2 Bakhtin (1981: 142).
3 For a critical appreciation of Pausch's studies on Suetonius (2004: 233–324) see below. Further exceptions are the contributions on biography in a volume on time in ancient Greek literature: Beck (2007a) on Xenophon's *Cyropaedia*, Beck (2007b) on Plutarch and Whitmarsh (2007) on Philostratus' *In Honour of Apollonius of Tyana*. See also Chrysanthou (2018: 8–10, 58–9, 108–10) on Plutarch and Garrett (2019) on Suetonius.
4 To put it in narratological terms, this concerns the well-known contrast of 'narrative time' vs. 'discourse time' as well as issues of order and frequency, cf. Genette (1972: 77–182).
5 Martinet (2014: 1201); cf. in a similar wording Della Corte (1967: 192): 'sistema a cassetti'. Suetonius made this method explicit in *Aug.* 9.1 where he states that he wants to 'set out the individual details [sc. of Augustus' life], not in order of events, but by topic' (*partes* [sc. *vitae*] *singillatim neque per tempora sed per species exsequar*). Cf. Bakhtin (1981: 142–3), Stadter (2007: 535) and Garrett (2018: *passim*).
6 On what follows see Pausch (2004: 258–75).
7 Cf. ibid. (256).
8 Cf. ibid. (268): 'Der Wechsel zwischen den beiden Darstellungsmodi der *narratio* und des Rubrikenschemas [...] ist allgemein charakteristisch für seine [sc. Suetons] biographische Technik.' The alternation of narrative and rubric is demonstrated in

Pausch's thorough analysis of the *Life of Vitellius* (2004: 275–317). On this alternation see also Cizek (1977: 59–62) and Hurley (2014).
9   The text is from Kaster's OCT (2016), translations are taken from Edwards (2000).
10 Vogt (1975: 207 *ad loc.*), referring to *TLL* 5/2, 1569,37–51: 'de ordine vel serie inde a capite repetendis'.
11 For more examples, cf. *TLL* 5/2, 1566,72–1567,37.
12 For a comparison with the parallel account in *Calig.* 12.4 see Gascou (1984: 380–1).
13 See Dihle (1987: 65–6).
14 On flashbacks in Suetonius see recently Garrett (2019: 381–3).
15 Cf. Suet. *Tib.* 63–4 and 69.
16 When speaking about the issues of chronology and narrative in biography Wallace-Hadrill rightly notes that 'the labels are not identical' (1983: 10).
17 For the Greek *bíos* see *LSJ* 316 s.v. I.: 'life' (and here esp. 3 'lifetime') and V.: 'a life, biography'.
18 Cf. e.g. Pausch (2004: 3–4), Stem (2012: 128–61) and Brenk (2008).
19 For the importance of careers on the representation of time in the genre of biography see Wallace-Hadrill (1983: 11).
20 Quotations from Nepos are from Marshall's Teubneriana (1991), translations are adapted from Watson (1886).
21 Schenk (2004).
22 For a more detailed discussion of this passage see Schenk (2004: 175 n. 26), who takes the rhetorical devices into account by which the narrator seeks to enhance the reputation of the office of secretary.
23 See Caes. *BGall.* 7.67.7; [Hirtius] 8.28.2, 8.48.1; Caes. *BCiv.* 2.42.3, 3.37.5, 3.38.4. (There are further examples referring to clearly Roman contexts in other historians such as Livy and Velleius.)
24 Cf. *OLD* s.v. *suffectus* 1a (quote from here) and *OLD* s.v. *sufficio* 2a and b.
25 *Vita* is here used in neither of the above mentioned meanings, but in the sense of 'manner . . . of life' (*OLD* s.v. *vita* 7). Nipperdey (1849: 136 *ad loc.*) is perhaps a bit overconfident when noting that Phocion's byname *chrēstós*/*bonus* was better explained by Nepos than by Valerius Maximus 3.8.ext.2. On Nepos' general interest in the character see Dihle (1987: 24) and Beneker (2009: *passim*).
26 Cf. Horsfall (1989: 52 *ad loc.*); Horsfall also mentions Mark Antony and further examples from the late Republic as possible targets of this remark. In the context of Nepos' *Lives of Foreign Generals* the issue of contemporary relevance has been treated at length by Dionisotti (1988: *passim*); cf. Stadter (2007: 533).
27 Quotations from Tacitus' *Agricola* are taken from Ogilvie's OCT (Winterbottom and Ogilvie 1975).
28 Cf. Sailor (2004: 144–5).
29 Sailor (2004: 139 and 156–7) stresses the formulation *hic interim liber* in the final sentence of the proem (*Agr.* 3.3).

30 For this scheme see Woodman and Kraus (2014: 65–7).
31 Kraus (2014: 238).
32 On intertextual influences from Caesar's *Bellum Gallicum* on this passage see Kraus (2014: 231–2). In general, it should not surprise us that non-Roman peoples have a prehistory and show awareness of it: Sallust, another model of Tacitus', has his African tribes possess historical records and seems to use these records even as a source of his own writing (Sall. *Iug.* 17.7).

9

Short Long / Long Short

Brevity, Power and Epigrammatic Temporality

Tom Geue
Australian National University

Time is always political. Under capitalist modernity especially, the chopping up, parcelling and distribution of time are crucial tools by which oppression is endlessly refreshed. Who has time? Who is denied it? How much time? What kind? These are particularly burning questions in an unjust economy which has all but abandoned the modest gains once won by labour movements across the globe. That shaky consensus of eight hours work, eight hours recreation and eight hours rest has dissolved (even before it could catch on for most of humanity) into an amorphous schedule of zero hours, two jobs, three jobs, round the clock. Many have no time, while a few have all the time in the world.

Versions of this unjust temporality existed in antiquity as well. This chapter will track one possible dispensation of temporal resources, and the political symbolism hung upon it, in the exchanges of two very different contemporary authors (Pliny and Martial) as they orbit round one of the hottest aesthetic topics of their day: brevity, or not. My point is a simple one: time tends to take sides, or tends to *be taken* by those with the means of doing so. And we can see this reflected in who can afford to be wordy, and who cannot but be brief.

In the fast-paced rhetorical culture of the early Roman principate, obsessed as it was with landing the perfect pointed dart, you could say that brevity was all the aesthetic rage throughout the first century CE.[1] From a rhetorical point of view, this is partly a function of new forensic practice requiring speakers to be more on point, under the strict surveillance of the dreaded water-clock (*clepsydra*), which supposedly whittled down the infinite drones of the Republic into the well-ordered clock-abiding apparatchiks of the principate. James Ker has written brilliantly on the politicization of this water-clock: how it comes to stand as a sort of barometer for the atmospherics of 'constraint' or 'freedom' under empire, an index of feeling boxed-in or liberated, depending on one's attitude to the measurement and monitoring of time.[2] In Tacitus' *Dialogus*, for example, the opposition is played out between Aper and Maternus: Aper the modernist who praises the new time constraints in speaking and their aesthetic knock-on in pointed brevity; Maternus the nostalgist mourning the loss of endless Republican yabbering.[3] Freedom conflated with free speech. We cannot say anything anymore! Sound familiar?

This active binary in the *Dialogus* also forks out, Ker shows, across two authors in active dialogue, namely Pliny and Martial. Whereas Pliny bristles against the water-clock and flaunts his ability to flout it, showing off his special imperial dispensations to flow overtime, Martial embraces the technology as a mechanism in the spirit of his poetics of brevity.[4] But there is more at stake than aesthetic 'choices' correlating with actively *chosen* politics here. As I hope to show below, the long-short Pliny-Martial cycle featured below[5] is a tussle around a certain point: that brevity and length are not just neutral items plucked from the marketplace of ideas, but aesthetic reflexes of relative power and social status. At Rome, the bigger you are, the more you can feel free to yawn, stretch the legs, take up space and *take your time*.

1. Pliny and Martial Go Long

As 'survivors' of the Domitianic night waking up in the Nervan-Trajanic dawn, Pliny and Martial are both faced with the classic (and much chattered-about)[6] problem of regime differentiation. How to signal, aesthetically, that the enlightened new regime produces a new form of art?[7] How to disinfect these words written *now* from the sordid space of *then*, the thou of yesterday from the you of today?[8] One ingenious way of underscoring an otherwise fairly faint political periodization[9] is through marking a new form of literary temporality, i.e. saying 'once we had to be brief; now we can relax'. Pliny, you could say, is committed to this project at glorious, tiresome *length*. Not only does he vaunt his long speaking time in the Priscus trial,[10] not only does he pen the interminable *Panegyricus*,[11] whose very length is the measure of new Trajanic indulgence: he also writes an extended tract in defence of length as a display piece in his first book of letters, 1.20. Taking a counter-intuitive stance against a long rhetorical tradition extolling brevity, and an even longer Callimachean tradition of 'big book, big evil', Pliny says no: actually, the bigger, the better.[12] Pliny calls the law onto his side, which apparently allows speakers all the time they need for a 'full treatment'; no impatient judge or passive-aggressive water-clock will be breaking his flow.[13] What is more, Pliny shades brevity with the darkness of the Domitianic terror: of course bugbear Regulus, that grim *delator* of the old regime, was a practitioner of violent verbal brevity, all the better to delate you as efficiently as possible.[14] To the objection that some people just prefer a short speech, Pliny cannot help stretching the concept to breaking point, with a *reductio ad absurdum* that raises the ghosts of the bad old days (Pliny, *Ep.* 1.20.23):

> 'At est gratior multis actio brevis.' Est, sed inertibus quorum delicias desidiamque quasi iudicium respicere ridiculum est. Nam si hos in consilio habeas, non solum satius breviter dicere, sed omnino non dicere.

> 'But many people prefer a short speech.' Yes, dullards prefer it, but it is stupid to think of their whims and distractions as an actual opinion. If you went with their advice, better not only to speak briefly, but to say absolutely nothing.[15]

If you're going to be brief, well, you might as well say nothing at all. Silence, of course, is a heavy concept in this early Trajanic moment setting up uncurbed verbal diarrhoea – feeling what we like and saying what we feel (Tacitus, *Histories*, 1.1.4), using our rusty voices again (Tacitus, *Agricola* 3.3), standing up and yelling after copping it in the audience for too long (Juvenal, *Satires* 1.1) – as the antidote to the enforced 'silence' of the Before Time.[16] Brevity, it seems, is on the wrong side of the asphyxiated, muted history we have gladly escaped. Finally we can breathe, finally we can talk – at length. So why ever would we want to be brief?

Despite Ker's very valid points about Martial standing on the other side of this debate – at least as far as the water-clock is concerned[17] – I think the picture of Martial on brevity, and his place in this discourse of freedom and constraint, is actually a little more flexible. In fact, I would say there is a particular moment where Martial himself tries to approximate this Plinian mode of marking a new politics with elongated time. And this comes with the arrival of Book 10, which is a special palimpsest of political revisionism: its first version initially circulated in 95, the book was recalled for product faults after Domitian's death in 96 and eventually rereleased – in new, improved, revised and expanded form – in 98. In other words, the brevity-length debate seems to take on new life precisely at this hinge point of literary history, straddling Domitianic and Nervan-Trajanic periods, the moment when Martial is himself tasked with the problem of how to wash one's historical periods of the suspicion that they just bleed into each other.

Up to Book 10, it is fair to say, Martial has made a career of and in brevity. He was an early adopter of the form, specializing in small scale guest-gifts (*xenia* and *apophoreta*) whose art lies in elegant processes of ekphrastic miniaturization. The *Epigrams* proper then become a bit more ambitious, alternating pithy two-liners with grander and longer bits. But it is only in the post-Domitianic version of *Epigrams* Book 10 that we see the self-curtailing dispenser of bits programmatically allow himself some more space and time.[18] The book opens with a direct flagging of the problem, complete with reader instructions for how to get around the product defect (Martial, *Ep.* 10.1):

> Si nimius videor seraque coronide longus
>   esse liber, legito pauca: libellus ero.
> terque quaterque mihi finitur carmine parva
>   pagina: fac tibi me quam cupis ipse brevem.
>
> If I seem too much, a long book with a late sign-off, read just a few things: bingo, a booklet again. Often my small page shares an end with the poem: DIY, make me brief as you like.

I shan't scratch the old sore point of whether the different quantities of *liber* (free) and *liber* (book) can resonate with each other in this post-96 hail to liberation; but suffice to say that Martial here marks his book as an unapologetic *book* (*liber*), rather than the equally common, more deprecatory book*let* (*libellus*).[19] As Victoria Rimell has nicely pointed out, there is long-short play-off encoded elegantly in the elegiac form here: hexameter 1 ending *longus* to mark the new departure, pentameter 2 ending *brevem* to remind us of the past.[20] The next epigram explains why this longer face (10.2.1–8):

> Festinata prius, decimi mihi cura libelli
>   elapsum manibus nunc revocavit opus.
> nota leges quaedam sed lima rasa recenti;
>   pars nova maior erit: lector, utrique fave,
> lector, opes nostrae: quem cum mihi Roma dedisset,
>   'nil tibi quod demus maius habemus' ait.
> 'pigra per hunc fugies ingratae flumina Lethes
>   et meliore tui parte superstes eris.
>
> The production of my tenth booklet, rushed before, has now recalled the work after it slipped from my hands. You'll read some bits which are already out there, now shaved down with a fresh file; the majority will be new: reader, be open to both, dear reader, you're my savings too: when Rome gave you to me, she said 'I have nothing more to give you. Thanks to him, you'll avoid the stagnant waters of thankless Lethe, and you (the better part of you) will survive.'

In this famous signal of the revised edition, note particularly how different temporalities and rhythms are grafted onto different temporal periods. In the Before Time, under Domitian, Martial was in a rush (*festinata . . . cura*), and the work slipped out of him prematurely.[21] Now, he has had proper time to polish *and* expand; which will let him please his reader so he can extend even further, into the future.[22] Some old, some new, some fame to come – but unquestionably, better and *bigger* than before. There is a sense that this new suspension of the constraints of brevity is a way of aesthetically signalling the inauguration of new freedoms – particularly striking as a departure, because epigram is meant to be one long toast to brevity. In this farewell to rush and time constraint, in this so-long to brevity, in this salute to expansion and time-taking, then, Martial and Pliny – shock horror – are on a strikingly similar page.

In other words, Martial Book 10 is the formerly brief-stricken epigrammatist's attempt at playing with the big boys: not so much in joining the chorus that is the 'Indignation Industry',[23] that grand exercise in sharp retrospective condemnation that defines Pliny and Tacitus' post-Domitianic jockeying; but rather, in joining the Length League. Interestingly, this bid for the big time plays out in a very direct manner, not long into this new expansive territory. In 10.20, Martial literally tells his muse to take his whole book – now looking markedly, modestly small again (*libellum*) – up to the Esquiline and knock on old Pliny's door. The temporal power dynamics of this home-call are fascinating, so let us read the whole thing (10.20):

> Nec doctum satis et parum severum,
> sed non rusticulum tamen libellum
> facundo mea Plinio Thalia i perfer:
> brevis est labor peractae
> altum vincere tramitem Suburae.   5
> illic Orphea protinus videbis
> udi vertice lubricum theatri
> mirantisque feras avemque regem,
> raptum quae Phryga pertulit Tonanti;
> illic parva tui domus Pedonis   10
> caelata est aquilae minore pinna.
> sed ne tempore non tuo disertam
> pulses ebria ianuam videto:
> totos dat tetricae dies Minervae,
> dum centum studet auribus virorum   15
> hoc quod saecula posterique possint

Arpinis quoque comparare chartis.
seras tutior ibis ad lucernas:
haec hora est tua, cum furit Lyaeus,
cum regnat rosa, cum madent capilli: 20
tunc me vel rigidi legant Catones.

Go on, Thalia my girl, take this little book – not particularly intellectual or serious, but not boorish either – to silver-tongued Pliny. With the Subura out of the way, it's short work getting up the hill. Up there you'll see Orpheus straightaway, slippery at the top of his wet theatre; also his wild beast admirers, and the royal bird who whisked off the stolen Phrygian to the Thunder-lord. Up there the modest house of your Pedo is engraved with an eagle's smaller wing. But don't rap drunkenly on the eloquent door when it's not your time: he gives dour Minerva whole days, keeping his head down writing for the ears of the Hundred Men material which the future could rank up there with the boy from Arpinum's pages. Safer for you to go later, at last lamps: this is *your* moment, when Lyaeus is off chain, when the rose reigns supreme, when hairs are lubricated. At that moment, even crank Catos are fine to read me.

The proposed journey is classic Martial at his most ambivalent: ambitious and irreverent, weeny and deferential all at the same time.[24] There is humility – the book is a *libellus*, lacking in learning next to Pliny, a little something altogether unserious – but there is pride too: at the same time, it is not *rusticulus*. The opening of the poem is almost a simultaneous embrace and denial of the diminutive. A humble brag, too, in that *brevis est labor*: a nod to the congenital brevity of epigram, but also a boast that the upper echelons of society are really now within reach, that Pliny's house is accessible, his door always open; the distances can be covered easily, the heights conquered (*vincere*) no sweat.[25] Partly, we infer, because Pliny has a thing for poets: his Orpheus is put on the pedestal, rolling out the red carpet for Martial's book, under the arm of his Thalia, to waltz right in.

Yet, it cannot be that easy. And it is not. While the distance is easily covered, the time is the tricky part. For Thalia cannot just burst in unannounced. Martial tells her not to go at a time 'not yours' (*tempore non tuo*, 12), i.e. a time that does not belong to her, but to Pliny. And that is a lot of time: entire days (*totos . . . dies*, 14), which our prolific Author of Substance spends on his lengthy compositions for the Centumviral court,[26] the material that will sprawl into posterity's nostalgia. Heaven forbid you disturb Pliny while he is knocking up his vast masterpieces in daylight hours;[27] rather, approach him at night, when things are laxer, Lyaeus the loosener rules, and even Catos have a perverse slot tucked aside for reading epigram. This, my muse, is your moment: a short time (*hora*) compared to the long and multiple days Pliny spends on his hundred-man enterprises. A very brief time to shine; a window perhaps reminiscent of a strained client forced to pick his patron's *kairos*. Indeed this temporal genuflection, the confining of Martial's product to a very restricted moment of late leisure, is an established way of signalling epigram's lowness: think the instructions to Domitian to read Martial's verse at the tenth (party) hour in 4.8.9–10, or the presentation of poems to Silius during the carnival of the Saturnalia (4.14.6–12).[28] Martial's circumscription of Pliny's visiting hours is just the latest incarnation of epigram's poetics of *sorry to bother you*.

2. Pliny Shorts Martial / Martial Shorts Himself

This request for just a little bit of time at the end of the day is granted by Pliny almost to the letter, when he gives his eventual reply to this poem in *Epistles* 3.21. Right at the end of Book 3, Pliny carves out some eschatological (and eulogistic) space for his recently deceased 'pal' Martial. BFFs always? In fact, as John Henderson points out, this epigram-epistle combination is the only time the two respectively mention each other,[29] so whatever bond we imagine should be taken with all sorts of condiment. In any case, Pliny pays the dead poet *some* kind of respect. But it is a respect that, crucially, puts Martial in his place, by denying him time; it is an honour that takes Martial's invitation at the beginning of Book 10 literally, and makes him as brief as Pliny likes.[30] In this naked time-grab, Pliny actually ends up clipping Martial's wings, and reducing him to the brief poet mould he was threatening to bust out of. Let us see how the cuts trim our plucky epigrammatist back down to size.

After a long preamble in which Pliny starts praising Martial only to make a point about his own untimely generosity – turns out he had shelled out for Martial's return trip to Bilbilis, as a nod back to the lost custom of rewarding poets materially for their work (*Epistles* 3.21.3–4), and the absence of patronage is itself a Martialian obsession[31] – Pliny responds to an assumed question of his addressee Cornelius Priscus: so, what are the actual 'verselets' (*versiculi*, 3.21.4) that made you reciprocate in cash? No problem, says Pliny. He digs them instantly from the file of memory (Pliny, *Ep.* 3.21.5):

> Adloquitur Musam, mandat ut domum meam Esquilis quaerat, adeat reverenter:
>
> Sed ne tempore non tuo disertam
> pulses ebria ianuam, videto.

> Totos dat tetricae dies Minervae,
> dum centum studet auribus virorum
> hoc, quod saecula posterique possint
> Arpinis quoque comparare chartis.
> Seras tutior ibis ad lucernas:
> haec hora est tua, cum furit Lyaeus,
> cum regnat rosa, cum madent capilli.
> Tunc me vel rigidi legant Catones.

He [Martial] is addressing the Muse, instructing her to look for my house on the Esquiline and approach it respectfully:

But don't rap drunkenly on the eloquent door when it's not your time: he gives dour Minerva whole days, keeping his head down writing for the ears of the Hundred Men material which the future could rank up there with the boy from Arpinum's pages. Safer for you to go later, at last lamps: this is *your* moment, when Lyaeus is off chain, when the rose reigns supreme, when hairs are lubricated. At that moment, even crank Catos are fine to read me.

For this extremely self-centred eulogy, Pliny has not only picked the verses that praise *him*; he has cut the poem down the middle, i.e. made it much snappier than the original,[32] and cleverly focussed only on the part that directly concerns him. It is as if he writes his own version of the piece from his own exclusive, aristocratic Plinian consciousness, which becomes aware of Martial's muse only at the point, late at night, when she rightfully comes knocking on his door, a locked-out lover trying her luck in the wee hours. The first bit of the poem, i.e. the sordid journey from the Subura, the admiring glances up to the Orpheus statue – none of that concerns or befits Pliny.[33] In Ilaria Marchesi's sharp analysis of the murky intertextual silences shading the hinterland of this passage, she comments that Pliny's nudging excerption actually makes time and timeliness the most important part of Martial's poem: 'By separating time from space (its logical and rhetorical counterpart in Martial's original), Pliny's selective quotation actually ends up reinforcing the sense that this is the dimension that matters more in the poem.'[34] True: but even more than this, it is a temporality defined by exclusion and restriction, a very stringent schedule determined by the relative values of social status. Pliny only has (very limited) time for Martial's praise, and that only at night;[35] the already short window of visiting hours is slammed shut through this act of abbreviation passed off as reciprocal 'gratitude'.

Nor is this the only way the poet is curtailed. First, there is the relative positionality necessarily attendant on a death notice, which already makes

Martial's time on earth patronizingly into a flash in the pan next to Pliny's sprawling longevity. Secondly, there is a sense in which Martial's epigrammatic time – that of the ephemera of this mortal world – is explicitly outdone by Pliny's own stretch into eternity. At the end of the letter and book, our long-winded fusspot writes (3.21.6):

> Meritone eum qui haec de me scripsit et tunc dimisi amicissime et nunc ut amicissimum defunctum esse doleo? Dedit enim mihi quantum maximum potuit, daturus amplius si potuisset. Tametsi quid homini potest dari maius, quam gloria et laus et aeternitas? At non erunt aeterna quae scripsit: non erunt fortasse, ille tamen scripsit tamquam essent futura. Vale.

> So was I justified in sending this man off in such a friendly manner, in mourning his death as one of my best friends – a man who wrote these verses about me? He gave me as much as he could, and would have given even more if it were in him. And yet what more can a man be given than glory, fame, eternity? But – goes the objection – his poetry won't be eternal: perhaps it won't, but he wrote it as if it would. Bye.

Martial could have given Pliny more, if he were capable. Read: he *did* actually give more in writing a fuller poem, but Pliny, posh Roman with a short attention span for lowly epigrammatists, cut him off along the strictest lines of relevance: a spatial demarcation of 'no Subura, only Esquiline' goes hand in hand with a slashing of verse length. Here there is a clear circumscription of a *right to length*, claimed by Pliny and denied to Martial; and this is somehow coordinated with a *right to duration*. The sting in the tail is that Martial's all-too-brief, all-too-material epigrams *will not last*. For all Martial's protestations otherwise – and there are a lot of them[36] – Pliny implies that these flash-in-the-pan, fun-size pieces *can't* stand the test of time.[37] If Pliny wants Martial's 'immortalizing' verses about him to survive, he actually has to do it himself, by incorporating their 'best bits' into the book of letters.[38] This is a moment of maximal upper class gentility, where Pliny looks quizzically upon Martial's one-time attempt to climb aboard the Esquiline with him, and says: OK, here's a small plot for a literary grave in my letters. No, it has to be half that size. Yes, it's the one about me. And the only way it will survive is if I put it in my letters. What's your name again? (*checks notes*) Martial, that's it.

It is hard to see this re-dimensioning of Martial's relative proportions, on Pliny's part, as anything less than an act of class aggression.[39] The lordly, senatorial Pliny sniffs out an equestrian upstart trying to jump on board the good ship 'LONG'. That upstart had written a poem seeking to stake out for himself and his book just a modicum of free time in Pliny's long and important day; he asks, in effect, whether he can come round once in a while and frolic with Rome's bigwigs. Pliny does not just shut his door; he sends him packing in the other direction, all the way back to Spain. The acts of 'thanks' which constitute this last letter in Book 3 – whether that be giving Martial money for the trip, or quoting his poetry – are designed to patronize a poet aiming at rights to length, and to plane him back to brevity. Only some people can keep talking, on and on, into the sunset of posterity.

Although the dating is of course impossible, it is tempting to take Pliny's brief rebuff as the thing that drove Martial hurtling back to his home turf of brevity in Book 12. Or at least to read Pliny's lordly rescaling as symptomatic of a *dynamic* that Martial would embrace again in his last book of poems, from Spain with love. Here the 'brief book' is back, composed supposedly 'in a few days' (*paucissimis diebus* – 12 *praef.*), and it fits snugly into a short winter hour of a reader with other stuff on his plate (Martial, *Ep.* 12.1):

> Retia dum cessant latratoresque Molossi
>   et non invento silva quiescit apro,
> otia, Prisce, brevi poteris donare libello.
>   hora nec aestiva est nec tibi tota perit.

> While the nets and Molossian barkers take a break, and the wood relaxes without a boar snuffed out, you'll be able to give some leisure to a brief booklet. It's not a summer hour, and you won't waste the whole thing.

Again, Martial plays the common gambit of the deferential, 'this book won't take too much of your time sir, and only downtime at that sir' – except Priscus is no Pliny.[40] How far we've fallen. A few poems later, Martial explicitly rubs this sharp return to brevity back up against the anomalies of Books 10 and 11 (*Ep.* 12.4):

> Longior undecimi nobis decimique libelli
>   artatus labor est et breve rasit opus.
> plura legant vacui, quibus otia tuta dedisti:
>   haec lege tu, Caesar; forsan et illa leges.

> The longer labour of Books 10 and 11 has been squeezed and shaved down my work to 'brief'. People with nothing to do – those you've granted leisure to – are allowed to read more; these ones are yours to read, Caesar; maybe you might read the others too?

Rimell rightly points out that Books 10–12 are a unified trio insofar as they have 'footholds in two or rather multiple worlds',[41] looking back and forward across historical flashpoints. But it seems that 12 is framed here almost as the mirror image of 10, to close: the 'expanded edition' of 10 becomes, in dying, the withered, 'contracted edition' of 12. Now we are really at rock bottom, i.e. degree zero brevity: the stasis of Spanish time has eaten away at Martial's creative capacities so much that he is now simply recycling material from Books 10 and 11, stuff that did not make the first cut. I know, Caesar – who has got the time to read those in full?! Have a selection instead. This beeline for brevity is really a bad case of back to square one. For this constellation of constraint is reprised from the little Martial's second ever epigram in the collection (1.2):

> Qui tecum cupis esse meos ubicumque libellos
> et comites longae quaeris habere viae,
> hos eme, quos artat brevibus membrana tabellis:
> scrinia da magnis, me manus una capit.

> You there who want my books with you wherever you go, seeking them as companions for a long journey, buy these, which the parchment squeezes into small page-faces: give book boxes to the Greats – I fit in one hand.

Back there, Martial was quick and mobile, the perfect portable companion for a long journey.[42] The material form of the codex enacts a compression (*brevibus . . . tabellis*) that is also a kind of constraint (*artat*; cf. *artatus*, 12.4.2). It looks a lot like Martial's fate to be held in the palm of a master's hand, pocketed away as a negligible means of filling out a spare moment he does not have, notionally stolen from a busy day. It is as if, from 1.2 to 12.4, no time has passed at all.

3. Short-Lived Long

When Martial tells his Thalia to take his book up the Palatine to Pliny's palace, he is clearly piping on the book-as-slave tune of Horace's *Epistles* 1.20. As I said above, there is an ambition to rise here: the book becomes a proper *liber*, and the entity charged with tucking the book under the arm is no slave, but a *muse*, a divine being responsible for firing that *liber* into the world. And yet through the double optics of oxymoron which characterize 'aspirational epigram', there is a danger that this Thalia will be taken not as a goddess, but as a whore – a dolled-up creature of the gutter, an enslaved woman with a Greek name threatening to rise above her station as she makes a brief visit to the elite punters late at night, catching the lads while deep in their cups. What this chapter has tried to show is how epigram is put *back in its place* as that second order creature, demoted from goddess back to whore, and how its position is marked by a withholding, a rationing, a reduction in time. The default brevity of epigram is just that: not chosen, but thrust upon it. A virtue of necessity made.

Martial is a long way from an enslaved person, and should never be conflated with one. But there is a sense in which this enforced condition of brevity, and the self-monitoring speech patterns surrounding it, approximate the status of the slave – among many other things, slavery is a state of having one's time controlled, constrained and policed.[43] There is something a little nasty in the way that Martial's time vis-à-vis patron(izing) Pliny is rationed along several temporal scales.[44] First, Martial must be brief in the immediate timescale of the poems we are reading; as soon as he experiments with being more expansive, he is slapped back down to size. Second, his already vanishingly short visiting hours are ruthlessly observed by Pliny, who chops out anything beyond them; epigram only ends up with a very negligible sliver of the elite day, and the boundary is reinscribed in Pliny's brutal editorial act of abbreviation. Third, Pliny denies Martial access to the elite time of literary immortality, the ability to endure beyond the end of one's mortal and material life and propagate oneself down the ages through poetry. Along all three axes from short to long, then – let us call them aesthetic or epigrammatic time, daily time and generational time – Martial is stripped back to the penury of brevity.

We only become aware of the social and political ordering of time at the moment such ordering groans under strain. This is exactly what Martial does in his 'expanded' Book 10: tries to lengthen to fill a time 'not his'. Pliny punishes him for the hubris by tapping his watch while dancing on his grave. When Pliny calls time, epigram's long is short-lived. Not everyone has the liberty of ignoring the water clock and running overtime. Not everyone has a ticket to eternity.

Notes

1 The aesthetic of brevity seems to explode especially around the late Augustan and Tiberian period; it is shared programmatic territory for Vitruvius, Velleius, Valerius Maximus and Phaedrus. See Woodman (1975: 285–6), Starr (1980: 298) and Geue (2022).
2 Ker (2009a). On the water-clock as a crucial watershed technology for the measurement and affect of 'short time' in Rome, see Wolkenhauer (2019).
3 Ker (2009a: 286–8).

4 Ker (2009a: 290–300).
5 The relationship between Martial *Ep.* 10.20 and Pliny *Ep.* 3.21 has got a lot of looks of late: see Henderson (2001) on Pliny's act of literary mediation in this letter and its place in the dynamics of the book; Marchesi (2013) on the diffuse intertextuality emerging from the interface; Edmunds (2015) on Martial's curious silence about Pliny's poetic output. Both Fitzgerald (2018) and Rimell (2018) start off with mentions of the exchange. My reading in this chapter merely rides on the coat-tails of all these trailblazers.
6 For the *locus classicus* on the strategy of 'denigration of predecessor' in the Trajanic-Hadrianic age, see Ramage (1989).
7 On this problem's commonness to Pliny and Martial, see Fitzgerald (2018: 120–2).
8 This delicate tussle of forgetting and remembering across a regime break is behind Rimell's comparison of Martial and Tacitus on survival (2018: 64).
9 At least according to the revisionists (Waters [1964], Waters [1969], Jones [1992] and Southern [1997]; see also Wilson's response [2003]), suspecting Domitian was not all that bad after all. Even if we refuse to go so far as to exculpate the old ba(l)d guy, it is certainly true that the intense periodization and hard break between Domitian and Nerva-Trajan, like most chunking of history, is a *retrospective* invention of the Pliny-Juvenal-Tacitus generation.
10 Ker (2009a: 293).
11 Pliny lays down the need for new speech to reflect the political tabula rasa in *Panegyricus* 2.2–3: *Nihil quale ante dicamus, nihil enim quale antea patimur; nec eadem de principe palam quae prius praedicemus, neque enim eadem secreto quae prius loquimur. Discernatur orationibus nostris diversitas temporum . . .*
12 Pliny, *Ep.* 1.20.5: *Et hercule ut aliae bonae res ita bonus liber melior est quisque quo maior.*
13 Pliny, *Ep.* 1.20.11.
14 On Regulus' shadowy presence in the Martial 10.20–Pliny 3.21 exchange, see Marchesi (2013: 110).
15 All translations mine, unless someone tells you otherwise.
16 Cf. the classic Tacitus *Agricola* 2.1.4: *memoriam quoque ipsam cum voce perdidissemus, si tam in nostra potestate esset oblivisci quam tacere.* Cf. Wilson (2003: 523–4).
17 Ker (2009a: 299).
18 On Book 10 as the hinge point and 'fault line' in Martial, see Rimell (2008: 65).
19 According to Larash (2008: 138), these two terms are fairly interchangeable in Martial – though she does not offer stats. On the Catullan baggage of the word *libellus*, see Roman (2001: 120–1).
20 Rimell (2008: 67).
21 See further Rimell (ibid., 69–70).

22 On the rebranding of Martial's *superstes* by Tacitus at the end of the *Agricola* (or vice versa), see Rimell (2018: 78–9).
23 Freudenburg 2001: 234–42.
24 Fitzgerald (2007: ch. 4) is excellent on the immense binary scope of Martial and his flair for juxtaposition, e.g. invective with praise.
25 On the different presentation of various visits to posh Roman households as pure schlep elsewhere in Martial, see Laurence (2011: 88).
26 Which were, we should remember, Pliny's pride and joy and his own main target for posterity's spotlight: see Mayer (2003).
27 On Martial's fairly well-sectioned daytime division of hours between early *negotium* and late *otium*, see Laurence (2011: 88–9).
28 See Garthwaite (1998: 161).
29 Henderson (2001: 61); but see Marchesi (2013) on the more diffuse intertextuality between them.
30 Cf. Rimell (2018: 64–5).
31 As it is of many authors in the ballpark (Juvenal and Calpurnius Siculus, too): for this motif of declining patronage in context, see Saller (1983: 255).
32 See Henderson (2001: 61); Rimell (2018: 64); and see also Marchesi (2013: 106–7), on the potentially awkward Domitianic baggage of the first part of the epigram.
33 Cf. Henderson (2001: 65) on this Martialian 'mini-trek' leading to someone – watch out Pliny – likely getting 'splashed with satire'.
34 Marchesi (2013: 109).
35 Although for a very different political reading of this temporality (identifying the cooler time of night with Trajanic temperateness, vs Flavian afternoon heat) see Rimell (2018: 75).
36 E.g. *Ep.* 10.2 (cf. Fitzgerald [2018: 111]). In fact this last part of Pliny's letter can be profitably read as a direct confutation of Martial's ubiquitous boasts about his own immortality and immortalizing power: see Garthwaite (1998: 163–5).
37 Rimell (2018: 83) reads Pliny as affirming Martial's self-monumentalization and survival strategy – but I am not sure this bears out in his genteel edit of a quotation and the backhanded *tamquam* (on which, see Fitzgerald [2018: 111–12]).
38 Cf. Edmunds (2015: 336) and Fitzgerald (2018: 111).
39 While Martial's whining about 'poverty' should be neutralized with scepticism, there was still a yawning distance between base level equestrian and senatorial status; on the likely financial limits Martial faced as a member of the former, see Saller (1983: 250–1). Tennant (2000) takes Martial's moans seriously.
40 While it is hard to pin Priscus' (= Terentius Priscus) precise profile down, Nauta (2002: 69–70) implies he might be in the non-high-flying-senatorial, more 'social equal' camp of Martial's patrons.
41 Rimell (2008: 191); cf. Rimell (2018: 73–4).

42 Although, as Larash (2008: 138) points out, this is a claim about the efficiency of the new codex: same amount of text in a smaller space.
43 See Moss (forthcoming) on slavery and/as 'chronometric violence'; cf. also Geue (2022).
44 For another way of triangulating these different forms of time (e.g. diurnal and 'historical-periodic') across Tacitus, Martial and Pliny, see Rimell (2018: 75–6).

Part Four

The End of Time

10

The Day of Reckoning

Seneca's Epistolary Time[*]

Catharine Edwards
Birkbeck, University of London

Letters, as a genre of writing, articulate a very particular kind of temporality. An individual letter is always (at least ostensibly) composed at a particular point in time; in a letter collection, each item is associated with a distinct moment of origin. Mikhail Bakhtin's notion of the 'chronotope' asserts the 'intrinsic connectedness of temporal and spatial relationships ... artistically expressed in literature'; importantly, 'it is precisely the chronotope', Bakhtin suggests, 'that defines genre and generic distinctions'. While the chronotope is an interconnection of space and time, for Bakhtin, 'the primary category in the chronotope is time';[1] literary genres, then, may be seen specifically as particular ways of *being in time*. The Younger Seneca's manipulation of the temporal distinctiveness of letters as a genre in relation to his own philosophical project is my focus in what follows.[2] Time – how we use it, how we misuse it and how we should think about it – is a recurrent concern in Seneca's letters. Seneca's epistolary time can also take on a spatial aspect (particularly relevant to the idea of the chronotope). Indeed, Seneca often chooses to represent time in spatial terms; the latter part of my discussion will home in on a selection of Seneca's spatial images in the letters and the ways these serve to reinforce his claims about the particular relationship of the good Stoic life to time.

1.

Whether or not Seneca's *Epistulae morales* were genuine letters, they present themselves as composed in sequence over an extended period.[3] Each individual letter apparently originates in an individual (if never fully specified) day. As

Emanuela Sangalli underlines, epistolary form is especially suited to underlining the reader's awareness of her own relationship to time, an awareness Seneca is particularly keen to promote.[4] These letters are overshadowed by the sense that time is running out. This collection is a work which repeatedly stresses the author's advanced age and often dwells on the proximity of death. From the outset Seneca presents time as something to be comprehended through its effects on the individual human body.

My particular focus here will be Letters 1 and 12, which demarcate the first book of the letters, but I shall also look forward to a number of later letters (in particular Letters 61, 74, 101) in which Seneca further explores the significance of the individual day as a unit of time.[5] Letter 1 immediately makes clear Seneca's preoccupation with time.[6] The opening sentence urges his addressee Lucilius to take possession of himself and his time, with parallel imperatives *vindica te tibi*, 'take possession of yourself', and *tempus . . . collige*, 'get hold of your time'; indeed to lay hold of one's time is to take possession of one's self.[7] We shall return shortly to the implications of this parallel. Wasting time, as Seneca underlines, is a failing by no means particular to Lucilius. The next sentence laments how time is snatched from us, *nobis*, a first-person plural encompassing Lucilius, Seneca himself, his readers – perhaps humanity in general, or slips away.

The central term (literally) in this first letter is *tempus*.[8] Seneca asserts at 1.3 that while *omnia . . . aliena sunt* ('all other things are outside our control'), *tempus tantum nostrum est* ('time alone belongs to us'). The time referred to here is specifically present time; future time, he often points out in the letters and elsewhere (most obviously in his treatise on the shortness of life, *De brevitate vitae*, for instance at 10.2) is always beyond our control.[9] *in huius rei unius fugacis ac lubricae possessionem natura nos misit* ('nature has put us in possession of this fleeting and slippery thing alone'). Noting our tendency to fritter away hours in pointless pursuits, Seneca adumbrates strategies by which we might gain more control over our time. A variety of metaphors used to conceptualize time are explored elsewhere in this volume;[10] Seneca proposes initially that we think of time as money, sharpening our sense of time as 'an expendable resource'.[11] Financial imagery figures prominently in sections 2, 4 and 5 of the first letter, through terms such as *pretium* ('price'), *aestimat* ('he estimates'), *imputari* ('to be entered as a debt'), *ratio* ('reckoning'), *constat* ('it comes out even'), *impensae* ('expenditure'), *perdere* ('to lose'), *reddam* ('I may render').[12] Though Seneca himself still wastes time, as he concedes with characteristic self-deprecation, he at least keeps a detailed account of how he spends it. At 1.4, he observes:

ratio mihi constat impensae ('the reckoning of my expenditure is correct')[13] propounding here an abbreviated, time-focused, version of the process of daily self-scrutiny, repeatedly advocated in the letters and elsewhere.[14]

The effort usually spent on scrutinizing one's finances, Seneca implies in Letter 1, is better devoted to keeping track of how one spends one's time. He presents as in some respects parallel our worries over having enough time and having enough money. Indeed, economic anxieties and how to control them are themselves a prominent concern in the letters, cropping up at Letter 2.6 and serving as a particular focus in the second book of the letters.[15] If we cultivate the right attitude to money, Seneca argues there, we can be satisfied with the barest minimum to keep body and soul together; similarly, in Letter 1, limited time is presented as no obstacle to living well, provided we are content with the time we have. For, while time should not be wasted, even the smallest amount of time, specifically the present, suffices for the exercise of virtue (and thus the achievement of happiness). Yet, in Letter 1, financial imagery also throws into relief the incommensurability of time and money; for time alone, it turns out, has true worth, so that the usual concerns of 'economic' thinking ultimately have no real significance.

Time (specifically present time) is personal in this letter and is the only thing, Seneca asserts, fugitive though it is, that one can properly be said to possess.[16] The legal imagery Seneca uses for taking possession of time has a strongly haptic dimension – 1.1 *vindica* ('claim!'); 1.2 *si . . . manum inieceris* ('if you lay hold'); 1.3 *possessionem* ('possession'). This conceptualization of time in concrete terms is ironic, given that Stoics regarded time as an 'incorporeal'.[17] Seneca himself, it is true, does not generally stress time's incorporeality, although he does observe elsewhere, in *De brevitate vitae* 8.1 (a passage which is in several respects echoed at Letter 1.2–3), that it is perhaps this characteristic which misleads people into regarding time as of no value. For Seneca, the value of time is to be considered primarily from a moral rather than a metaphysical perspective, as Mireille Armisen-Marchetti underlines.[18] What matters in the Letters is not time as an abstraction but human time, lived time.

Seneca's work insistently draws our attention to the positioning of the good life in time. Indeed, as Gregor Vogt-Spira comments, 'an awareness of the flow of time is never absent in Seneca.'[19] Seneca's attitude to the importance of the individual day, discussed further below, is to be distinguished sharply from that recommended, for instance, in Horace's *Odes* 1.11, where the addressee is (famously) exhorted to seize the day, *carpe diem*, but also to avoid a calculating engagement with time. Horace's symposiastic present is precisely a moment to forget about the passage of time, as Vogt-Spira underlines.[20] Seneca's present, by contrast, entails perpetual vigilance, ensuring that no moment is wasted.

In his opening letter, Seneca presents as crucial to making good use of one's time a proper understanding of death.[21] The reader is reminded (1.2) *se cotidie mori* ('he dies each day'). This is, of course, a paradoxical message. Seneca's reader is to find reassurance in the idea of death as a cumulative process; the days we have already experienced are already in death's hands, he suggests.[22] The idea of 'dying every day' will be elaborated in later letters, as James Ker underlines, in relation both to the importance of the individual day and to the perpetual presence of death.[23] Sharing with his addressee the importance of not counting on the future, Seneca declares: *ecce hic dies ultimus est. ut non sit; prope ab ultimo est* ('imagine this is the last day of life; or else as nearly the last', *Ep*. 15.11). Already at Letter 4.7–8, the possibility that any day may be our last is explored in some detail. How can we hope to anticipate the circumstances of our own death when as many people have been killed by angry slaves in their own homes, Seneca asserts, as by angry kings?[24] – the latter option, we might note, knowingly foreshadows the likely conclusion of his own story.

Yet, this sequence of letters, composed by an elderly man in poor health, is necessarily open-ended. The last letter will most likely be written without the knowledge that it *is* the last letter (in fact the last letters of the series known in Aulus Gellius' day have not survived to ours). Seneca reminds his reader that, just as any day may be one's last, *any* letter may be the last: *hanc epistulam scribo, tamquam me cum maxime scribentem mors evocatura sit* ('I am writing you this letter, as if death were about to summon me in the very middle of writing', 61.2), although, assuming they appear in the order in which they were written – which may be a big assumption – he would go on to write at least sixty-three more.

Seneca does not make explicit precisely what he understands by 'present' time, the *tempus* that Lucilius is exhorted to seize hold of in the opening sentence of Letter 1; Armisen-Marchetti plausibly suggests that, at least sometimes in his writing, it is the present day, *dies*, which has this sense.[25] Having invoked the Virgilian phrase *optima quaeque dies . . . prima fugit* ('the fairest day is ever first to flee', *Georgics* 3.66–7), Seneca observes at *De brevitate vitae* 10.4: *singuli tantum dies, et hi per momenta, praesentes sunt* ('only single days – and those only in minutes – are present'). For Seneca, although he is concerned with the longer-term philosophical development of his addressee (and indeed himself), the individual day – the present day – is the unit of time on which a philosophical approach to life should focus.[26] He repeatedly presents embodied habit, *exercitatio*, crucial to philosophical progress, as embedded through daily routine.[27] Relentless vigilance over one's behaviour is actualized through 'daily meditation': 4.5 *cotidie meditari*, 16.1 *cotidiana meditatio*. The anchoring of the individual letter in an individual day is reinforced through such terms as *hodiernum*, to characterize the 'daily' quotations from Epicurus and others, with which Letters 2 to 29 conclude (for instance, 2.5). The individual day, indeed, is crucial to the temporal character of the letter as a genre. Epistolary writing thus offers the ideal medium through which to put Seneca's philosophical approach to time into practice.

In Letter 8, developing the claims of Letter 1, Seneca prides himself on making the most of each day (8.1–2):[28]

> nullus mihi per otium dies exit. partem noctium studiis vindico. non vaco somno sed succumbo, et oculos vigilia fatigatos cadentesque in opere detineo.
>
> I never spend a day in idleness; I appropriate even a part of the night for study. I do not allow time for sleep but yield to it when I must, and when my eyes are wearied with waking and ready to fall shut, I keep them at their task.

This concern to extract maximum value from the individual day recurs in later letters. Letter 122, for instance, opens with a comment that the hours of light are growing shorter. This is all the more reason to rise early, even before dawn, to make the most of the day: *circumscribatur nox et aliquid ex illa in diem transferatur* ('Cut short the night; use some of it for the day's business'),[29] though Seneca is ferocious in his criticism of those who protract the day merely for pleasure.[30] His concern to make the most effective use of time, as Ker notes, is shared with the Elder Pliny, who boasts of his efficient use of time in the preface to the *Natural Histories* (*NH* pr. 18). Indeed, the latter's nephew presents his uncle as notorious for his temporal frugality, *parsimonia temporis* (Pliny, *Ep.* 3.5.13). Turning one day into two, he would rise from a nap and begin his studies again, 'as if it were another day', *quasi alio die*, Younger Pliny records (3.5.11).[31] Seneca himself returns repeatedly to the question of how exactly the individual day is to be spent, setting out his own daily routine (exercise, meals, bath – in cold water ideally – and, most importantly, study), for instance at 65.1–2 and 83.1–7, the latter ostensibly in response to a request from Lucilius.[32]

2.

Letter 12 (the last letter of the first book of the *Epistulae morales*) opens with a poignant acknowledgement of the effects of time on the individual human body.[33] Seneca casts himself as an old man, visiting his villa and lamenting its parlous condition. His *vilicus* reminds him that the villa and its decaying plane trees merely show the effects of their age – and Seneca remembers that he built the house and planted the trees himself, while the ancient wreck of a slave who looks about to depart this life is none other than the sweet little boy he used to play with – Seneca's 'abjected reflection', as John Henderson puts it.[34] Ker observes, 'The distinct and normally incommensurate life-cycles of villa, tree, and slave all somehow reach their end simultaneously, heralding the ruin of the master.'[35]

But the letter then shifts mood. While the analogies of the following sections (12.4–5) may be in some respects reminiscent of Horatian admonitions to seize ephemeral pleasure before old age supervenes, Seneca's concern is more particularly with savouring the pleasures particular to old age, even or especially, while mortality is recognized (notably the paradoxical pleasure of no longer desiring pleasures).[36] As Victoria Rimell observes, in the course of this letters 'anxieties about aging are voiced but also processed.'[37] Cicero, in his *De senectute* (§24), a work with which Seneca engages closely in Letter 12, has Cato insist that no-one is so old he cannot hope to live for another year; Seneca, at Letter 12.6, comments rather that no-one is so old he cannot hope for another day.[38] Here, too, the individual day has a particular resonance.

Whatever letter turns out to be Seneca's last will perhaps also be the product of his last day. Seneca reminds his addressee Lucilius that death may strike him in the midst of composition (61.2, quoted above). In the same passage, he observes (61.1):

> id ago, ut mihi instar totius vitae dies sit. nec mehercules tamquam ultimum rapio, sed sic illum aspicio, tamquam esse vel ultimus possit.

> I am endeavouring to live every day as if it were a complete life. I do not indeed snatch it up as if it were my last; I do regard it, however, as if it might perhaps be my last.

The awareness of death's proximity informs his resolve that a well-used day should be valued just as much as a well-used life; it offers enough scope for virtue.[39] A later letter, 101, opens with another reminder of the passage of time (101.1):

> Omnis dies, omnis hora quam nihil simus ostendit at aliquo argumento recenti admonet fragilitatis oblitos; tum aeterna meditatos respicere cogit ad mortem.

> Every day and every hour show us what a nothing we are and remind us of our fragility with some fresh evidence when we had forgotten it; then, as we plan for eternity, they make us look back at death.

The individual day offers scope for the exercise of virtue but each day also brings reminders of mortality (at this point, indeed, with increasing urgency, Seneca is monitoring the hours, too). The chilling image of death at one's shoulder here recalls Seneca's treatise *De brevitate vitae*.[40] Jacques Derrida (who draws on this latter text particularly in his *Aporias: dying-awaiting (one another at) the 'limits of truth'*) characterizes this as a 'rear-view mirror of waiting for death at every moment'.[41]

Letter 101 goes on offer the example of the sudden death of Seneca's friend Senecio, an unexpected end which makes a mockery of all Senecio's plans for the future (the similarity of their names reinforces the potency of this *memento mori*), serving as a prompt for Seneca's further reflection on the need to focus on each individual day (101.7–8):

> sic itaque formemus animum, tamquam ad extrema ventum sit. nihil differamus. cotidie cum vita paria faciamus. maximum vitae vitium est, quod imperfecta semper est, quod aliquid ex illa differtur. qui cotidie vitae suae summam manum imposuit, non indiget tempore.

> Therefore, let us so order our minds as if we had come to the very end. Let us postpone nothing. Let us balance life's account every day. The greatest flaw in life is that it is always imperfect, and that a certain part of it is postponed. One who daily puts the finishing touches to his life is never in want of time.

We might note here Seneca's accounting imagery, *paria faciamus* (OLD s.v. *par* 2), reminding us of the concerns of Letter 1. More strikingly, however, this passage suggests the idea of one's self, perhaps even one's life, as a work of art over which one can exert a kind of authorial control. This conceit recurs at a number of points in the letters, notably at 77.20, where the life of an individual is compared to a play (*quomodo fabula, sic vita*); each of us should take care that his life has an appropriate conclusion: *bonam clausulam impone* ('give it a good ending!') – Seneca exhorts his reader. Elsewhere (11.8, 26.8), he comments light-heartedly on the need for the individual letter to have a good *clausula*. If the day is the letter's temporal correlate, a proper *clausula* is also a daily requirement.

In a later section of Letter 101, Seneca returns to the theme of treating each day as entire life. The point, sharpened by the tale of Senecio's sudden end, is repeated and developed (101.10):

> ideo propera, Lucili mi, vivere et singulos dies singulas vitas puta. qui hoc modo se aptavit, cui vita sua cotidie fuit tota, securus est.

> Therefore, my dear Lucilius, begin at once to live, and count each separate day as a separate life. He who has thus prepared himself, he whose daily life has been a rounded whole, is easy in his mind.

Interestingly, Senecio is presented as having met his death stricken by angina, after he had eaten his dinner, at the end of a full day. Epicurean texts compare the individual who is ready to meet his end to a satisfied dinner guest, now prepared to take his leave. Lucretius, for instance, has his personified Nature reproach one who cannot bear the prospect of death: *cur non ut plenus vitae conviva recedis | aequo animoque capis securam, stulte, quietam?* ('why not, like a banqueter fed full of life, withdraw with contentment and rest in unworried peace, you fool?', *De rerum natura* 3.938–9). Yet this is not an analogy which appeals to Seneca, for whom the pleasures of the table are generally a source of disgust.[42] Caught up in his plans for the future, Senecio experienced his life as *imperfectus*, his full stomach notwithstanding.[43] Senecio, we should note, is no voluptuary but a man of frugal habits. His last day followed a measured routine, beginning with a visit to his friend Seneca. Indeed, Senecio had sat at the bedside of another friend, *graviter adfecto et sine spe iacenti* ('one gravely ill and lying without hope', 101.3). Senecio did not imagine for a moment his dying friend would outlive him. And yet, he should have countenanced this possibility.[44] His own end took him wholly by surprise, his life in consequence lacking the completeness he could have attained, had he only been more attentive to the ever-present nature of death.

3.

In Letter 101 and elsewhere, Seneca advises that we should treat each day as if it were a whole life. The latter part of this essay will reflect further on this rather counter-intuitive advice, which is closely related to Seneca's claim (articulated, for instance, at *Ep.* 49.10) that a long life is not intrinsically preferable to a short one. Seneca often considers time in spatial terms, as Armisen-Marchetti underlines, comparing life with the flow of a river (as at *Ep.* 58.22–3) or characterizing it as a linear journey with a particular destination.[45] These are relatively common strategies; D. Casasanto and L. Boroditsky's work, for instance, underlines the ways our mental representations of time are asymmetrically (but not unidirectionally) dependent on our mental representations of space.[46] Nevertheless, the combination of multiple spatial analogies readily gives rise to paradox; alongside the linear analogy, suggesting a journey from one distinct location to another, Seneca also uses circles to characterize human life.

In common with many other writers, Seneca often emphasizes the circularity of the temporal cycles of the sun and moon and the workings of the cosmos.[47] At 36.11, for instance, he remarks:

> observa orbem rerum in se remeantium; videbis nihil in hoc mundo extingui, sed vicibus descendere et surgere. aestas abit, sed alter illam annus adducet; hiemps cecidit, referent illam sui menses; solem nox obruit, sed ipsam statim dies abiget. stellarum iste discursus quidquid praeterit, repetit; pars caeli levatur assidue, pars mergitur.

> Mark how the round of the universe repeats its course; you will see that no star in our firmament is extinguished but that they all set and rise in alternation. Summer has gone, but another year will bring it again; winter lies low but will be restored by its own proper months. Night has overwhelmed the sun but day will soon rout the night again. The wandering stars retrace their former courses; a part of the sky is rising unceasingly, and a part is sinking.

It is not surprising to find planetary movements or the repeated succession of the seasons described in terms of a circle.[48] In relation to human life, however, Seneca makes the image of the circle work much harder.[49]

One of Seneca's most developed discussions of the cyclical nature of time features in Letter 74.[50] Here he is again making the argument that, since virtue is the only thing that matters, a longer life is not intrinsically superior to a shorter one (74.26–7):

> sive illi senectus longa contigit sive citra senectutem finitus est, eadem mensura summi boni est, quamvis aetatis diversa sit.
> utrum maiorem an minorem circulum scribas, ad spatium eius pertinet, non ad formam. licet alter diu manserit, alterum statim obduxeris et in eum in quo scriptus est pulverem solveris, in eadem uterque forma fuit ... quod rectum est, nec magnitudine aestimatur nec numero nec tempore; non magis produci quam contrahi potest. honestam vitam ex centum annorum numero in quantum voles corripe et in unum diem coge; aeque honesta est.

> Whether a long old age falls to one's lot, or whether the end comes on this side of old age – the measure of the supreme good is unvaried, in spite of the difference in years.

> Whether you draw a larger or a smaller circle (*circulus*), its size affects its area, not its shape (*forma*). One circle may remain as it is for a long time, while you may contract the other forthwith, or even merge it completely with the sand in which it was drawn; yet each circle has had the same shape ... That which is straight is not judged by its size, or by its number, or by its duration; it can no

more be made longer than it can be made shorter. Scale down the honourable life as much as you like from the full hundred years, and reduce it to a single day; it is equally honourable.

Importantly, it is the *forma* of the circle which signifies, not the *spatium*.[51] Here the form of the circle serves a dual purpose to indicate both the completeness of a life (whatever its length it may be viewed as complete, *perfecta*)[52] and also its 'goodness', *honestas*. Virtuous character can make a single day equivalent, on Seneca's view, to a hundred years.[53] It is striking that here once again it is the single day, for Seneca, which is the shortest unit of time within which virtue may be fully exemplified.

This equivalence in virtuous character between the single day and a much longer period may, I think, help us to make sense of the complex image of circles set out at 12.6–9. This letter's earlier sections – in which the elderly Seneca visits his ruinous villa – repeatedly deploy imagery of turning (12.1 *quocumque me verti*, 'wherever I turned'; 12.3 *conversus ad ianuam*, 'turned to face the door'; 12.4 *quocumque adverteram*, 'wherever I had turned my attention'), reinforcing the sense of circularity as the Seneca character is spun around, aware of his life eddying away. From 12.6, Seneca articulates a complex set of images relating to the phases of human life and to the conceptualization of units of time. The day is a key unit here. He declares: *unus autem dies gradus vitae est*, ('For one day is a step along life's journey'); the term *gradus* can mean simply step, or a measured unit of length, though it can also mean a stair or rung of a ladder.[54] He then continues (12.6–7):

> tota aetas partibus constat et orbes habet circumductos maiores minoribus: est aliquis qui omnis complectatur et cingat (hic pertinet a natali ad diem extremum). est alter, qui annos adulescentiae excludit. est qui totam pueritiam ambitu suo adstringit. est deinde per se annus in se omnia continens tempora, quorum multiplicatione vita componitur. mensis artiore praecingitur circulo. angustissimum habet dies gyrum, sed et hic ab initio ad exitum venit, ab ortu ad occasum.

> The totality of our life is divided into parts; it consists of large circles (*orbes*) enclosing smaller ones. One circle embraces and circumscribes the rest; it extends from birth to the final day of life. The next circle limits the period of our adolescence. The third confines all of childhood in its circumference. Again, there is the year, in a class by itself; it contains within it all the temporal divisions through the multiplication of which we arrive at life's total. The month is defined by a narrower ring (*circulus*). The smallest circle (*gyrus*) of all is the day; but the day too passes from its beginning to its ending, its sunrise to its sunset.

Here, too, Seneca describes time in terms of geometric shape, conceptualizing both solar time and human time in terms of circles.[55] The idea of the year as a circle can be traced back to Homer.[56] Cicero's contemporary Varro goes so far as to derive the Latin word *annus* 'year' from a word for circle: *vocatur annus quod ut parvi circuli anuli, sic magni dicebantur circites ani, unde annus* ('[it] is called an *annus*, "year", because just as little circles are *anuli*, "rings", so big circuits were called *ani*, whence comes *annus*, "year"', Varro, *Ling.* 6.8).[57] The circling seasons and the cycle of day and night, too, are relatively familiar ideas (as was noted above in relation to 36.11). Yet, the conceptualization of human life in terms of concentric circles (if that is the right way to imagine them) is one not paralleled in extant classical texts.[58] It is particularly difficult, I think, to make sense of the idea of childhood, or of adolescence, as enclosed in a circle. Gretchen Reydams-Schils would relate such a conception to the ever-increasing circle of human connections that the individual Stoic forms over the course of her life through the process of oikeiosis, so that the day of one's birth is the central point with ever increasing circles surrounding it.[59] Carlos Lévy's similar suggestion, that Seneca evokes a graduated cone, perhaps goes too far in concretizing Seneca's imagery.[60] We might rather think of a large circle and within it smaller separate circles. But in the end, even this reading may be too concrete; Seneca's focus is surely on analogy rather than spatial relationships.

Seneca goes on (12.7) to quote a saying attributed to Heraclitus (while also reminding us that he is known for his obscurity), *unus . . . dies par omni est* ('one day is equal to every day').[61] Seneca suggests two different ways of understanding this. The first is in terms of the simple number of hours in each day. The second is in relation to each day's balance between light and darkness; all days thus resemble one another in terms of their trajectory, insofar as each alternates from dark to light to dark (though the text is corrupt here).[62] We might read him as proposing that, as regards the alternation between light and darkness at least, the very longest space of time offers nothing more than the individual day.

A further implication of the resemblance might be that because each day of your life is *like* the last day of your life, it should not be too onerous to treat it as if it *were* the last day of your life.[63] Seneca then concludes (though it is not perhaps wholly clear how this follows from the interpretations he has offered): *itaque sic ordinandus est dies omnis, tamquam cogat agmen et consummet atque expleat vitam* ('every day should be regulated as if it concluded the series, as if it consummated and filled out our life', 12.8).[64] The verb *consummet* (12.8) recurs a number of times in the letters in the sense of 'rounds out'.[65] It also recalls both the *summa manus* of the author/artist's final touches (as at 101.7) – and perhaps, too, the *summum bonum* whose measure is unvaried, whatever life's length, as Seneca will underline at 74.26. At 92.25, he highlights a key characteristic of *virtus* as follows: *futuro non indigere nec dies suos* **computare**; *in quantulo libet tempore bona aeterna consummat* ('the quality of not needing a single day beyond the present, and of not **reckoning** up the days that are ours; in the slightest possible moment of time virtue completes an eternity of good'). It is the individual day here which corresponds to the *quantulum*; and once again Seneca underlines the liberating *securitas* to be derived from letting go of the future. It is perhaps relevant to remember here the Stoic insistence that virtue is to be reckoned in terms of intention rather than result (as Seneca regularly reminds his reader, e.g. at *Ep.* 14.16). We do not need to complete our virtuous actions for them to count as virtuous.

An individual life seen as a circle may be experienced as complete, perfect, whenever it comes to an end.[66] The equivalence in the form of the individual day and the individual human life underwrites the contention that the smallest of the chronological circles in Letter 12, the day, can on one level be equated to the largest of circles experienced by the human individual. Verbal parallels underline the resemblance (in 12.6–7, human life runs *a natali ad diem extremum*, 'from birth to the final day', the individual day *ab ortu ad occasum* 'from sunrise to sunset'). This equivalence is both metaphysical and moral. The idea of the individual human life as a circle serves to render its end as one with its beginning.[67] Indeed, Seneca repeatedly stresses in the letters (for instance at 54.6 and 74.34) that to die is to return to the state we were in before birth; our end is our beginning.[68] Time here is collapsible, telescope-like – to modify Lévy's imagery of the graduated cone.

4.

Certainly, there are tensions between different senses of temporality in the letters, in particular the quotidian and the maturational (with occasional invocations of the cosmic). We might track an oscillation in this text, on the Bakhtinian model, between these multiple, interrelated senses of time, with the struggle or dialogue between them animating Seneca's philosophical project.[69] For all their preoccupation with the atomized time of the individual day, the letters also showcase the development over a more extended time of both writer and addressee – showing what it should mean to exist in time.[70] Philosophical self-development is a major undertaking – and not something to be achieved in one day. Yet, the fixation on daily time itself offers a measured optimism. Time is paradoxically renewable; tomorrow is another day. It is never too late to embark on the road to self-improvement.

There is a suggestive contrast here between Seneca's epistolary time and that of the novel (the genre of greatest interest to Bakhtin himself, of course), whose form implies the author has envisaged the conclusion of her narrative, so that the characters' apparent freedom of action is illusory. Letters, however, each (at least ostensibly) originating in a particular (if not fully specified) point in time, are composed individually without knowledge of what will happen in future. With these particular letters we may also conceive the possibility of their having been retrospectively edited and rearranged so as to generate a disingenuous kind of emplotment (even if the circumstances of the author's actual death could not have been precisely anticipated).[71] Seneca sometimes expresses the desire to assert a kind of authorial control over his own life, as we have seen; certainly, we cannot help but read the letters in the light of their author's own violent end.[72] At the same time, through their assertion of the paramount importance of the present day and its power to round out perfectly any life, the *Epistulae morales* challenge, at least implicitly, the shadow cast by imperial displeasure over their author's immediate future.

Notes

[*] I am most grateful to participants in the Venice conference, especially Ahuvia Kahane and Duncan Kennedy, for their comments on an earlier version of this paper. Particular thanks are due to Bobby Xinyue for bringing us all together so brilliantly, both in person and on the page.

[1] Bakhtin (1981: 84–5). On the usefulness of the notion of 'chronotope' in relation to ancient conceptualizations of 'short time', see Miller and Symons (2019: 6).

[2] For some of the complex ways in which Seneca engages with space and place in the letters, see Edwards (2018).

[3] Scholars disagree as to the length of time over which they were composed. Some scholars argue for a period of composition over two years 62–4 CE, see Mazzoli (1989: 1850–3) and Grimal (1991: 219–39, 443–56). Others take the view that Seneca embarked on the project only in 63, so that the spring of 23.1 and the spring of 67.1 refer to the same year, see Griffin (1992: 400). There remains the possibility that such references to markers of the passage of time are themselves fictive elements, designed to reinforce the epistolary character of the collection.

[4] Sangalli (1988: 53).

5   For a more comprehensive discussion of Letters 1 and 12, see Edwards (2019).
6   A text especially favoured in the early modern period, as Panizza (1983) underlines.
7   This is a pairing which recurs often, e.g. 71.36.
8   As Hijmans (1976: 136) notes in his analysis of *Ep.* 1's structure.
9   Cf. e.g. *Ep.* 101.4. *Quam stultum est aetatem disponere ne crastini quidem dominum!* ('But how foolish it is to set out one's life, when one is not even owner of tomorrow!'). See also Ker in this volume.
10 See e.g. Kahane, Fearn and Batty in this volume.
11 A conceptual metaphor which informs many conventional metaphorical statements about time in the twenty-first century. See Gibbs (2017: 188–9). On people's failure to set a proper value on time, see also *Brev.* 8.2.
12 See Armisen-Marchetti (1995) and Vogt-Spira (2017: 205–6).
13 Cf. also in relation to time: *Brev.* 17.5, *Tranq.* 3.8, Pliny, *Ep.* 1.9.1 *singulis diebus in urbe ratio aut constet aut constare videatur* ('if one takes a single day passed in Rome, one can give or at least have the impression of giving an account of it'), a comment perhaps influenced by Seneca.
14 And in greatest detail in *Ira* 3.36; see Ker (2009b). See also *Ep.* 83.2.
15 And frequently in the second book of the letters, on which see Soldo (2021).
16 As Vogt-Spira notes (2017: 203), 'characterising it as *res fugax et lubrica* ... emphasises the difficulty in adopting the right attitude to time'.
17 Goldschmidt (1977: 37–45), Sangalli (1988) and Reydams-Schils (2005: 29–34). Seneca expresses a more metaphysical interest in time at *Ep.* 58.22 and 88.33.
18 Armisen-Marchetti (1995). Cf. Delpeyroux (2002: 204): 'dans le "temps abstrait" des développements philosophiques les plus spéculatifs intervient toujours une composante humaine'.
19 Vogt-Spira (2017: 197).
20 A contrast subtly explored by Vogt-Spira (ibid., 198–201).
21 On the interrelationship of death and time in Seneca, see further Edwards (2014).
22 Cf. 24.20, 58.23.
23 Ker (2009c: 161).
24 Cf. e.g. 74.3.
25 Armisen-Marchetti (1995: 563). Elsewhere, however, we can find Seneca characterizing the entire duration of the Roman state as a *punctum* (*NQ* 1. pr. 11). The term *punctum* is also used to underline the trivial length of any human life at *Ep.* 49.3: *punctum est quod vivimus et adhuc puncto minus* ('the time we spend in living is but a moment'). See Vogt-Spira (2017: 196–7). Cf. M. Aur. *Med.* 2.17. On this approach to the conceptualization of time, see Porter (2020: 264–5).
26 Earlier Stoics were more interested in the conceptualization of time in terms of physics. Chrysippus observed that no time is present as a whole or exactly (*SVF* II 509); cf. Plutarch *On common conceptions* 1081c–1082a (= L–S 51C). This claim is

helpfully discussed by Schofield 1988. Posidonius characterized the present as the least perceptible time dividing the past from the future (fr. 98.9–12 E–K). Like Seneca, Marcus Aurelius makes clear the mind should be concerned only with the present (6.32), in his concern with 'quotidianità', 'everydayness', as Sangalli (1988: 53) underlines.

27 Cf. e.g. 108.4.
28 On claims of this kind (for which there are parallels in Pliny *NH* pr. 18, Gell. pr. 4), see Ker (2004). Quintilian (*Inst*. 10.3.26) recommends night as the best time to write, free of distractions. Ker sees Seneca's concern with making good use of the night as having a significant influence on Gellius.
29 *Ep*. 122.3. This concern is analyzed by Ker (2004). Cf. *NQ* 1. pr. 2–4, discussed by Williams (2012: 31–2).
30 At 122.14–17, those who misuse night-time in the interests of pleasure are described as *lucifugae* ('avoiders of sunlight'). See also Ker (2019).
31 We might see the Younger Pliny as perhaps influenced by the concerns of Seneca's letters here.
32 We might follow Miller and Symons (2019: 5–6) in characterizing the individual's daily regimen as a 'chronotype'. Seneca describes himself as an afficionado of cold-water baths at *Ep*. 53.3. Their moral superiority is further celebrated at 51.6 and 86.10–12.
33 For the continuously changing body, see 58.24. On this aspect of the letters, see further Edwards (2005).
34 Henderson (2004: 25).
35 Ker (2009c: 335). The plane tree, we might note, was celebrated in antiquity for its longevity (see e.g. Mart. 9.61), as Watson and Watson observe (2009: 215).
36 In particular, Seneca can be seen as responding to two of the complaints against old age set out (and answered) in Cicero, *Cat. mai*. 15: *quod privet fere omnibus voluptatibus ... quod haud procul absit a morte* ('that it deprives us of almost all physical pleasures ... that it is not far removed from death'). Seneca also draws on Plato's *Republic* (esp. 328d). The topic of old age is developed further in Letters 26, 45, 58, 67, 78, 83 and 104.
37 Rimell (2017: 778).
38 See Ker (2009b: 336). At *Brev*. 11.1, Seneca explicitly criticizes old men who pray for a few more years. Sometimes even to wish for a day is treated by Seneca as over-ambitious; at *Ep*. 54.7, having described an experience of intense breathlessness and becoming reconciled to the unpredictability of death's arrival, he presents his expectations as even more circumscribed: *nihil cogito de die toto* ('I do not plan a whole day ahead').
39 Cf. *Brev*. 7.9. For the reminder that each day may be one's last, see also e.g. *Ep*. 93.6.
40 On which see Williams (2003).

41 Derrida (1993: 55). See further 1993: 2–4 on the *De brevitate vitae*.
42 The closest Seneca comes to such a characterization is in his vignette of the perfect life of the Stoic sage, from which nothing is lacking; at *Ep.* 98.15, Seneca observes, *ipse vitae plenus est* ('he has lived a complete life'); cf. 85.23. This motif is suggestively analyzed, in relation particularly to Sen. *Ep.* 61.4 (*mortem plenus expecto*, 'having had my fill, I await death'), by Berno (2008).
43 On Seneca's exploration in Letter 101 and elsewhere of the impact of the imminent prospect of annihilation on our sense of self see Porter (2020: esp. 271–2).
44 Seneca reproaches himself for failing to be aware that his younger friend might predecease him (63.15).
45 Armisen-Marchetti (1995: 550–3). E.g. 70.1–3, cf. Armisen-Marchetti (1989: 86–9), Lavery (1980) and Richardson-Hay (2006: 98). The day as a *gradus vitae* at 12.6 might be interpreted in this light. For the stages of life as *gradus*, cf. 49.3.
46 Casasanto and Boroditsky (2008), building on the classic study by Lakoff and Johnson (1980).
47 *OLD* s.v. 1 defines *circus* as 'a circle or zone in the sky', citing Cic. *Arat.* 512 (266), *Rep.* 6.16; cf. *Rep.* 6.15 on the orbits of the stars: *circos suos orbesque conficiunt* ('they complete their circular courses and orbits'). Lyle (1984) discusses the use of the circus track as an analogy; while in reality not strictly circular in shape, the ideal circus was discussed as if it were a circle.
48 Though in Letter 36 this circularity is harnessed to the assertion that nothing is ever fully annihilated; death merely interrupts life and 'the day will return when we shall be restored to the light' (*veniet iterum, qui nos in lucem reponat dies*, 36.10).
49 Armisen-Marchetti (1995: 551) traces a link between the *cursus*, the course of a river or of a race, and the sense of life's journey as a circle (or ellipse) derived from the racetrack, the *circus*. The term *gyrus* (Sen. *Ep.* 12.7) has a similar range of meanings (see below).
50 Discussed by Ker (2009c: 338–9).
51 Isomorphism is key, as Ker notes (ibid.: 338), rather than breadth.
52 For human life made *imperfecta* because business is postponed see 101.7 (quoted above).
53 On the irrelevance of length of life, cf. 93.8, 78.29 *Posidonius ait, 'unus dies hominum eruditorum plus patet quam imperitis longissima aetas'* ('Posidonius says, "for the wise, one day offers more than the longest lifetime offers the ignorant"'); 85.22 on the *beata vita*: *itaque in aequo est longa et brevis, diffusa et angustior, in multa loca multasque partes distributa et in unum coacta. qui illam numero aestimat et mensura et partibus, id illi, quod habet eximium, eripit. quid autem est in beata vita eximium? quod plena est* ('And so there is equality between the long life and the short, between the extended life and that which is more limited, between one whose influence extends far and wide and one restricted to a single sphere. Those who assess life in

terms of number or measure deprive it of its distinctive quality. What is the distinctive quality of the happy life? Completeness.').

54 For the stair/ladder-rung meaning see *OLD* s.v. *gradus* 3.
55 *Gyrus* is often used for the orbits of heavenly bodies (*OLD* s.v. *gyrus* 4), e.g. Man. 1.234, as well as for the circular course on which horses are trained (*OLD* s.v. *gyrus* 1).
56 E.g. *Il.* 23.833. See Habinek (1982: 66). We might note also e.g. Virgil, *Aeneid* 1.269–70 *triginta magnos volvendis mensibus orbis | imperio explebit* ('he shall fulfil in his reign thirty great circles of rolling months').
57 Cited by Maltby s.v. *annus*.
58 Habinek (1982: 66) notes there may be a precedent in Heraclitus but the fragmentary nature of the relevant text makes it impossible to be certain. Ker (2009c: 338) explores the possible implications of concentric circle models in terms of differentiation, inclusion and hierarchization.
59 Reydams-Schils (2005: 31). Relevant here is Hierocles' model of concentric circles to represent relations to self and to others (Long and Sedley 1987, 57G = Stob. 4. 671–673.11). As Ker notes (2009c: 339), here too 'the assimilation of broader circles to the smaller circles is to be effected through the technique of metaphorical utterances'.
60 Lévy (2003), noting the ambiguity of *gradus* at 12.6 (which can also mean 'stair'), argues that these concentric circles should be seen in three dimensions, forming a sort of graduated cone, with the day of one's birth at the apex, though it is hard to see how the circle of each individual day could then be accommodated. Viparelli (2000: 36–41) and Reydams-Schils (2005) also favour a conical interpretation. Ker (2009c: 336) proposes reading *gradus* rather as 'span'.
61 We might see this as a paradoxical inversion of another celebrated observation of Heraclitus 'you never step into the same river twice' (Heraclitus B49a D–K). The latter Heraclitean *sententia* is itself picked up by Seneca at *Ep.* 58.22–3, where he notes that no one is the same person when old as he was when young.
62 On the possible readings, see Slégen (1972). We might note the relevance here of 24.26 where Seneca underlines the repetitive sameness of our daily experience.
63 This thought recurs repeatedly; cf. *Brev.* 7.9 *qui omnes dies tamquam vitam ordinat, nec optat crastinum, nec timet* ('one who plans out every day as if it were his last, does not long for or fear tomorrow'), *Ep.* 61.1–2, 93.6, 101.8.
64 Habinek (1982: 68) contends that the moral follows from both interpretations of the saying of Heraclitus.
65 cf. 32.3 *quam pulchra res sit consummare vitam ante mortem* ('what a noble thing it is to round out your life before the advent of death'), 74.20, 92.2, *Ira* 3.36.1. *consummo* as *OLD* notes derives from *summa* (fem. of *summus*).
66 The idea (though not preceded by a structured argument) is to be found in Hor. *Epist.* 1.4.13–14 *omnem crede diem tibi diluxisse supremum. | grata supervenies quae*

non sperabitur hora ('believe that every day that has dawned is your last. The unhoped-for hour will be welcome to you when it comes').

67 We might compare the image of the snake biting its tail as a representation of an aion, which Politian attributes to the Egyptian Orus.
68 In some passages he suggests we ourselves may return to the light again (e.g. 36.10), though elsewhere he presents death as final. Different possibilities are articulated at 71.16. See Busch (2009).
69 Burton (1996: 9) highlights this aspect of Bakhtin. See Bakhtin (1981: 252).
70 As Armisen-Marchetti comments (1995: 545), 'la parénétique, parce qu'elle est ascèse spirituelle et lente maturation, s'exerce dans le temps et grâce à lui'. See also Edwards (2019: 4).
71 An issue to be related to the debate over the degree to which these letters are 'fictive'. See Griffin (1992: 347) and Edwards (2019: 5–6).
72 As Ker (2009c) underlines.

11

Engendering the Christian Age

Ovid's *Fasti* and the Annunciation in Renaissance Poetic Calendars[*]

Bobby Xinyue
King's College London

The renewed interest in Ovid's *Fasti* among Italian humanists in the late fifteenth century led to the appearance of several Neo-Latin Christian calendar poems.[1] Replicating the structure of the Ovidian poem, these Renaissance poetic *fasti* chronicled the feasts of the ecclesiastical year and displayed a wealth of religious and antiquarian learning. While these Renaissance poems varied considerably in metre, length and style, nearly all of them made a serious attempt to reclaim March – named after the Roman god Mars and once considered the first month of the Roman year – for Christianity. This chapter enquires into the literary and wider cultural and political significance of this act of reclamation. I will examine in sequence the *Fasti christianae religionis* of Ludovico Lazzarelli (*c.* 1483/4); the *Fasti libri* of Battista Mantovano (Lyon, 1516); and the *Sacri Fasti* of Ambrogio 'Novidio' Fracco (Rome, 1547). In particular, I will focus on these poems' treatment of the Feast of the Annunciation (25 March), which historically marked the first day of the new year for Christians since the Middle Ages.[2] It will be argued that the Renaissance poets' account of this major Christian feast day engaged closely with the displacement of Mars from Book 3 of Ovid's *Fasti*, as well as the Ovidian poem's emphasis on the interventions and creative powers of women and female goddesses in Rome's early history. Of course, not every Renaissance poetic calendar sought to recreate the style of the Ovidian model; but the *Fasti* was clearly an intertext in the sense that it constituted part of the literary discourse upon which these Renaissance texts were produced. As will be seen, the humanist poets' response to Ovid's *Fasti* 3 is particularly pronounced in their depiction of Mary as the *genetrix* of Christianity, and in their assertion of the Annunciation as the moment that a new *saeculum* took over from and surpassed pagan antiquity. By handling the Annunciation in this way, the Italian humanists used their poetic calendars to reinforce not only the status of Mary in Christian thought but also the authority of the Roman church as the call for religious reform gathered pace in the sixteenth century.

1. Beginnings and Authorities in Ovid's *Fasti* 3

Book 3 of Ovid's *Fasti* is deeply concerned with new beginnings. In the course of a lengthy prologue (3.1–166) followed by a rich episode on the March Kalends (3.167–396), which amount to nearly half of the book, Ovid recounts Rhea Silvia's conception of Romulus and Remus by Mars (3.9–58); the foundation of Rome (3.59–78); the creation of the ten-month calendar by Romulus (3.79–98); the formation of the twelve-month calendar by Numa (3.99–154); the introduction of the Julian calendar (3.155–66); and the springtime reawakening of nature (3.235–42). These narratives of human, civic and natural creation cumulatively draw attention to the primacy of March on the Roman calendar (notwithstanding the later introduction of January and February) and the month's historical importance to the Romans.

Despite this however, the status and presence of the month's patron god, Mars, are notably subdued. Book 3 opens with a striking request from the poet for Mars to drop his weapons: *Bellice, depositis clipeo paulisper et hasta, | Mars, ades et nitidas casside solve comas* ('Warlike Mars, lay down your shield and spear for a brief while, and come, loosen your glistering locks from your helmet,' 3.1–2). The disarming of Mars is a key symbol of the book's movement from war to peace, foreshadowing the privileging of *sacra* over *arma* which subsequent episodes bear out.[3] Moreover, while Mars is credited as the divine ancestor of warlike Romans (cf. *Bellice*, 3.1), his authority soon diminishes: immediately after the call for disarmament, Ovid asks Mars to learn from Minerva, a goddess who is in command of the arts of war and peace equally (3.5–8).[4]

As the prologue proceeds, the relegation of Mars' status is coupled with a heightened focus on female figures. Recounting the conception of Romulus and Remus, Ovid paints Mars simply as a violent rapist (3.21–2). By contrast, Silvia's experience, in particular her inability to grasp the significance of her pregnancy (3.23–6, esp. 25 *nec scit*) and the apprehension she felt when she recounted her disturbing dream (3.27–38), receives special focus. The book's interest in female subjects can also be detected later when Ovid traces the post-Romulean history of the calendar. While ostensibly praising Numa's reform of the ten-month

Romulean calendar (3.151–4), Ovid ends his eulogy by suggestively attributing the introduction of January and February to Numa's wife, Egeria (*Egeria sive monente sua*, 'or because his Egeria was giving him advice', 3.154).

Women play an even larger part in the episode of the Matronalia, which begins with the poet asking Mars to explain why *women* celebrate the first day of his month (3.169–70).[5] Mars' reply (3.179–228) culminates in the story that the new Roman wives (formerly Sabine women) – led by Romulus' wife, Hersilia – successfully stopped the war between their fathers and husbands by putting their babies between the battlelines; and that this peace-making intervention was the reason behind the celebration of the March Kalends by women, especially mothers. Mars' own description of the Matronalia thus serves as an annual reminder of women's effectiveness against his primary function as god of war.[6] But more than that, this episode acts as a counterpoint to the rape of Silvia and the conception of the twins. In their capacity as mothers, the Roman wives and Hersilia in particular conceived a plan that would secure Rome's future, while their offspring helped to bring about peace.[7] The important role played by Hersilia and the children at this crucial juncture in Rome's early history underscores the shift of creative power from an Olympian deity to mortal women.

In the coda to this episode, Mars' authoritative status is undermined further by his inability to settle on a definitive explanation for the Matronalia. In addition to the action of the Roman wives, the god suggests that the Matronalia may also have come about because he made Silvia a mother (3.233–34); or because it was fitting for mothers to celebrate fertility at a time when nature was reawakening and reproducing again (3.235–44); or because Roman women founded a temple to his own mother, Juno, on this day (3.245–8); or because Juno had an affinity with brides (3.249–52). Mars' merry-go-round of possible *causae* hints at his own lack of grip on the situation;[8] and as a result, Ovid's narrative on the traditional first day of the Roman year appears to contest the primacy of Mars, highlighting his inadequacy as the divine originator of Rome. Indeed, these images of motherhood, fertility, piety and human-divine *concordia* at the end of the Matronalia contrast sharply with and gradually displace the divine sexual violence with which Book 3's narrative began.

Furthermore, as readers encounter stories of female reproductivity, calendrical advancement, epochal progress and seasonal cycle in the course of the first half of *Fasti* 3, the variety of rhythms and modes of time multiply. On the one hand, Ovid tries to tie them all together by highlighting their connections. The thematic movement from the book's prologue to the Matronalia episode labours the point that there is harmony, rather than conflict, between Mars' patronage of the month and the festival of women on the traditional first day of the year. Mars' impregnation of Silvia marks the beginning of Rome, so the story goes; and Romulus honours his father by placing a month named after him at the start of the year, which also happens to be the time when nature reproduces, and thus the March celebration of women and female reproductivity is fitting. On the other hand, these different temporal rhythms and modes simply do not neatly align. Even Ovid himself acknowledges this in *Fasti* 1 when he asks Janus: *dic, age, frigoribus quare novus incipit annus, | qui melius per ver incipiendus erat?* ('Tell me, how come the new year begins in the cold season, when it would have been better for it to start in spring?', 1.149–50).[9] The contrived alignment of different temporal modes in *Fasti* 3 only serves to underline the difficulty of achieving total synchrony. As we shall see, Ovid's poetic exploration of the contestability of time, the alignment of calendrical and other modes of time, and the mutability of calendrical authority – all of which packed into a passage that focuses intensely on beginnings and creations – are not lost on the authors of Renaissance *fasti*, whose treatment of the Annunciation engage in a lively dialogue with the opening sequence of Book 3 of Ovid's *Fasti*.

2. The Annunciation and the Start of Christian Time

The Feast of the Annunciation was by all measures a highly significant occasion on the Christian calendar. Celebrated on 25 March, this day embodied the synchronization of natural, theological and calendrical time, and it, too, was associated with 'new beginnings'. Early Christians accepted the conventional Roman date for the spring equinox, 25 March, and used it to determine the date of Easter.[10] When the Feast of the Annunciation was first introduced (probably in the fourth or fifth century), it was held that this feast commemorated the idea that the spring equinox was both the day of God's Creation and the beginning of Christ's Redemption.[11] Already in the mid-third century, it was thought that the Incarnation also took place on this date. The Pseudo-Cyprianic *De pascha computus*, which attempted to calculate the date of Easter for 243 CE, argued that since the world was created in spring and the coming and redemption of Jesus must have coincided with the creation and fall of Adam, the conception and death of Christ thus took place shortly after the spring equinox.[12] Later, when the Anno Domini dating system was introduced in 525 CE, its inventor, the polymath monk Dionysius Exiguus, assigned the first day of the new year to 25 March on the basis that according to Catholic theology the era of grace began with the Incarnation of Christ.[13] In the Middle Ages, attempts were made to establish the Feast of the Annunciation as also the exact date of God's Creation and Christ's Crucifixion. By the time the *Legenda Aurea* was being compiled (c. 1259–66), a compendium of hagiographies that exercised an enormous influence on Christian *fasti* of the Renaissance, its author, Jacobus de Voragine, firmly assigned 25 March as not only the date of the Annunciation and God's Creation, but also the Friday of Christ's crucifixion and death.[14]

Despite its importance for Christian thought and the ecclesiastical calendar, however, the Annunciation is narrated only briefly in the Bible. The primary source for the story is the Gospel of Luke (1.26-38), while a shorter and different version, in which the Annunciation was delivered to Joseph, is told in the Gospel of Matthew (1.18-25). What this tells us is that Mary's revered status as virgin, mother and heavenly queen was developed through other means. A common motif in early literary accounts of Mary was the 'Eve–Mary antithesis', first established by Justin Martyr (c. 100–c. 165) and later expanded upon by Irenaeus of Lyon (c. 130–202). This antithesis, which was to become a central component of Marian theology,[15] secured Mary's image as a virgin (even though she was betrothed), whose obedience was the source of her own salvation as well as humanity's.[16] Mary's status as mother par excellence was also established by early Christian literature, as we find her being referred to as 'Theotokos' ('Bearer of God') from the middle of the third century, and 'Dei genetrix' or 'mater Dei' in later Latin texts. Meanwhile, the tradition of Mary's Assumption, which may have originated in as early as the late second century,[17] gave rise to her designation as 'Regina coeli' ('Queen of Heaven'). These honorific titles were reflected in prayers and liturgies of Mary: in particular a group of Marian hymns (including the eleventh-century 'Salve Regina'), known collectively as the 'Marian antiphons', became widely used in the Latin West. In addition to these representational traditions, another important source on the life of Mary was the apocryphal Gospel of Pseudo-Matthew, a Latin compilation written probably in the early or mid-seventh century.[18] The various Marian episodes in the Pseudo-Matthew, which significantly supplemented the brief accounts of Mary in the Gospels and Acts, foregrounded her chastity as a unique form of worship and religious commitment that earned her a special convenant with God;[19] and these stories strengthened Christian belief in the Church's teachings about the Immaculate Conception and the Virgin Birth.[20] The incorporation of these Marian episodes into medieval hagiographies and devotional works subsequently assured that the Pseudo-Matthew would become a foundational text for depictions of Mary and popular beliefs about her for several centuries after.[21]

Starting from the early fourteenth century, poets and artists from Italy became increasingly interested in exploring the significance of the Annunciation and the question of how to depict Mary's various virtues and identities. In Dante's *Commedia* (*c*. 1308–20), Mary was both an exemplary human woman who uttered the words 'Ecce ancilla Dei' (cf. Luke 1.38) at the moment of the Annunciation (*Purgatorio*, 10.44) and the *regina augusta* of Heaven (*Paradiso*, 33.19) – 'a paradoxical combination of humility with outstanding merit and divine election', as Botterill succinctly puts it.[22] Dante's characteristic fusion of the classical and the biblical, evident in his depiction of Mary, established a template for later poets. Battista Mantovano (or 'Mantuan'), whose *Fasti libri* (1516) will be discussed below, composed in 1488 an immensely popular Latin epic about Mary, *Parthenice Mariana*, in which the Annunciation was a major episode in its second book. The Annunciation itself then became the subject of Jacopo Sannazaro's *De partu Virginis* (1526), which displaced Mantovano's *Parthenice Mariana* as *the* Latin epic about Mary in the sixteenth century. Indeed, Sannazaro's poem may be seen as part of a broader intellectual interest in the Annunciation that intensified in the late-fifteenth and early-sixteenth centuries, as Brazeau shows that not only poets but also artists such as Sandro Botticelli and Lorenzo Lotto appeared to have incorporated elements of contemporary sermons on Mary's emotional state during the Annunciation into their artistic compositions.[23]

Set against this background, we may say that the authors of Renaissance poetic calendars were writing at a unique moment when the significance of both the Feast of the Annunciation and Mary, which had long been established in Christian theology, was receiving renewed cultural interest in Italy. The calendrical poets thus had at their disposal an increasing body of work on Mary and the Annunciation, which supplemented the meagre data of the Gospels and enriched their creative imagination. Furthermore, the temporal importance of the Annunciation for not only the ecclesiastical calendar, but also the start of the year and indeed the very notion of 'Christian time', made it an especially appealing topic for the poets of Renaissance *fasti*. As we shall see, while none of the Renaissance poetic calendars deviates substantially from the version of the story told in Luke, a number of them embellish the gospel account by asserting the 'foundational' significance of Mary and the primacy of her feast day in relation to pagan antiquity. The authors of these early modern *fasti* engage closely with Ovid's reflections on new beginnings and Roman time, as well as Christian and Renaissance discourses about the mother of Christ. In doing so,

Engendering the Christian Age 201

these Renaissance poems constitute more than just a Christianization of a classical literary form. Rather, they play an important role in reasserting the significance of the Annunciation for Christian conceptions of time and decidedly reinforce Mary's position at the very centre of the narrative of the birth of Christianity.

3. The *Fasti* of Lazzarelli, Mantovano and Fracco

(i) Ludovico Lazzarelli

Completed in the late fifteenth century, Ludovico Lazzarelli's *Fasti christianae religionis* is the earliest Renaissance calendar poem to provide an extended account of the Annunciation.[24] Lazzarelli's *fasti* consists of sixteen books: Books 1–3 treat the Church's movable feasts, Books 4–15 then narrate fixed feasts from March through to February, and the final book (entitled *Iudicium*) focuses on the Last Judgement. By setting March as the starting point of his central twelve books, Lazzarelli already gestures at the antiquarian learning of his poem.[25] The book on March (Book 4) begins with the poet declaring that, in his poem, the Christian God displaces Mars from the first position in the year (1–8):

> Annua cum referam quae sint decreta Tonanti
>   Festa, genethliacos sacrificosque dies,
> Qui datus est Marti, sit mensis in ordine primus:
>   Aetere tunc etenim nuntius ima petit,
> Prima dedit miseris mortalibus orsa salutis,   5
>   Tunc Deus intacta Virgine factus homo.
> Morte etiam Christi tunc facta redemptio nobis,
>   Anni igitur merito sit datus iste caput.

As I recount the annual feasts which were credited to God, and the natal and the sacred days, the month dedicated to Mars must come first: that is the time [of the year] when an angel travelled from heaven to earth; that is when God, made man through the chaste Virgin, gave wretched mortals the beginning of their salvation; that is when we were redeemed through Christ's death. Therefore, this [month] is rightfully treated as the start of the year.

We can see here straightaway that Lazzarelli is working with both pre-Christian and Christian ideas about the primacy of March. The poet acknowledges the ancient etymology of what was once the first month on the Roman year (cf. *datus est Marti … mensis*, 3), but then immediately justifies the month's first position in his festal poem by citing early Christian doctrines on the Annunciation as the beginning of Christ's Redemption of mankind (cf. *orsa salutis*, 5; *etiam . . . tunc facta redemptio*, 7).

The importance of the Annunciation is then fully brought out in Lazzarelli's presentation of the event, which constitutes the longest episode of the book on March (745–992). The poet begins by retelling the gospel account (745–874), but then digresses with the Genesis story of Adam and Eve and the doctrine of the fall of man (875–938; cf. Gen. 3.1-24). This digression, which draws on the early Christian 'Eve–Mary antithesis' to contrast Eve's sinfulness with Mary's purity, marks the conception of Christ as the day when the fortune of man is reversed (cf. *Qua luce eiecti fuimus, revocamur eadem,* | *Omnibus o salve, concelebranda dies!*, 'On that day we were ejected: on that same day we are called back, o hail, day that is celebrated by all', 939–40). At this point, Lazzarelli resumes the gospel story with an extended speech by Mary (951–72), in which she emphasizes not only her chastity, but also her willingness to bear God's son: *Facta parens et sponsa Dei . . .* | *Votivum dederam virgo pudoris opus . . .* | *Virgo in ventre tuli, peperi quoque virgo Tonantem,* | *Virgineus semper me redimivit honor* ('I was made both mother and bride of God . . . as a virgin I had made a vow of chastity . . . as a virgin I bore God in my womb and as a virgin I gave birth to Him; the honour of being a virgin has always surrounded me,' 967–72). Lazzarelli's account of the Annunciation up to this point can almost be seen as an outline of the representational history of Mary, as the poet weaves together the gospel story with Mary's image as the anti-Eve mother of Christ in early Christian texts and the Pseudo-Matthew's depiction of her exceptional chastity.

However, what makes Lazzarelli's Mary particular interesting is the final part of her speech, where she explicitly asks poets to praise *her* instead of the women of classical antiquity (975–82):

> Vos nunc ergo omnes, lectissima turba, poetae,
>   Cantibus Aonias qui celebratis aquas,
> Desinite antiquas mentiri carmine nymphas,
>   Huc pia Castaliae vertite plectra lyrae.
> Priscarum ficta pro maiestate dearum,
>   Haec resonet veri numinis una Dea.
> Carmine digna Dea est, mecum cantate poetae,
>   Dicite concordes: carmine digna Dea est.
>
> Now, therefore, all you poets – the choicest crowd – you who frequent the Aonian waters with songs: cease to lie about ancient women in your song. Turn the pious plectrums of the Castalian lyre to here instead of the fictitious greatness of

ancient goddesses. Let this goddess of true divinity alone resound. 'She is a goddess worthy of song,' sing with me, poets, and say in harmony: 'She is a goddess worthy of song.'

Here Mary designates herself as a divine female authority worthy of poetic fame, which contrasts sharply with her brief and humble self-portrayal as the *ancilla Dei* at the end of Luke 1.26-38.[26] Moreover, by setting herself apart from the classical past and claiming that her virtues should enable her to displace the suspect pre-eminence of ancient women and pagan deities, Mary draws attention to her importance as the woman who engendered a new and better Christian age.

The implied contrast between the mother of Christ and the women of antiquity at the end of Lazzarelli's book on March also facilitates a comparison between Mary and Silvia. Unlike the mother of Romulus, who lost her virginity through Mars' rape and carried the sons of an Olympian god without truly knowing that one of them would become the founder of Rome, Mary kept her virginity and willingly conceived God's son, the founder of Christianity. Whereas Ovid's Silvia was deeply ambivalent about what she saw in her dream, Mary's speech here shows that she is well aware of what is asked of her and the significance of her pregnancy. Indeed, Lazzarelli's calendrical poem lends Mary an authoritative voice and a clear sense of her own historical importance which her character ostensibly lacked in the gospel account of the Annunciation. In doing so, Lazzarelli's *fasti* makes Mary the focus of the story of the conception of Christ, underscoring her significance at the start of Christianity and the Church's year.

(ii) Battista Mantovano

Both the displacement of pagan antiquity and the elevation of Mary's status at the point of the Annunciation find further expressions in the *Fasti libri* of Battista Mantovano (1516). Mantovano's interest in Marian narratives, already attested by his earlier composition of the *Parthenice Mariana*, stems from his close affiliation with the Carmelite order, which counts Mary as its patroness.[27] In his hexameter calendrical poem, the poet offers essentially a condensed version of the Annunciation narrative from his Marian epic; but on this occasion he frames the story explicitly as the moment when pagan gods began to be expelled by Christianity (fol. h i v–h ij r):[28]

> cum Deus extremi vellet primordia secli
> texere, progeniem divinae mentis alumnam
> misit, et humanae vestivit imagine formae.

> propterea missus summo legatus olympo
> coelica qui matri ferret mandata futurae.
> haec foetura recens Coelo mirabilis, Orco
> terribilis, quia diis priscis fatale ferebat
> exilium, traxit Phoebo primordia ab isto.

> When God wished to create the beginning of the last age, He sent an offspring nursed by His divine mind and clothed [him] in the image of human form. For that cause, a messenger was sent from the lofty sky, who carried the celestial order to a mother-to-be. This new offspring – wonderful for Heaven, terrible for Hell, since it was bringing a fatal exile for the ancient gods – drew forth the beginning from that day.

This notion that pagan divinities are set to be banished from the forthcoming Christian age is developed further in the episode's next movement. Mantovano imaginatively depicts Mercury spotting and following the angel Gabriel as he made his way to Mary, listening in on their conversation, and detecting its relevance for pagan gods even though he could not catch every word (fol. h ij r).[29] The presentation of the exchange between Gabriel and Mary from the perspective of the pagan messenger-god, who is not privy to divine revelations as he watches another messenger deliver God's plan, pointedly emphasizes that Mercury no longer holds his primary role as heaven's emissary. This, in turn, hints at the idea that the pagan gods on the whole are about to lose their function. Furthermore, by explicitly showing that the task of narrating divine knowledge no longer belongs to the pagan authority of reporting but to a Christian messenger, the shift from Mercury to Gabriel mirrors the shift from Ovid as the reporter of pagan *causae* and *sacra* to Mantovano as the new reporter of Christian religion.

In the next scene, Mantovano expands on the displacement of pagan authorities by depicting an assembly of the Olympian gods who, upon hearing the news from Mercury, agitated at their impending overthrow (fol. h ij r):

> tum se proripiens Romam prope Leuctra deorum
> repperit in gentem cuneum, quibus omnia fatus.
> illi autem magno inter se trepidare tumultu
> incepere, Venus flevit, Saturnia Iuno
> flevit, et abiecta Pallas contabuit hasta.

> Then hurrying on to Rome, [passing] near Leuctra,[30] he found a large assembly of the gods, to whom he confessed everything. However, they began to agitate among themselves with a great tumult: Venus wept, Saturnian Juno wept, and Pallas pined away by her cast-aside spear.

More than merely demonstrating his familiarity with a key classical literary trope, Mantovano's inventive portrayal of the Olympian gods lamenting at their demise draws attention to the fact that the 'divine council' motif is used predominantly in ancient epics to underline the enormous influence of the gods on human affairs. As the symbolic image of divine power and ancient religion itself, the 'divine council' encapsulates the attempt made by classical literature to inquire into the workings of the world.[31] Seen against this background, Mantovano's depiction of the powerlessness of the Olympians, reinforced by the lament of the three goddesses and the notable absence of Jupiter, not only foregrounds their displacement by Mary and the Christian God but also hints at the obsolescence of classical texts as the source of religious knowledge. In doing so, Mantovano implicitly asserts his own text – a hexameter poem about the Church's calendar, saints and rites – as a new literary authority on religion.

In the next part of the episode, Mantovano makes a case for seeing the Feast of the Annunciation as the rightful beginning of the year; and through this exposition the poet further underlines the superiority of the Christian calendar. The passage opens with an image of the convergence of seasonal time and religious time on 25 March: this day, Mantovano says, marks the spring equinox with the first rising of Aries (*princeps signorum Aries ... primo surgebat ab ortu*, fol. h ij v); it is a time when nature reawakens and new lives begin (*exonerata gelu tellus gaudebat, et omnes | floribus et tenero vernabant gramine campi*, fol. h ij v). The poetic emphasis on the day's synchronicity with various 'beginnings' and 'firsts' in the natural world (cf. *princeps ... primo*) then goes to substantiate Mantovano's claim that the Annunciation is in fact the starting point of Christian time: *haec igitur praeclara dies ... aetati fecit primordia sanctae* ('thus this famous day made the beginning of the sacred age', fol. h ij v). By highlighting this felicitous temporal synchrony, this passage presents the Christian calendar as a supreme time-measuring instrument, which in turn draws attention to one of the major problems with the Roman calendar: namely, the start of the year and spring do not align. As I mentioned above, the question of why the Roman year began in the dead of winter is asked by Ovid himself in his address to Janus in *Fasti* 1 (1.149–50). When Mars spoke in Book 3, the god's account of Rome's foundation myth and his description of spring (3.234–42) only reinforced the impression that the Roman year ought to, and once did indeed, start on the March Kalends. Seen against this background, Mantovano's exposition of the timing of the Annunciation, where seasonal, calendrical and religious-epochal time all harmonize, works to underline the supremacy of Christian *scientia*.

Like Lazzarelli, Mantovano's account of the Annunciation culminates by focusing on Mary. Whereas in Lazzarelli's poem Mary seeks to secure her poetic fame among Christian poets, here the mother of Christ becomes the subject of Mantovano's hymnic appeal (fol. h iij r):

> sancta parens cui luce Deus communicat ista
> splendorem regnumque suum, cui subiicit orbem
> terrarum mundique polos, dignare tuorum
> exaudire preces et nostra piacula solve.

> Holy mother, to whom God on that day imparts His splendour and kingdom, to whom He has subjugated the earth and the poles of the world: deign to hear out your people's prayers and expiate our sins.

While Mantovano does not assimilate Mary to a *dea* as Lazzarelli does, her prominent status in the present poem is still noteworthy. Quite remarkably, Mary is here imagined as having a stake in God's kingdom (cf. *cui luce Deus communicat ista | … regnumque suum*); and her image as both the celestial queen and expiator of human sins (cf. *nostra piacula solve*) – alluding to her hymnic titles 'Regina Coeli' and 'Mater misericordiae', respectively – underscores her significance to Christian beliefs in the afterlife and the Redemption. Mantovano's appellation of Mary as *sancta parens*, moreover, recalls the opening of the first hymn in the Gradual for the feast of the Nativity of Mary (*Salve sancta parens enixa puerpera regem qui caelum terramque regit in saecula saeculorum*, 'Hail, Holy Mother, who in childbirth brought forth the King who rules heaven and earth, world without end'). By incorporating a liturgical hymn into his poetic calendar in this way, Mantovano on the one hand accentuates the religiosity of his poetic account of the Annunciation, while on the other hand highlighting the idea that his *fasti* is not just another versified calendar, but a literary counterpart to the Church's rituals.

(iii) Ambrogio 'Novidio' Fracco

Composed in elegiac couplets, the *Sacri fasti* (Rome, 1547) of Ambrogio 'Novidio' Fracco, as John Miller accurately observes, 'exudes Ovidian spirit on every page'.[32] Fracco's close imitation of and constant dialogue with Ovid's *Fasti* can be seen clearly in the opening of Book 3. The poet begins by telling the Virgin Mary that he intends to dedicate this month to her and Christ instead of Mars (*hoc quia tu natum conceptum mense tulit, | utque huius sic hunc credimus esse tuum*, 'since in this month you conceived your son, thus we believe this month to be yours as much as his', 24b);³³ and in reply, the Blessed Virgin assures Fracco of his poetic direction and inspires him to sing (24b):

> vix ea finieram pia quum regina deorum
>   protinus ad vatem rettulit ora suum.
> parteque qua roseum vertit pulcherrima vultum:
>   purpureum niveo venit ab ore iubar.
> atque suum gremio natum complexa serenum
>   cum foret ex alto talia visa loqui.
> 'quod prius ad proprium mensem vocor, accipe, vates,
>   et tibi tu causas temporis ede mei.'
> dixerat et nati pectus mihi contigit hasta,
>   visus eram causas et mihi posse loqui.
> ergo suo funem solvat de littore puppis:
>   quaque vocat ventus, vela secunda ferat.

> I had scarcely finished saying these things, when the queen of heaven immediately lifted her face to her poet; and turning the most beautiful part of her rosy face to him, a brilliant light shone from her snowy-white face. And when she appeared holding her serene Child on her lap, she seemed to speak these words from above: 'Since I was earlier called upon to my own month, undertake [this task], poet, and bring forth for yourself the causes of my time.' She had spoken and touched my chest with her son's spear, and I seemed to be able to speak of the causes for myself. Therefore, let my boat loosen its rope from the shore: wherever the wind calls, let it bring favourable sails.

Fracco's depiction of Mary clearly recalls the Ovidian Venus in the opening of *Fasti* 4. There, the goddess of love turned to the Roman poet as he sought for her inspiration (*ad vatem voltus rettulit illa suos*, Ov. *F.* 4.2); a brightness then accompanied her appearance (*aether | protinus ex illa parte serenus erat*, 4.5–6); and when Venus touched the poet's temple with her myrtle (4.15–16), Ovid suddenly found his voice and set sail on his poetic ship (4.17–18).³⁴ The close correspondence between Mary and Venus shines a light on both the religious outlook and literary ambition of the Renaissance poem. The Venus of *Fasti* 4 is not merely associated with erotic love and elegiac poetry, but is also the goddess of creation. In his lengthy praise of Venus following the *invocatio*, Ovid presents the goddess as the divine mother of the *gens Iulia* (4.21–60, esp. 57–60) and the nourishing force behind nature's fertility (4.87–94), even claiming at one point that 'she created all the gods' (*illa deos omnes ... creavit*, 4.95). By incorporating these aspects of the Ovidian Venus into his depiction of Mary as a supreme goddess and mother (cf. *pia ... regina deorum*; *suum gremio natum complexa serenum*), Fracco firstly highlights that pagan models of femininity and fertility have been surpassed by the Christian ideal of love and motherhood. Secondly, the dramatic entry of Mary as a poetic initiator and temporal authority (cf. *causas temporis ede mei*) in Book 3 of Fracco's poem draws attention to the way that Ovid's *Fasti* 3 gravitates towards female intervention. As discussed above, Ovid's book of March gradually shifts power away from Mars onto female figures who are better suited to the month's primary festival, the Matronalia, which celebrates women's creative power and motherhood. Fracco's appeal to Mary at the corresponding point of his *Sacri fasti* thus reflects the extent to which his poem is attuned to the poetic programme of Ovid's *Fasti* 3, as the Renaissance poet caps the Ovidian displacement of Mars and makes Mary, 'the quintessential maternal figure of Christianity',[35] the focal point and inspiration of his book on March.

Fracco's dialogue with Ovid's *Fasti* 3 becomes both more combative and more explicit as the book goes on. Following the invocation to Mary, Fracco presents a long narrative in which Mars is pitted against Christ. The Roman god, we are told, learns of a plan by Christ to destroy the pagan gods and to appropriate March for his mother (24b); Mars then begins to plan a war against Christ by riling up a crowd in Jerusalem, which ends with the Crucifixion (24b–25a); but Christ returns from the dead and proclaims victory (25a). At this point, Fracco offers a vivid portrait of Christ bearing spear, aegis and shield (cf. *cornibus hasta tribus, nonisque ex orbibus aegis, | factaque de spinis aurea cassis erat*, 'he had a tripled-headed spear, and an aegis from the nine realms, and a golden helmet made from thorns', 25a). Then, Fracco reworks Ovid's request for Mars to disarm (cf. Ov. *F.* 3.1–10) by staging a lively exchange between Christ and the Roman god, during which Christ appropriates the name 'Mars' (on account of the victorious 'war' he waged against death and sin),[36] and then tells the Roman god to drop his weapons: *tu tua tela iace, | pone hastam et clypeum* ('you discard your weapon; put down the spear and shield', 25b). This narrative of Mars' submission to Christ is, first and foremost, symbolic of the Renaissance poem's attempt to Christianize and outdo Ovid's *Fasti*. But more than that, by contrasting Mars' eagerness for war with Christ's bloodless victory, and by showing Christ bearing Mars' customary weapons and replacing the Roman god in the process, Fracco underlines the triumph of Christianity over paganism, of faith over force. In doing so, Fracco's book on March deposes Mars from the throne of his own time and looks ahead to Rome's rebirth under Christianity.

Just as Christ wields authority over Mars, Fracco's Mary eclipses the women celebrated by Ovid in the story of the Matronalia. While Hersilia, Silvia, and Juno can each be associated with the Matronalia in Ovid's poem (cf. Ov. *F.* 3.229–58), in the *Sacri fasti* Fracco puts forward Mary as the only and ultimate honouree in his book: *femineas Martis nam quas dixere calendas: | accepit meritis sanctius illa suis* ('for they said that the Kalends of March was a festival of women; she has received this honour by her merits more inviolably', 26a). The Renaissance poet goes on to suggest that, as the embodiment of peace and motherhood, Mary is the sum total of Hersilia and Silvia/Ilia: *pace nurus Martis iuvit, fuit Ilia mater: | haec nos pace iuvat, haec ea mater erat* ('the daughter-in-law of Mars delighted in peace, and Ilia was a mother; Mary too aids us with peace, Mary too was a mother', 26a). In a final act of literary and theological one-upmanship, Fracco then asks women to turn to Mary in the way that ancient women worshipped Juno Lucina on 1 March (*ite, nurus, igitur meliori numine fretae: | Iuno ante, Esquiliis haec modo vestra manet*, 'Go, then, women, relying on a better divinity: Juno previously, now your Mary resides on the Esquiline,' 26a; cf. Ov. *F.* 3.253–6).[37]

In his retelling of the Annunciation (32b–34a) later in Book 3, Fracco expands the range of his intertextual activity to establish a dialogue with the poetry of Virgil and biblical narrative, as well as with Ovid's *Fasti*. Fracco's engagement with Virgil can be felt most strongly in Mary's reaction to Gabriel's prophecy, where the Virgin says: *nota mihi: magni veniet patris incrementum* ('these things are known to me: a progeny of Our Mighty Father will come', 33b). The words here clearly allude to Virgil's praise of the miraculous child in the 'Messianic' Fourth *Eclogue* (cf. *cara deum suboles, magnum Iovis incrementum*, 'dear offspring of the gods, a great progeny of Jupiter', Verg. *Ecl.* 4.49), who is imagined by Virgil as the initiator of a new Golden Age. A few lines later, Fracco combines allusions to the Gospel of Luke and Virgil's *Aeneid* as the poet describes a prodigious light radiating around Mary: *'fiat' ait; subito quum circum lumine fusa est: | perque comam flammae virginis arsit apex* ('"Let it be," she said; when suddenly a light poured around her and the tip of its glow blazed through the Virgin's hair,' 33b). The verb *fiat* evokes the Latin text of Mary's response to Gabriel (cf. *fiat mihi secundum verbum tuum*, Luke 1.38), while the description of the light recalls the omens that appeared above Iulus' head at the end of *Aeneid* 2, omens which Anchises took to mean divine favour and bright future for the Trojans (cf. *ecce levis summo de vertice visus Iuli | fundere lumen apex, tactuque innoxia mollis | lambere flamma comas et circum tempora pasci*, 'see a gentle light seemed to shine from the crown of Iulus' head, and a soft flame, harmless in its touch, licked his hair and grazed around his temples', Verg. *Aen.* 2.682–4). In the final part of Fracco's version of the Annunciation, Mary recounts a dream she had after being impregnated by the Holy Spirit; here, both the trope of the dream narrative and the specific imagery are redolent of Silvia's dream about the fate of her twins at the beginning of Ovid's *Fasti* 3:

> 'vitis erat,' dixit, 'seges illi iuncta: sed amni
>   proxima: quae multas pinguis alebat aves.
> indeque erant visae bis senae astare columbae:
>   quae segeti, et viti, limitis instar erant.
> pampinus attigerat producto palmite coelum:
>   sidera texebat gramine summa seges.
> ecce ferox miles ferrum properabat in illas

Fracco, 33b

> She said: 'There was a vine – next to a field, yet close to a stream – that nourished many birds abundantly. Then, twelve doves appeared to stand, on the field and on the vine in equal number. A vine-tendril with an extending branch had touched the sky; the field weaved together stars with its top grass. But look! A fierce soldier was making for the knife towards them.

> inde duae pariter, visu mirabile, palmae
>   surgunt; ex illis altera maior erat
> et gravibus ramis totum protexerat orbem
>   contigeratque sua sidera summa coma.
> ecce meus ferrum patruus molitur in illas.

Ov. *F.* 3.31–5

> From it, a strange sight, two palm trees sprang at once: one of the trees was taller than the other and covered all the world with its heavy branches, touching the topmost stars with its crown. But look! My uncle is wielding an axe against the trees.

These episodes from *Eclogue* 4, *Aeneid* 2 and *Fasti* 3 are all to do with the inauguration of a new age; indeed, in each instance the sense of a new beginning is tied up with the momentous emergence of a divinely favoured child (the anticipated *puer* in *Eclogue* 4, Ascanius/Iulus in *Aeneid* 2, and foetal Romulus in *Fasti* 3). Fracco's multiplying allusions to these natal moments allow him to position his poem as a learned successor to the classical literary tradition on epochal change. The resulting polyphony underscores the *Sacri fasti*'s ability to synthesize different ideas about the birth of a new age and put them in service of a new Christian master-narrative. The synthesis of multiple myths, figures and inaugural moments into one story about the birth of God's son mirrors the historical shift from polytheism and competing pagan narratives of divine fate to

Christian monotheism and theological oneness. In this way, Fracco's account of the Annunciation reinscribes into the calendar Christianity's simultaneous incorporation of and dominance over its pagan antecedents.

4. Annunciation, Reformation and the Poetic Calendar

The representation of Mary as the *genetrix* of Christianity in these Renaissance poetic calendars, and their forceful assertion of the Annunciation as the beginning of Christian greatness, appeared during a time when the Church of Rome – and Mary's cult in particular – came under the scrutiny of reformers from both within and outside the Church. Even before the spread of Protestantism, Catholic reformers in the early sixteenth century had demanded that the Church embark on a spiritual revival and a renewal of its discipline.[38] While Mary's theological status as the mother of God was not a matter of dispute, the Church's glorification of the Virgin and the kind of devotion she received became new points of contention in addition to long unresolved disputes concerning Mary's Assumption and Immaculate Conception. Following Martin Luther's publication of his *Ninety-Five Theses* in 1517, the scrutiny directed towards Marian cult intensified. Luther's denial of papal authority led to the Protestant reliance on the Scriptures alone; and on this basis Mary's significance was no more than the instrument of the Incarnation.[39] Later, Erasmus attacked the excessive invocation of Mary, arguing that her increased prominence would not only lead to idolatry, but even undermine the centrality of Christ in Christian theology and devotional practice.[40] In response to the spread of Protestantism, the Church convoked the Council of Trent (1543–65); and over the course of twenty years the Council passed a number of decrees that directly or indirectly reasserted Mary's rightful place in Christian theology and legitimized the devotion paid to her cult.[41] By the end of the Council of Trent, Mary, in the words of Susan Haskins, had become 'the unassailable focus of new piety, triumph, and exaltation' in the Church's fightback against Protestantism.[42]

Since Mary's status was at this time a key battleground for the Roman Church and the Protestant reformers, and knowing that the Counter-Reformation Church would later reassert its authority through a robust defence of Marian devotion, we are now well placed to elucidate the political implications of the treatment of Mary and the Annunciation episode in Renaissance poetic calendars. By highlighting the significance of Mary for the beginning of Christianity, these poems explicitly underline the theological importance of the mother of Christ at a time when her status is being contested. Less explicitly, but no less acutely, these poems also make the point that, if Mary's status were to diminish or be challenged, the Christian world would revert back to a less enlightened age. As I have shown above, the authors of these poetic calendars repeatedly sought to establish the Annunciation as the moment that Christianity displaced paganism, and they drove this point home in two ways. First, the poets developed parallels between Mary and *genetrix*-figures in Ovid's poem (such as Silvia, Juno and Venus) in order to emphasize Mary's role as the new exemplary figure of maternal creation. Second, the poets engaged in competitive dialogues with the part of Ovid's *Fasti* where the poem was most concerned with new beginnings. By asserting – via combative exchanges with Ovid – the significance of Mary at the inception of Christianity, the Renaissance poets firmly embed the mother of Christ into the foundation of the Christian world, making her an indispensable part of cultural and religious progress. Therefore, far more than simply adding their voices to the Church's glorification of Mary, these calendrical poets' treatments of the Annunciation synthesize the figure of Mary with the notion of Christian progress, and in doing so frame any attempt to diminish Mary's status as culturally and religiously regressive.

To take this argument a step further, if these poems' depiction of Mary and the Annunciation were an attempt to intervene in the contemporary theological debate surrounding Mary's status, then the genre of the Christian *fasti* must amount to more than a reworking of a classical literary form. I would suggest that calendrical poetry was at this point increasingly weaponized by Italian humanists against the Protestant Reformation, and that the genre was taking on a politically combative role. Just as Ovid in the *Fasti* marshals his aetiological and antiquarian knowledge to comment on the transformation of Roman religion under Augustus,[43] the Christian *fasti* presses theological learning and classical erudition into political service at a moment when both the Church's authority and classicizing humanism were being challenged. Indeed, the Protestant rejection of the intercession of saints and the proliferation of vernacular translations of the Bible meant that both the Church's calendar of saints and the Christian language, Latin, were under threat from the Reformation. The composition of a Christian calendrical poem *in Latin* was therefore no mere imitation, but an ideologically charged cultural activity. Seen from this perspective, the weaponization of the figure of Mary and of the Feast of the Annunciation in calendrical poetry may be said to have prefigured how Mary would soon become the focal point of the Counter-Reformation Church's reassertion of its doctrines and practices.

Notes

* I would like to thank Ingrid De Smet and Bryan Brazeau for commenting on an earlier version of this paper. All translations of Latin are my own.
1 For an overview of the genre, see Miller (2003).
2 In Christian Europe, the starting point of the year varied at different times and depended greatly on location. The most commonly used dates were 25 March and 25 December. The practice of beginning the year on 1 January became common from the mid-sixteenth century and was reinforced by the Gregorian calendar reform of 1582, which effectively established 1 January as New Year's Day henceforth. In England and Ireland, the Feast of the Annunciation, which came to be known as Lady Day, marked the first day of the year until 1752. See further Steel (2000: 137–42) and Holford-Strevens (2005: 127–8).
3 Heyworth (2019: 21). On the generic implications of this opening couplet, see esp. Hinds (1992a) and Hinds (1992b).
4 Heyworth (2019: 22–3) notes well that in *Fasti* 3 Ovid finds far more to celebrate in other deities.
5 On the March Kalends, see esp. Hinds (1992a: 87–112) and Hinds (1992b: 117–31). Dolansky (2011) argues that the Matronalia was not so much a women's festival, but one focused on the *domus*.
6 Chiu (2016: 97).
7 See also Heyworth (2019) on 3.207–12.
8 Chiu (2016: 97).
9 See further Feeney (2007: 204).
10 The Roman dates for the equinoxes and solstices became on the Christian calendar the Annunciation (25 March), the Nativity of St John the Baptist (24 June), the Conception of St John the Baptist (24 September) and the Nativity of Jesus Christ (25 December). See further Steel (2000: 71) and Holford-Strevens (2005: 33, 84).
11 Steel (2000: 109, 138) and Holford-Strevens (2005: 63).
12 On the *De pascha computus*, see Ciccolini (2020). See Goldhill (2022) on the extent to which late antique literature was preoccupied with new Christian conceptualizations of time.
13 Steel (2000: 238).
14 On the influence of the *Legenda Aurea* on Christian *fasti*, see Soldati (1903: 414–15) and Trümpy (1979: 9–10).
15 See further Graef (1963: I.39–40).
16 Irenaeus, *Against the Heresies*, 3.22.4; with further discussion by Haskins (2008: 11).
17 Shoemaker (2016: 24–5).
18 Ehrman and Pleše (2011: 75).
19 Ibid. (2011: 76).

20 Haskins (2008: 27).
21 Ibid. and Ehrman and Pleše (2011: 76).
22 Botterill (1994: 152, detailed discussion on 153–60).
23 See Brazeau (2014: 234–6) on the influence of the sermons of Fra Roberto Caracciolo da Lecce on Botticelli's *Annunciazione di Cestello* (1489-90), Lotto's *Annunciazione di Recanati* (1534–5) and Sannazaro's *De partu Virginis*.
24 Lazzarelli began work on the poem in 1469 or shortly after; the *terminus post quem* for its publication is 1484. Four versions of the text exist: an autograph manuscript showing signs of multiple revision and in an unfinished state (*Vat. lat.* 2853); a copy dedicated to Ferdinand of Aragon and his son Alfonso (Beinecke MS 391); and two copies dedicated to Charles VIII (Septempedanus 207 and 3). Lazzarelli's text has been edited by Bertolini (1991), which I quote here. Key scholarship on the poem includes: Fritsen (2000), Fritsen (2015: 165–70), Corfiati (2003) and Miller (2003: 178–84).
25 See also Miller (2003: 179).
26 Luke 1.38: *dixit autem Maria ecce ancilla Domini fiat mihi secundum verbum tuum* ('"I am the Lord's servant," Mary answered. "May your word to me be fulfilled." Then the angel left her.') All references to Luke in Latin refer to the Vulgate; English translations are taken from the New International Version.
27 On Mantovano's Carmelite affiliation, see Saggi (1954).
28 The text is taken from the 1518 edition of the poem printed in Strasbourg. In the absence of numerical pagination, I use the folio signature instead. The first letter of a new verse is uncapitalized for ease of reading; punctuation is modernized.
29 *Mercurius qui tunc casu veniebat ab Orco | vidit ut ex summo Carmeli vertice sanctum | Gabriel allabi versus florentia rura | Nazaret, insidias metuens post illius ivit | Virginis ad thalamos celeri vestigia gressu, | limineque in primo residens audivit eorum | colloquium. nec cuncta tamen verba auribus hausit, | sed quia versutus, quiddam deprehendit in illis | arcani quod se, divos quod tangeret omnes.* ('Mercury, who by chance at that time was coming from the underworld, saw holy Gabriel gliding from the highest summit of Mount Carmel and turning to the blossoming fields of Nazareth. Fearing his designs, he went after the tracks of his swift course to the chamber of the Virgin. At first sitting on the threshold, he heard their conversation, but did not drink up every word with his ears. However, since he was clever, he apprehended a certain secrecy between them that mattered to him and all the [pagan] deities.)
30 The mention of Leuctra appears to reflect the fact that a direct flight from Nazareth to Rome passes over Leuctra.
31 For an overview of divine council scenes in Greek and Roman epics, see Reitz (2019: 719–46).

32 Miller (2003: 176). The poet's chosen nickname for himself, Novidio (= *Novus Ovidius*), points to his literary aspiration.
33 Text and pagination come from the 1547 edition printed in Rome; punctuation modernized.
34 There are further verbal parallels: *Alma fave dixi* (Fracco, 24a) and *'Alma, fave', dixi* (Ov. F. 4.1); *scis dea* (Fracco, 24b) and *'scis, dea'* (Ov. F. 4.5).
35 Miller (2003: 178).
36 Note especially (25a): *Mars mihi sit nomen: sum belliger. hasta cruore | aspice, victori quam madet ista mihi.* ('Let Mars be my name: I am the wager of war. Look at the bloodied spear: how it drips for me, the victor'.)
37 For further discussion of Fracco's reworking of Ov. F. 3.243–5, see Miller (2003: 178). The mention of the Esquiline is undoubtedly an allusion to the Basilica di Santa Maria Maggiore.
38 Haskins (2008: 33–4).
39 Ibid. (34); see further discussion by Graef (1963: II.6–12) on Luther's views on Mary.
40 *Pilgrimages of Pure Devotion* (1536, anonymous Tudor translation); see further Haskins (2008: 34) and Graef (1963: II. 2–6).
41 As outlined by Haskins (2008: 35), these include: (a) a decree passed in the fourth session (8 April 1546) that asserted the equal validity of the Scriptures as well as the unwritten tradition, thus implicitly granting canonical authority to traditional beliefs that had informed the figure of Mary; (b) a second decree passed in the fifth session (17 June 1546) that exempted Mary from original sin; (c) a third decree passed in the twenty-fifth session (3–4 December 1563) that defended the efficacy of invoking saints.
42 Haskins (2008: 35).
43 Barchiesi (1997: esp. 159–64); see also Wallace-Hadrill (1987: 228–9) and Newlands (1995: 12, 68–9).

12

Respice finem

Fast-Forwarding to the End of Time in Lucretius, Virgil, Ovid, Milton and Early Eighteenth-Century Poems on the Last Judgement

Philip Hardie
University of Cambridge

1.

One of the many ways in which Milton's *Paradise Lost* overgoes its classical model the *Aeneid* is in the reach of its temporal scope.[1] The *Aeneid* begins with a local storm in the Mediterranean that allusively suggests a return to the Chaos out of which the ordered cosmos was formed. Its proleptic ending, on the Shield of Aeneas, is an image of a perfected Roman cosmos, in which disturbance in the human and natural worlds has been brought to an end with the *pax Augusta*, an 'end of history', sealed by the triple triumph of Octavian in 29 BCE. Virgil plays games with time to reinforce the sense of finality. In 29, Octavian was not yet 'Augustus', although he is anachronistically called by that name in the preceding scene of the Battle of Actium (*Aen.* 8.678). He watches the nations parading before him from the threshold of the Palatine Temple of Apollo, a temple that was not dedicated until the year following the triple triumph. Apollo is the god of the sun, and Octavian/Augustus is seated beneath a pedimental group of Apollo as the sun-god in his four-horse chariot (*quadriga*). Implied is the claim that Augustus is a sun-king whose gaze, like that of the Sun, extends in *space* over the whole world; but the rapidly moving *quadriga* is also a reminder of the never-ending motion of the sun as it measures *time*. The effects of time's motion on Virgil's attempt to write an end to history are registered at the end of the Parade of Heroes, set in a 'timeless' Underworld, in *Aeneid* 6, where all history is somehow present for a single synoptic view, but where Aeneas learns that the younger Marcellus will be dead 'before his time', in 23 BCE.

The narrative of *Paradise Lost* begins at a point even before the creation of our world out of chaos, the point in the 'eternal empire' (*PL* 7.96) of God in which the rebel angels have been defeated and hurled down to the burning lake. The proleptic survey of future history in the last two books, corresponding to the Virgilian Parade of Heroes and Shield of Aeneas, takes Adam and the reader down to the actual end of history, the Last Judgement. In one unbroken sentence, Michael's words trace the continuing course of history down to the fulfilment of the promise made just now to Eve in the 'protevangelium' at the beginning of human history,² in the second coming of Christ and the 'dissolution' of Satan (*PL* 12.537–56):³

> So shall the world go on,
> To good malignant, to bad men benign,
> Under her own weight groaning, till the day
> Appear of respiration to the just,   540
> And vengeance to the wicked, at return
> Of him so lately promised to thy aid,
> The woman's seed, obscurely then foretold,
> Now ampler known thy saviour and thy Lord,
> Last in the clouds from heaven to be revealed   545
> In glory of the Father, to dissolve
> Satan with his perverted World, then raise
> From the conflagrant mass, purged and refined,
> New heavens, new earth, ages of endless date⁴
> Founded in righteousness and peace and love   550
> To bring forth fruits, joy and eternal bliss.
>   He ended; and thus Adam last replied.
> How soon hath thy prediction, seer blest,
> Measured this transient world, the race of time,
> Till time stand fixed: beyond is all abyss,   555
> Eternity, whose end no eye can reach.⁵

The world 'goes on' in time, macrocosmic time measured figuratively by the breathing of the human microcosm, 'groaning', 'respiration'. The span of historical time is articulated by successive manifestations of Christ – 'obscurely **then** foretold' – '**Now** ampler known' – '**Last** ... to be revealed'. The end will come with a 'return', the second coming of Christ, which will put a stop to the passage of time, and usher in a peace that is truly eternal, in contrast to the *pax Augusta*. Eternity is an 'abyss' of temporal undifferentiation, a return, with respect to time, to the undifferentiation, with respect to matter, of the abyss that preceded creation, when 'thou O Spirit … Dove-like satst brooding on the vast abyss' (*PL* 1.17–21).[6] But the language of temporality is reintroduced in Michael's final image of 'bringing forth fruits', a process of growth and ripening.

There is also a synchronism between universal time and the time of narrating. 'He ended; and thus Adam last replied': Michael ends his speech with the end of history, and this is Adam's last verbal response to Michael's preview of history, and these are also the opening words of Adam's last speech (12.553–73) in the poem as a whole.[7] 'How soon' registers the rapidity of Michael's survey of all time in less than two books, but also expresses a sense that time will indeed pass quickly, measured against measureless eternity. That sense is reinforced by 'transient' and 'race' (of time).

The juxtaposition of 'prediction, seer' corresponds, inversely, to the sequence of Books 11 and 12: in Book 11 Michael supernaturally empowers Adam's eyes with a vision of human history down to the Flood (11.368 'foresight', literally; 12.7 'Thus thou hast **seen** one world begin and end'). At that point Adam's mortal vision begins to fail, and Book 12 takes the form of a verbal 'relation' (12.11 'Henceforth what is to come I will relate'). Michael narrates the final revelation (12.545 'revealed') of Christ, but neither he nor Milton seizes the opportunity to work up verbal *enargeia* of the terrifying last day.

The *Aeneid* does not offer any direct predictions of the end of the world, and such would be a disturbing intrusion in the Augustan teleology of the poem. Virgil's silence is in contrast with Lucretius' fearless, and liberating, predictions of the end of the world, in accordance with Epicurean doctrine.[8] Aeneas does, however, allude to a Lucretian formulation in his eye-witness account of the destruction of the city of Troy: *urbs antiqua ruit multos dominata per annos* ('the ancient city, that had lorded it for many years, collapsed', *Aen.* 2.363). Compare the account of the destruction, in a single day, of the three divisions of the world, sea, earth and heavens, at *De rerum natura* 5.94–6, ending **multosque per annos** | *sustentata* **ruet** *moles et machina mundi* ('the mass and fabric of the world, which has held up for many years, will collapse'). For Aeneas, the destruction of his city, before his eyes, is equivalent to a 'world destroyed', from which will issue, eventually, a 'world restored', Rome and her empire, to use the language with which Milton punctuates Michael's pause after revealing to Adam the destruction of the world through the Flood: 'so here the angel paused | Betwixt the world destroyed and world restored' (*PL* 12.2–3).

In Ovid's *Metamorphoses*, Jupiter has also been reading these lines of Lucretius, when he refrains from using the thunderbolt to punish mankind for the sins of Lycaon, for fear that this might bring about the total conflagration of the heavens and the end of the world: 'He also remembered that a time was fated, when sea, earth and the palace of the sky would catch fire and burn up, and the world's elaborate structure would be in trouble' (Ov. *Met.* 1.256–8). Instead, Jupiter decides to destroy the race of mortals with a deluge, from which the only survivors, Noah-like, are the best and most just of men, Deucalion, and the most god-fearing of women, his wife Pyrrha: 'There was no man better than he, nor more attached to justice, and no woman more god-fearing than she' (*Met.* 1.322–3) – compare *PL* 11.874–8 (Adam speaks): 'Far less I now lament for one whole world | Of wicked sons destroyed, than I rejoice | For one man found so perfect and so just, | That God vouchsafes to raise another world | From him...'

In the last book of the *Metamorphoses*, Jupiter has full access to the records of fate, including the precise timing of fated events, when he tells Venus that the time has come for Julius Caesar to enter the heavens as a god: 'He for whom you distress yourself, Venus, has filled up his allotted time, and completed the years he owed to the earth' (15.816–17). It might be thought strange if he does not, in Book 1, know the hour of the end of the world. But perhaps Jupiter does have reason to be uncertain of the date of that final conflagration, since it almost comes about in the next book, as a result of the disastrous chariot-ride of Phaethon. In her terrified appeal to Jupiter, Mother Earth (Tellus) fears that the last day has indeed come: 'See, Atlas himself is in trouble, and hardly bears up on his shoulders the burning sky. If the sea, if the earth, if the palace of the sky are perishing, we are reduced to the confusion of the Chaos of old. If anything still survives, snatch it from the flames, and take thought for the sum of things (*rerum consule summae*)' (2.296–300). Through the reactions of the character in the text, the reader is drawn into the vivid experience of what the last day might be like. Again, the Lucretian account of the end of the world is in play. *Summa rerum* is a common phrase, used to refer to 'the interests of the state' in the historians and Cicero, and to 'the totality of the material world' in Lucretius, including a passage in which Lucretius demonstrates the possibility of the destruction of our world through a storm of atoms issuing from the infinite void, *De rerum natura* 5.368: *corruere hanc rerum uiolento turbine summam* ('to overthrow this totality of the world in a violent storm'). A few lines later in Book 5, Lucretius retells the story of Phaethon, correcting the mythological account by allegorizing it as a description of the end of the world through fire, in accordance with atomic doctrine.

In Ovid's account, Phaethon's chaotic ride in the chariot that measures the sun's daily course in the sky does not lead to the end of time, but to disruptions in the linear sequence of time.[9] This temporal disorder is in strong contrast to the ekphrastic images of cosmic order in the description of the Palace of the Sun at the beginning of *Metamorphoses* Book 2, an order both spatial (5–16, divisions of the universe) and temporal (17–18 'an image of the shining sky', with the twelve signs of the Zodiac; 25–30 'Day and Month and Year, and Centuries, and the Hours placed at equal intervals' and the four Seasons). Ovid here also comments on the stability, or instability, of the cosmic order, spatial and temporal, paraded on the Virgilian Shield of Aeneas, since the Palace of the Sun is in the image of the solar Palatine Temple of Apollo from which Augustus views the triumph in the last scene on the Shield.[10]

2.

In the rest of this paper I will look at the handling of time in the eighteenth-century fashion for poems on the Last Judgement, a taste for hyperbolical images of catastrophe and disorder which might appear at odds with that period's 'Augustan' rage for order. The poets share in a wider taste for cataclysmic upheavals of nature, also evidenced in prose treatises on the history of the earth, such as those by Thomas Burnet and John Ray. The poems draw repeatedly on Milton's great epic of sacred history, and they also look back to classical models, which are overtly signalled in epigraphs taken from Virgil, Ovid and Lucan.[11]

Like Ovid's Jupiter, the Christian reader is uncertain as to the hour of the Last Judgment, when 'the day of the Lord will come like a thief in the night',[12] but he or she can be certain that it will come, 'Sooner or later, in some future date, | (A dreadful secret in the book of fate!),' as Edward Young puts it in his *A Poem on the Last Day* (Oxford 1713), 1.69–70. The anxiety aroused by the uncertain date of the certain event[13] is exploited by Samuel Catherall, a Fellow of Oriel College, Oxford, in *An Essay on the Conflagration in Blank Verse* (Oxford 1720), p. 6: 'That last, tremendous day, when, lo! the heav'ns | Shall pass away in thunder, elements | With fervent heat dissolve, no angel knows, | No, nor the Son of Man. To God alone | Omniscient it is known, or when, or how | He has decree'd to set the world on fire. | But that he will, is fix'd and certain.' Very similar is the formulation of a more significant writer, Joseph Trapp, Church of England clergyman, whose works include a blank verse translation of Virgil, and a Latin translation of *Paradise Lost*, in his *Thoughts upon the Four Last Things: Death;*

Judgment; Heaven; Hell. A Poem in Four Parts (1734–5; third edition 1749): 'Of that great day indeed, that day, and hour | Knows no man; not ev'n he th' almighty pow'r, | The awful judge himself, as son of man; | (As God, he all things knows, and all things can:) | When it will come, in darkness is concealed; | But come it will; that clearly is revealed' (2.27–32; cf. also 2.586–91).

Uncertainty as to the hour bestows an urgency on the need to be prepared.[14] Thomas Newcomb concludes the *Preface* ('To the right honourable the Earl of March') of his *The Last Judgment of Men and Angels. A Poem in Twelve Books: After the Manner of Milton* (London 1723) by stating his aim 'to dispose the reader to make a due and early preparation to appear without dread in that great and terrible day of the Lord; before whose presence the heavens and the earth shall melt away; and before whose throne the best, and the greatest of the sons of men shall one day tremble'. In this long pastiche of Milton, Newcomb, a friend of Edward Young from their student days in Oxford, narrates at great length, and, in the last two books, through the consciousness of the resurrected Adam, the last things sketched briefly in prophecy in *Paradise Lost*.

In the urgency of the task to call the reader's mind to an awareness of the last day, the poet leaps over the intervening time – however long that may be – to make that moment present, in exercises of *enargeia*, mental visions of the end of the world and the second coming. Vision rather than verbal relation is the favoured mode, in contrast to the Miltonic Michael's narrative to Adam of the end of time in Book 12 of *Paradise Lost*. In the Preface to his *An Essay on the Conflagration*, Samuel Catherall, opining that only Milton would be equal to the task, notes

> how ... difficult must it be, when things future are to be represented, to use colours strong enough to give them real life, and make them appear present to the mind! ... I wish some great pen would undertake so vast a work, and by his lofty, and lively descriptions make us, as it were, anticipate that day, wherein the heav'ns being on fire shall be dissolved, and the elements shall melt with fervent heat.

Edward Young practises the art of the scene-painter in *A Poem on the Last Day*, recommending that if only, against the smiles of beauty or the charms of grandeur, 'The conscious soul would this great scene [of the last day] display ... Such deep impression would the picture make | No power on earth her firm resolve could shake' (1.119–24). Fortified by the certainty of the conquest of death, 'More boldly we our labours may pursue, | And all the dreadful image set to view' (133–4). When he comes to narrate the Last Judgement, Young announces, 'This mighty scene I next presume to draw' (2.153), and offers the reader a striking vision, 'Lo! the wide theatre, whose ample space | Must entertain the whole of human race' (161–2).

Tenses switch between future and present in order to jolt the reader into the immediacy of that day. Joseph Trapp projects his living voice forward into a less distant future in order to magnify the power of that voice in its impact on the unresponsive reader. His *Thoughts upon the Four Last Things* are prefaced by 'Verses written by the author, and design'd for his tomb-stone', addressed to 'You [who] stand on vast eternity's dread brink.' 'Thus, while my tomb the solemn silence breaks, | And to the eye this cold, dumb marble speaks, | Tho' dead, I preach: if e'er with ill success, | Living, I strove th' important truths to press; | Your precious, your immortal souls to save; | Hear me, at least, O! hear me, from my grave!' The absent presence in the reader's here and now of the dead author from the grave corresponds to the living author's attempt to make vividly present the last day in an uncertain future.

The last day's sudden interruption in the onwards flow of time finds expression in contrasts between the moment *then* and the preceding flow of time of which the *now* is a part. In *A Poem on the Last Day*, Edward Young is particularly energetic in his attempts to conjure up the experience of that moment, set against the long stretches of preceding time (3.91–9, 114–15):

> That hour, on which the' Almighty King on high
> From all eternity has fix'd His eye,
> Whether His right hand favour'd, or annoy'd,
> Continued, alter'd, threaten'd, or destroy'd;
> Southern or eastern sceptre downward hurl'd,
> Gave north or west dominion o'er the world;
> The point of time, for which the world was built,
> For which the blood of God Himself was spilt,
> That dreadful moment is arrived …
>
> Such is the scene; and one short moment's space
> Concludes the hopes and fears of human race.

Young screws up the intensity of the experience of that moment by projecting himself and his reader, in imagination, into the mind of the sinner who realises that this moment will seal the fate of his soul for eternity, *Last Day* 3.47–54:

> What millions wouldst thou give
> For one more trial, one day more to live!

> Flung back in time an hour, a moment's space,
> To grasp with eagerness the means of grace;
> Contend for mercy with a pious rage,
> And in that moment to redeem an age!
> Drive back the tide, suspend a storm in air,
> Arrest the sun; but still of *this* despair.

This reimagining of the predicament of Faustus at the end of Marlowe's *The Tragical History of Dr Faustus* is followed by an extensive prosopopoeia, putting words into the mouth of the guilty breast newly resurrected to face the Last Judgement. The imagined despairing speech of the condemned soul is penned by the trembling poet, who invites the reader to share his own mental vision: 'I see, I see, the Judge's frowning brow: | Say not, 'tis distant; I behold it now. | I faint, my tardy blood forgets to flow, | My soul recoils at the stupendous woe; | That woe, those pangs, which from the guilty breast, | In these, or words like these, shall be express'd' (118–23). Young concludes with the horror of the thought of the unending pain that will follow this futile plea: 'Deep anguish, but too late! The hopeless soul, | Bound to the bottom of the burning pool, | Though loath, and ever loud blaspheming, owns, | He's justly doom'd to pour eternal groans …' (208–11).

Another kind of cancellation of historical time results from the general resurrection of the dead at the last trump, leading to the simultaneous living presence of all humans who have ever lived and died in the past. In Aaron Hill's (1685–1750) *The Judgment-Day. A Poem* (*Works*, 1753), 294–5: 'Armies, unnumber'd, throng th' ætherial space, | Paternal Adam views, at once, his whole collected race …'. In Edward Young's *The Last Day* 2.167–9, 'And every age and nation pours along; | Nimrod and Bourbon mingle in the throng; | Adam salutes his youngest son; no sign | Of all those ages which their births disjoin.' At the end of history, Adam is thus able to review all of his descendants in a single survey, after their deaths and subsequent resurrection. This mirrors, and inverts, the Virgilian Aeneas' review of the unborn souls of his descendants in *Aeneid* 6, at a point before the beginning of Roman history proper. But whereas the Parade of Heroes is a parade of the fame of outstanding individuals in their future lives, a coming fame with love for which Anchises fires his son (*Aen.* 6.889 *incenditque animum famae uenientis amore*), those who have achieved fame in the course of history are now lost in the throning masses of all of humanity, indistinguishable and undistinguished, at a point in a history of the world where fame, that which preserves the memory of the great through time, no longer has any meaning. In this 'one distinct survey' of all Adam's family, Edward Young bids the 'vain-glorious Muse, and you whoe'er | Devote yourselves to Fame, and think her fair', to 'look round' (*Last day* 3.79–80); they will find that those 'Whose shining acts Time's brightest annals grace' are now (89–90) 'All lost! all undistinguish'd! nowhere found! | How will this truth in Bourbon's palace sound?' In his *The Last Judgment* Thomas Newcomb warns the rulers of the world of the loss of all distinction at the last day, with particular reference to the hall of fame that is Westminster Abbey: 'Thou, with the boastful marbles that resound | The sovereign's glory, and the hero's fame, | (Tho' Anna's relicks, and Maria's urn, | Lodg'd in thy sacred vaults) alas, must yield, | And undistinguish'd, to the common flame ...' (9. 730–4; alluding to Lucan's *communis rogus*, *Civil War* 7.814).

Edward Young comments of the vast throng of the resurrected dead, that 'not in number more | The waves that break on the resounding shore, | The leaves that tremble in the shady grove, | The lamps that gild the spangled vault above' (*Last Day* 2.181–4). Rather than directing the reader's attention to the ordered catalogue of history and fame in the Virgilian Parade of Heroes, Young rings the changes on the much-imitated similes applied by Virgil to the crowd of innumerable and unnamed shades thronging at the bank of Acheron, at the beginning of Aeneas' passage through the Underworld in *Aeneid* 6.309–12: 'Thick as the leaves in autumn strow the woods, | Or fowls, by winter forc'd, forsake the floods, | And wing their hasty flight to happier lands' (Dryden's translation). Young concludes the scene with: 'They all are here, and here they all are lost: | Their millions swell to be discern'd in vain, | Lost as a billow in th' unbounded main' (*Last Day* 2.194–6).

The contrast between the last day and the preceding length of time leads to a recurrent focus on the cyclical alternation of seasons, which will be brought to an end in that day. Compare the images of cyclical time on the Ovidian Palace of the Sun, which will be violently disrupted by Phaethon's chariot ride. In *Paradise Lost* God's covenant after the Flood (the end of 'one world', *PL* 12.6) includes the assurance that the seasons will hold their course until the world is finally destroyed by the universal conflagration: 'Day and night, | Seed-time and harvest, heat and hoary frost, | Shall hold their course; till fire purge all things new, | Both Heaven and Earth, wherein the just shall dwell' (*PL* 11.898–901). At that time, in the Last Judgement poems, the seasonal variety and vicissitude will come to an end. The round of seasons on earth is the effect of changes to the cosmic system brought about by God after the Fall, putting an end to the perpetual spring of the unfallen world (*PL* 10.649–706). But for human beings in the present world, that round of seasons is something familiar, and indeed pleasurable.

In Book 5 of Newcomb's *The Last Judgment*, Michael shows Zephon, one of those angels who does not frequently descend to earth like Michael, the features and places of the earth soon to be destroyed, and asks Zephon: 'Say, for soon | The mournful trial hastens, can your hand | Without reluctance launch the living flame | Across yon beauteous empires, which in smiles | Rejoice, and hope a thousand springs shall bloom | Yet o'er their flowry vales, which still with joy | wait for the sun's approach to crown each field | With summer's pride, and autumn's rich return | To bless the peasant's labour?' (735–42). In Book 5, Michael's host of angels arrives at earth to recall 'her watchful guardians', and hears the guardian angels' morning hymn, a rewriting of Adam's morning hymn at *Paradise Lost* 5.153–208. The angels pray for the continuation of the 'grateful vicissitude' of day and night, a likeness of which is also to be found in Milton's heaven: 'Oh still continue bounteous; nor deny | To this thy favourite world the blissful change | Of light and silent darkness; eve and morn' (*The Last Judgment* 5.170–2); 'still may yonder lamp of day | Glorious upon his axle turn, and guide | The year, the circling months, and days, and hours...' (185–7). Compare the description of dawn in heaven at the beginning of *PL* 6, where we learn of 'a cave | Within the mount of God, fast by his throne, | Where light and darkness in perpetual round | Lodge and dislodge by turns, which makes through heaven | Grateful vicissitude, like day and night' (*PL* 6.4–8).

Edward Young begins *The Last Day* with the appeal 'Man, bear thy brow aloft; view every grace | In God's great offspring, beauteous Nature's face: | See Spring's gay bloom; see golden Autumn's store; | See how Earth smiles, and hear old Ocean roar' (1.31–4). A survey of the beauties and wonders of the world and the heavens ends with the sobering reminder that (63–8):

> Yet all must drop, as autumn's sickliest grain,
> And earth and firmament be sought in vain;
> The tract forgot where constellations shone,
> Or where the Stuarts fill'd an awful throne:
> Time shall be slain, all Nature be destroy'd,
> Nor leave an atom in the mighty void.

Young alludes to Milton's 'grateful vicissitude' when he mourns the 'one universal ruin' that will return the universe to 'a second chaos' (1.167–8), bringing to an end time, 'While thousand golden planets knew no rest, | Still onward in their circling journey press'd; | A grateful change of seasons some to bring, | And sweet vicissitude of fall and spring' (151–4).

The *ubi sunt* topos ('Where are the snows of yesteryear?') normally draws attention to the swift and relentless, and indefinitely continuing, passage of time.

From the perspective of the last day, the present tense of *ubi sunt* takes on a new complexion, marking an absolute divide between a time when the world was in time, and a time when time has ceased. In Newcomb's *The Last Judgment* the Son looks down from his tribunal on 'The world, no more a world, a sea of flame | Rolling without restraint, without a shore' (10.58–9); 'Where are now the groves | Of Arabia? Where breathe her spicy gales, | Scented far off at sea[15] . . . Can the eye | Of angels now unfold, where blazed the thrones | Of earthly monarchs?' (79–85). Aaron Hill, in his *The Judgment-Day* (151–8), exclaims 'How low, proud earth, are all thy honours laid! | Where are thy late-contested empires found? | Where the big boasts of arts and arms display'd! | Where are the dreadful pomps, which hemm'd thee round! | What difference, now, 'twixt rich and poor, remains? | The ruler's sceptre, and the captive's chains? | Where lie the properties of boastful wealth? | Distinction, and degrees, now clash no more!'

The abolition of seasonal variety is, however, in counterpoise with an image of ripening fruit that is applied in Last Judgement poems to the reader who is properly prepared for the last things, and also to the condition of the just who will experience the new heaven and new earth that will be created in the millennium after the Last Judgement and the destruction of our world. This is the point at which the image of fruit that runs through *Paradise Lost* reaches its final term: 'New heavens, new earth, ages of endless date | Founded in righteousness and peace and love | To bring forth fruits, joy and eternal bliss' (*PL* 12.549–51). That final image has already appeared in the Father's prophecy to the Son of Christian history, at *PL* 3.334–7: 'The world shall burn, and from her ashes spring | New heaven and earth, wherein the just shall dwell | And, after all their tribulations long, | See golden days, fruitful of golden deeds . . .'[16] A ripening into a new Golden Age.

Yet, the static and unchanging joys of the new paradise may be just a little boring, a problem confronted in Newcomb's *The Last Judgment*, when Adam asks the angel how they should spend their time, and reaches for the notion of temporal process contained in the image of ripening fruit: 'How wandring thro' these vales, which may afford | Scene after scene fresh transport, shall the hours | And days, and months, and years, not glide away | With some anxiety, and tedious wings, | Till we select those pleasures which may yield | The mind eternal and unchanging joys, | Still new, tho' still repeated, and more sweet | From long fruition; he who guides our thought | To find what thus shall please, nor satiate, found, | Merits his share of praise' (11.397–406).

Edward Young uses the image of ripening fruit as a closural device in *A Poem on the Last Day*. Following a climactic account of the destruction of the world at the last day, Young turns to contemplate the fact that these 'revolutions' in nature are all for the sake of man, whose gaze is now turned from that distant conflagration to a gaze directed, here and now, to the inner man (3.310–27):

> Enter the sacred temple of thy breast,   310
> And gaze, and wander there, a ravish'd guest;
> Gaze on those hidden treasures thou shalt find,
> Wander through all the glories of thy mind.
> Of perfect knowledge, see, the dawning light
> Foretells a noon most exquisitely bright!   315
> Here springs of endless joy are breaking forth!
> There buds the promise of celestial worth!
> Worth, which must ripen in a happier clime,
> And brighter sun, beyond the bounds of time.
> Thou, minor, canst not guess thy vast estate,   320
> What stores, on foreign coasts, thy landing wait:
> Lose not thy claim: let virtue's path be trod;
> Thus glad all heaven, and please that bounteous God,
> Who, to light thee to pleasures, hung on high
> Yon radiant orb, proud regent of the sky;   325
> That service done, its beams shall fade away,
> And God shine forth in one eternal day.

From this point of view the future holds not sudden rupture, but a gradual dawning and ripening, natural processes that are followed by images of the realization, in time, of gain in the human spheres of property law (coming into an inheritance) and mercantilism (trading voyages). At the end of time, 'beyond the bounds of time', the sun will 'fade away' (rather than being suddenly extinguished), 'And God shine forth in one eternal day.'

The gradual fade-out and fade-in of light which close Young's *A Poem on the Last Day* are in strong contrast to the closing lines of his major poem, the nine-book *Night Thoughts*. A first point of closure seems to have been reached with a paragraph (9.2378–410) that performs an *envoi* to the 'night' of *Night Thoughts*, to be replaced by the 'eternal day' that is the last two words of *A Poem on the Last Day*: 'Then farewell, NIGHT! Of darkness now no more: | Joy breaks, shines, triumphs; 'tis eternal day'; 'Eternity [is] the prize', for those who follow Christ, 'And leave the racers[17] of the world their own, | Their feather, and their froth, for endless toils' (toils without closure). This paragraph ends with what appears to be a final call to the backsliding Lorenzo to seize the moment, 2404–6. 'Lorenzo! 'tis not yet too late: Lorenzo! | . . . That is, seize wisdom, ere she seizes thee . . .'

What is really the final paragraph (2411–34) plunges the reader back in the darkness which is the *sine qua non* for 'Night Thoughts', the nocturnal darkness in which what is really the final appeal to Lorenzo is made:

> Thus, Darkness aiding intellectual light,
> And sacred Silence whispering truths Divine,
> And truths Divine converting pain to peace,
> My song the midnight raven has outwing'd,
> And shot, ambitious of unbounded scenes,   2415
> Beyond the flaming limits of the world,
> Her gloomy flight. But what avails the flight
> Of Fancy, when our hearts remain below?
> Virtue abounds in flatterers and foes;
> 'Tis pride to praise her, penance to perform.   2420
> To more than words, to more than worth of tongue,
> Lorenzo! rise at this auspicious hour:
> An hour when Heaven's most intimate with man;
> When, like a falling star, the ray Divine
> Glides swift into the bosom of the just;   2425
> And just are all, determined to reclaim;[18]
> Which sets that title high, within thy reach.
> Awake then; thy Philander calls; awake!
> Thou who shalt wake when the creation sleeps;
> When, like a taper, all these suns expire;   2430
> When Time, like him of Gaza, in his wrath,
> Plucking the pillars that support the world,
> In Nature's ample ruins lies entomb'd;
> And Midnight, universal Midnight, reigns.

Finis. The here and now is connected with the there and then, in another example of the rhetoric whereby Last Judgement poems attempt to jolt the reader from the quotidian and mundane into the tremendous presence of the last things. There is a spatial contrast between a Lucretian flight of fancy into 'unbounded scenes', and the narrower space 'below', where our hearts remain. There is a temporal contrast between 'this auspicious hour', the time of utterance when the poet calls on Lorenzo to awake, and that dreadful hour when Lorenzo will wake with all other humans who have ever died, including Philander, who already calls from beyond the grave in this auspicious hour (like Joseph Trapp from his tombstone).[19] There is also a contrast in verbal moods, between the imperatives 'rise' and 'awake', which Lorenzo can choose to heed or not, and the future indicative, 'Thou who shalt awake,' a certainty that cannot be resisted. At that distant hour of the awakening of the dead in the general resurrection, those who are 'just' will receive their reward, while those who are not will be damned for eternity. That hour will set a limit to the time travel of Last Judgement poems, when time itself reaches the end of its lifespan and is buried in the darkness of the tomb. Comparing small things to great, the final extinction of the stars will be like the extinguishing of a taper such as one might burn in any night, such as this night in which the poet calls to Lorenzo.[20] Then the darkness of recurring nights will give way to 'universal Midnight', and the clocks will have stopped.

Young reinforces the closure of (the often Miltonic) *Night Thoughts* with allusion to the closing scene of *Samson Agonistes*. He also engages with some opening and closing lines of another poet with whom *Night Thoughts* is intermittently in conversation, Alexander Pope. Young ends, with a call to Lorenzo to awake, where Pope had begun his essay on (mortal) man with the same call to his patron, *Essay on Man* 1.1–2: 'Awake, my St. John! leave all meaner things | To low ambition, and the pride of kings.'[21] The synchronism of narrative closure with eschatological closure alludes to the closing words of another of Pope's works, the *Dunciad*, 4.653–6: 'Lo! thy dread Empire, Chaos! is restor'd; | Light dies before thy uncreating word: | Thy hand, great Anarch! lets the curtain fall; | And Universal Darkness buries All.'[22] Young's universal darkness also signals the end of God's created world, the end of created time, to be replaced by Midnight's universal reign. But for Young the final end is not a return to Chaos, Milton's 'old anarch' (*PL* 2.988), since, as we know by this point in the poem, beyond universal Midnight lies the dawning of Eternity. Book 4 of the *Dunciad* was written in 1742, and Pope may parody Last Judgement poems. Young ends *Night Thoughts* (1742–5) with topics of Last Judgement poems, and with a corrective rewriting of Pope.

Some Early Eighteenth-Century Poems on the Last Day (not an exhaustive list)

Catherall, Samuel, Fellow of Oriel College, Oxford (1720), *An Essay on the Conflagration in Blank Verse*, Oxford.

Hill, Aaron (1685–1750) (1721), *The Judgment-Day: A Poem*, London.

Newcomb, Thomas (1682?–1765) (1723), *The Last Judgment of Men and Angels. A Poem in Twelve Books: After the Manner of Milton*, London.

Pomfret, John (1667–1702) (1724), *Dies Novissima: OR, THE LAST EPIPHANY. A Pindarick Ode, on Christ's Second Appearance to Judge the World*. (In *Poems upon Several Occasions*, London.

Rowe, Elizabeth Singer (1674–1737) (1739), *The Conflagration: An Ode*, London.
Swift, Jonathan (1667–1745) (1774), *The Day of Judgment* (parody). London.
Trapp, Joseph (1679–1747) (1734/5), *Thoughts upon the Four Last Things: Death; Judgment; Heaven; Hell. A Poem in Four Parts*, London.
Watts, Isaac (1674–1748) (1706), *The Day of Judgment, AN ODE, Attempted in English Sapphic*, in *Horae Lyricae*, 40–2, London.
Young, Edward (1683–1765) (1713), *A Poem on the Last Day*. Oxford.

Notes

1 In general on *Paradise Lost*'s dealings with time see Boesky (2016). On the Christian 'invention of time' in late antiquity see Goldhill (2022).
2 Genesis 3.15; *PL* 10.175–81.
3 On the mimetic structures in the syntax of 537–51 see Corns (1994: 116–18).
4 Loewenstein (1990: 119–20) compares the apocalyptic conclusion of *Of Reformation*, (*YP* i. 616) 'the faithful in supereminence of beatific vision progressing the dateless and irrevoluble circle of eternity shall clasp inseparable hands with joy'.
5 Milton gives a second account of the whole course of Christian time in the Father's account of the last things to the Son, *PL* 3.323–41. Cf. the retrospective version of the Miltonic Michael's relation, to the newly resurrected Adam, in Newcomb's *Last Judgment*, when Adam retires to sleep, and his still waking fancy is visited by a celestial shape: 'While my voice | Instructs thee, what has e'er befell thy race | Since mortal, or hereafter shall befall, | Till time shall cease to run, and in the stream | Lost of eternity rolls on no more | In days, and months, and years, which soon shall end | In one great ocean, without depth or bounds!' (10.958–64).
6 *OED* s.v. *abyss* n. 1a 'primal formless chaos out of which the earth and the heavens were created'. Cf. also *PL* 2.405 'The dark, unbottomed, infinite abyss' of Chaos.
7 Cf. 12.574 'To whom thus also the angel last replied'; 624–6 (after Eve's last speech) 'So spake our mother Eve, and Adam heard | Well pleased, but answered not; for now too nigh | The archangel stood . . .' On the closure of narrative time in *PL* see Shumaker (1967: 58–9).
8 On Lucretius' apocalyptic imagination see Schiesaro (2020).
9 As shown by Zissos and Gildenhard (1999).
10 Barchiesi (2005: 237).
11 See e.g. the classical epigraphs in: (i) Catherall, *An Essay on the Conflagration*: Lucan 7.814 *Communis mundo superest rogus*; (ii) Young's *Poem on the Last Day*, Book 1: *Geo.* 1.328–31 *ipse pater media nimborum in nocte corusca | fulmina molitur dextra, quo maxima motu | terra tremit, fugere ferae et mortalia corda | per gentis humilis strauit pauor*; Book 3: *Met.* 1.256–8 *esse quoque in fatis reminiscitur*; and

(iii) Newcomb's *Last Judgment*, title page: *Geo.* 1.328-31 and *Aen.* 9.7 *uoluenda dies en attulit*; Book 4: Lucan 7.814-15 *communis mundo superest rogus ossibus astra misturus*, and Lucan 1.72-7 *cum compage soluta . . . excutietque fretum – &c.*; Book 6: *Aeneid* 6.273-9 (the personifications *in faucibus Orci*); Book 7: *Aeneid* 6.172 *Vocat in certamina Divos*; Book 12: *Aen.* 6.638-41 *deuenere locos laetos, & amoena uirecta | fortunatorum nemorum . . . sua sidera norunt.*

12 Peter 3.10 'But the day of the Lord will come as a thief in the night; in the which the heavens shall pass away with a great noise, and the elements shall melt with fervent heat, the earth also and the works that are therein shall be burned up. But of that day and hour knoweth no man, no, not the angels of heaven, but my Father only.' Cf. also Matthew 24.36-44, 'Therefore be ye also ready: for in such an hour as ye think not the Son of man cometh'; 1 Thessalonians 5.1-3.

13 That anxiety and that urgency are already registered in Paulinus of Nola, *Carmen* 10.293-318, justifying to Ausonius his need to make full use of the *tempus praesens* to prepare himself for the second coming.

14 Amos 4.12, 'Prepare to meet thy God, O Israel.'

15 Cf. *PL* 4.159-65

16 On 'fruit' as a keyword in *PL*, see MacCaffrey (1959: 83-6).

17 Cf. perhaps Milton's 'race of time', *PL* 12.554.

18 *OED* s.v. *reclaim* v. 2e intrans. 'To improve oneself morally or spiritually; to mend one's ways, repent, reform. *Obsolete*.'

19 With the final call to Lorenzo to awake cf. *Last Day* 1.81 '(Ye sublunary worlds, awake, awake!)', at the last trump; 1.98 'The living die with fear, the dead awake'; 2.1-6 'Now man awakes, and from his silent bed, | Where he has slept for ages, lifts his head; | Shakes off the slumber of ten thousand years, | And on the borders of new worlds appears. | Whate'er the bold, the rash adventure cost, | In wide Eternity I dare be lost.'

20 Cf. 9.1978-9 'How, like a widow in her weeds, the Night, | Amid her glimmering tapers, silent sits!'

21 Young contrasts Pope's *Essay on* [mortal] *Man* with his own poem on 'immortal man' at *NT* 1.452-60 'Or his who made Mæonides [Homer, referring to Pope's translation of the *Iliad*] our own! | Man, too, he sung: immortal man I sing . . .'

22 As Cornford (1989: 337, 359) notes, Young also alludes to, and inverts the sense of, the last line of the *Dunciad* at *NT* 5.131-2 'There lies our Theatre; there sits our Judge. | Darkness the Curtain drops o'er Life's dull Scene,' introducing the reign of Reason and Virtue'; and at 9.1302 'And One eternal Curtain cover All!' (at the last trump). On *Night Thoughts* and Pope's *Essay on Man* see Odell (1972). Pope in turn alludes to Shakespeare, *Henry IV*, Part 2, I. i. 154, 160, 'Let Order die . . . And darkness be the burier of the dead.' Northumberland's outburst on news of death of Hotspur, 'Now let not Nature's hand | Keep the wild flood confin'd! Let order die! . . .' (cited by Sutherland [1953] on *Dunciad* 4.656).

Bibliography

Adam, B. (1998), *Timescapes of Modernity: The Environment and Invisible Hazards*, London and New York: Routledge.
Agócs, P. (2020), 'Pindar's *Pythian* 4: Interpreting History in Song', *Histos* Supplement 11: 87–154.
Allen, T. M., ed. (2018), *Time and Literature (Cambridge Critical Concepts)*, Cambridge: Cambridge University Press.
Allen, T. W., W. R. Halliday and E. E. Sikes (1963), *The Homeric Hymns*, 2nd edn, Amsterdam: Adolf M. Hakkert.
Altheim, F. (1924), 'Die Entstehungsgeschichte des homerischen Apollonhymnus', *Hermes* 59: 430–49.
Anderson, W. S. (1997), *Ovid's Metamorphoses Books 1–5*, Norman, OK: University of Oklahoma Press.
Arend, W. (1933), *Die typischen Scenen bei Homer*, Hildesheim: Olms.
Armisen-Marchetti, M. (1989), *Sapientiae facies: étude sur les images de Sénèque*, Paris: Les Belles Lettres.
Armisen-Marchetti, M. (1995), 'Sénèque et l'appopriation du temps', *Latomus* 54: 545–67.
Atack, C. (2020), 'Plato's Queer Time: Dialogic Moments in the Life and Death of Socrates', *Classical Receptions Journal* 12: 10–31.
Auffarth, C. (1991), *Der Drohende Untergang*, Berlin: De Gruyter.
Bachelard, G. (1984), *The New Scientific Spirit*, Boston, MA: Beacon Press.
Bailey, C. (1947), *Titi Lucreti Cari De Rerum Natura Libri Sex*, 3 vols, Oxford: Clarendon Press.
Bakhtin, M. M. (1981), *The Dialogic Imagination: Four Essays*, ed. M. Holquist, trans. C. Emerson and M. Holquist, Austin, TX: University of Texas Press.
Bakker, E. J. (2002a), '*Khronos, Kléos*, and Ideology from Herodotus to Homer', in A. Rengakos and M. Reichel (eds), *Epea Pteroenta: Beitrage zur Homerforschung: Festschrift für Wolfgang Kullmann zum 75 Geburtstag*, 11–30, Stuttgart: Steiner.
Bakker, E. J. (2002b), 'Remembering the God's Arrival', *Arethusa* 35: 63–81.
Baltes, M. (1981), 'Die Kataloge im homerischen Apollonhymnus', *Philologus* 125: 25–43.
Barad, K. (2007), *Meeting the Universe Halfway: Quantum Physics and the Entanglement of Matter and Meaning*, Durham, NC: Duke University Press.
Barchiesi, A. (1997), *The Poet and the Prince: Ovid and Augustan Discourse*, Berkeley and Los Angeles, CA: University of California Press.
Barchiesi, A. (2005), *Ovidio Metamorfosi* vol. i *Libri I–II*, Rome: Fondazione Valla.

Barnes, J. (1982), *The Presocratic Philosophers*, London and New York: Routledge.
Barthes, R. (1974), *S/Z*, trans. R. Miller, New York: Hill & Wang.
Barthes, R. (1982), *Camera Lucida: Reflections on Photography*, trans. R. Howard, London: Vintage.
Bartsch, S. and D. Wray, eds (2009), *Seneca and the Self*, Cambridge: Cambridge University Press.
Bassi, K. (2005), 'Things of the Past: Objects and Time in Greek Narrative', *Arethusa* 38: 1–32.
Beard, M. (1987), 'A Complex of Times: No More Sheep on Romulus' Birthday', *Proceedings of the Cambridge Philological Society* 33: 1–15.
Beck, B. (2017), 'Lost in the Middle: Story Time and Discourse Time in the *Iliad*', *Yearbook of Ancient Greek Epic* 1: 46–64.
Beck, M. (2007a), 'Xenophon', in de Jong and Nünlist (eds), 383–96.
Beck, M. (2007b), 'Plutarch', in de Jong and R. Nünlist (eds), 397–411.
Ben-Dov, J. and L. Doering, eds (2017), *Constructions of Time in Antiquity: Ritual, Art, and Identity*, Cambridge: Cambridge University Press.
Bender, J, and D. E. Wellbery, eds (1991), *Chronotypes: The Construction of Time*, Stanford, CA: Stanford University Press.
Beneker, J. (2009), 'Nepos' Biographical Method in the Lives of Foreign Generals', *Classical Journal* 105: 109–21.
Benjamin, W. (1999), *The Arcades Project*, Cambridge, MA: Belknap Press.
Bergmann, W. (1983), 'Das Problem der Zeit in der Soziologie: Ein Literaturüberblick zum Stand der "zeitsoziologischen" Theorie und Forschung', *Kölner Zeitschrift für Soziologie und Sozialpsychologie* 35: 462–504.
Bergren, A. (2008), *Weaving Truth: Essays on Language and the Female in Greek Thought*, Washington, DC: Center for Hellenic Studies.
Bergson, H. (1913), *Time and Free Will: An Essay on the Immediate Data of Consciousness*, London: G. Allen & Company.
Bernabé, A. (1995), 'Una cosmogonía cómica (Aristófanes Aves 695 ss.)', in J. A. Lopez Ferez (ed.), *De Homero a Libanio: Estudios actuales sobre textos griegos*, 195–211, Madrid: Ediciones Clásicas.
Berno, F. R. (2008), 'Seneca e la semantica della pienezza', *Bolletino di Studi Latini* 38: 549–66.
Bernstein, M. A. (1996), *Foregone Conclusions: Against Apocalyptic History*, Berkeley and Los Angeles, CA: University of California Press.
Bertolini, M. (1991), *Ludovico Lazzarelli: Fasti Christianae Religionis*, Naples: M. D'Auria.
Bettini, M. (1991), *Anthropology and Roman Culture: Kinship, Time, Images of the Soul*, trans. J. van Sickle, Baltimore, MD: Johns Hopkins University Press.
Bianchi, E., S. Brill and B. Holmes, eds (2019), *Antiquities Beyond Humanism*, Oxford: Oxford University Press.
Bielfeldt, R. (2014), 'Gegenwart und Vergegenwärtigung: dynamische Dinge im Ausgang von Homer', in R. Bielfeldt (ed.), *Ding und Mensch in der Antike: Gegenwart und Vergegenwärtigung* (Akademiekonferenzen 16), 15–48, Heidelberg: Winter.

Blondell, R. (2002), *The Play of Character in Plato's Dialogues*, Cambridge: Cambridge University Press.
Boesky, A. (2016), '*Paradise Lost* and the Multiplicity of Time', in T. N. Corns (ed.), *A New Companion to Milton*, 380–92, Chichester: John Wiley and Sons.
Boetzkes, A. (2010), *The Ethics of Earth Art*, Minneapolis, MN: University of Minnesota Press.
Bonazzi, M. (2020), 'Protagoras', *Stanford Encyclopedia of Philosophy*. Available online: https://plato.stanford.edu/archives/fall2020/entries/protagoras/ (accessed 12 June 2023).
Bonnechere, P. (2003), 'Trophonius of Lebadea: Mystery Aspects of an Oracular Cult in Boeotia', in M. B. Cosmopoulos (ed.), *Greek Mysteries: The Archaeology of Ancient Greek Secret Cults*, 185–208, London: Routledge.
Bonnechere, P. (2013), 'Les dieux du Trophonion lébadéen: panthéon ou amalgame?', in V. Pirenne-Delforge (ed.), *Les Panthéons des cités: Des origines à la Périégèse de Pausanias*, 91–108, Liége: Presses universitaires de Liège.
Bordo, J. (2008), 'The Homer of Potsdamerplatz – Walter Benjamin in Wim Wenders' *Sky Over Berlin/Wings of Desire*, A Critical Topography', *IMAGES* 2: 86–109.
Botterill, S. (1994), *Dante and the Mystical Tradition*, Cambridge: Cambridge University Press.
Bowie, A. M. (2019), *Homer. Iliad. Book III*, Cambridge: Cambridge University Press.
Bowin, J. (2009), 'Aristotle on the Order and Direction of Time', *Apeiron* 42: 33–62.
Boyd, B. W. (1987), 'Propertius on the Banks of the Eurotas (A Note on 3.14.17–20)', *Classical Quarterly* 37: 527–8.
Brazeau, B. (2014), '"Emotional Rescue": Heroic Chastity and Devotional Practice in Iacopo Sannazaro's *De partu Virginis*', *California Italian Studies* 5: 225–46.
Breglia Pulci Doria, L. (2000), 'Ferecide di Siro tra orfici e pitagorici', in M. Tortorelli Ghidini, A. Storchi Marino and A. Visconti (eds), *Tra Orfeo e Pitagora. Origini e incontri di culture nell'antichità: atti dei seminari napoletani 1996–1998*, 161–94, Napoli: Bibliopolis.
Brenk, F. E. (2008), 'Setting a Good Exemplum. Case Studies in the *Moralia*, the *Lives* as Case Studies', in A. G. Nikolaidis (ed.), *The Unity of Plutarch's Work: 'Moralia' Themes in the 'Lives', Features of the 'Lives' in the 'Moralia'*, 237–53, Berlin and New York: De Gruyter.
Brisson, L. (1997), 'Chronos in Column XII of the Derveni Papyrus', in A. Laks and G. W. Most (eds), *Studies on the Derveni Papyrus*, 149–65, Oxford: Clarendon Press.
Bruneau, P. (1970), *Recherches sur les cultes de Délos à l'époque hellénistique et à l'époque impériale*, Paris: De Boccard.
Bruner, J. (1987), 'Life as Narrative', *Social Research* 54: 11–32.
Budelmann, F. and T. Phillips, eds (2018), *Textual Events: Performance and the Lyric in Early Greece*, Oxford: Oxford University Press.
Bundy, E. L. (1962), *Studia Pindarica*, Berkeley and Los Angeles, CA: University of California Press.

Burkert, W. (1972), *Lore and Science in Ancient Pythagoreanism*, Cambridge, MA: Harvard University Press.
Burkert, W. (1979), 'Kynaithos, Polycrates and the *Homeric Hymn to Apollo*', in G. W. Bowersock, W. Burkert and M. C. J. Putnam (eds), *Arktouros: Festschrift B. M. W. Knox*, 59–62, Berlin: De Gruyter.
Burnyeat, M. (1976a), 'Protagoras and Self-Refutation in Later Greek Philosophy', *The Philosophical Review* 85 (1): 44–69.
Burnyeat, M. (1976b), 'Protagoras and Self-Refutation in Plato's *Theaetetus*', *The Philosophical Review* 85 (2): 172–95.
Burt, S. (2014), '"Like": A Speculative Essay about Poetry, Simile, Artificial Intelligence, Mourning, Sex, Rock and Roll, Grammar, Romantic Love, William Shakespeare, Alan Turing, Rae Armantrout, Nick Hornby, Walt Whitman, William Carlos Williams, Lia Purpura, and Claire Danes', *Poetry Review* 43: 17–21.
Burton, S. (1996), 'Bahktin, Temporality, and Modern Narrative: Writing "the Whole Triumphant Murderous Unstoppable Chute"', *Comparative Literature* 48.1: 39–64.
Busch, A. (2009), 'Dissolution of the Self in the Senecan Corpus', in Bartsch and Wray (eds), 255–81.
Butler, S. (2016), 'Introduction: On the Origin of "Deep Classics"', in S. Butler (ed.), *Deep Classics: Rethinking Classical Reception*, 1–19, London: Bloomsbury.
Calame, C. (2009), *Poetic and Performative Memory in Ancient Greece: Heroic Reference and Ritual Gestures in Time and Space*, Washington, DC: Center for Hellenic Studies.
Calame, C. (2011), 'The *Homeric Hymns* as Poetic Offerings: Musical and Ritual Relationships with the Gods', in Faulkner (ed.), 334–57.
Callahan, J. F. (1948), *Four Views of Time in Ancient Philosophy*, Cambridge, MA: Harvard University Press.
Campbell, B. (2012), *Rivers and the Power of Ancient Rome*, Chapel Hill: University of North Carolina Press.
Capponi, M. (2003), 'Fins d'hymnes et sphragis énonciatives', *Quaderni Urbinati di Cultura Classica* 75: 9–35.
Carson, A. (1986), *Eros the Bittersweet: An Essay*, Princeton, NJ: Princeton University Press.
Casasanto, D. and L. Boroditsky (2008), 'Time in the Mind: Using Space to Think about Time', *Cognition* 106: 579–93.
Casaubon, I., T. Aldobrandini and M. Casaubon, eds (1692), *Diogenis Laertii de vitis, dogmatibus et apophthegmatibus clarorum philosophorum libri X: Graece et Latine*, Amsterdam: Henricus Wetstein.
Casey, E. S. (2001), 'Between Geography and Philosophy: What Does It Mean to Be in the Place-World?', *Annals of the Association of American Geographers* 91: 683–93.
Cassin, B. (2014), *Sophistical Practice: Toward a Consistent Relativism*, New York: Fordham University Press.
Càssola, F. (2010), *Inni omerici*, 9th edn, Milan: Mondadori.

Cavarero, A. (2005), *For More than One Voice: Toward a Philosophy of Vocal Expression*, trans. P. A. Kottman, Stanford, CA: Stanford University Press.
Chappell, M. (2006), 'Delphi and the *Homeric Hymn to Apollo*', *Classical Quarterly* 56: 331–48.
Chappell, M. (2011), 'The *Homeric Hymn to Apollo*: The Question of Unity', in Faulkner (ed.), 59–81.
Chase, M. (2013), 'Discussions on the Eternity of the World in Antiquity and Contemporary Cosmology', *Schole* 7: 20–68.
Cherniss, H. (1962), *Aristotle's Criticism of Plato and the Academy*, New York: Russell & Russell.
Chiu, A. (2016), *Ovid's Women of the Year*, Ann Arbor, MI: University of Michigan Press.
Christopoulos, M., E. D. Krantzakis and O. A. Levaniouk, eds (2010), *Light and Darkness in Ancient Greek Myth and Religion*, Lanham, MD: Lexington Books.
Chrysanthou, A. (2020), *Defining Orphism: The Beliefs, the teletae and the Writings*, Berlin and New York: De Gruyter.
Chrysantou, C. S. (2018), *Plutarch's Parallel Lives: Narrative Technique and Moral Judgment*, Berlin and Boston, MA: De Gruyter.
Ciccolini, L. (2020), 'Scripture in the North African Treatises of Pseudo-Cyprian', in J. Yates and A. Dupont (eds), *The Bible in Christian North Africa, Part I*, 142–67, Berlin and Boston, MA: De Gruyter.
Cizek, E. (1977), *Structures et idéologies dans 'Les vies des douze Césars' de Suétone*, Paris: Les Belles Lettres.
Clack, B. and B. R. Clack (2008), *Philosophy of Religion: A Critical Introduction*, Cambridge: Polity.
Clay, D. (2000), *Platonic Questions: Dialogues with the Silent Philosopher*, University Park, PA: Pennsylvania State University Press.
Clay, J. S. (1981), 'Immortal and Ageless Forever', *Classical Journal* 77: 112–17.
Clay, J. S. (1983), *The Wrath of Athena: Gods and Men in the Odyssey*, Princeton, NJ: Princeton University Press.
Clay, J. S. (1989), *The Politics of Olympus: Form and Meaning in the Major Homeric Hymns*, Princeton, NJ: Princeton University Press.
Clay, J. S. (1994), 'Tendenz and Olympian Propaganda in the *Homeric Hymn to Apollo*', in J. Solomon (ed.), *Apollo: Origin and Influences*, 23–36, Tucson, AZ: University of Arizona Press.
Clay, J. S. (2003), *Hesiod's Cosmos*, Cambridge: Cambridge University Press.
Clay, J. S. (2009), 'The Silence of the Pythia', in L. Athanassaki, R. P. Martin and J. F. Miller (eds), *Apolline Politics and Poetics. International Symposium*, 5–17, Athens: European Cultural Centre of Delphi.
Clay, J. S. (2011), 'The *Homeric Hymns* as Genre', in Faulkner (ed.), 232–53.
Connors, C. and C. Clendenon (2016), 'Mapping Tartaros: Observation, Inference, and Belief in Ancient Greek and Roman Accounts of Karst Terrain', *Classical Antiquity* 35: 147–88.

Conrad, J. (1856), *De Pherecydis Syrii Aetate Atque Cosmologia*, diss., Ex typographia Hildenbrandtii.
Conybeare, C. and S. Goldhill, eds (2020), *Classical Philology and Theology Entanglement, Disavowal, and the Godlike Scholar*, Cambridge: Cambridge University Press.
Coope, U. C. M. (2005), *Time for Aristotle: Physics IV, 10-14*, Oxford: Oxford University Press.
Corfiati, C. (2003), 'Il cod. Vat. lat. 2853: per una storia dei *Fastorum christianae religionis libri* di Ludovico Lazzarelli', *Roma nel Rinascimento*: 256-76.
Cornford, F. M. (1997), *Plato's Cosmology: The Timaeus of Plato*, Indianapolis, IN: Hackett Publishing.
Cornford, S., ed. (1989), *Edward Young: Night Thoughts*, Cambridge: Cambridge University Press.
Corns, T. N. (1994), *Regaining Paradise Lost*, Harlow: Longman.
Csapo, E. and M. C. Miller (1998), 'Democracy, Empire, and Art: Toward a Politics of Time and Narrative', in K. A. Raaflaub and D. Boedeker (eds), *Democracy, Empire and the Arts in Fifth-Century Athens*, 87-125, Cambridge, MA: Harvard University Press.
Culler, J. (2015), *Theory of the Lyric*, Cambridge, MA: Harvard University Press.
Dahlstrom, D. O. (2013), *The Heidegger Dictionary*, London and New York: Bloomsbury.
Daston, L., ed. (2000), *Biographies of Scientific Objects*, Chicago, IL: University of Chicago Press.
de Beistegui, M. (2005), *The New Heidegger*, London and New York: Continuum.
de Jong, I. J. F. (1987), *Narrators and Focalizers: The Presentation of the Story in the Iliad*, Amsterdam: Grüner.
de Jong, I. J. F. and R. Nünlist, eds (2007), *Time in Ancient Greek Literature*, Leiden: Brill.
De Landa, M. (2000), *A Thousand Years of Nonlinear History*, New York: Zone Books.
Degani, E. (1961), *ΑΙΩΝ da Omero ad Aristotele*, Padua: Antonio Milani.
Deichgräber, K. (1940), 'Anaximander von Milet', *Hermes* 75: 10-19.
Deleuze, G. (1989), *Cinema 2: The Time-Image*, trans. H. Tomlinson and R. Galeta, Minneapolis, MN: University of Minnesota Press.
Della Corte, F. (1967), *Suetonio eques romanus*, Florence: La Nuova Italia.
Delpeyroux, M.-F. (2002), 'Temps, philosophie et amitié dans les *Letters à Lucilius*', in L. Nadjo and E. Gavoille (eds), *Epistulae antiquae: actes du IIe colloque international 'le genre epistolaire antiue et ses prolongements européens'*, 203-21, Louvain: Peeters.
Derrida, J. (1992), 'Given Time: The Time of the King', *Critical Inquiry* 18: 161-87.
Derrida, J. (1993), *Aporias: Dying - Awaiting (One Another at) the 'Limits of Truth'*, trans. T. Dutoit, Stanford, CA: Stanford University Press.
Derrida, J. (1994), *Spectres of Marx*, London: Routledge.
Derrida, J. (2005), *Rogues: Two Essays on Reason*, Stanford, CA: Stanford University Press.
Diels, H. (1969), *Kleine Schriften zur Geschichte der antiken Philosophie: Hrsg. von Walter Burkert*, Darmstadt: Wissenschaftliche Buchgesellschaft.
Dihle, A. (1987), *Die Entstehung der historischen Biographie*, Heidelberg: Winter.

Dimock, W. C. (2008), 'After Troy: Homer, Euripides, Total War', in R. Felski (ed.), *Rethinking Tragedy*, 66–81, Baltimore, MD: Johns Hopkins University Press.
Dionisotti, A. C. (1988), 'Nepos and the Generals', *Journal of Roman Studies* 78: 35–49.
Dolansky, F. (2011), 'Reconsidering the Matronalia and Women's Rites', *Classical World* 104: 191–209.
Drerup, E. (1937), 'Der homerische Apollonhymnos. Eine methodologische Studie', *Mnemosyne* 5: 81–134.
Du Four, M. (1941), 'C. Suetonii Tranquilli Vita Tiberii. Chapters I to XXIII, edited with parallel passages and a historical commentary', diss., University of Pennsylvania, Philadelphia.
Dunn, F. M. (2007), *Present Shock in Late Fifth-Century Greece*, Ann Arbor, MI: University of Michigan Press.
Edelman, L. (2004), *No Future: Queer Theory and the Death Drive*, Durham, NC: Duke University Press.
Edmonds, R. G. (2018), 'Misleading and Unclear to the Many: Allegory in the Derveni Papyrus and the Orphic Theogony of Hieronymus', in M. A. Santamaría Álvarez (ed.), *The Derveni Papyrus*, 77–99, Leiden: Brill.
Edmunds, L. (2015), 'Pliny the Younger on His Verse and Martial's Non-Recognition of Pliny as a Poet', *Harvard Studies in Classical Philology* 108: 309–60.
Edwards, C. (2000), *Suetonius: Lives of the Caesars*, translated and with Introduction and Notes, Oxford: Oxford University Press.
Edwards, C. (2005), 'Archetypally Roman? Representing Seneca's Ageing Body', in A. Hopkins and M. Wyke (eds), *Roman Bodies: Antiquity to the Eighteenth Century*, 13–22, Cambridge: Cambridge University Press.
Edwards, C. (2014), 'Death and Time', in G. Damschen and A. Heil (eds), *Brill's Companion to Seneca: Philosopher and Dramatist*, 323–41, Leiden: Brill.
Edwards, C. (2018), 'On Not Being in Rome: Exile and Displacement in Seneca's Prose', in W. Fitzgerald and E. Spentzou (eds), *The Production of Space in Latin Literature*, 169–94, Oxford: Oxford University Press.
Edwards, C. (2019), *Seneca: Selected Letters*, Cambridge: Cambridge University Press.
Ehrman, B. D. and Z. Pleše (2011), *The Apocryphal Gospels: Texts and Translations*, Oxford: Oxford University Press.
Falcon, A., ed. (2016), *Brill's Companion to the Reception of Aristotle in Antiquity*, Leiden: Brill.
Farrar, C. (1988), *The Origins of Democratic Thinking: The Invention of Politics in Classical Athens*, Cambridge: Cambridge University Press.
Faulkner, A., ed. (2011), *The Homeric Hymns. Interpretative Essays*, Oxford: Oxford University Press.
Faure, R., S.-P. Valli and A. Zucker, eds (2022), *Conceptions of Time in Greek and Roman Antiquity*, Berlin and Boston, MA: De Gruyter.
Fearn, D. W. (2003), 'Mapping Phleious: Politics and Myth-Making in Bacchylides 9', *Classical Quarterly* 53: 347–67.

Fearn, D. W. (2017), *Pindar's Eyes: Visual and Material Culture in Epinician Poetry*, Oxford: Oxford University Press.

Fearn, D. W. (2020), *Greek Lyric of the Archaic and Classical Periods: From the Past to the Future of the Lyric Subject*, Leiden: Brill.

Feeney, D. (1999), '*Mea Tempora*: Patterning of Time in the *Metamorphoses*', in P. Hardie, A. Barcheisi and S. Hinds (eds), *Ovidian Transformations: Essays on Ovid's Metamorphoses and Its Reception*, 13–30, Cambridge: Cambridge Philological Society.

Feeney, D. (2007), *Caesar's Calendar*, Cambridge, MA: Harvard University Press.

Feeney, D. (2010), 'Time and Calendar', in M. Peachin (ed.) *The Oxford Handbook of Roman Studies*, 882–94, Oxford and New York: Oxford University Press.

Feldherr, A. (2010), *Playing Gods: Ovid's Metamorphoses and the Politics of Fiction*, Princeton, NJ: Princeton University Press.

Felson, N. (2011), 'Children of Zeus in the *Homeric Hymns*: Generational Succession', in Faulkner (ed.), 254–79.

Fenik, B. (1968), *Typical Battle Scenes in the Iliad: Studies in the Narrative Techniques of Homeric Battle Description*, Wiesbaden: Steiner.

Fitzgerald, W. (1988), 'Power and Impotence in Horace's *Epodes*', *Ramus* 17: 176–91.

Fitzgerald, W. (2007), *Martial: The World of the Epigram*, Chicago, IL: University of Chicago Press.

Fitzgerald, W. (2018), 'Pliny and Martial: Dupes and Non-Dupes in the Early Empire', in König and Whitton (eds), 108–25.

Foley, J. M. (1991), *Immanent Art: From Structure to Meaning in Traditional Oral Epic*, Bloomington, IN: Indiana University Press.

Forderer, M. (1971), *Anfang und Ende der abendländischen Lyrik: Untersuchungen zum Homerischen Apollonhymnus und zu Anise Koltz*, Amsterdam: Grüner.

Förstel, K. (1979), *Untersuchungen zum Homerischen Apollonhymnos*, Bochum: Brockmeyer.

Foucault, M. (1972), *The Archaeology of Knowledge*, London: Tavistock.

Fowler, D. P. (2000), 'Postmodernism, Romantic Irony, and Classical Closure', in D. P. Fowler, *Roman Constructions: Readings in Postmodern Latin*, 5–33, Oxford: Oxford University Press.

Foxhall, L., H.-J. Gehrke and N. Luraghi (2010), *Intentional History: Spinning Time in Ancient Greece*, Stuttgart: Steiner.

Fränkel, H. (1931), 'Die Zeitauffassung in der frühgriechischen Literatur', *Zeitschrift für Ästhetik und allgemeine Kunstwissenschaft: 4.Kongress-Bericht*, 97–118.

Fränkel, H. (1955), *Wege und Formen frühgriechischen Denkens: literarische und philosophiegeschichtliche Studien*, Munich: Beck.

Fratantuono, L. (2015), *A Reading of Lucretius' De Rerum Natura*, Lanham, MD: Lexington Books.

Freudenburg, K. (2001), *Satires of Rome: Threatening Poses from Lucilius to Juvenal*, Cambridge and New York: Cambridge University Press.

Fritsen, A. (2000), 'Ludovico Lazzarelli's *Fasti Christianae Religionis*: Recipient and Context of an Ovidian Poem', in G. Tournoy and D. Sacre (eds), *Myricae: Essays on Neo-Latin Literature in Memory of Jozef IJsewijn*, 115–32, Leuven: Leuven University Press.

Fritsen, A. (2015), *Antiquarian Voices: The Roman Academy and the Commentary Tradition on Ovid's Fasti*, Columbus, OH: Ohio State University Press.

Gabriel, M. (2015a), *Fields of Sense: A New Realist Ontology*, Edinburgh: Edinburgh University Press.

Gabriel, M. (2015b), *Why the World Does Not Exist*, Cambridge: Polity Press.

Gabriel, M. (2018), *Neo-Existentialism*, Cambridge: Polity Press.

Gagliardi, D. (1998), *Il tempo in Seneca filosofo*, Naples: M. D'Auria.

Galison, P. L. (2003), *Einstein's Clocks, Poincaré's Maps: Empires of Time*, New York: WW Norton & Company.

Garcia, L. F. J. (2013), *Homeric Durability: Telling Time in the Iliad*, Washington, DC: Center for Hellenic Studies.

Garcia, T. (2014), *Form and Object: A Treatise on Things*, trans. M. A. Ohm and J. Cogburn, Edinburgh: Edinburgh University Press.

Garcia, T. (2018), *The Life Intense: A Modern Obsession*, trans. A. RayAlexander, C. RayAlexander and J. Cogburn, Edinburgh: Edinburgh University Press.

Garrard, G. (2012), *Ecocriticism*, London: Routledge.

Garrett, P. (2018), 'Structure and Persuasion in Suetonius' *De vita Caesarum*', *Ramus* 47: 197–215.

Garrett, P. (2019), 'Foreshadowing and Flashback: Childhood Anecdotes in Suetonius' *Caesars*', *Classical Quarterly* 69: 378–83.

Garthwaite, J. (1998), 'Patronage and Poetic Immortality in Martial, Book 9', *Mnemosyne* 51: 161–75.

Gascou, J. (1984), *Suétone Historien*, Rome: École Française à Rome.

Gatz, B. (1967), *Weltalter, goldene Zeit und sinnverwandte Vorstellungen*, Hildesheim: Olms.

Genette, G. (1972), *Figures III*, Paris: Éditions du Seuil.

Genette, G. (1980), *Narrative Discourse: An Essay in Method*, trans. J. Lewin, Ithaca, NY: Cornell University Press.

Gentili, B., C. Catenacci, P. Giannini and L. Lomiento (2013), *Pindaro: Le Olimpiche*, Milan: Mondadori.

Germany, R. (2014), 'The Unity of Time in Plautus' *Captivi*', abstract of paper delivered at Society for Classical Studies meeting, New Orleans, January 2015. Available online: https://classicalstudies.org/annual-meeting/146/abstract/unity-time-plautus%E2%80%99-captivi (accessed 12 June 2023).

Geue, T. (2022), 'Rush Job: Slavery and Brevity in the Early Roman Principate', *Cambridge Classical Journal* 68: 83–111.

Gibbs, R. W. (2017), *Metaphor Wars: Conceptual Metaphors in Human Life*, Cambridge: Cambridge University Press.

Gildenhard, I. and A. Zissos (2004), 'Ovid's "Hecale": Deconstructing Athens in the *Metamorphoses*', *Journal of Roman Studies* 94: 47–72.

Goldhill, S. (2017), 'The Limits of the Case Study: Exemplarity and the Reception of Classical Literature', *New Literary History* 48: 415–35.

Goldhill, S. (2022), *The Christian Invention of Time*, Cambridge: Cambridge University Press.

Goldschmidt, V. (1977), *Le Système stoicien et l'idée de temps*, 3rd edn, Paris: Vrin.

Graef, H. (1963), *Mary: A History of Doctrine and Devotion*, 2 vols, New York: Sheed & Ward.

Graf, F. and Johnston, S. I. (2007), *Ritual Texts for the Afterlife: Orpheus and the Bacchic Gold Tablets*, London and New York: Routledge.

Granger, H. (2007), 'The Theologian Pherecydes of Syros and the Early Days of Natural Philosophy', *Harvard Studies in Classical Philology* 103: 135–63.

Gratwick, A. S. (1979), 'Sundials, Parasites, and Girls from Boeotia', *Classical Quarterly* 29: 308–23.

Greensmith, E. (2020), *The Resurrection of Homer in Imperial Greek Epic*, Oxford: Oxford University Press.

Grethlein, J. (2007), 'The Poetics of the Bath in the *Iliad*', *Harvard Studies in Classical Philology* 103: 25–49.

Grethlein, J. (2014), '"Future Past": Time and Teleology in (Ancient) Historiography', *History and Theory* 53: 309–30.

Grethlein, J. and L. Huitink (2017), 'Homer's Vividness: An Enactive Approach', *Journal of Hellenic Studies* 137: 67–91.

Grethlein, J. and C. B. Krebs, eds (2012), *Time and Narrative in Ancient Historiography: The 'Plupast' from Herodotus to Appian*, Cambridge: Cambridge University Press.

Griffin, J. (1980), *Homer on Life and Death*, Oxford: Oxford University Press.

Griffin, M. (1992), *Seneca: A Philosopher in Politics*, 2nd edn, Oxford: Oxford University Press.

Grimal, P., ed. (1991), *Sénèque et la prose latine*, Geneva: Fondation Hardt.

Gurd, S. A. (2016), *Dissonance: Auditory Aesthetics in Ancient Greece*, New York: Fordham University Press.

Güthenke, C. (2020), '"For Time is / nothing if not amenable" – Exemplarity, Time, Reception', *Classical Receptions Journal* 12: 46–61.

Güthenke, C. and B. Holmes (2018), 'Hyperinclusivity, Hypercanonicity, and the Future of the Field', in M. Formisano and C. S. Kraus (eds), *Marginality, Canonicity, Passion*, 57–74, Oxford: Oxford University Press.

Guthrie, W. K. C. (1965), *A History of Greek Philosophy: Volume 2, The Presocratic Tradition from Parmenides to Democritus*, Cambridge: Cambridge University Press.

Habinek, T. (1982), 'Seneca's Circles: *Ep.* 12.6–9', *Classical Antiquity* 1: 66–9.

Hacking, I. (1994), 'The Looping Effects of Human Kinds', in D. Sperber, D. Premack and A. J. Premack (eds), *Causal Cognition: A Multidisciplinary Approach*, 351–94, Oxford: Clarendon Press.

Hacking, I. (1995), *Rewriting the Soul: Multiple Personality and the Sciences of Memory*, Princeton, NJ: Princeton University Press.

Hacking, I. (1996), 'The Disunities of the Sciences', in P. Galison and D. J. Stump (eds), *The Disunity of Science: Boundaries, Contexts, and Power*, 37–74, Stanford, CA: Stanford University Press.
Hacking, I. (2002), *Historical Ontology*, Cambridge, MA: Harvard University Press.
Hadot, P. (1995) '"Only the Present is Our Happiness": The Value of the Present Instant in Goethe and in Ancient Philosophy', in A. I. Arnoldson (ed.), *Philosophy as a Way of Life*, 217–37, Malden, MA: Blackwell.
Hahn, R. (2012), *Anaximander and the Architects: The Contributions of Egyptian and Greek Architectural Technologies to the Origins of Greek Philosophy*, Albany, NY: State University of New York Press.
Halberstam, J. (2005), *In a Queer Time and Place: Transgender Bodies, Subcultural Lives*, New York and London: New York University Press.
Hamilton, J. T. (2003), *Soliciting Darkness: Pindar, Obscurity, and the Classical Tradition*, Cambridge, MA: Harvard University Press.
Hannah, R. (2009), *Time in Antiquity*, London and New York: Routledge.
Hannam, J. (2009), *God's Philosophers: How the Medieval World Laid the Foundations of Modern Science*, London: Icon Books.
Harman, G. (2018), *Object-Oriented Ontology: A New Theory of Everything*, London: Penguin Random House.
Harrison, S. J. (2007), *Generic Enrichment in Vergil and Horace*, Oxford: Oxford University Press.
Haskins, S. (2008), *Who Is Mary? Three Early Modern Women on the Idea of the Virgin Mary. Vittoria Colonna, Chiara Matraini and Lucrezia Marinella*, Chicago, IL and London: University of Chicago Press.
Heidegger, M. (1962), *Being and Time*, trans. J. Macquarrie and E. Robinson, Oxford: Blackwell.
Heidegger, M. (2002), 'The Origin of the Work of Art', in M. Heidegger, *Off the Beaten Track*, ed. and trans. J. Young and K. Haynes, 1–56, Cambridge: Cambridge University Press.
Heiden, B. (2013), 'Coordinated Sequences of Analogous Topics in the Delian and Pythian Segments of the Homeric Hymn to Apollo', *Trends in Classics* 5: 1–8.
Henderson, J. (2001), 'On Pliny on Martial on Pliny on Anon. . . : (*Epistles* 3.21 / *Epigrams* 10.19)', *Ramus* 30: 56–87.
Henderson, J. (2004), *Morals and Villas in Seneca's Letters*, Cambridge: Cambridge University Press.
Herring, S. (2020), 'The Ancients and the Queer Moderns', in C. Looby and M. North (eds), *Queer Natures, Queer Mythologies*, 271–87, New York: Fordham University Press.
Heubeck, A. (1972), 'Gedanken zum homerischen Apollonhymnus', in *Timetikon Aphieroma: Festschrift für Konstantinos J. Merentitis*, 131–46, Athens.
Heyworth, S. J. (2019), *Ovid: Fasti. Book III*. Cambridge: Cambridge University Press.
Hierche, H. (1974), *Les Épodes d'Horace: Art et Signification*, Brussels: Latomus.

Hijmans, B. L. (1976), *Inlaboratus et facilis: Aspects of Structure in Some Letters of Seneca*, Leiden: Brill.
Hilbert, D. R. (1984), *The Oxford Handbook of Philosophy of Perception*, Oxford: Oxford University Press.
Hinds, S. (1992a), 'Arma in the *Fasti* Part 1: Genre and Mannerism', *Arethusa* 25: 81–112.
Hinds, S. (1992b), 'Arma in the *Fasti* Part 2: Genre, Romulean Rome and Augustan Ideology', *Arethusa* 25: 113–53.
Holford-Strevens, L. (2005), *The History of Time: A Very Short Introduction*, Oxford: Oxford University Press.
Holmes, B. (2020), 'At the End of the Line: On Kairological History', *Classical Receptions Journal* 12: 62–90.
Honig, B. (2009), *Emergency Politics: Paradox, Law, Democracy*, Princeton, NJ: Princeton University Press.
Horsfall, N. (1989), *Cornelius Nepos: A Selection, Including the Lives of Cato and Atticus*, Oxford: Oxford University Press.
Hurley, D. W. (2014), 'Suetonius' Rubric Sandwich', in T. Power and R. K. Gibson (eds), *Suetonius the Biographer: Studies in Roman Lives*, 21–37, Oxford: Oxford University Press.
Hutton, J. (1788), 'Theory of the Earth', *Transactions of the Royal Society of Edinburgh* 1: 215.
Hutton, M. and R. M. Ogilvie (1970), 'Agricola', trans. M. Hutton, rev. R. M. Ogilvie, in *Tacitus in Five Volumes. I: Agricola – Germania – Dialogus*, 3–115, Cambridge, MA: Harvard University Press.
Ildefonse, F. (1997), *La Naissance de la Grammaire dans l'Antiquité grecque*, Paris: Vrin.
Ilievski, V. (2015), 'Eternity and Time in Plato's Timaeus', *Antiquite Vivante* 65: 5–22.
Ingarden, R. (1973), *The Literary Work of Art*, Evanston, IL: Northwestern University Press.
Jaeger, W. (1947), *The Theology of the Early Greek Philosophers*, Oxford: Clarendon Press.
James, W. (1981), *The Works of William James*, ed. F. H. Burkhardt et al., vol. 8. = James, W. *Principles of Psychology*, vol. 1, Cambridge, MA: Harvard University Press.
Janko, R. (1981), 'The Structure of the Homeric Hymns: A Study in Genre', *Hermes* 109: 9–24.
Janko, R. (1982), *Homer, Hesiod, and the Hymns: Diachronic Development in Epic Diction*, Cambridge: Cambridge University Press.
Janko, R. (2011), *Philodemus, On Poems Books 3-4, with the Fragments of Aristotle, On Poets*, Oxford: Oxford University Press.
Johnson, D. M. (1999), 'Hesiod's Descriptions of Tartarus (*Theogony* 721–819)', *Phoenix* 53: 8–28.
Jones, B. W. (1992), *The Emperor Domitian*, London: Routledge.
Jones, P. (2005), *Reading Rivers in Roman Literature and Culture*, Oxford: Lexington Books.

Kahane, A. (2018a), 'Cognitive Functional Grammar and the Complexity of Early Greek Epic Diction', in P. Meineck, W. M. Short and J. Devereaux (eds), *The Routledge Handbook of Classics and Cognitive Theory*, 21–38, London: Routledge.

Kahane, A. (2018b), 'The Complexity of Epic Diction', *Yearbook of Ancient Greek Epic* 2: 78–117.

Kahane, A. (2019), 'Oral Theory and Intertextuality: The Case of the *Homeric Hymns*', in S. Bär and A. Maravela (eds), *Narratology and Intertextuality: New Perspectives on Greek Epic from Homer to Nonnus*, 234–66, Leiden: Brill.

Kahane, A. (2021), 'Disagreement, Complexity and the Politics of Homer's Verbal Form', in P. Vasunia (ed.), *The Politics of Literary Form*, 23–48, London: Bloomsbury.

Kahane, A. (2022a), 'A Narratology of the Emotions: Method, Temporality, and Anger in Homer's *Iliad*', in M. de Bakker, B. van den Berg and J. Klooster (eds), *Emotions and Narrative in Ancient Literature and Beyond*, 27–47, Leiden: Brill.

Kahane, A. (2022b), 'Homer and Ancient Narrative Time', *Classical Antiquity* 41: 1–50.

Kahane, A. (forthcoming), 'The Future of the Past and the Futures of Antiquity', in M. Telò and S. A. Gurd (eds), *The Before and the After*, Punctum Books.

Kahn, C. H. (1994), *Anaximander and the Origins of Greek Cosmology*, Indianapolis, IN: Hackett Publishing.

Kahn, C. H. (2009), *Essays on Being*, Oxford: Oxford University Press.

Kakridis, J. T. (1937), 'Zum homerischen Apollonhymnus', *Philologus* 92: 104–8.

Kaster, R. A. (2016), *C. Suetoni Tranquilli De Vita Caesarum Libros VIII et De Grammaticis et Rhetoribus Librum*, Oxford: Oxford University Press.

Keizer, H. M. (2010), 'Life Time Entirety: A Study of AIΩN in Greek Literature and Philosophy, the Septuagint and Philo', PhD diss., University of Amsterdam, Amsterdam.

Kennedy, D. F. (2013), *Antiquity and the Meanings of Time: A Philosophy of Ancient and Modern Literature*, London: Bloomsbury.

Kennedy, D. F. (2020), 'On Not Being Modern: Exploring Historical Ontology with Bruno Latour', in A. Turner (ed.), *Reconciling Ancient and Modern Philosophies of History*, 43–82, Berlin: De Gruyter.

Ker, J. (2004), 'Nocturnal Writers in Imperial Rome: The Culture of *Lucubratio*', *Classical Philology* 99: 209–42.

Ker, J. (2007), 'Roman *Repraesentatio*', *American Journal of Philology* 128: 341–65.

Ker, J. (2009a), 'Drinking From the Water-Clock: Time and Speech in Imperial Rome', *Arethusa* 42: 279–302.

Ker, J. (2009b), 'Seneca on Self-Examination: Reading *On Anger* 3.36', in Bartsch and Wray (eds), 160–87.

Ker, J. (2009c), *The Deaths of Seneca*, New York: Oxford University Press.

Ker, J. (2019), 'Diurnal Selves in Ancient Rome', in Miller and Symons (eds), 184–213.

Ker, J. (2023), *The Ordered Day: Quotidian Time and Forms of Life in Ancient Rome*, Baltimore, MD: Johns Hopkins University Press.

Kim, L. Y. (2008), 'Time', in T. Whitmarsh (ed.), *The Cambridge Companion to the Greek and Roman Novel*, 145–61, Cambridge: Cambridge University Press.

Kingsley, P. (1995), *Ancient Philosophy, Mystery, and Magic: Empedocles and Pythagorean Tradition*, Oxford: Clarendon Press.

Kirk, G. S. (1981), 'Orality and Structure in the Homeric "Hymn to Apollo"', in C. Brillante, M. Cantilena and C. O. Pavese (eds), *I poemi epici rapsodici non omerici e la tradizione orale: Atti del Convegno di Venezia, 28–30 settembre 1977*, 163–82, Padua: Antenore.

Kirk, G. S. (1985), *The Iliad: A Commentary. Volume I, Books 1–4*, Cambridge: Cambridge University Press.

Kirk, G. S., J. E. Raven and M. Schofield (1983), *The Presocratic Philosophers: A Critical History with a Selection of Texts*, 2nd edn, Cambridge: Cambridge University Press.

Kolk, D. (1963), *Der pythische Apollonhymnus als aitiologische Dichtung*, Meisenheim am Glan: Anton Hain.

Kondoleon, C. (1999), 'Timing Spectacles: Roman Domestic Art and Performance', in B. Bergmann and C. Kondoleon (eds), *The Art of Ancient Spectacle*, 320–41, New Haven, CT: Yale University Press.

König, A. and C. Whitton, eds (2018), *Roman Literature under Nerva, Trajan and Hadrian: Literary Interactions, AD 96–138*, Cambridge: Cambridge University Press.

Koselleck, R. (2002), *The Practice of Conceptual History: Timing History, Spacing Concepts*, Stanford, CA: Stanford University Press.

Koselleck, R. (2004), *Futures Past: On the Semantics of Historical Time*, trans. and with an Introduction by K. Tribe, New York: Columbia University Press.

Kowalzig, B. (2007), *Singing for the Gods: Performances of Myth and Ritual in Archaic and Classical Greece*, Oxford: Oxford University Press.

Kraggerud, E. (1984), *Horaz und Actium: Studien zu den politischen Epoden* (Symbolae Osloenses Suppl. 26), Oslo: Universitetsforlaget.

Kraus, C. S. (2014), 'Long Ago and Far Away: The Uses of the Past in Tacitus' *Minora*', in J. Ker and C. Pieper (eds), *Valuing the Past in the Greco-Roman World: Proceedings from the Penn–Leiden Colloquia on Ancient Values VII*, 219–42, Leiden: Brill.

Lakoff, G. and M. Johnson (1980), *Metaphors We Live By*, Chicago, IL: University of Chicago Press.

Laks, A. and G. Most (2016), *Early Greek Philosophy*, 9 vols, Cambridge, MA: Loeb Classical Library, Harvard University Press.

Lamarque, P. (2009), 'Poetry and Abstract Thought', in P. A. French, H. K. Wettstein and E. Lepore (eds), *Philosophy and Poetry: Midwest Studies in Philosophy 33*, 37–52, Malden, MA: Wiley-Blackwell.

Larash, P. (2008), 'Martial's Short Poems and Catullus' Long Poems', *The Classical Outlook* 85: 136–40.

Lateiner, D. (2014), 'Homer's Social-Psychological Spaces and Places', in M. Skempis and I. Ziogas (eds), *Geography, Topography, Landscape: Configurations of Space in Greek and Roman Epic*, 63–94, Berlin: De Gruyter.

Latour, B. (1988), *The Pasteurization of France*, trans. A. Sheridan and J. Law, Cambridge, MA: Harvard University Press.
Latour, B. (1993), *We Have Never Been Modern*, trans. C. Porter, Cambridge, MA: Harvard University Press.
Latour, B. (1999), *Pandora's Hope: Essays on the Reality of Science Studies*, Cambridge, MA: Harvard University Press.
Latour, B. (2000), 'On the Partial Existence of Existing *and* Nonexisting Objects', in Daston (ed.), 247–69.
Latour, B. (2013), *An Inquiry into Modes of Existence: An Anthropology of the Moderns*, trans. C. Porter, Cambridge, MA: Harvard University Press.
Lavery, G. B. (1980), 'Metaphors of War and Travel in Seneca's Prose Works', *Greece & Rome* 27: 147–57.
Laurence, R. (2011), 'Literature and the Spatial Turn: Movement and Space in Martial's *Epigrams*', in R. Laurence and D. J. Newsome (eds), *Rome, Ostia, Pompeii: Movement and Space*, 81–99, Oxford: Oxford University Press.
Lawson, J. (2011), 'Chronotope, Story, and Historical Geography: Mikhail Bakhtin and the Space-Time of Narratives', *Antipode* 43: 384–412.
Leighton, A. (2018), *Hearing Things: The Work of Sound in Literature*, Cambridge, MA: Harvard University Press.
Leo, F. (1901), *Die griechisch-römische Biographie nach ihrer litterarischen Form*, Leipzig: Teubner.
LeVen, P. A. (2018), 'Echo and the Invention of the Lyric Listener', in Budelmann and Phillips (eds), 213–33.
Lévy, C. (2003), 'Sénèque et la circularité du temps', in B. Bakhouche (ed.), *L'Ancienneté chez les anciens. Tome 2: Mythologie et religion*, 491–509, Montpellier: Presses Universitaires de la Méditerranée.
Loewenstein, D. (1990), *Milton and the Drama of History*, Cambridge: Cambridge University Press.
Long, A. A. and D. Sedley (1987), *The Hellenistic Philosophers*, 2 vols, Cambridge: Cambridge University Press.
Lopez-Ruiz, C. (2010), *When the Gods Were Born: Greek Cosmogonies and the Near East*, Cambridge, MA: Harvard University Press.
Louden, D. B. (2002), 'Eurybates, Odysseus, and the Duals in Book 9 of the *Iliad*', *Colby Quarterly* 38: 62–76.
Lowrie, M. (1997), *Horace's Narrative Odes*, Oxford: Clarendon Press.
Lucci, C. (2011), *Le diverse percezioni del tempo nell'epica greca arcaica: studi sull'Iliade e l'Odissea*, Pisa: Edizioni EDS.
Luckmann, T. (1991), 'The Constitution of Human Life in Time', in J. Bender and D. Wellbery (eds), *Chronotypes: The Construction of Time*, 151–66, Stanford, CA: Stanford University Press.
Lyle, E. B. (1984), 'The Circus as Cosmos', *Latomus* 43: 827–41
Lynn-George, M. (1988), *Epos, Word, Narrative and the Iliad*, London: Palgrave Macmillan.

MacCaffrey, I. G. (1959), *Paradise Lost as Myth*, Cambridge, MA: Harvard University Press.
Macé, A. (2017), 'Nature Among the Greeks: Empirical Philology and the Ontological Turn in Historical Anthropology', in P. Charbonnier, G. Salmon and P. Skafish (eds), *Comparative Metaphysics: Ontology After Anthropology*, 201–20, London: Rowman & Littlefield Publishers.
Macleod, C. M. (1974), 'Two Comparisons in Sappho', *ZPE* 15: 217–20.
Mankin, D. (1995), *Horace: Epodes*, Cambridge: Cambridge University Press.
Mansfeld, J. (2018), *Studies in Early Greek Philosophy*, Leiden: Brill.
Marchesi, I. (2013), 'Silenced Intertext: Pliny on Martial on Pliny (on Regulus)', *American Journal of Philology* 134: 101–18.
Marshall, P. K. (1991), *Cornelii Nepotis Vitae cum Fragmentis*, Stuttgart and Leipzig: Teubner.
Martinet, H. (2014), *C. Suetonius Tranquillus: Die Kaiserviten, Berühmte Männer*, 4th edn, Berlin and Boston, MA: De Gruyter.
Maslov, B. (2015), *Pindar and the Emergence of Literature*, Cambridge: Cambridge University Press.
Matlock, A. (2020), 'Relationality, Fidelity, and the Event in Sappho', *Classical Antiquity* 39: 29–56.
Mayer, R. G. (2003), 'Pliny and *gloria Dicendi*', *Arethusa* 36: 227–34.
Mazzoli, G. (1989), 'Le *Epistulae morales ad Lucilium* di Seneca: valore letterario e filosofico', *Aufsteig und Niedergang der Römischen Welt* II.36.3: 1823–77.
McInerney, M. (2020), 'Queer Time for Heroes in the *Roman d'Enés* and the *Roman de Troie*', in W. Rogers and C. M. Roman (eds), *Medieval Futurity*, 107–28, Berlin and Boston, MA: Medieval Institute Publications.
Meisner, D. A. (2018), *Orphic Tradition and the Birth of the Gods*, Oxford: Oxford University Press.
Meister, J. C. and W. Schernus, eds (2011), *Time: From Concept to Narrative Construct: A Reader*, Berlin and Boston, MA: De Gruyter.
Merleau-Ponty, M. (2012), *Phenomenology of Perception*, trans. D. A. Landes, London: Routledge.
Meuli, K. (1975), *Gesammelte Schriften*, Basel and Stuttgart: Schwabe.
Michael, J. (2017), 'Lyric History: Temporality, Rhetoric, and the Ethics of Poetry', *New Literary History* 48: 265–84.
Miller, F. J. (1916/77), *Ovid. Metamorphoses*, 2 vols, rev. G. P. Goold, Cambridge, MA: Harvard University Press.
Miller, A. M. (1979), 'The "Address to the Delian Maidens" in the *Homeric Hymn to Apollo*. Epilogue or Transition?', *Transactions of the American Philological Association* 109: 173–86.
Miller, A. M. (1986), *From Delos to Delphi: A Literary Study of the Homeric Hymn to Apollo*, Leiden: Brill.
Miller, D. A. (1981), *Narrative and Its Discontents: Problems of Closure in the Traditional Novel*, Princeton, NJ: Princeton University Press.

Miller, J. F. (2003), 'Ovid's *Fasti* and the Neo-Latin Christian Calendar Poem', *International Journal of the Classical Tradition* 10: 173–86.

Miller, K. J. and S. L. Symons, eds (2019), *Down to the Hour: Short Time in the Ancient Mediterranean and Near East*, Leiden and Boston, MA: Brill.

Mitchell, A. J. (2011), 'Heidegger's Poetics of Relationality', in D. O. Dahlstrom (ed.), *Interpreting Heidegger: Critical Essays*, 217–31, Cambridge: Cambridge University Press.

Molde, K. (2020), 'Towards a Theory of Poetic License: Lyric Enchantment and Lyric Embarrassment', *Poetics Today* 41: 561–93.

Momigliano, A. (1993), *The Development of Greek Biography*, expanded edn, Cambridge, MA: Harvard University Press.

Moore, C. (2020), *Calling Philosophers Names: On the Origins of a Discipline*, Princeton, NJ: Princeton University Press.

Morgan, K. A. (2015), *Pindar and the Construction of Syracusan Monarchy in the Fifth Century B.C.*, Oxford: Oxford University Press.

Morson, G. S. (1994), *Narrative and Freedom: The Shadows of Time*, New Haven, CT: Yale University Press.

Morton, T. (2013), *Hyperobjects: Philosophy and Ecology after the End of the World*, Minneapolis, MN: University of Minnesota Press.

Moss, C. (forthcoming), 'Chronometric Violence: Sleeplessness, Enslavement, and the Mechanics of Control'.

Most, G. W. (2005), 'How Many Homers?', in A. Santoni (ed.), *L'Autore multiplo – Pisa, Scuola Normale Superiore, 18 ottobre 2002*, 1–14, Pisa: Scuola Normale Superiore.

Müller, T. (2016), 'The Ecology of Literary Chronotopes', in H. Zapf (ed.), *Handbook of Ecocriticism and Cultural Ecology*, 590–604, Berlin: De Gruyter.

Nagy, G. (2011), 'The Earliest Phases in the Reception of the *Homeric Hymns*', in Faulkner (ed.), 280–333.

Nail, T. (2019), *Being and Motion*, New York: Oxford University Press.

Nauta, R. R. (2002), *Poetry for Patrons: Literary Communication in the Age of Domitian*, Leiden: Brill.

Nersessian, A. (2020), *The Calamity Form: On Poetry and Social Life*, Chicago, IL: University of Chicago Press.

Nethercut, J. S. (2021), *Ennius Noster: Lucretius and the Annales*, New York: Oxford University Press.

Newlands, C. (1995), *Playing with Time: Ovid and the Fasti*, Ithaca, NY: Cornell University Press.

Nightingale, A. W. (1995), *Genres in Dialogue: Plato and the Construct of Philosophy*, Cambridge: Cambridge University Press.

Nightingale, A. W. (2004), *Spectacles of Truth in Classical Greek Philosophy*, Cambridge: Cambridge University Press.

Niles, J. D. (1979), 'On the Design of the *Hymn to Delian Apollo*', *Classical Journal* 75: 36–9.

Nipperdey, K. (1849), *Cornelius Nepos*, Leipzig: Weidmann.
Nisbet, R. G. M. (1978), 'Virgil's Fourth Eclogue: Easterners and Westerners', *Bulletin of the Institute of Classical Studies* 25: 59–78.
Nisbet, R. G. M. (1984), 'Horace's *Epodes* and History', in T. Woodman and D. West (eds), *Poetry and Politics in the Age of Augustus*, 1–18, Cambridge: Cambridge University Press.
Norfolk, S. (2002), *Afghanistan: Chronotopia*, Arles: Actes Sud.
Norwood, G. (1945), *Pindar*, Berkeley and Los Angeles, CA: University of California Press.
Nowotny, H. (1994), *Time: The Modern and Postmodern Experience*, trans. N. Plaice, Cambridge: Polity Press.
Odell, D. W. (1972), 'Young's *Night Thoughts* as an Answer to Pope's *Essay on Man*', *Studies in English Literature 1500–1900*, 12: 481–501.
O'Donnell, J. (2019), 'The Power of Forgetting', *Transactions of the American Philological Association* 149: 235–46.
Ogle, V. (2019), 'Time, Temporality and the History of Capitalism', *Past and Present* 243: 312–27.
Oliensis, E. (1998), *Horace and the Rhetoric of Authority*, Cambridge: Cambridge University Press.
O'Meara, L. (2013), '"Not a Question But a Wound": Adorno, Barthes, and Aesthetic Reflection', *Comparative Literature* 65: 182–99.
Owen, G. E. L. (1966), 'Plato and Parmenides on the Timeless Present', *The Monist* 50: 317–40.
Palmer, J. (2009), *Parmenides and Presocratic Philosophy*, Oxford: Oxford University Press.
Palmer, J. (2016), 'Elemental Change in Empedocles', *Rhizomata* 4: 20–54.
Panizza, L. (1983), 'Textual Interpretation in Italy, 1350–1450: Seneca's Letter 1 to Lucilius', *Journal of the Warburg and Courtauld Institutes* 46: 40–62.
Papadopoulou, Z. and I. Papadopoulou-Belmehdi, (2002): 'Musique et culte: Le cas des Déliades', in F. Labrique (ed.), *Religions méditerranéennes et orientales de l'Antiquité: actes du colloque des 23–24 avril 1999, Institut des sciences et techniques de l'Antiquité*, 155–76, Le Caire: Institut français d'archéologie orientale.
Papaioannou, S. (2004), '*Ut non [forma] cygnorum, sic albis proxima cyginis*: Poetology, Epic Definition, and Swan Imagery in Ovid's *Metamorphoses*', *Phoenix* 58: 49–61.
Passmore, O. (2019), 'Present, Future and Past in the *Homeric Hymn to Apollo*', *Ramus* 47: 123–51.
Pausch, D. (2004), *Biographie und Bildungskultur: Personendarstellungen bei Plinius dem Jüngeren, Gellius und Sueton*, Berlin and New York: De Gruyter.
Payne, M. (2006), 'On Being Vatic: Pindar, Pragmatism, and Historicism', *American Journal of Philology* 127: 159–84.
Payne, M. (2014), 'The Natural World in Greek Literature and Philosophy', in G. Williams (ed.), *Oxford Handbooks Online in Classical Studies*, Oxford: Oxford

University Press. Available online: 10.1093/oxfordhb/9780199935390.013.001 (accessed 12 June 2023).

Payne, M. (2018a), 'Fidelity and Farewell: Pindar's Ethics as Textual Events', in Budelmann and Phillips (eds), 257–74.

Payne, M. (2018b), *Hontology: Depressive Anthropology and the Shame of Life*, Winchester: Zero Books.

Pelling, C. B. R. (2012a), 'Biography, Greek', in S. Hornblower and A. Spawforth (eds), *The Oxford Classical Dictionary*, 4th edn, 232–3, Oxford: Oxford University Press.

Pelling, C. B. R. (2012b), 'Biography, Latin', in S. Hornblower and A. Spawforth (eds), *The Oxford Classical Dictionary*, 4th edn, 233–4, Oxford: Oxford University Press.

Peponi, A.-E. (2009), 'Choreia and Aesthetics in the *Homeric Hymn to Apollo*: The Performance of the Delian Maidens (Lines 156–64)', *Classical Antiquity* 28: 39–70.

Peterle, G. and Visentin, F. (2017), 'Performing the Literary Map: "Towards the River Mouth" Following Gianni Celati', *Cultural Geographies* 24: 473–85.

Petrovic, I. (2013), 'The Never-Ending Stories: A Perspective on Greek Hymns', in F. F. Grewing, B. Acosta-Hughes and A. Kirichenko (eds), *The Door Ajar: False Closure in Greek and Roman Literature and Art*, 203–28, Heidelberg: Winter.

Phillips, T. (2016), *Pindar's Library: Performance Poetry and Material Texts*, Oxford: Oxford University Press.

Phillips, T. (2020), *Untimely Epic: Apollonius Rhodius' Argonautica*, Oxford: Oxford University Press.

Pinkster, H. (2015), *The Oxford Latin Syntax. Vol. 1: The Simple Clause*, Oxford: Oxford University Press.

Porter, J. I. (2004), 'Homer: The History of An Idea', in R. L. Fowler (ed.), *The Cambridge Companion to Homer*, 324–43, Cambridge: Cambridge University Press.

Porter, J. I. (2019), 'Hyperobjects, OOO, and the Eruptive Classics – Field Notes of an Accidental Tourist', in E. Bianchi, S. Brill and B. Holmes (eds), *Antiquities Beyond Humanism*, 189–209, Oxford: Oxford University Press.

Porter, J. I. (2020), 'Living on the Edge: Self and World *in extremis* in Roman Philosophy', *Classical Antiquity* 39: 225–83.

Porter, J. I. (2021), *Homer: The Very Idea*, Chicago, IL: University of Chicago Press.

Preller, L. (1846), 'Studien zur griechischen Litteratur', *Rheinisches Museum für Philologie* 4: 377–405.

Protevi, J. (1996), *Time and Exteriority: Aristotle, Heidegger, Derrida*, London: Bucknell University Press.

Purves, A. (2006), 'Falling into Time in Homer's *Iliad*', *Classical Antiquity* 25: 179–209.

Purves, A. C. (2010a), *Space and Time in Ancient Greek Narrative*, Cambridge: Cambridge University Press.

Purves, A. C. (2010b), 'Wind and Time in Homeric Epic', *Transactions of the American Philological Association* 140: 323–50.

Purves, A. (2021), 'Sappho's Lyric Sensibility', in P. J. Finglass and A. Kelly (eds), *The Cambridge Companion to Sappho*, 175–89, Cambridge: Cambridge University Press.

Ramage, E. S. (1989), 'Juvenal and the Establishment: Denigration of Predecessor in the *Satires*', *Aufstieg und Niedergang der Römischen Welt* II.33.1: 640–707.
Reece, S. (2010), 'Epithets', in M. Finkelberg (ed.), *The Homer Encyclopedia*, 257–59, Malden, MA: Wiley-Blackwell.
Reitz, C. (2019), 'Divine Council Scenes in Ancient Epic', in C. Reitz and S. Finkmann (eds), *Structures of Epic Poetry*, vol. II, pt 2, 719–46, Berlin and Boston, MA: De Gruyter.
Renfrew, A. (2014), *Mikhail Bakhtin*, London: Routledge.
Reydams-Schils, G. (2005), *The Roman Stoics: Self, Responsibility and Affection*, Chicago, IL: University of Chicago Press.
Richardson, N. (2010), *Three Homeric Hymns: To Apollo, Hermes, and Aphrodite. Hymns 3, 4, and 5*, Cambridge: Cambridge University Press.
Richardson-Hay, C. (2006), *First Lessons: Book 1 of Seneca's Epistulae Morales. A Commentary*, Bern et al.: Peter Lang.
Richardson-Hay, C. (2009), 'Dinner at Seneca's Table: The Philosophy of Food', *Greece & Rome* 56: 71–96.
Ricoeur, P. (1984–8), *Time and Narrative*, Chicago, IL: University of Chicago Press.
Rietra, J. R. (1928), 'C. Suetonii Tranquilli Vita Tiberii. C. 24–C. 40', diss., Amsterdam: H. J. Paris.
Rijksbaron, A. (2011), 'Introduction', in J. Lallot, A. Rijksbaron, B. Jacquinod and M. Buijs (eds), *The Historical Present in Thucydides: Semantics and Narrative Function*, 1–18, Leiden: Brill.
Rimell, V. (2008), *Martial's Rome: Empire and the Ideology of Epigram*, Cambridge: Cambridge University Press.
Rimell, V. (2017), 'Philosophy's Folds: Seneca, Cavarero and the History of Rectitude', *Hypatia* 32: 768–83.
Rimell, V. (2018), 'I Will Survive (You): Martial and Tacitus on Regime Change', in König and Whitton (eds), 63–85.
Riverso, E. (1979), *Filosofia Analitica del Tempo*, Rome: Armando.
Roark, T. (2011), *Aristotle on Time: A Study of the Physics*, Cambridge: Cambridge University Press.
Roller, M. (2004), 'Exemplarity in Roman Culture: The Cases of Horatius Cocles and Cloelia', *Classical Philology* 99: 1–56.
Roman, L. (2001), 'The Representation of Literary Materiality in Martial's *Epigrams*', *Journal of Roman Studies* 91: 113–45.
Rood, T., C. Atack and T. Phillips (2020), *Anachronism and Antiquity*, London and New York: Bloomsbury.
Rouse, W. H. D. (1890), 'δολιχόσκιος = Zd. dareghaarstaya', *Classical Review* 4: 183.
Ryberg, I. S. (1958), 'Vergil's Golden Age', *Transactions of the American Philological Association* 89: 112–31.
Saggi, L. (1954), *La congregazione mantovana dei Carmelitani sino alla morte del B. Battista Spagnoli (1516)*, Rome: Institutum Carmelitanum.

Sailor, D. (2004), 'Becoming Tacitus: Significance and Inconsequentiality in the Prologue of *Agricola*', *Classical Antiquity* 23: 139–77.
Saller, R. P. (1983), 'Martial on Patronage and Literature', *Classical Quarterly* 33: 246–57.
Salmon, P. (2020), *An Event, Perhaps: A Biography of Jacques Derrida*, New York and London: Verso.
Sangalli, E. (1988), 'Tempo narrato e tempo vissuto nelle *Epistulae ad Lucilium* di Seneca', *Athenaeum* 78: 53–67.
Santamaría, M. A. (2019), 'Pherecydes of Syros in the Papyrological Tradition', in C. Vassallo (ed.), *Presocratics and Papyrological Tradition*, 91–107, Berlin and Boston, MA: De Gruyter.
Santamaría, M. A. (2021), 'The Emergence of the World in Early Greek Theogonies from Hesiod to Acusilaus', in A. B. Pajares and R. M. Hernández (eds), *Narrating the Beginnings*, 117–38, Wiesbaden: Springer.
Sattler, B. M. (2017), 'How Natural is a Unified Notion of Time?', in I. Phillips (ed.), *The Routledge Handbook of Philosophy of Temporal Experience*, 19–29, London and New York: Routledge.
Šćepanović, S. (2012), 'Αἰών and χρόνος: Their Semantic Development in the Greek Poets and Philosophers Down to 400 BC', PhD diss., University of Oxford, Oxford.
Schenk, P. (2004), '*At id quidem nostris moribus nefas habetur*: Rhetorische Kunst und interkultureller Diskurs in der *praefatio* des Cornelius Nepos', *Göttinger Forum für Altertumswissenschaft* 7: 163–83.
Schibli, H. (1990), *Pherekydes of Syros*, Oxford: Oxford University Press.
Schiesaro, A. (2014), '*Materiam superabat opus*: Lucretius Metamorphosed', *Journal of Roman Studies* 104: 73–104.
Schiesaro, A. (2020), 'Lucretius' Apocalyptic Imagination', *Materiali e discussioni per l'analisi dei testi classici* 84: 27–93.
Schiller, J. C. F. von (1993), 'On Naïve and Sentimental Poetry', in J. C. F. von Schiller, *Essays*, ed. and trans. W. Hinderer and D. O. Dahlstrom, 179–260, New York: Continuum.
Schofield, M. (1988), 'The Retrenchable Present', in J. Barnes and M. Mignucci (eds), *Matter and Metaphysics*, 329–74, Naples: Bibliopolis.
Sedley, D. (1998), *Lucretius and the Transformation of Greek Wisdom*, Cambridge: Cambridge University Press.
Sentesy, M. (2018), 'The Now and the Relation between Motion and Time in Aristotle: A Systematic Reconstruction', *Apeiron* 51: 279–323.
Shaw, B. (2019), 'Did the Romans Have a Future?', *Journal of Roman Studies* 109: 1–26.
Shoemaker, S. J. (2016), *Mary in Early Christian Faith and Devotion*, New Haven, CT and London: Yale University Press.
Short, W. (2016), 'Spatial Metaphors of Time in Roman Culture', *Classical World* 108: 381–412.
Shumaker, W. (1967), *Unpremeditated Verse: Feeling and Perception in Paradise Lost*, Princeton, NJ: Princeton University Press.

Smyth, H. W. (1920), *A Greek Grammar for Colleges*, New York et al.: American Book Company.

Snell, B. (1953), *The Discovery of the Mind*, trans. T. G. Rosenmeyer, Oxford: Blackwell.

Soldati, B. (1903), 'Gl'inni sacri d'un astrologo del' Rinascimento', in *Miscellanea di studi in onore di A. Graf*, 405–29, Bergamo: Instituto italiano d'arti grafiche.

Soldo, J. (2021), *Seneca: Epistulae Morales. Book 2*, Oxford: Oxford University Press.

Solmsen, F. (1982), 'The Earliest Stages in the History of Hesiod's Text', *Harvard Studies in Classical Philology* 86: 1–31.

Sorabji, R. (1983), *Time, Creation and the Continuum: Theories in Antiquity and the Early Middle Ages*, London: Duckworth.

Sorall, M. F. (1990), 'Place, Voice, Space: Mikhail Bakhtin's Dialogical Landscape', *Environment and Planning D: Society and Space*, 8: 256–74.

Southern, P. (1997), *Domitian: Tragic Tyrant*, London and New York: Routledge.

Sowa, C. B. A. (1984), *Traditional Themes and the Homeric Hymns*, Chicago, IL: Bolchazy-Carducci.

Spelman, H. L. (2018a), 'Event and Artefact: The *Homeric Hymn to Apollo*, Archaic Lyric, and Early Greek Literary History', in Budelmann and Phillips (eds), 151–71.

Spelman, H. L. (2018b), *Pindar and the Poetics of Permanence*, Oxford: Oxford University Press.

Spelman, H. L. (2020), 'The View from Olympus: The Muses' Song in the *Homeric Hymn to Apollo*', *Classical Quarterly* 70: 1–9.

Spencer, D. (2010), *Roman Landscape: Culture and Identity*, Cambridge: Cambridge University Press.

Stadter, P. (2007), 'Biography and History', in J. Marincola (ed.), *A Companion to Greek and Roman Historiography*, 528–40, Malden, MA: Wiley–Blackwell.

Stamatellos, G. (2012), *Plotinus and the Presocratics: A Philosophical Study of Presocratic Influences in Plotinus' Enneads*, Albany, NY: State University of New York Press.

Stamatopoulou, Z. (2017), *Hesiod and Classical Greek Poetry: Reception and Transformation in the Fifth Century BCE*, Cambridge: Cambridge University Press.

Starr, R. J. (1980), 'Velleius' Literary Techniques in the Organization of His History', *Transactions of the American Philological Association* 110: 287–301.

Steel, D. (2000), *Marking Time: The Epic Quest to Invent the Perfect Calendar*, New York: Wiley and Sons.

Stégen, G. (1972), '*Vnus dies par omni est* (Héraclite fr.1063 Diels dans Sén. Epist. 12.7)', *Latomus* 31: 829–32.

Stehle, E. (1996), *Performance and Gender in Ancient Greece: Nondramatic Poetry in Its Setting*, Princeton, NJ: Princeton University Press.

Stein, N. (2015), 'Aristotle on Parts of Time and Being in Time', *Review of Metaphysics* 69: 495–518.

Stem, S. R. (2012), *The Political Biographies of Cornelius Nepos*, Ann Arbor, MI: University of Michigan Press.

Stephens, S. A. (2015), *Callimachus: The Hymns*, Oxford: Oxford University Press.

Stocks, C. (2016), 'Monster at Night: Hannibal, *Prodigia*, and the Parallel Worlds of *Epode* 16 and *Ode* 4.4', in P. Bather and C. Stocks (eds), *Horace's Epodes: Contexts, Intertexts, and Reception*, 153–74, Oxford: Oxford University Press.

Sutherland, J., ed. (1953), *Alexander Pope: The Dunciad*, revised edn, London and New Haven, CT: Methuen.

Syrad, K. (2019), 'Introduction', in P. Hughes, *Tracks: Walking the Ancient Landscapes of Britain*, 6–17, London: Thames & Hudson.

Tanaka, S. (2016), 'History Without Chronology', *Public Culture* 28: 161–86.

Tarán, L. (1979), 'Perpetual Duration and Atemporal Eternity in Parmenides and Plato', *The Monist* 62: 43–53.

Tarán, L. and D. Gutas (2012), *Aristotle: Poetics. Editio Maior of the Greek Text with Historical Introductions and Philological Commentaries*, Leiden: Brill.

Tennant, P. M. W. (2000), 'Poets and Poverty: The Case of Martial', *Acta Classica* 43: 139–56.

Thalmann, W. G. (1984), *Conventions of Form and Thought in Early Greek Epic Poetry*, Baltimore, MD: Johns Hopkins University Press.

The Postclassicisms Collective (2020), *Postclassicisms*, Chicago, IL: University of Chicago Press.

Theunissen, M. (2002), 'Griechische Zeitbegriffe vor Platon', *Archiv für Begriffsgeschichte* 44: 7–23.

Trümpy, H. (1979), *Die Fasti des Baptista Mantuanus von 1516 als volkskundliche Quelle: Textauswahl, Übersetzung und Kommentar*, Nieuwkoop: B. de Graaf.

Unte, W. (1968), 'Studien zum homerischen Apollonhymnos', diss., FU Berlin, Berlin.

Ustinova, Y. (2009), *Caves and the Ancient Greek Mind: Descending Underground in the Search for Ultimate Truth*, Oxford: Oxford University Press.

van Berkel, T. A. (2020), 'The Ethical Life of a Fragment: Three Readings of Protagoras' Man Measure Statement', in D. C. Wolfsdorf (ed.), *Early Greek Ethics*, 74–109, Oxford: Oxford University Press.

Versnel, H. (1993), *Inconsistencies in Greek and Roman Religion, Volume 2: Transition and Reversal in Myth and Ritual*, Leiden: Brill.

Viparelli, V. (2000), *Il senso e il non senso del tempo in Seneca*, Naples: Loffredo.

Vlastos, G. (1952), 'Theology and Philosophy in Early Greek Thought', *The Philosophical Quarterly* 2: 97–123.

Vlastos, G (1965a), 'Creation in the Timaeus: Is It a Fiction?', in R. E. Allen (ed.), *Studies in Plato's Metaphysics*, 401–19, London and New York: Routledge.

Vlastos, G. (1965b), 'The Disorderly Motion in the Timaeus', in R. E. Allen (ed.), *Studies in Plato's Metaphysics*, 379–99, London and New York: Routledge.

Vogt, W. (1975), 'C. Suetonius Tranquillus, Vita Tiberii. Kommentar', diss., Würzburg.

Vogt-Spira, G. (2017), 'Time in Horace and Seneca', in M. Stöckinger, K. Winter and A. Zanker (eds), *Horace and Seneca: Interactions, Intertexts, Interpretations*, 185–210, Berlin and Boston, MA: De Gruyter.

Volk, K. (1997), 'Cum carmine crescit et annus: Ovid's *Fasti* and the Poetics of Simultaneity', *Transactions of the American Philological Association* 127: 287–313.
von Leyden, W. (1964), 'Time, Number, and Eternity in Plato and Aristotle', *The Philosophical Quarterly* 14 (54): 35–52.
von Wilamowitz-Moellendorff, U. (1922), *Pindaros*, Berlin: Weidmann.
Wallace-Hadrill, A. (1983), *The Scholar and His Caesars*, London: Duckworth.
Wallace-Hadrill, A. (1987), 'Time for Augustus: Ovid, Augustus and the *Fasti*', in Michael Whitby, P. R. Hardie and Mary Whitby (eds), *Homo Viator: Classical Essays for John Bramble*, 221–30, Bristol: Bristol Classical Press.
Walter, A. (2020), *Time and Ancient Stories of Origin*, Oxford: Oxford University Press.
Ward, M. (2019), 'Glory and Nostos: The Ship-Epithet ΚΟΙΛΟΣ in the *Iliad*', *Classical Quarterly* 69: 23–34.
Warren, J. (2006), 'Epicureans and the Present Past', *Phronesis* 51: 362–87.
Waters, K. H. (1964), 'The Character of Domitian', *Phoenix* 18: 49–77.
Waters, K. H. (1969), 'Traianus Domitiani Continuator', *American Journal of Philology* 90: 385–404.
Watson, J. S. (1886), 'Cornelius Nepos: Lives of Eminent Commanders' in J. S. Watson, *Justin, Nepos, and Eutropius*, 305–450, London: Henry Bohn. Available online: https://www.tertullian.org/fathers/nepos.htm (accessed 12 June 2023).
Watson, L. (2003), *A Commentary on Horace's Epodes*, Oxford: Oxford University Press.
Watson, P. and L. Watson (2009), 'Seneca and Felicio: Imagery and Purpose', *Classical Quarterly* 59: 212–25.
Weinreich, O. (1937), *Phöbus, Aurora, Kalender und Uhr: Über eine Doppelform der epischen Zeitbestimmung in der Erzählkunst der Antike und Neuzeit*, Stuttgart: Kohlhammer.
West, M. L. (1963), 'Three Presocratic Cosmologies', *Classical Quarterly* 13, 154–76.
West, M. L. (1971), *Early Greek Philosophy and the Orient*, Oxford: Oxford University Press.
West, M. L. (1975), 'Cynaethus' Hymn to Apollo', *Classical Quarterly* 25: 161–70.
West, M. L. (1978), *Hesiod: Works and Days. Edited with Prolegomena and Commentary*, Oxford: Clarendon Press.
West, M. L. (1983), *The Orphic Poems*, Oxford: Clarendon Press.
West, M. L. (2003), *Homeric Hymns. Homeric Apocrypha. Lives of Homer*, Cambridge, MA: Harvard University Press.
Wheeler, S. M. (1999), *A Discourse of Wonders: Audience and Performance in Ovid's Metamorphoses*, Philadelphia, PA: University of Philadelphia Press.
Wheeler, S. M. (2000), *Narrative Dynamics in Ovid's Metamorphoses*, Tübingen: Gunter Narr.
Whitmarsh, T. (2007), 'Philostratus', in de Jong and Nünlist (eds), 413–30.
Whittaker, J. (1968), 'The "Eternity" of the Platonic Forms', *Phronesis* 13: 131–44.
Wilberding, J. G. (2016), 'Eternity in Ancient Philosophy', in Y. Y. Melamed (ed.), *Eternity: A History*, 14–55, Oxford: Oxford University Press.

Wilcox, D. J. (1987), *The Measure of Times Past: Pre-Newtonian Chronology and the Rhetoric of Relative Time*, Chicago, IL: University of Chicago Press.
Williams, G. D. (2003), *Seneca: De Otio, De Brevitate Vitae*, Cambridge: Cambridge University Press.
Williams, G. D. (2012), *The Cosmic Viewpoint: A Study of Seneca's Natural Questions*, Oxford: Oxford University Press.
Wilson, M. (2003), 'After the Silence: Tacitus, Suetonius, Juvenal', in A. J. Boyle and W. J. Dominik (eds), *Flavian Rome: Culture, Image, Text*, 523–42, Leiden: Brill.
Wings of Desire (1987) [Film] Dir. Wim Wenders, France: Argos Films.
Winterbottom, M. and R. M. Ogilvie (1975), *Cornelii Taciti Opera Minora*, Oxford: Oxford University Press.
Wolkenhauer, A. (2011), *Sonne und Mond, Kalender und Uhr: Studien zur Darstellung und poetischen Reflexion der Zeitordnung in der römischen Literatur*, Berlin and New York: De Gruyter.
Wolkenhauer, A. (2019), 'Time, Punctuality and Chronotopes: Concepts and Attitudes Concerning Short Time in Ancient Rome', in Miller and Symons (eds), 214–38.
Woodman, A. J. (1975), 'Questions of Date, Genre, and Style in Velleius: Some Literary Answers', *Classical Quarterly* 25: 272–306.
Woodman, A. J. and C. S. Kraus (2014), *Tacitus, Agricola*, Cambridge: Cambridge University Press.
Zanker, A. T. (2019), *Metaphor in Homer: Time, Speech, and Thought*, Cambridge: Cambridge University Press.
Zapf, H., ed. (2016), *Handbook of Ecocriticism and Cultural Ecology*, Berlin and Boston, MA: De Gruyter.
Zeller, E. (1932), *La filosofia dei Greci nel suo sviluppo storico*, Florence: La Nuova Italia.
Zinn, P. (2016), 'Lucretius On Time and Its Perception', *Kriterion* 30: 125–151.
Zissos, A. and I. Gildenhard (1999), 'Problems of Time in *Metamorphoses 2*', in P. Hardie, A. Barchiesi and S. Hinds (eds), *Ovidian Transformations: Essays on Ovid's Metamorphoses and its Reception,* 31–47, Cambridge: Cambridge Philological Society.
Zucker, A. (2016), 'Themistius', in A. Falcon (ed.), *Brill's Companion to the Reception of Aristotle in Antiquity*, 358–73, Leiden: Brill.
Zumthor, P. (1990), *Oral Poetry: An Introduction*, Minneapolis, MN: University of Minnesota Press.

Index of Passages

Anaximander
  fr. B1 D–K: 98, 100

Aristophanes
  Birds
  468–9: 96
  693–702: 94–6

Aristotle
  Metaphysics
  XIV.4, 1091b4–14: 96

  Nicomachean Ethics
  X.4, 1174a19–22: 19

  On Generation and Corruption
  I.3, 317b34: 40

  Physics
  IV.11, 219a22–6: 18

  Poetics
  9, 1451b6: 47
  25, 1461a3: 33 n.32

  Politics
  VII.16, 1335a6–7: 31 n.7
  VII.16, 1335a28–37: 31 n.7

Bacchylides
  9.27–32: 122 n.41
  fr. 7.1: 104 n.31

Bible
  Genesis 3.1-24: 202
  Genesis 3.15: 231 n.2
  Amos 4.12: 232 n.14
  Matthew 1.18-25: 199
  Matthew 24.36-44: 232 n.12
  Luke 1.26-38: 199, 203, 214 n.26
  Luke 1.38: 209
  1 Thessalonians 5.1-3: 232 n.12
  Peter 3.10: 232 n.12

Caesar
  Civil War
  2.42.3: 156 n.23
  3.37.5: 156 n.23
  3.38.4: 156 n.23

  Gallic War
  7.67.7: 156 n.23
  8.28.2 (Hirtius): 156 n.23
  8.48.1 (Hirtius): 156 n.23

Catherall, Samuel
  An Essay on the Conflagration
  epigraph: 231 n.11
  Preface: 222
  p. 6: 221

Chrysippus
  Long and Sedley 51B3–4: 65
  SVF II 509: 190 n.26

Cicero
  Aratea
  512: 192 n.47

  Cato Maior de senectute
  15: 191 n.36
  24: 182

  De inventione
  1.20: 145

  De re publica
  6.15–16: 192 n.47

Dante Alighieri
  Commedia
  Purgatorio 10.44: 200
  Paradiso 33.19: 200

Diogenes Laertius
  8.32: 105 n.72

Euphorion
  P.Oxy. 3830 fr. 3: 106 n.77

Euripides
  Heraclidae
  37: 105 n.71

Supplices
545: 105 n.71
926: 105 n.71

Troades
952: 105 n.71

fragments
484.2–6: 104 n.41

Fracco, Ambrogio 'Novidio'
Sacri Fasti
III, p. 24a: 215 n.34
III, p. 24b: 206–7, 215 n.34
III, p. 24b–25b: 208, 215 n.36
III, p. 26a: 209
III, p. 32b–34a: 209–10

Gellius, Aulus
Noctes Atticae
Praef.4: 191 n.28
3.3.5: 57

Heraclitus
B49a D–K: 187, 193 n.61

Herodotus
1.30: 44–5, 47
2.19: 140 n.25
2.51: 105 n.70
8.65: 105 n.70

Hesiod
Theogony
34: 104 n.34
119: 105 n.71
728: 105 n.61
807–10: 105 n.61

Works and Days
134–7: 2
236–7: 2

Hierocles
Long and Sedley 57G: 193 n.59

Hill, Aaron
The Judgment-Day: A Poem
151–8: 227
294–5: 224

Hirtius. *See under* Caesar

Homer
Iliad
1.290: 104 n.34
1.494: 104 n.34
2.461–7: 141 n.32
5.15–19: 17, 20–3, 26–7
5.596–600: 140 n.14
5.616–18: 24
11.200–377: 137
11.572: 26
13.506–11: 24–5
16.384–93: 140 n.14
17.26–37: 140 n.14
18.94–100: 34 n.43
23.833: 193 n.56
Scholia ad 2.783: 105 n.68
Scholia ad 6.44 (D scholia): 21
Scholia ad 8.479: 106 n.77

Odyssey
1.127–8: 23
5.226: 105 n.71
8.306: 104 n.34
10.151–4: 23, 33 n.32
11.134–5: 29
12.371: 104 n.34
13.363: 105 n.71
17.29: 23
22.92–6: 24
24.6: 105 n.71

Homeric Hymn to Apollo
1–13: 73
131–3: 76
132: 75, 80
135: 74
137: 73
14–15: 84 n.21
141–2: 73, 76
147: 73
150–2: 73
151: 84 n.26
153: 72
156: 74
160: 74–5
162: 74
162–95: 80
165–6: 84 n.21
173–4: 74

186: 84 n.17
187–206: 73
189–90: 81
192: 84 n.26
193: 75
214–15: 76
218: 76
222–3: 76
229: 76
229–38: 83 n.13
281: 76
297–9: 77
300–54: 85 n.35
363: 77
368–9: 77
371–4: 77
375: 76
377: 76
388–90: 76
388–92: 86 n.47
388–96: 78
393: 86 n.49
394: 78–9
400–1: 78
409: 79
412: 79
425: 79
484–5: 79–80
490–6: 78
496: 86 n.43
508–10: 78
514–19: 86 n.46
526–44: 80

Horace
Epistles
1.2.41–3: 140 n.11
1.4.13–14: 193 n.66
1.20: 169

Epodes
16.41–66: 1–2

Odes
1.11: 179–80
4.14: 141 n.31
4.14.25–6: 140 n.14

Irenaeus
Against the Heresies
3.22.4: 213 n.16

Juvenal
1.1: 161

Lazzarelli, Ludovico
Fasti christianae religionis
4.1–8: 201–2
4.745–992: 202–3

Lucan
Bellum civile
1.72–7: 231 n.11
7.814: 225, 231 n.11

Lucretius
1.1: 62
1.41: 62
1.432: 59
1.459–60: 53
1.459–63: 59–60
1.464–6: 60–1
1.466: 53
1.467–70: 61
1.470: 53
1.471–7: 62
1.478–80: 61
1.479: 60
1.482: 61
3.938–9: 184
3.947–8: 62
5.94–6: 219
5.368: 220
5.1446–7: 60

Manilius
Astronomica
1.234: 193 n.55

Mantovano, Battista
Fasti libri
fol. h i v–h ij r: 203–4
fol. h ij r: 204–5, 214 n.29
fol. h ij v: 205
fol. h iij r: 206

Marcus Aurelius
Meditations
2.17: 190 n.25
4.43: 140 n.11
6.32: 190 n.26

Martial
1.2: 169

4.8.9–10: 165
4.14.6–12: 165
9.61: 191 n.35
10.1: 162
10.2: 172 n.36
10.2.1–8: 162–3
10.20: 163–5, 171 n.5, 171 n.14
12.Praef.: 168
12.1: 168
12.4: 168–9

Milton, John
Of Reformation
YP i.616: 231 n.4

Paradise Lost
1.17–21: 219
2.405: 231 n.6
2.988: 230
3.323–41: 231 n.5
3.334–7: 227
4.159–65: 232 n.15
5.153–208: 226
6.4–8: 226
7.96: 218
10.649–706: 225
10.958–64: 231 n.5
11.368: 219
11.874–8: 220
11.898–901: 225
12.2–3: 219
12.6: 225
12.7: 219
12.11: 219
12.537–56: 218–19
12.549–51: 227
12.553–73: 219
12.554: 232 n.17
12.574: 231 n.7

Nepos
Life of Atticus
6.2: 149

Life of Cato
1.2–2.3: 149
2.2: 152
3.5: 149

Lives of Foreign Generals: 149–52
Datames 6.3: 150
Eumenes 1.5: 150
Hannibal 3.1: 150
Phocion 1.1: 151

Newcomb, Thomas
The Last Judgment of Men and Angels
Title page epigraph: 231 n.11
Preface, end of: 222
4.epigraph: 231 n.11
5.170–72: 226
5.185–7: 226
5.735–42: 226
6.epigraph: 231 n.11
7.epigraph: 231 n.11
9.730–4: 225
10.58–9: 227
10.79–85: 227
11.397–406: 227
12.epigraph: 231 n.11

Ovid
Amores
1.7.43: 140 n.14
3.6: 141 n.33

Ex Ponto
1.5.21–4: 140 n.23
4.5.41–4: 140 n.23
4.6.45–50: 140 n.23

Fasti
1.149–50: 205
2.1: 56
3.1–10: 208
3.1–396: 196–8
3.31–5: 210
3.229–58: 209
3.234–42: 205
3.243–5: 215 n.37
4.1: 215 n.34
4.2: 207
4.5: 215 n.34
4.15–18: 207
4.21–60: 207
4.87–95: 207

Heroides
5.27–34: 140 n.23

Metamorphoses
1.34–42: 132
1.256–8: 220, 231 n.11

Index of Passages   263

1.279–92: 127
1.283: 135
1.285–7: 136
1.285–92: 130–1
1.291–6: 131
1.310: 132
1.322–3: 220
1.324–47: 132–3
1.347: 133
1.545: 140 n.12
1.568–87: 129
2.5–18: 221
2.25–30: 221
2.220–1: 135
2.241–59: 127, 134–5
2.245: 137
2.252–3: 137
2.254–6: 135
2.259: 136–8
2.263–71: 135
2.272–300: 134
2.296–300: 220
3.342–3: 140 n.12
5.386–7: 141 n.32
5.572–614: 140 n.12
6.396: 140 n.12
11.50: 140 n.12
12.111: 140 n.12
14.462: 140 n.12
14.598–604: 140 n.12
15.816–17: 220

Tristia
1.8.1–14: 140 n.23

Oxyrhynchus Papyri
3830 fr. 3 (Euphorion): 106 n.77

Parmenides
B8: 104 n.33, 104 n.41

On Nature
fr. 8.6–11: 42–3

Paulinus of Nola
Carmina 20.293–318: 232 n.13

Pausanias
39.4: 106 n.76

Pherecydes (Schibli numeration)
fr. 2: 89, 104 n.38, 105 n.65

fr. 7: 104 n.38, 105 n.65
fr. 14: 92–9
fr. 14.1: 89
fr. 60: 99–100, 104 n.43, 105 n.62,
fr. 61: 99, 105 n.59
fr. 68: 92
fr. 78: 92, 96, 104 n.44
fr. 88: 100, 104 n.38, 105 n.63

Pindar
Nemea
8.5: 119 n.6

Olympia
2.17: 100, 105 n.68
2.68–72: 101, 106 n.75
6.55: 122 n.46
7.33: 122 n.46
10: 109–19
10.1–12: 111–13
10.1–3: 107, 110
10.9–12: 107
10.24–85: 107
10.49–51: 110, 116–18
10.72–5: 110, 114–16
10.95–105: 107–8

Scholia ad Ol. 10.15ab: 121 n.28

Plato
Phaedo
107d–114c: 91, 103 n.15

Republic
328d: 191 n.36

Theaetetus
142c: 47
151e9–160d2: 49
152a: 46
152a–171d: 47
152a–b: 44, 47
152c: 47
152d: 48
166a–168c: 48
171c–d: 48–9

Timaeus
22: 140 n.24
37–8: 89–91
37e3–38a3: 104 n.33
41e: 89–90

Plautus
  Boeotia
  fr. 1: 57–9
Pliny the Elder
  Natural History
  Praef. 18: 191 n.28
Pliny the Younger
  Epistulae
  1.9.1: 190 n.13
  1.20: 160–1
  3.21: 165–8, 171 n.5, 171 n.14
  3.5.11, 13: 181

  Panegyricus
  2.2–3: 160, 171 n.11
Plutarch
  On Common Conceptions
  1081c–1082a (= L–S 51C): 190 n.26
Pope, Alexander
  Dunciad
  4.653–6: 230
  4.656: 232 n.22

  Essay on Man
  1.1–2: 230
Porphyry
  Life of Pythagoras
  17: 105 n.72
Posidonius
  fr. 98.9–12 Edelstein-Kidd: 190 n.26
  Long and Sedley 51E5: 65
Protagoras
  D–K 80 B1: 44

Quintilian
  4.1.1: 145
  10.3.26: 191 n.28

Rhetorica ad Herrennium
  1.4: 145

Sallust
  Bellum Iugurthinum
  17.7: 157 n.32
Sappho
  fr. 96.6–10: 115

Scholia in Homeri Iliadem
  ad 2.783: 105 n.68
  ad 6.44 (D scholia): 21
  ad 8.479: 106 n.77
Scholia in Pindarum
  ad Ol. 10.15ab: 121 n.28
Seneca
  Apocolocyntosis
  2: 55

  De brevitate vitae
  1.3: 63
  2.1: 63
  3.1: 64
  7.9: 191 n.39
  7.10: 63
  8.1: 63–5, 179
  8.2: 190 n.11
  10.2: 64, 178
  10.3–6: 65
  10.4: 180
  10.4–6: 64
  11.1: 191 n.38
  15.5: 66
  17.5: 190 n.13

  De Constantia Sapientis
  5.5: 64

  De Ira
  3.36: 190 n.14
  3.36.1: 193 n.65

  De Tranquillitate Animi
  3.8: 190 n.13

  Epistulae morales
  1: 178–81, 183
  1.3: 64
  2.5: 181
  2.6: 179
  4.5: 181
  4.7–8: 180
  8.1–2: 181
  11.8: 183
  12: 178, 181–2, 186–8
  12.6: 192 n.45
  12.7: 192 n.49
  14.16: 188
  15.11: 180
  16.1: 181

23.1: 189 n.3
24.20: 190 n.22
24.26: 193 n.62
26.8: 183
32.3: 193 n.65
36.10: 192 n.48, 194 n.68
36.11: 185, 187
49.3: 190 n.25, 192 n.45
49.10: 184
51.6: 191 n.32
53.3: 191 n.32
54.6: 188
54.7: 191 n.38
58.22: 64, 190 n.17
58.22–3: 184, 193 n.61
58.23: 190 n.22
58.24: 191 n.33
61: 178
61.1–2: 182, 193 n.63
61.4: 192 n.42
61.12: 180
63.15: 192 n.44
65.1–2: 181
67.1: 189 n.3
70.1–3: 192 n.45
71.16: 194 n.68
71.36: 190 n.7
74: 178
74.3: 190 n.24
74.20: 193 n.65
74.26: 188
74.26–7: 185–6
74.34: 188
77.20: 183
78.29: 192 n.53
83.1–7: 181
83.2: 190 n.14
85.22: 192 n.53
85.23: 192 n.42
86.10–12: 191 n.32
88.33: 190 n.17
92.2: 193 n.65
92.25: 188
93.6: 191 n.39, 193 n.63
93.8: 192 n.53
98.15: 192 n.42
101: 178, 183–4
101.1: 182–3
101.7: 187, 192 n.52

101.8: 193 n.63
108.4: 191 n.27
117.7: 61
122.3: 181, 191 n.29
122.14–17: 181, 191 n.30

Quaestiones Naturales
1.pr.11: 190 n.25
1.pr.2–4: 191 n.29

Sextus Empiricus
Adversus Mathematicos
10.218: 61

Shakespeare, William
II *Henry IV*
I.i.154, 160: 232 n.22

Sonnets
60.1–4: 113

Simplicius
In Aristotelis Physica Commentaria
24.25: 98, 105 n.57

Solon (Gerber numeration)
fr. 4.15–16: 98, 105 n.56, 106 n.74
fr. 36.3–6: 98, 105 n.56, 106 n.74

Sophocles
Oedipus at Colonus 607–15: 104 n.31

Stobaeus
4.671–673.11: 193 n.59

Suetonius
Divus Iulius
2–23: 149

Divus Augustus
9.1: 155 n.5

Tiberius: 144–5
9.1: 145
9.1–11.1: 149
42–67: 145–6
63–4: 156 n.15
69: 156 n.15

Caligula
12.4: 155 n.12

Galba
6.1: 149

Otho: 144

Divus Vespasianus
2.3: 149

Divus Titus
4: 149

Tacitus
  Agricola
  1.1–3.2: 152
  2.1–3.1: 154
  2.1.4: 171 n.16
  3.3: 161
  5–6: 149
  11.4: 153
  30–2: 153–4
  46.4: 153

  Histories
  1.1.4: 161

Thucydides
  1.22.4: 45–6
  3.104.4: 83 n.13

Trapp, Joseph
  Thoughts upon the Four Last Things
  prefatory verses: 223
  2.27–32: 221–2
  2.586–91: 222

Valerius Maximus
  3.8.ext.2: 156 n.25

Varro
  De Lingua Latina
  6.8: 187

Virgil
  Aeneid
  1.269–70: 193 n.56
  2.304–8: 140 n.14
  2.363: 219
  2.494–9: 140 n.14
  2.682–4: 209
  6.88: 137
  6.172: 231 n.11
  6.273–9: 231 n.11
  6.309–12: 225
  6.638–41: 231 n.11
  6.889: 224
  7.698–702: 141 n.32
  8.678: 217
  9.7: 231 n.11
  10.60: 137
  10.601–4: 140 n.14

  Eclogues
  4.49: 209

  Georgics
  1.328–31: 231 n.11
  3.66–7: 180

Xenophanes
  B14: 104 n.36

Young, Edward
  A Poem on the Last Day
  1.epigraph: 231 n.11
  1.31–4: 226
  1.63–8: 226
  1.69–70: 221
  1.119–24: 222
  1.133–4: 222
  1.151–4: 226
  1.167–8: 226
  2.153: 223
  2.161–2: 223
  2.167–9: 224
  2.181–4: 225
  2.194–6: 225
  3.epigraph: 231 n.11
  3.47–54: 223–4
  3.79–80: 225
  3.89–90: 225
  3.91–9: 223
  3.114–15: 223
  3.118–23: 224
  3.208–11: 224
  3.310–27: 228

  Night Thoughts
  1.452–60: 232 n.21
  5.131–2: 232 n.22
  9.1302: 232 n.22
  9.2378–410: 228
  9.2411–34: 229

General Index

*Numbers in **bold** refer to figures*

absence 38, 39, 41, 42, 56, 66, 132
Achelous 129, 151 n. 41
Acheron 225
Achilles 26, 28–9, 34 n. 32, n. 43, 137
Adam 198, 202, 218–19, 220, 222, 224–7
Aeneas 62, 219, 224, 225
    shield of 217, 218, 221
Aeneid (Virgil) 10, 137, 209–10, 217–19, 224–5
    Parade of Heroes 217–18, 224–5
aesthetics 118–19, 120 n. 24, 121 n. 30
Afghanistan 109–10, 118
Afghanistan: Chronotopia (Norfolk) 109–10, 118
Agricola (Tacitus) 8, 144, 151–4, 155, 161, 171 n. 16, 172 n. 22
Ajax 24, 25, 34 n. 32
Alciphron 58
Alcman 112
alētheia / Alētheia 33 n. 31, 47–8, 50
'am-being' 44, 45, 48, 50
Amphinomus 24
Amphios 24
Anaximander 98, 100, 102, 105 n. 51, n. 54, n. 55
angels 113–14, 201, 218, 221, 226, 227. *See also individual names*
Anno Domini dating system 198–9
Annunciation, the 9–10, 195–6, 198–206, 209–12, 213 n. 2
apocalypse 127, 129, 133–6, 139
Apollo 28, 71–87, 147, 217. *See also* Delphi; oracle at Delphi; Temple of Apollo
Aristophanes 94–6
Aristotle 19, 20, 30, 35, 40, 43, 47, 96
    on time 18, 19, 31 n. 3, n. 7
Armisen-Marchetti, M. 179, 180, 184, 192 n. 49, 194 n. 70
Ascanius / Iulus 209, 210
Athens 46, 58, 94, 102

atoms 40, 60, 61, 220
    and void 53, 59, 61, 62, 220, 226
attachments 37, 38, 41, 42
Attic Nights (Gellius) 59
audiences 45, 74–5, 107–8, 112, 132–3, 138, 144, 154, 161
Augustine 31 n. 12, 38
Augustus. *See* Octavian / Augustus

Bacchylides 115, 117
Bakhtin, Mikhail 4, 8, 108–9, 127–9, 131–3, 136, 139, 143, 177, 188–9
battle scenes 17, 20–1, 23, 26–7
Being and Time (Heidegger) 19
Biographies of Scientific Objects (Daston) 39–40
biography 8, 26, 143–57
Birds (Aristophanes) 94–6
Blessed Isles, the 1–2, 11 n. 4, 101
body, human 9, 46, 57–8, 178–9, 181–2
Bonazzi, Mauro 45, 46
Botticelli, Sandro 200, 214 n. 23
Breglia Pulci Doria, L. 91, 92
brevity 8–9, 63, 65, 159–64, 168–70
Burnet, Thomas 221

Caesar, Julius 149, 150, 152, 157 n. 32, 220
Caesars. *See* emperors
calendar poems 195–6, 200–6, 211–12
calendars 3, 9, 56, 196–8, 205
Calgacus 153–4
Callimachus 72, 80, 82, 160
Campbell, B. 133–4, 141 n. 31
capitalism 159
Carmelite order 203, 214 n. 27
Casey, Edward S. 117, 120 n. 9
Catherall, Samuel 221, 222, 230
Catholic church 10, 196, 199, 211
Cato (the Elder) 149, 152, 182
caves 100, 101, 226

Caÿster 135, 137
Chaos 95–6, 135–6, 217–18, 220, 226, 230, 231 n. 6
Christianity / Christian theology 9–10, 91, 195, 198–206, 208, 211, 212, 227
Christ, Jesus 10, 198–202, 206–8, 211, 212, 218–19, 227
chronology 7–8, 18–20, 117, 128, 134–9, 144–8, 154
Chronos / Kronos / Χρόνος 88–91, 93–8, 100–2
  embodiment of time 88–90, 92, 93, 99, 101
  judge of the dead 101, 102
  mixing of the gods 95, 99, 100
  name change 90, 92, 99, 101
  ordinance of 98–9, 101, 102
chronotopes 4, 8, 12 n. 14, 54, 108, 133–6, 137, 177
  ecological 127–30
  liquid 127, 129–30, 131, 134, 137, 138
chronotype 12 n. 15, 54, 67 n. 4, 191 n. 32
Chrysippus 65, 200 n. 26
Chthoniē / Gē 89–93, 95, 97, 99
Cicero 100, 182, 187, 191 n. 36, 220
clepsydra. *See* water-clock
climate change 39
clocks / clock-time 57–9, 230. *See also* sundials; water-clocks
cognition 7, 17–18, 20–8, 110
combat scenes. *See* battle scenes
coming-to-be / coming-into-being 35–42, 44, 46, 115, 118
Commedia Divina (Dante) 200
comprehension 38–9
Confessions (Augustine) 38
contemplation 107–23
cosmic regions 90, 99, 101, 105 n. 61
cosmologies 94–7, 102–3
Council of Trent 211
creation 90–2, 99, 102, 132–3, 135–6, 196, 198–9, 207, 212, 218–19
Croesus 44–5, 47
Cronia 102
cursus honorum 149
cycles / cyclicity / cyclicality 127–9, 131–3, 139, 185, 187, 197, 225
Cynthus 73, 76

Dante 200
darkness 30 n. 1, 187, 222, 226, 228–30, 232 n. 22
Daston, Lorraine 39–40
day(s) 9, 64, 164, 178–82, 186–9, 228
De brevitate vitae (Seneca) 63–6, 178, 179, 180, 183
'Deep Classics' 110
Delos 71–5, 80, 81, 82, 84 n. 23, 85 n. 28
  Festival / Maidens 71–5, 81
Delphi 71–2, 76, 78–80, 82
democracy 30, 32 n. 13, 46
De partu Virginis (Sannazaro) 200, 214 n. 23
De pascha computus (Pseudo-Cyprian) 198
De rerum natura (Lucretius) 53, 59–62, 184, 219, 220
Derrida, Jacques 32 n. 13, 41–2, 47, 183
De senectute (Cicero) 182
determination(s) 41–2, 49
Deucalion 133, 220
De uiris illustribus (Nepos) 148–51
Dialogus (Tacitus) 160
Diels, H. 91, 94, 97
Diogenes Laertius 97
Diomedes 17, 20, 27, 32 n. 16, 33 n. 32
Dionysius Exiguus 198–9
divine council 204–5, 214 n. 31
δολιχόσκιος / δολιχόσκιον ἔγχος 17–18, 20–2, 24–5, 27, 29, 32 n. 16
Domitian 8, 9, 152–4, 160–3, 165, 171 n. 9, 172 n. 32
Dunciad, The (Pope) 230, 232 n. 22
duration 19, 26, 90, 93, 98–9, 167, 185–6

Easter 198
ecclesiastical year 195, 199, 200, 201, 203. *See also* Annunciation; Easter
Eclogue IV (Virgil) 2, 11 n. 4, 209–10
ecocriticism 7, 8, 107, 117, 119, 120 n. 20, 129
Egeria 197
eighteenth-century poetry 221–31
ekphrasis 162, 221
ekstases 19, 25
Empedocles 44, 48
emperors 55, 144, 146, 147, 154. *See also individual names*

enargeia 33 n. 20, 219, 222
endpoints 9, 20
environment 8, 54, 116, 127–9, 131, 133, 136, 139
environmental philosophy 7, 117–19
epic 5, 21–3, 29–30, 61, 94, 97, 200
  Ovidian 127–39
Epicureanism 53, 60, 62, 63, 65, 184, 219
Epicurus 59, 181
epideixis 45, 46, 121 n. 35
Epigrams (Martial) 9, 162–5, 167–70, 172 n. 32
epistemic transparency 18, 22
epistemology 22, 28–9, 38, 40, 49, 59–62, 66
Epistles (Horace) 169
Epistles (Pliny) 9, 165–6
Epistulae morales (Seneca) 9, 64, 65, 177–94
epithets 5, 17, 21–3, 25, 28, 97
Epode 16 (Horace) 1–2, 11 n. 4
equinox, spring 198, 205, 213 n. 10
Erasmus 211
Erebus 95–6, 101
Eros 95
Essay on Man (Pope) 230, 232 n. 22
Essay on the Conflagration in Blank Verse (Catherall) 221, 222, 230, 231 n. 11
eternal being / existence 89, 91, 93–8, 101–2
eternity (αἰον / Αἰον) 1, 90–7, 102, 113–14, 167, 170, 219, 223, 228, 230
ethics 18, 20, 27–9, 63–7
Eumenes 150
Euphorion 101
Euripides 101
Eurotas 134–6
Eve 202, 218, 231 n. 7
existential change 97
exordium 145

fame (κλέος) 21, 23, 74–5, 107, 115, 167, 203, 224–5
Fasti (Ovid) 9–10, 56, 195–8, 206–10, 212
fasti (Renaissance) 195–215
Fasti christianae religionis (Lazzarelli) 195, 201–3
Fasti libri (Mantovano) 195, 203–6
fate 29, 220

Feeney, D. 139, 141 n. 37
fields of sense 36–43, 47, 49, 50, 50 n. 5, n. 6, 51 n. 17, n. 18
fire 89, 100, 220, 221, 222
Flood, the 219, 225
form 108, 110, 114, 178, 189
Fracco, Ambrogio 'Novidio' 9, 195, 206–11, 215 n. 37
freedom 29, 153–4, 159–73
fruit 10, 218–19, 227–8

Gabriel (archangel) 204, 209, 214 n. 29
Gabriel, Markus 35–7, 50 n. 4
Garcia, Tristan, 35, 37–9, 41, 42, 49, 50 n. 8
Gē. *See* Chthoniē / Gē
Gellius, Aulus 59, 180, 191 n. 28
generated / ungenerated beings 94, 96–7, 99
genre 3–5, 128, 130, 133, 136–9, 177
geology / geological time 110, 138, 140 n. 6
Georgics (Virgil) 180
Gildenhard, I. 135–6, 141 n. 36
gnomai 116, 122 n. 45
Gorgias 44
Grenfell Papyrus 93
guest gifts 161–2

Hacking, Ian 37, 40, 50 n. 4, n. 6
Hadot, P. 62, 63
Hagesidamos 107–8
Hannibal (Nepos) 150
Harman, Graham 35, 37
Haskins, Susan 211, 215 n. 41
Heidegger, Martin 19, 25, 31 n. 12, 33 n. 31, 108, 109
Helen 60–1, 62, 136
Henderson, John 165, 182
Hephaestus 137
Heptamychos (Pherecydes) 7, 89–106
Heraclitus 48, 187, 193 n. 58, n. 61, n. 64
Herakles 114–15
Herodotus 44–5, 47, 135
heroes / heroic life 21, 23, 25–6, 28, 29, 144
Hersilia 197, 208–9
Hesiod 2, 11 n. 5, 76, 94–5, 101, 105 n. 61
Hill, Aaron 224, 227, 230
historical ontology 3, 6, 35–6, 39–42, 44, 49, 50
Histories (Tacitus) 161

historiography 12 n. 13, 119, 122 n. 54, 146, 148, 155
history 2, 10, 39–43, 47, 60–1, 153, 218–19
Homer 5, 17–30, 76, 117, 187
   ethics 20–1, 27–9
   formulae 5, 8, 21, 25–9, 115–16
   temporality 18, 23, 27–30
   victory and death in 17, 18, 20–1, 29
Homeric Hymn to Apollo 6–7, 71–87
Honig, Bonnie 18, 28, 31 n. 11
Horace 1–2, 11 n. 4, 62, 169, 179–80, 182
horological time 57–9
'Horse Gallop' (Muybridge) 25–6, **26**
hours 57–8, 164–6, 168, 170, 178, 181–3, 187, 220–30
hubris (ὕβρις) 72, 79–82, 87 n. 55, 170
humanism (Italian) 9–10, 195, 196, 212
Hymn to Delos (Callimachus) 72, 80, 82

Idomeneus 24
Iliad (Homer) 17, 19–22, 24–5, 28–9, 33 n. 29, 137
image(s) 17–34
   of cognition 18, 20–3, 25, 27
imagery 21, 112, 115–17, 210. See also under Seneca
immortality 75, 77, 170, 172 n. 36
Incarnation, the 198–9, 211
intensity 39, 42
Irenaeus of Lyon 199
'is'-being 43, 44, 45, 48, 50
isegoria 46

Jones, P. 129, 136
Judgment-Day, The (Hill) 224, 227
Juno 197, 204, 208–9, 212
Jupiter 132–3, 138, 205, 220, 221. See also entries under Zeus
Justin Martyr 199

katabasis 101
Ker, James 6, 9, 159–60, 161, 180, 181, 182
knowledge 22, 25, 27, 29, 47–8
Kronos. See Chronos / Kronos

land artists 117
landscape 4, 109–10, 117–18, 129–30, 134–9
Last Judgement 10, 201, 218, 221–30

Last Judgement poems 221–31
Last Judgment of Men and Angels, The (Newcomb) 222, 225, 226, 227, 230
Last Things 221–3, 227, 229, 231 n. 5
Latour, Bruno 35, 37, 38, 39, 50 n. 2, n. 3, n. 4
layering 4, 110, 112, 118, 137, 144, 152–3
Lazzarelli, Ludovico 9, 195, 201–3, 206, 214 n. 24
Legenda Aurea 199, 213 n. 14
length 8–9, 160–4, 167–8, 170, 186, 188. See also brevity
Leto 72, 74
letters 9, 160, 165–7, 177–94
libertas. See freedom
Life of Atticus (Nepos) 149
Life of Eumenes (Nepos) 150
Life of Julius Caesar (Suetonius) 149, 150
Life of Otho (Suetonius) 144
Life of Phocion (Nepos) 151
Life of Tiberius (Suetonius) 8, 144–8
light 17, 27, 187, 209
Lives of Foreign Generals (Nepos) 149, 151, 154–5
'long-shadowed' (δολιχόσκιος) 5, 17, 20–7, **22, 23**, 33 n. 26
looping effects 37, 50 n. 4
Lorenzo (*Night Thoughts*) 228–30
Lucan 10, 221, 225, 231 n. 11
Lucilius (*Epistulae*) 64, 178, 180–2, 184
Lucretius 53, 59–62, 66, 135, 184, 217, 219–20
Luke, gospel of 199, 200, 203, 209, 214 n. 26
Luther, Martin 211
lyric poetry 7, 107–33

Mantovano, Battista 9–10, 195, 200, 203–6, 214 n. 27
March (month of) 10, 195–9, 201–3, 205, 208–9
Marlowe, Christopher 224
Mars 195–8, 201, 203, 205, 206, 208–9
Martial 159–73
Mary (mother of Jesus) 10, 195–6, 199–212
   Eve–Mary antithesis 199, 202
Matronalia 197, 208–9, 213 n. 5
Matthew, gospel of 199

Melissus of Elea 43–4
Menander 58
Mercury 204, 214 n. 29
Metamorphoses (Ovid) 8, 127–41, 220–1
metaphysics 39–40, 50 n. 5, 91
Metaphysics (Aristotle) 35
metempsychosis 7, 90, 94, 100–2, 105 n. 66
methodology 5, 29, 37, 109
Michael (archangel) 218–19, 222, 226
Middle Comedy 58
Milton, John 10, 217, 219, 221–2, 226, 230
Minerva 163, 164, 166, 196
Moral Epistles (Seneca). *See Epistulae morales*
mortality 40, 61, 66, 75, 77, 99, 182–3
Morton, Tim 117–18, 122 n. 50
Mount Ida 101
Müller, T. 127–9, 133, 137, 139
muses 74, 163–4, 166, 169
Muybridge, Eadweard 25–6, **26**

Nail, Thomas 35, 42, 43, 49
narrative 19, 26, 61, 127–9, 131–3, 139, 144, 148
    narratology 4–5, 94
Natural Histories (Pliny) 181
nature imagery 107, 112, 115, 116
neo-existentialism 35
Nepos, Cornelius 144, 148, 150–2, 154, 156 n. 20, n. 25. n. 26
Neptune 130, 132, 135
Nerva 8, 160, 161, 171 n. 9
Newcomb, Thomas 222, 225–7, 230
new materialism 35
new realism 35
Nicomachean Ethics (Aristotle) 19
Night 95, 96, 228
Night Thoughts (Young) 228–30
Nile 8, 135, 136, 140 n. 24, 141 n. 31
Ninety-Five Theses (Luther) 211
nooks, cosmic (μυχοί) 7, 90, 92, 99–103
Norfolk, Simon 109–10, 118
novel, the 12 n. 4, 128, 189
'now' (*nunc* / νῦν) 54, 56, 58, 81, 111–14
Numa 196–7

object-oriented ontology 7, 35, 119, 120 n. 23
occupati (time-wasters) 63–6

Octavian / Augustus 138, 141 n. 37, 212, 217, 221
Odes (Horace) 179–80
Odysseus 28, 29
Odyssey 23, 24, 26, 28–9, 85 n. 31
Oinomaus / Oenomaus 24, 25, 116–17
Olympia 7, 113, 116, 117, 119
Olympiad 107, 114–15
Olympian 10 (Pindar) 7, 107–19
    moonlight 114–16
    pebble 107, 110–14
    snow 116–18, 122 n. 50
Olympus 71–6, 79, 81, 82, 84 n. 16, n. 17, 85 n. 28
omens 147–8
On Generation and Corruption (Aristotle) 40
On Nature (Parmenides) 42–3
On Nature, or on What there Is (Melissus) 43–4
On the Brevity of Life (Seneca). *See De brevitate vitae*
On the Nature of Things (Lucretius). *See De rerum natura*
On the Nature of Things that Are (Empedocles) 44
ontology 22, 28, 29, 35–51, 59–62. *See also* historical ontology; object-oriented ontology
On What there Is Not, or on Nature (Gorgias) 44
open-ended present 55
Ophioneus / Ophion 90, 96, 101–2
oracle at Delphi 71–2, 75–81
Orphism 94, 95, 100
Ovid 8–10, 56, 127–41, 195–215, 220, 221, 225
    adynata 138–9, 140 n. 23
    the female in 196–8, 208–9
    Palace of the Sun 221, 225

Paradise Lost (Milton) 10, 217–19, 221–2, 225–7
Parmenides 6, 35, 40, 42–8, 50, 90
Parthenice Mariana (Mantovano) 200, 203–6
pax Augusta 217, 218–19
Payne, Mark 115–16, 122 n. 45
Peloponnesian War 45

Peneus 129, 135, 136
perception 3, 21–2, 28, 46–8, 60, 61
Phaedo (Plato) 100
Phaethon 8, 129, 133, 135–6, 220–1, 225
Phegeus 17, 20–2, 26–7, 32 n. 16
phenomenology 3, 5, 19, 27–8, 107–9, 117
Pherecydes 7, 89–106
Philander 229
philology 7, 50 n. 7, 107, 110, 118
Phocion 151
photography 109–10, 113, 118, 120 n. 18, n. 24
Pindar 7, 100, 101, 107–23
Plato 35, 43–4, 46–50, 90–1, 98, 100
    dialogues 47, 49 (*see also individual dialogues*)
    Forms 40, 43
Platonism 7, 89–91, 94, 96–8, 102
Plautus 53, 57–9
Pliny the Elder 181
Pliny the Younger 9, 159–73, 181, 191 n. 31
plot 4, 19, 20, 29, 33 n. 29, 189
pneuma 89, 100
Po (river) 129
Poem on the Last Day (Young) 221, 222–8, 241
Poetics (Aristotle) 19, 31 n. 19, 47
politics of time 9, 28–9, 159–73
Pompeius 152
Pope, Alexander 230, 232 n. 21, n. 22
portents 146–8
Posidonius 65, 191 n. 26
Poussin, Nicolas 118
Praefatio (Nepos) 150
presence 39, 41, 42
present, the 6, 53–68
Protagoras 6, 36, 42–50, 51 n. 12
Protestantism 211–12
Pseudo-Matthew, gospel of 199–200, 202
Ptolemy II 80–1
Pyrrha 133, 220
Pythagoras 100, 101
Python 76, 77, 85 n. 42

Ray, John 221
reception studies 107, 110
Reformation, the 10, 211–12
Regulus 161, 171 n. 14
Renaissance poetry (Italian) 10, 195–215

renewal 128–30, 132–3, 137, 139
repetition 29, 113, 127–30, 132–3, 137–9, 139 n. 2
res gestae 60, 61, 151. *See also* history
resurrection of the dead 224–5, 229–30
revocatio 65
Rhea Silvia 196–8, 203, 208–9, 210, 212
rhetoric 111–12, 143, 156 n. 22, 159–60, 166, 229
Rhine 8, 135, 136, 141 n. 31
Rhone 135, 136, 141 n. 31
Ricoeur, Paul 19, 31 n. 12
rivers 8, 127–41. *See also individual names*
    catalogue of 129, 135–8
    flooding / drying 8, 127–39
Roman church. *See* Catholic church
Rome 8, 58, 137–8, 150, 208
    foundation / history 1, 2, 10, 152, 195–8, 203, 205, 224
Romulus and Remus 10, 196–8, 203, 210
Rouse, W. H. D. 21, 22
routine 180–1, 184
rubrics 144, 146, 148, 155 n. 8

Sabine women 197
Sacri Fasti (Fracco) 195, 206–11
Samson Agonistes (Milton) 230
Sannazaro, Jacopo 200, 214 n. 23
Sappho 114–17
Satan 218
Schibli, H. 89–94, 99, 100, 102, 103 n. 2, n. 3
Schliemann, Heinrich 109, 120 n. 22
sea / seashore 112, 130–2, 135
seasons 95–6, 128, 134–5, 185, 187, 197, 205, 221, 225–7
Seneca the Younger 9, 53, 63–6, 177–94
    circle imagery in 184–8
    on death / old age 178, 180, 182–3, 184, 186
    financial imagery in 178–9
Senecio 183–4
senses / sensation / *sensus* 53, 59–62
shadow(s) 17, 21–3, **22**, **23**, 25–7, 33 n. 26, 58
Silvia. *See* Rhea Silvia
simile(s) 111–13, 115–16, 122 n. 54, 130, 137, 225
Simplicius 98

slip box principle 144
Socrates 46–9, 51 n. 15
Solon 44–5, 47
song 26, 71, 73, 74–5, 77, 84 n. 21, 117, 202–3
Sonnet 60 (Shakespeare) 113
souls 100–2, 222–4. *See also* metempsychosis
space / spatiality 39, 54–5, 108, 113, 128–33, 135–9, 166, 177, 184
space-time 54, 108–10, 115, 128. *See also* chronotopes
spears 17, 20–7, **22**, **23**, 29, 32 n. 16, 33 n. 32
specious present, the 55
spectrality 42
speculative realism 35
Stoicism 61, 63–5, 177, 179, 187–8
styles of thinking / reasoning 35–6, 38, 40, 42–4, 47, 51 n. 18
succession narratives 96–7
Suetonius 8, 143–5, 148–50, 155 n. 3, n. 5, 156 n. 14
summa rerum 220
sundials 57–8

Tacitus 8, 143–4, 151–5, 156 n. 27, 157 n. 32, 160, 161, 163
Tanaka, Stephen 18, 28–9
Taq-e Zafar archway 118
Tartarus 95–6, 101
Temple of Apollo 76–7, 79, 81, 85 n. 41, 86 n. 46, 217, 221
temporalities of presence 53–68
temporality
  and chronology 18–30
  Homeric 18, 23, 27–30
  outlined 2–3
  plurality of 19–20, 27, 28, 30
texts 40–2, 47, 49–50, 114, 128
Thalia 163–4, 169
Theaetetus (Plato) 44, 46–9, 51 n. 12
Theodorus 47–9, 51 n. 15, n. 16
theogonies 89, 94–6, 103
Theogony (Hesiod) 94, 95, 97
Theogony (Pherecydes). *See Heptamychos*
Theokrasia (Pherecydes). *See Heptamychos*
Theseus 129
'things in themselves' 35, 45, 48, 53

Thoughts upon the Four Last Things (Trapp) 221–2, 223, 231
Thucydides 45–6, 83 n. 13
Tiber 8, 135, 136, 137–8, 140 n. 12, n. 28
Tiberius 145–8
Timaeus (Plato) 90, 91, 94
time
  'archaic' 82, 93
  cyclical 128, 185, 225
  definitions 38, 53–4, 66
  divine / human 6–7, 71–87, 89
  historical 2, 6–7, 30, 82, 108, 128, 133–4, 136, 218, 224
  as intensive variation of presence 38–9
  natural 128, 129, 132, 134, 139
  as number of change 18–20, 26
  presence of 6, 53–68
  Roman conceptions of 6, 55–7
  sacred 71, 76–7, 81–2, 83 n. 4
  wasting of 63–6, 178–80
Time and Narrative (Ricoeur) 19
time-orientation 54
timescape 54
'to be' 35, 42–3
topography 100, 103
The Tragical History of Dr Faustus (Marlowe) 224
Trajan 8, 160, 161, 171 n. 9, 172 n. 35
Trapp, Joseph 221–2, 223, 229, 231
Trojan War 53, 61, 62, 136
Troy / Trojans 28, 60, 62, 109, 120 n. 22, 137, 209, 219
truth 28–30, 47–50

underworld 101, 217–18, 225. *See also* Erebus; Tartarus

values / value systems 8, 18–19, 20, 21, 25, 153, 166
Varro 187
Venus 62, 204, 207–8, 212, 220
vices 65, 145–6
victory 17, 18, 20, 29, 107–9, 114–15, 208
victory odes 109
Virgil 2, 10, 180, 209, 217–19, 221, 224–5
virtue(s) 64, 145, 179, 182–3, 185–6, 188, 200, 203

Vita Catonis (Nepos) 149, 150, 152
Vogt-Spira, Gregor 179–80, 190 n. 16

water 89, 100, 129–33, 135
water-clock 9, 159–61, 170, 170 n. 2
'we'-being 44, 46, 48, 50
Wenders, Wim 113–14
Westminster Abbey 225
Wheeler, S. M. 127, 129, 138, 139 n. 2
Wings of Desire 113–14, 121 n. 36

Xanthus 135, 136, 137

Yeats, W. B. 109
Young, Edward 221–31, 232 n. 21, n. 22

Zas 89–93, 95, 97, 99
Zephon 226
Zeus 73–5, 79–81, 97, 101, 102. *See also entries under* Jupiter